T0226252

Lecture Notes in Artificial Intelligence   11034

Subseries of Lecture Notes in Computer Science

More information about this series at http://www.springer.com/series/1244

Sarah Creem-Regehr · Johannes Schöning
Alexander Klippel (Eds.)

Spatial Cognition XI

11th International Conference, Spatial Cognition 2018
Tübingen, Germany, September 5–8, 2018
Proceedings

 Springer

Editors
Sarah Creem-Regehr
University of Utah
Salt Lake City, UT
USA

Alexander Klippel
Pennsylvania State University
University Park, PA
USA

Johannes Schöning
University of Bremen
Bremen
Germany

ISSN 0302-9743   ISSN 1611-3349   (electronic)
Lecture Notes in Artificial Intelligence
ISBN 978-3-319-96384-6   ISBN 978-3-319-96385-3   (eBook)
https://doi.org/10.1007/978-3-319-96385-3

Library of Congress Control Number: 2018948640

LNCS Sublibrary: SL7 – Artificial Intelligence

This Springer imprint is published by the registered company Springer Nature Switzerland AG
The registered company address is: Gewerbestrasse 11, 6330 Cham, Switzerland

Preface

Welcome to the proceedings of the International Conference on Spatial Cognition 2018 which was held during September 5–8, 2018, in Tübingen, Germany. Spatial Cognition took place in Germany for the eighth time, after being held in the USA in 2016, and it was hosted by the University of Tübingen and the Max Planck Institute for Biological Cybernetics.

The University of Tübingen, founded in 1477, has been an institute of excellence in research and teaching for over 500 years. The university has over 25,000 students and supports numerous collaborative research centers and DFG-funded research training programs. The MPI for Biological Cybernetics is internationally known for the Department of Human Perception, Cognition, and Action directed by Professor Heinrich Bülthoff, which combines traditional psychophysics methods with computer simulations and realistic virtual environments to address innovative questions relating to spatial cognition.

Over 30 years, the Spatial Cognition conference series has brought together researchers from different scientific fields insofar as they are concerned with cognitive agents and space, such as cognitive psychology, linguistics, computer science, geography, philosophy, or education. The conference is concerned with the acquisition, organization, and utilization of knowledge about spatial objects and environments, be it real, virtual, or abstract, human or machine. Research issues in the field range from the investigation of human spatial cognition to mobile robot navigation, including aspects such as wayfinding, spatial planning, spatial learning, internal and external representations of space, and communication of spatial information. SC 2018 gathered together researchers working on spatial cognition from all of these perspectives.

The conference brings together researchers and practitioners from a variety of backgrounds and interest areas. The intimate size of this single-track conference provides an ideal venue for leading researchers, practitioners, and students to share research results and experiences. As always, our main goal has been to provide an engaging and high-quality program. We retained the successful format of previous years: a three-day conference event preceded by one day of workshops, tutorials, and a doctoral symposium. This year we were delighted to receive 44 paper submissions of which we accepted 22 papers (resulting in overall acceptance rate of 50%) and 76 posters! Submissions were assessed in early 2018 by an international and diverse Program Committee (PC) and finally at a remote meeting of the PC chairs. The topics of this year's papers and posters reflect the diversity of ideas and perspectives that comprise the spatial cognition community, ranging from the study of agents to navigation to language. What brings this all together is a commitment to innovation that expands our understanding of how humans perceive and interact in space. We were especially pleased to have three exciting keynote speakers this year. Prof. Nira Liberman is a professor of social psychology at Tel Aviv University (from 2001). She studies psychological distance, including temporal distance, spatial distance, social distance, and probability. Her research encompasses questions of how distances affect mental representation, decision-making, and motivation, how distances affect intellectual performance, generalization in learning, as well as how distances are interrelated. William H. Warren is a professor of cognitive, linguistic, and psychological science at Brown University and Director of the Virtual Environment Navigation Lab (VENLab). He uses virtual reality techniques to investigate the visual control of human action, including locomotion, path integration, spatial navigation, crowd behavior, and the dynamics of perceptual-motor coordination. Warren is the author of over 110 research articles and chapters and the recipient of a Fulbright Research Fellowship, an NIH Research Career Development Award, and Brown's Teaching Award for Excellence in the Life Sciences. Prof. Luc Van Gool is a professor of computer vision at ETH Zurich (1998) and KU Leuven (1991). His main interests include 3D capture, object recognition, motion and action analysis, as well as their combination. He has co-authored more than 250 publications on these topics. In 2016 he was awarded the Jan Koenderink Award for the lasting influence of his work on SURF features, and in 2017 he was given a Distinguished Researcher Award by the IEEE Computer Society.

As ever, a large number of people have contributed to the organization, reviewing, venue arrangement, Web and media presence, and publicity for Spatial Cognition 2018, and we would like to express our deepest gratitude to the many dozens of volunteers whose efforts have contributed to what we hope will be a memorable event. We would in particular like to thank our local chairs and our corporate sponsors for their continued support for this conference series.

June 2018

Sarah Creem-Regehr
Johannes Schöning
Alexander Klippel

Organization

General Chair

Alexander Klippel   The Pennsylvania State University, USA

Program Chairs

Sarah Creem-Regehr   University of Utah, USA
Johannes Schöning   University of Bremen, Germany

Local Chairs

Hanspeter Mallot   University of Tübingen, Germany
Heinrich Bülthoff   Max Planck Institute for Biological Cybernetics, Tübingen, Germany
Marianne Stickrodt   Max Planck Institute for Biological Cybernetics, Tübingen, Germany
Tobias Meilinger   Max Planck Institute for Biological Cybernetics, Tübingen, Germany

Poster Chairs

Lace Padilla   University of Utah, USA
Bodo Winter   University of Birmingham, UK

Workshop and Tutorial Chair

Heather Burte   Tufts University, USA

Doctoral Colloquium Chair

Elizabeth Chrastil   University of California, Santa Barbara, USA

Program Committee

Thomas Barkowsky
Anna Belardinelli
Michela Bertolotto
Stefano Borgo
Martin Butz
Christophe Claramunt
Michel Denis
Sara Irina Fabrikant
Paolo Folgliaroni
Christian Freska
Dedre Gentner
Nicholas Giudice
Klaus Gramann
Mary Hegarty
Stephen Hirtle
Toru Ishikawa
Petra Jansen
Tomi Kauppinen
Peter Kiefer
Markus Knauff
Werner Kuhn
Susan Levine
Antonio Lieto
Mark May
Timothy McNamara
Chiara Meneghetti

Daniel Montello
Bernd Neumann
Nora Newcombe
Francesca Pazzagila
Albert Postma
Ian Pratt-Hartmann
Marco Ragni
Kai-Florian Richter
Andrea Rodriguez-Tastets
Holger Schultheis
Angela Schwering
Jeanine Stefanucci
Andrew Stull
Holly Taylor
Thora Tenbrink
Sabine Timpf
Martin Tomko
David Uttal
Nico Van de Weghe
Maria Vasardani
Constanze Vorwerg
Jan Oliver Wallgrün
Stephan Winter
Diedrich Wolter
Joost Zwarts

Contents

Navigating in Space I

Spatial Features of Terrain Reflected in Pigeon Flights

Margarita Zaleshina and Alexander Zaleshin[(✉)]

Moscow Institute of Physics and Technology, Moscow, Russia
terbiosorg@gmail.com

Abstract. In this work, we studied the properties of pigeon flight trajectories over combined cross-country and urban terrain. We considered GPS tracks of pigeons returning home from two distant sites; birds flew separately and finished at the same endpoint. Spatial analysis of flight paths and directions was used to identify "flight corridors" and regions of interest along the bird trajectories. The visual characteristics of the territories over which pigeons flew were calculated using remote sensing data from open sources. The resulting distinctive zones along flight trajectories and visual features of the landscape were compared. It was found that the "flight corridors" correspond to real objects and areas in the terrain. The results of study showed that spatial features of the terrain can be reflected in the routes of pigeon flights and it is possible to identify sets of significant objects and areas based on the data about flight paths. In the study spatial data were processed using the geographical information system QGIS.

Keywords: Spatial cognition · Navigation · Wayfinding · Pigeon flight Geographic information systems · QGIS

1 Introduction

Aspects of the spatial cognition of pigeons in flights over combined terrain are presented in this paper. As the initial data were used GPS tracks of pigeons returning home from distant sites. Calculated points of proximity of flight trajectories were compared with significant landmarks on the terrain. The same endpoint determined the general direction of all flights, but at any moment the values of flight directions and pathways varied depending on the spatial features of the terrain under the flying birds. Significant objects for the flying pigeons were presented both points of interest (such as a home or feeding spot) and notable landmarks (such as a lake or road).

The areas which were most often visited by different birds during separate flights were identified based on analysis of data on the pigeons' flight paths. It has been found that extended objects can attract the attention of flying birds and affect the flight path. Moreover, flight paths over significant landmarks can form extended "flight corridors".

The pigeons' tracks were compared with spatial features of the terrain which can be visually detected. For this purpose, specific areas and objects were identified, based on remote sensing data from open sources at different scales.

For spatial data processing of GPS tracks and information about the terrain surface the geographical information system QGIS was used.

S. Creem-Regehr et al. (Eds.): Spatial Cognition 2018, LNAI 11034, pp. 3–14, 2018.
https://doi.org/10.1007/978-3-319-96385-3_1

2 Background and Related Works

2.1 Features of Pigeon Flight Pathways in Different Cases

What information about pigeon flight may be obtained not by looking at a map, but using data on its flight path only? Do pigeon flight paths vary depending on whether they fly near a lake or above a road?

The navigational behavior of pigeons in different situations is described in many publications. Blaser et al. [1] proved that pigeons are able to remember routes and fly to the objects which are important to them, such as home or feeding spots, and that they also can choose where to turn depending on the degree of their satiety. Moreover, observation of pigeons' flight paths shows that they tend to fly round significant natural obstacles, such as lakes or hills. Lipp et al. [2] discovered that pigeons can select extended linear objects and use them as landmarks. Ortega et al. [3] reported similar results: pigeons occasionally fly home in a straight line, but more often fly along well-known routes, preferring to be guided by familiar landmarks. Schiffner et al. [4] analyzed pigeons' GPS tracks and discussed whether a pigeon requires visual perception in order to accurately determine its location. Vyssotski et al. [5] showed that when flying from the sea to the shore in good visibility conditions, pigeons move straight to the goal, while in bad visibility conditions they choose the direction of the closest landmark on the shore. In papers [1, 6, 7] it has been shown that in an unknown place untrained pigeons first try to explore the area, and perform survey flights in different directions, while trained pigeons head straight to the goal. This is also true of pigeons flying in groups.

It is worth noting that pigeon flight paths may reflect areas and objects in the terrain, as well as points of interest for the pigeons, such as feeding or sleeping places. Elements of the terrain to which pigeons react may include extended ones – roads, rivers, or borders of dissimilar territories – or point-areal ones. Significant terrain elements may set of various flight "corridors" or distort flight paths even in case of the same starting and final route points.

A range of possible of pigeon flight path is shown in the diagram in Fig. 1.

Figure 1 shows that in cases (a) and (d) a common movement direction remains, in case (b) the movement direction changes after the "beacon", in case (c) movement is directed to the point of interest until it is closely approached, and in case (e) movement with no definite direction occurs near a point of interest.

2.2 Particularities of Pigeon Visual Cognition When Orienting Themselves During Flight

The biological features of a pigeon allow it to use active visual stimuli when orienting itself. The flicker threshold value at which separate moving stimuli seem to be continuous is higher for a pigeon than a human and equal to 75 frames per second [8, 9]. When flying, a pigeon can determine distance and conditions and orient itself within a short time. A pigeon has color vision, its viewing angle is 340° and it successfully tracks direction. Herbranson et al. [10] described features of the cognition of pigeons during visual orientation in relation to angles. The authors discovered that information

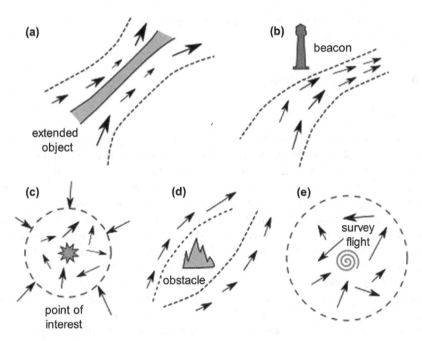

Fig. 1. Typical pigeon flight paths in relation to external factors: (a) "flight corridor" along an extended object; (b) flight with the "beacon" as a landmark which is not directly approached; (c) movement around the "point of interest", with no definite direction of movement near the point of interest; (d) skirting around obstructions; (e) survey flight, with no definite direction of movement.

about angles in terms of a direction of movement may be more important for pigeons than information about the angle of orientation of static stimuli.

The significance of visual stimuli is different for investigatory flights, when a pigeon surveys unknown terrain, than for purposeful flights, when a pigeon flies along the known path to the known goal. The path of the investigatory survey flight may cover a large territory. It is during the survey flight that a pigeon actively reacts to the terrain features in a way that is noticeable based on its flight. A trained pigeon mostly flies almost directly to the goal with insignificant deviations from a set route. Biro et al. [11] state that when orienting itself while flying above known terrain, a pigeon may combine purposeful movement in a chosen direction with landmark guidance.

Moreover, the way in which a pigeon orients itself based on visual data is directly influenced by the degree to which the landscape is filled with separate stimuli. Mann et al. [12] studied the influence of landscape complexity on pigeon navigational behavior. The authors concluded that pigeons orient themselves better when flying above territory where landscape complexity is neither too high nor too low.

It is also important to understand that the objects determined as landmarks may exist simultaneously at different scales. Stimuli may include both separate trees in the forest and the extended forest area itself, in which trees can only be interpreted as a texture fill. Characteristic distance values for pigeon "flight corridors" and characteristic "beacon" stimuli sizes are determined in the present paper for flights above combined cross-country and urban terrain.

3 Materials and Methods

3.1 Materials

We performed spatial analysis of pigeons' trajectories using the geographical information system QGIS. Calculation within the investigation of pigeons' flights was performed using the Dryad data package published in the Dryad Digital Repository [13] (publication [7]). Flights of poorly trained pigeons above the varied terrain were selected for processing (the first, second and third pigeon flights above the known terrain). Flight paths of pigeons flying separately were reviewed. Pigeons flew over cross-country terrain (site 1) and over urban terrain (site 2). Analysis was performed for two different points of departure from site 1 and 2, with the same final landing point. Calculation was made for 24 flights from site 1 and for 27 flights from site 2. The areas of departure and landing of pigeons were reviewed separately (in these areas paths crossed themselves more often and movement direction was constantly changing). Characteristic parameters of pigeons' flights were measured using QGIS tools, indicating that for site 1 the distance from the departure point to the final point was 11.3 km, and for site 2 it was 12.6 km. The characteristic distance between separate coordinate values of pigeons' GPS tracks is in the range of 20–40 m, and the coordinates of separate points on GPS tracks were measured once per second.

Remote sensing data (satellite images) in the form of OpenLayers (http://openlayers.org) was used for ground surface information about the chosen terrain. The original coordinate system of the project was WGS 84.

3.2 Methods

This work was performed in the following steps:

1. Creation of Data Layers.

- Creation of point and line vector layers with pigeon flight data based on GPS tracks that were presented in the CSV file format. Creation of linear Vector layers featuring pigeons' trajectories.
- OpenLayers (http://openlayers.org) embedding. Creation and reference of raster layers with satellite image materials for the area of pigeon flights.

2. Flight Corridor Identification.

Flight corridor identification was calculated in three different ways on the basis of the characteristic features of pigeon trajectories, such as (i) common intersections, (ii) similar directions, and (iii) overlapping buffer zones of different tracks:

- Intersection corridors were identified based on selection of intersection points of different flight paths. Figure 2(a) shows an example of the intersection points in which the trajectories of pigeons were crossed in pairs.
- Directional corridors were identified based on selection of points, where different pigeons were flying in similar directions. The movement directions were identified using the angle of movement from one GPS point to the next on the same track. The intervals of the direction angles were set as (0–30), (30–60), (60–90), (90–120), (120–150), (150–180), (180–210), (210–240), (240–270), (270–300), (300–330) and (330–360) degrees. The movement directions were considered similar if they fell into the same interval in terms of the direction angle. The entire flight area was split into equal segments; the GPS track points with a similar direction were selected if there were at least eight of them in one segment. Figure 2(b) shows an example of how movement in a specific direction was identified.
- Proximity corridors were identified based on the buffers with 35 m distance from the tracks. The buffers were built at a 35 m distance from the pigeon GPS-tracks. Figure 2(c) displays an example of buffers near tracks. The union buffer layer contains all pairwise intersections of the original buffers.

3. Regions of Interest Identification.

Certain regions of pigeons' interest were discovered in addition to the flight corridors. If a heterogeneous direction of movement corresponding to the "survey flight" (as shown in Fig. 1(e)) is found in the area in which pigeon trajectories converged, it is presumed to be a region of interest (ROI). ROIs could be identified if the trajectories of at least five pigeon flights were close to each other and there was multidirectional movement near ROI. Figure 3 shows an example of ROI identification.

4. Identification of Visual Features of the Landscape.

Visual features of the landscape were identified according to the concentration of visually observed objects. Firstly, boundaries of individual homogeneous surfaces were identified by constructing isolines. A density map of the existing terrain inhomogeneities was then constructed based on the resulting clusters of isolines for characteristic inhomogeneity dimensions of 50 and more meters. The specified accuracy for the inhomogeneity map corresponds to typical distance between two neighboring points of the GPS pigeon tracks. Figure 4 displays an example of the area under analysis and the corresponding inhomogeneity map.

5. Comparison of the pigeon flight corridors and terrain features.

- The pigeon flight corridors that had been found using the three methods specified in Steps 2 were compared to the areas of visual terrain features identified using the methods specified in Step 4.

3.3   QGIS Plugins

Batch processing was applied while performing the spatial analysis. The data were processed using the open source software program QGIS (http://qgis.org), including

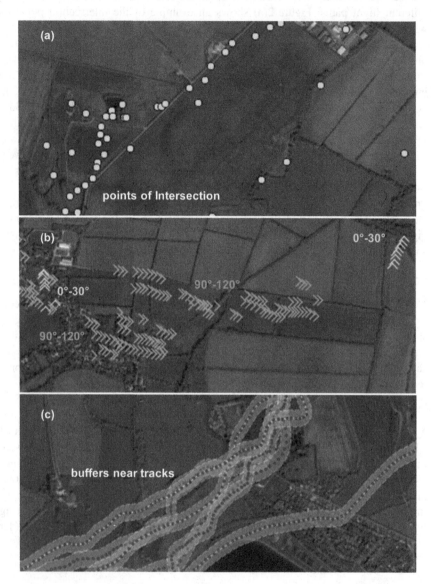

Fig. 2. Selection of characteristic features in the flight corridors: (a) intersection of the trajectories: the points of intersection show the places where crossed two GPS-tracks of pigeons; (b) similar directions movements: the upwards arrows indicate the points at which the pigeons were flying 0 to 30 degrees to the north, and the rightwards arrows indicate the points at which the pigeons were flying 90 to 120 degrees to the north; (c) buffer areas: pigeon tracks are represented by dotted lines, and buffers with 35 m distance from the tracks are represented by light solid fills.

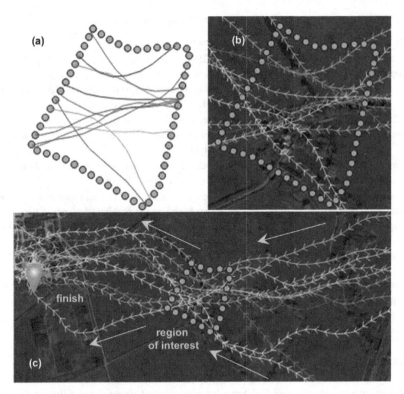

Fig. 3. Pigeon trajectories in the region of interest (indicated with dotted circles in the figure): (a) pigeon tracks; (b) pigeon tracks with OpenLayers data; (c) tracks displayed within the wider area near the region of interest, with general directions of movement indicated by the arrows.

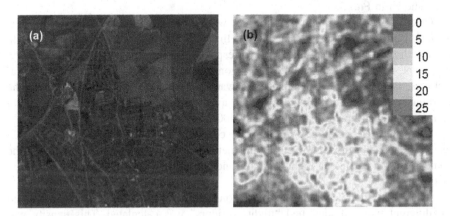

Fig. 4. Construction of the terrain inhomogeneity map: (a) the area under analysis; (b) the calculated inhomogeneity map; the range shows the concentration of diversified landmarks in the territory.

Table 1. Applied QGIS tools and external plugins

Plugin	Description
OpenLayers plugin https://github.com/sourcepole/qgis-openlayers-plugin	QGIS plugin embeds OpenLayers (http://openlayers.org) functionality. I. It allows to obtain Google Maps, Bing Maps, OpenStreetMap and another open source layers
Points2One http://plugins.qgis.org/plugins/points2one	Create lines and polygons from vertices. Connects points in a layer to form lines and polygons
Line intersections https://www.qgis.org/en/docs/index.html	Locate intersections between lines, and output results as a point shapefile
Heatmap plugin http://www.qgistutorials.com/en/docs/creating_heatmaps.html	Create a density raster of an input point vector layer based on the number of points in a location, with larger numbers of clustered points resulting in larger values

additional analysis plugins: QGIS geoalgorithms and GDAL tools (http://www.gdal.org) integrated into QGIS. The applied external tools and plugins are presented in Table 1.

4   Results

Map layers of movement corridors have been computed using three different methods: (i) with flight trajectories crossing most often; (ii) with matching movement directions for different pigeons; (iii) with a number of pigeons traveling in the vicinity of other flight trajectories. Direction and proximity corridors for flights with departing from site 1 are shown in Fig. 5.

Calculations of distribution of corridor widths, where the pigeons flew, were performed using the Delaunay triangulation. In QGIS, this algorithm creates a polygon layer with the Delaunay triangulation corresponding to point layers of object density. After that, the sides of the resulting polygons intersected with the selected flight trajectories, the width of each intersection was determined. The average width of the corridors was determined as the weighted average of obtained results. Typical flight corridors are distributed in width of 200–400 m.

Then, the pigeon flight corridors were compared to the areas with visual terrain features that had been identified using the methods specified in Step 3. The result of the comparison for the pigeon flight corridors and density of visual landmarks is displayed in Fig. 6.

In addition, the relative density of pigeon flights over different types of terrain and for different types of identified "flight corridors" was calculated. This density was calculated as the number of registration of GPS tracks of pigeons in the "flight corridor", normalized by area. Figure 7 shows the diagrams of the dependence of the

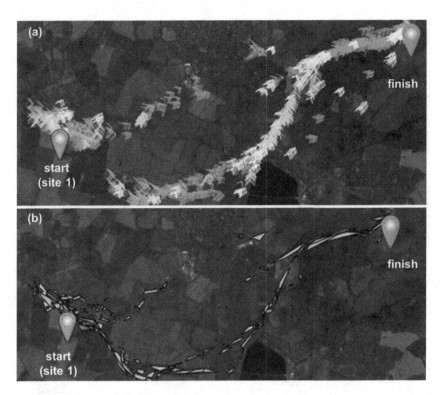

Fig. 5. Direction and proximity corridors for flights departing from site 1. (a) Direction corridors based on the similarity in direction of pigeon flights in the selected area. The movement directions were identified using the angle of movement from one GPS point to the next on the same track. Arrows indicate directions for the intervals of (0–30), (30–60), (60–90) and (90–120) degrees. (b) Proximity corridors based on whether there is a common buffer for the trajectories of different flights. The summary buffer is constructed using buffer intersections.

density of pigeon flights on the density of landmarks in the terrain, for the intersection corridors. As a result of comparison of the landscape flown over by the pigeons and their trajectories, it has been found that pigeons prefer the average density of landmarks during the flight over poorly oriented "cross-country" terrain (Fig. 7a). In contrast, pigeons flying over a terrain with a large number of landmarks (buildings, a network of roads) often fly over a terrain with a high density of objects (Fig. 7b).

At once, calculations made from data on direction corridors show that the directions of the pigeons are more pronounced in a locality with a high density of reference objects.

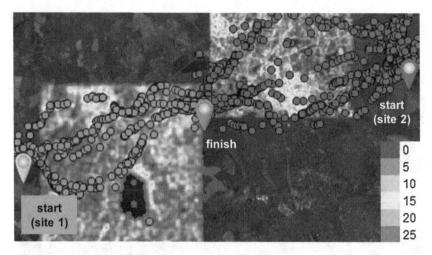

Fig. 6. Comparison of the pigeon flight corridors and density of visual landmarks. Intersection corridors have been identified where flight trajectories cross each other frequently, for flights departing from sites 1 (west) and 2 (east). The flight corridors usually correspond to the average density of isolines. The range shows the density of diversified landmarks in the territory.

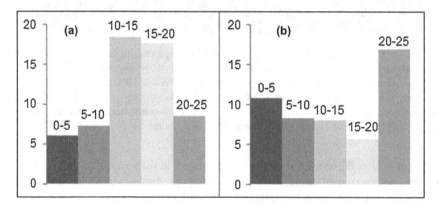

Fig. 7. Diagrams of the density of flights of pigeons, depending on the concentration of objects in the territory, calculated according to "intersection corridors". The abscissa shows the concentration of landmarks in the territory, the ordinate shows the normalized density of the flight of pigeons over the territory with a given concentration of landmarks (a) flight over a poorly oriented ("cross-country") terrain - site 1; (b) flight over a terrain with a large concentration of objects ("urban" area with a building and a network of roads) - site 2.

5   Conclusions

The paper explored the flights of different pigeons flying along a route with given points of departure and destination, over combined cross-country and urban terrain that was previously little known. Similarities and differences in the trajectories of the bird flights have been identified, and track features were attributed both to the visual features of the landscape birds fly over and to specific locations that are significant for the pigeons.

It was revealed that the spatial orientation of pigeons when flying over a terrain with a low density of objects differs from the orientation when flying over a territory with a large density of different landmarks. The birds preferred not to fly over a built-up area with high density of visual reference points, or – in contrast – to fly with making a lot of multidirectional survey movements over high density terrain.

The results of the study prove that it is possible to identify the location of points and extended areas that are of significance for the pigeons only by processing spatial data on the birds' GPS trajectories, even in the absence of an appropriate cartographic map. Identified points and areas correspond to particular places on the real terrain.

Unlike movement on the road network, birds traveling in the air have less need to tie themselves to certain movement corridors. However, they can use such corridors, including taking into account the visual perception of the terrain. Thus, the study of bird flight path properties makes it possible to fully reveal general principles of spatial orientation during navigation.

References

1. Blaser, N., Dell'Omo, G., Dell'Ariccia, G., Wolfer, D.P., Lipp, H.-P.: Testing cognitive navigation in unknown territories: homing pigeons choose different targets. J. Exp. Biol. **216**, 3123–3131 (2013). https://doi.org/10.1242/jeb.083246
2. Lipp, H.-P., Vyssotski, A.L., Wolfer, D.P., Renaudineau, S., Savini, M., Tröster, G., et al.: Pigeon homing along highways and exits. Curr. Biol. **14**, 1239–1449 (2004). http://linkinghub.elsevier.com/retrieve/pii/S0960982204005160
3. Jiménez Ortega, L., Stoppa, K., Güntürkün, O., Troje, N.F.: Vision during head bobbing: are pigeons capable of shape discrimination during the thrust phase? Exp. Brain Res. **199**, 313–321 (2009). https://doi.org/10.1007/s00221-009-1891-5
4. Schiffner, I., Siegmund, B., Wiltschko, R.: Following the sun: a mathematical analysis of the tracks of clock-shifted homing pigeons. J. Exp. Biol. **217**, 2643–2649 (2014). http://www.ncbi.nlm.nih.gov/pubmed/24803461
5. Vyssotski, A.L., Dell'Omo, G., Dell'Ariccia, G., Abramchuk, A.N., Serkov, A.N., Latanov, A.V., et al.: EEG responses to visual landmarks in flying pigeons. Curr. Biol. **19**, 1159–1166 (2009). https://doi.org/10.1016/j.cub.2009.05.070
6. Wiltschko, R., Wiltschko, W.: Avian navigation: a combination of innate and learned mechanisms. Adv. Study Behav. **47**, 229–310 (2015). https://doi.org/10.1016/bs.asb.2014.12.002
7. Pettit, B., Flack, A., Freeman, R., Guilford, T., Biro, D.: Not just passengers: pigeons, Columba livia, can learn homing routes while flying with a more experienced conspecific. Proc. R. Soc. B Biol. Sci. **280**, 20122160 (2012). https://doi.org/10.1098/rspb.2012.2160

8. Bovet, D., Vauclair, J.: Picture recognition in animals and humans. Behav. Brain Res. **109**, 143–165 (2000). http://linkinghub.elsevier.com/retrieve/pii/S0166432800001467

9. D'Eath, R.B.: Can video images imitate real stimuli in animal behaviour experiments? Biol. Rev. **73**, 267–292 (2007). https://doi.org/10.1111/j.1469-185X.1998.tb00031.x

10. Herbranson, W.T., Karas, E., Hardin, G.: Perception of angle in visual categorization by pigeons (Columba livia). Anim. Behav. Cogn. **4**, 286–300 (2017). http://www.animalbehaviorandcognition.org/article.php?id=1093

11. Biro, D., Freeman, R., Meade, J., Roberts, S., Guilford, T.: Pigeons combine compass and landmark guidance in familiar route navigation. Proc. Natl. Acad. Sci. **104**, 7471–7476 (2007). https://doi.org/10.1073/pnas.0701575104

12. Mann, R.P., Armstrong, C., Meade, J., Freeman, R., Biro, D., Guilford, T.: Landscape complexity influences route-memory formation in navigating pigeons. Biol. Lett. **10**, 20130885 (2014). https://doi.org/10.1098/rsbl.2013.0885

13. Pettit, B., Flack, A., Freemain, R., Guilford, T., Biro, D.: Not just passengers: Pigeons, Columba livia, can learn homing routes while flying with a more experienced conspecific. Proc. R. Soc. B. Dryad Digital Repository (2012). https://doi.org/10.5061/dryad.53f4b

Humans Construct Survey Estimates on the Fly from a Compartmentalised Representation of the Navigated Environment

Tobias Meilinger[1](✉), Agnes Henson[1,2], Jonathan Rebane[1,3],
Heinrich H. Bülthoff[1], and Hanspeter A. Mallot[4]

[1] Max Planck Institute for Biological Cybernetics, Tübingen, Germany
tobias.meilinger@tuebingen.mpg.de
[2] Leeds Beckett University, Leeds, UK
[3] Stockholm University, Stockholm, Sweden
[4] Cognitive Neuroscience, Eberhard-Karls-University, Tübingen, Germany
hanspeter.mallot@uni-tuebingen.de

Abstract. Despite its relevance for navigation surprisingly little is known about how goal direction bearings to distant locations are computed. Behavioural and neuroscientific models proposing the path integration of previously navigated routes are supported indirectly by neural data, but behavioral evidence is lacking. We show that humans integrate navigated routes post-hoc and incrementally while conducting goal direction estimates. Participants learned a multi-corridor layout by walking through a virtual environment. Throughout learning, participants repeatedly performed pairwise pointing from the start location, end location, and each turn location between segments. Pointing latency increased with the number of corridors to the target and decreased with pointing experience rather than environmental familiarity. Bimodal pointing distributions indicate that participants made systematic errors, for example, mixing up turns or forgetting segments. Modeling these error sources suggests that pointing did not rely on one unified, but rather multiple representations of the experimental environment. We conclude that participants performed incremental on-the-fly calculations of goal direction estimates within compartmentalised representations, which was quicker for nearby goals and became faster with repeated pointing. Within navigated environments humans do not compute difference vectors from coordinates of a globally consistent integrated "map in the head".

Keywords: Spatial learning · Survey knowledge · Virtual environments

1 Introduction

For survey estimates, such as novel shortcutting or distal pointing, navigators must utilise their memory to relate their current location to a distant, non-perceivable target location. A straight-forward mechanism to achieve this is read-out of current and target coordinates from an integrated memory and computation of a difference vector. Such a computationally simple process does not depend on distance to target or familiarity with an environment, but requires that locations are represented within a coordinate

© Springer Nature Switzerland AG 2018
S. Creem-Regehr et al. (Eds.): Spatial Cognition 2018, LNAI 11034, pp. 15–26, 2018.
https://doi.org/10.1007/978-3-319-96385-3_2

system. Other behavioral [1, 2] and neuroscientific models [3–5] propose path integration of previously navigated routes, for example, in the form of a mental walk. These assumptions are supported by neural data such as successive activation of hippocampal place cells along a path to the goal [6] and medial temporal lobe activity correlating with goal distance [7, 8]. A related account does not assume mental walk, but constructing a mental model of a non-visible area by integrating successive corridors until a goal location is reached [9]. Both mental walk and mental model assume an increase in computation with route distance and both would predict speed-up with repeated survey estimation demands. In contrast to read-out from a cognitive map these two models are hereafter referred to as 'constructive'.

In order to test these assumptions we conducted a learning experiment within an immersive virtual environment (VE) consisting of a route of eight corridors presented via a head-mounted display (HMD) (Figs. 1 and 2A). Participants repeatedly walked through the environment from start to end and back. Throughout learning, they were repeatedly asked to point from each of the nine route locations (Fig. 1B) to each other location. Participants either conducted pointing tasks interspersed throughout the whole environment familiarisation period, or later on in the navigational task. We used latency data as well as an analysis of systematic errors to draw conclusions about the alternative models explored above. Latency was measured to probe whether distance influenced location processing (i.e., read-out vs. constructive) and also whether learning was contingent on repeated survey task demands or mere exposure. The systematic error analysis characterised whether errors could be specifically modelled as non-random deviations from the correct pointing direction, such as on the basis of incorrect turns or deleting sections during integration.

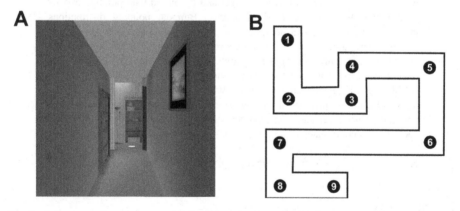

Fig. 1. Experimental environment (A) Participant's view. (B) Bird's eye view of environmental layout. Circles represent target and test locations for the pointing task numbered from start across the center of all turn to the end of the route.

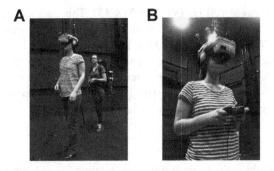

Fig. 2. Experimental procedure. (A) A participant walking through the environment during the learning phase. (B) A participant performing the test phase using an input device. The persons on the photo consented to publication.

2   Methods

2.1   Participants

Twenty-five participants (12 females and 13 males) aged between 23 and 65 ($M = 32.2$ years, $SD = 11$ years) participated in this experiment. They were randomly assigned to the *early pointing* condition (12 participants) and the *late pointing* condition (13 participants). We expected large effect sizes for the between group comparisons in addition with precise measurements due to many repetitions. Twelve participants per group should be sufficient to find them. All participants were recruited via a subject database, were paid for their participation, and signed an informed consent approved by the ethical committee of the University Clinics in Tübingen before participating in the experiment.

2.2   Material

The Virtual Environment. Figure 1 shows a snapshot of the environment as seen during walking, as well as a map of the route. The route consisted of a start and endpoint, as well as seven turning locations along the route. During the first two learning trials, all nine of these 'target locations' were named by the experimenter as the participant arrived at the location. These target locations were named after salient landmarks at the locations. The locations were named as follows: Filing Cabinet, Bay Window, Mirror, Vase, Potted Plant, Bookcase, Painting, Grandfather Clock, Fishbowl. The corridor design and environmental landmarks were distinct at each location, with sufficient information to identify and distinguish each location from one another.

The Setup. Participants walked within a 12×12 m space, of which the VE covered a 10×10 m area. This allowed them to explore the space, without the possibility of walking into any obstacles and provided realistic proprioceptive and vestibular feedback, as well as efference copies while walking in VEs (see Fig. 2A). To obtain participants' location in the space, their head position was tracked by 16 high-speed motion capture cameras at 120 Hz (Vicon® MX 13). This data was used to update the visualization of the VE. The visual surrounding at a location was rendered in real time (60 Hz) using a NVIDIA Quadro FX 3700 graphics card with 1024 MB RAM in a standard laptop. Participants viewed the scene in stereo using an nVisor SX 60 head-mounted display that provided a field of view of 44 × 35 degrees at a resolution of 1280 × 1024 pixels for each eye with 100% overlap. This setup provided important visual depth cues such as stereo images and motion parallax.

2.3   Procedure

There were 10 walkthroughs in each direction, totaling 20 walkthroughs of the environment. Participants were instructed to follow a moving ball throughout the space in order to constrain exploration time. The virtual ball moved at an average speed of 1 m per second, stopping to hover for 3 s over white circles on the ground at each turning location and at both ends of the environment.

During the *pointing task* in *the test phase*, participants were teleported to target locations. Here they were asked to successively point to all other target locations. During these trials, participants could look and rotate around, but not walk. This was enforced by placing participants in a circular handrail with 0.48 m diameter to prevent them from leaving their location. Participants were asked to press a button on their gamepad once they recognised their location (Fig. 2B). The time required to "self-localise" was recorded for each participant. Participants were then instructed on the display to point to a named location, as if the walls were transparent. They were provided with a black midline through the display and informed to move their head until the line corresponded to the estimated target location. The name of the target location was displayed on the screen for each pointing. When participants believed they were facing the target, they pressed a button to move on to the next pointing. At each testing location all eight target locations were presented in a random order, that was newly determined for each location. No feedback on accuracy was given. After they had pointed to all targets from one location, participants were teleported to a new position. This was repeated, in random order, until participants had pointed to all target locations from all nine locations along the route. This resulted in 72 pointings per pointing task.

The final section of the *test phase* consisted of a *sequence task*. Participants were again transported to each location and were required to detail the turning sequence from that location to each end location by pressing the 'left' and 'right' keys on the gamepad corresponding to the turning sequence from their location to one of the end locations. This was collected for both directions from every location except the end locations themselves, and the penultimate locations before an end location. For these locations, only one sequence direction was recorded, as one end location is always visible for each penultimate location. Data from this task is not further reported here.

Participants were randomly assigned to two conditions, which dictated when they experienced the pointing task. Participants in *the early pointing group* were given the complete test phase (pointing task followed by sequence task) every four trials. Participants in the *late pointing condition* performed only the sequence section of the test phase after learning trials 4, 8 and 12. They eventually experienced the full test phase after 16 and then 20 trials. Additional post hoc tasks and questionnaires are not reported here. The whole experiment with in between breaks lasted approximately 3.5 h in the early pointing and 2.5 h in the late pointing group.

2.4 Analysis

For the analysis we used pointing time and computed the absolute pointing error. Values deviating more than three standard deviations from a participant's mean were not analyzed. Accuracy and latency were analyzed with ANOVAs using the between-participants factor pointing group (early vs. late) and either the within-participants factor learning trial (4, 8, 12, 16 & 20), or distance to the target expressed as the number of corridors (1–8). When deviating from sphericity we applied the Greenhouse-Geisser correction.

2.5 Error Modeling

First, it was determined if participants made qualitative errors, characterised as systematic, non-random deviations from the correct pointing direction. We expected correct pointing directions derived from pairwise pointings (i.e., pointing from location X to location Y) to have Von Mises distribution (i.e., the circular equivalent of normal distribution) with peaks centered near the correct pointing directions. To test for prevalent Von Mises distribution we conducted v-tests [10]. Then Rayleigh tests examined if any deviation was due to uniform data (i.e., point equally often in each direction) or instead a result of an additional Von Mises distribution peak at another location (Fig. 3). In order to establish the origin of any such errors, we conducted modelling to distinguish between possible representational strategies. A read-out strategy relies on co-ordinate look-up from a single unified representation, while mental model construction allows for multiple local representations that may vary across locations pointed from, pointed to or direction of pointing.

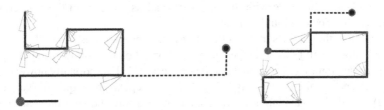

Fig. 3. Example pointing distributions. Solid red circles denote correct point location. Circular histograms plots are shown at pointing locations and reflect directions pointed towards. The black and red circles denote the final pointing location assuming a subject mixes up a turn.

According to constructive theories, sources of systematic error might include: wrong turns, forgetting or inserting elements, mixing up current location or target location, and estimating on the basis of a smaller number of turns. Such qualitative errors were assumed as the most logical explanation of any bimodality observed in the pointing data, compared to other continuous sources of error, such as leg-length adjusting.

In order to identify such turning and forgetting errors, new mazes were generated in MATLAB by alternating single turn directions (e.g., at location 4 or 6 as in Fig. 3) resulting in 7 alternative mazes or by eliminating legs (e.g., between location 3 and 4) resulting in 6 alternative mazes. Correct and alternative mazes were tested for best fit per subject and trial period on the basis of minimal absolute error. For each subject and period this was done three times, for all pointings together, as well as separately, for both forward and backward directions. Forward vs. backward can be considered as the simplest compartmentalization which keeps complexity of the pointing tasks constant (i.e., each pair of locations A and B occurs in each sub-set).

3   Results and Discussion

3.1   The Generation of Survey Estimates

We used pointing latency as a function of target distance and familiarity to distinguish between read out from a cognitive map and constructive accounts (i.e., mental walk and mental model). A distance effect on pointing latency would support predictions of constructive strategies, since greater integration demands entail greater processing, either in form of a longer mental walk or a larger constructed mental model. However, a read-out strategy would assume constant cognitive effort for all estimations, and thus predict constant latency. Pointing latency indeed differed as a function of distance, $F(2.34, 161) = 9.72$, $p < .001$, $\eta_p^2 = .30$, and increased with distance to the target up to a distance of four corridors, F's > 8.1, p's $< .010$, before plateauing (Fig. 4A). Error also differed, $F(2.22, 161) = 39.8$, $p < .001$, $\eta_p^2 = .63$, and increased up to six corridors, F's > 19.5, p's $< .001$ (Fig. 4B). Similar error increase has been demonstrated previously [11] and might stem simply from learning, as larger travelled distance results in larger average errors [12]. While the current data do not differentiate between models, the latency increase with distance nevertheless aligns with the predictions of constructive theories of spatial processing.

Constructive theories assume an effortful estimation processes via walkthroughs or segmental integration; however, repeated estimations should result in speeded pointing due to increased familiarity with these active processes [13]. Importantly however, such training effects should occur only when such strategies are required (i.e., during pointing), not during navigation itself. Simple exposure to the environment does not make demands on these estimation practices. To test this prediction we compared two groups of navigators. The early pointing group completed a pointing task after four learning trials (i.e., walkthroughs through the environment), and were then tested after every four learning trials throughout the experiment. The late pointing group completed 16 learning trials before the first pointing task and were tested again after the 20th learning trial.

Pointing latency decreased with pointing experience (Fig. 4C), as opposed to experience navigating an environment. During their first pointing trial, early and late pointers pointed equally quickly, $F(1,23) = 0.008$, $p = .929$, despite the greater environmental experience of late pointers. Afterwards, latencies decreased both for late poin-ters, $F(1,12) = 38, p < .001$, and for early pointers up to the 16th learning trial, $F(1,11)$'s $> 4.24, p$'s $< .065$. We also observed improvement from the first to the second half of the first pointing test, $F(1,23) = 5.51, p = .028$. Comparing the first halves, after 16 learning trials (i.e., same familiarity with the environment), the early learners pointed more quickly, $F(1,23) = 5.68, p = .026$, profiting from their prior pointing experience. Pointing error (Fig. 4D), however, was inversely related to familiarity with the environment, rather than experience in pointing estimates. The error of learning groups did not differ at the same level of environmental familiarity, $F(1,23) = 0.363, p = .553$, although late pointers were more accurate at their first pointing than early pointers, $F(1,23) = 6.01, p = .022$. This indicates that the quality of the representation improved with navigation, though the estimation process itself only improved with repeated opportunities to point. This dissociation of pointing errors and latencies also excludes an explanation that larger errors result in lower confidence, which results in longer latencies. Late pointers show low error, but high latencies which then cannot be explained by low confidence.

While these results strongly support the predictions of constructive theories of survey estimation, we also propose that this procedure is consistent with accounts of the biological mechanism of place cell pre-play. Pre-play is a process that has been documented in place cells which identify locations, for example, along a route. During pre-play place cells along a route successively fire as if the animal was walking along the route towards the goal while being physically located at one spot [6]. Pre-play is

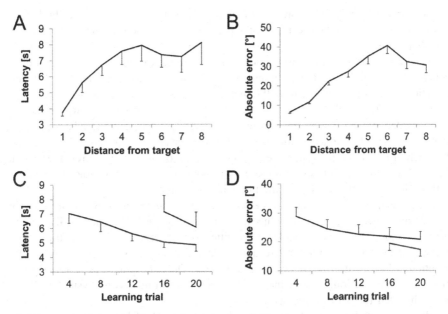

Fig. 4. Pointing results. (A) Latency and (B) pointing error as a function of distance (number of corridors). (C) Latency and (D) absolute pointing error as a function of learning trials for early and late pointers. Error bars indicate 1 standard error as estimated from the marginal means.

more consistent with an account of integration via mental walk. Mental walk would assume that before a navigator conducts a survey task, they mentally walk through an environmental representation, where place cells encode self-location [3]. This would explain the distance effect in time, as mentally walking longer distances should also result in longer estimation times. However, in order to account for latency reduction as a function of testing, the mental walk account would be forced to conceptually decouple mental and physical walking.

The cognitive demand initially burdening latency could conceivably be due to either spatial processing or handling the pointing task. Handling is unlikely to have significantly increased cognitive load, as the task of aligning a black line to a target was basic, and no subject experienced issues performing the task. Handling demands would also predict a parallel decrease in both error and latency over learning, while both dissociate for late pointers. Finally, the plateau that occurs in pointing latency as a function of distance could reflect estimation based on a truncated number of segments, since further estimation will not have a large impact on pointing accuracy. Alternatively, there could be cognitive capacity limitations that prevent more distant estimations.

Pointing latency improvement with experience could originate from an enhanced estimation process or from recalling previous pointing responses, thereby skipping the estimation process. While memorising vectors read out from a map can similarly explain such a latency reduction, the difference vectors predicted by this account cannot explain latency increase with target distance

3.2   Compartmentalization in Spatial Memory

In addition to the underlying process of survey navigation as indicated in the latency data, we wished to probe the types of representations formed during such tasks via systematic errors.

Most pointings showed a distribution centered around the correct target direction as indicated by significant circular v-tests (Figs. 3 and 5). However, there were clear deviations to that pattern at least at the first testing in 14% of location-target pairs (i.e., $2 \to 7$, $3 \to 7$, $2 \to 8$, $3 \to 8$, $1 \to 9$, $2 \to 9$, $3 \to 9$ and $4 \to 9$). Rayleigh tests demonstrated that in all cases this was not due to uniform data, but instead a result of an additional Von Mises distribution peak at another location (p's < 0.01). It is unlikely that such bimodal distributions were merely the result of quantitative error. Please note that for bimodal distributions with close-by peaks (e.g., Fig. 3 right side) this analysis will not identify deviations from the predicted orientation.

To investigate whether these systematic errors originated from one representation or multiple underlying representations we compared forward vs. backward navigation. Figure 6 shows such mazes which were fitted per subject and learning trial to the pointing data separately for forward and backward pointing. We then compared distributions of best fitting mazes using Fisher tests. Only the pointings across leg segments of three and longer were included in the maze fittings, as no systematic errors were observed for the two leg cases.

We observed deviations from the correct map in 40% of the mazes for forgetting one corridor leg and 29% for single turn errors. In both cases forward and backwards maze fits differed (both p < .001, Fig. 6). This suggests that forward and backward

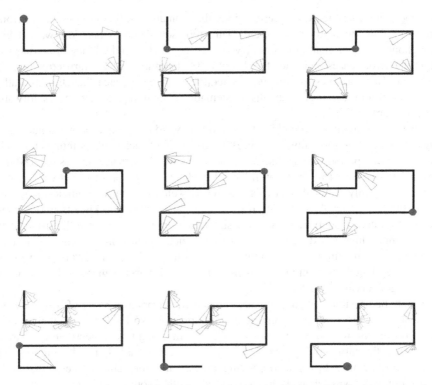

Fig. 5. Pairwise pointings. Solid circles denote correct point location. Circular histograms plots from early and late pointing groups are shown at pairwise pointing locations between selected landmark locations and the desired goal.

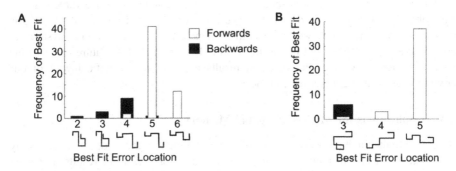

Fig. 6. Frequencies of best fit maze models. (A) Maze fits for forgetting error. (B) Maze fits for single turn errors. Below the x-axis are the types of mazes formed assuming an error of the corresponding type was made at the designated location (i.e., 3 would denote the 3rd landmark location from the start of the maze as indicated in Fig. 1B).

pointing estimates relied on representations that contained different systematic errors and were thus qualitatively different. This representational separation was stable throughout the experiment; it was observed after the 8th, 16th and 20th learning trials for forgetting error mazes and after the 4th and 20th learning trial for turn error mazes, p's < .05. This indicates that navigators require more experience than the 20 walk-throughs (20 min learning) to equalise systematic errors in representations for forward and backward walking.

Mazes were fitted for a combined forward backward representation when making a single turn error and forgetting one leg. Both forward and backwards pointings for each subject and trial period were included for analysis. Fits with separate mazes reduced the error in average by 24% for forgetting and 18% for turns (p's < .001). Fit was greater than for randomly shuffled data (p's < .001) as well as fitting one single map only (p's < .009). In general, fitting the data to new forward and backwards mazes con-siderably reduced the error. However a significant amount of error still existed after maze fitting, which could perhaps best be explained by allowing for more than one single error in the maze, and combining forgetting and turning errors as well as incorrect leg-length estimation or handling errors, and working memory limitation in generating a survey estimate.

It may be possible that subjects made systematic errors as a result of being unable to self-localise. However, the pointing distributions for two leg-length segments were all unimodal with relatively low variance (Fig. 5), meaning that subjects were accurate in assessing the current and adjacent target locations. It is unlikely that having to point further resulted in subjects incorporating positional error. This suggests that self-localization error was relatively low compared to other sources of error.

We used forward vs. backward pointing mainly because comparing both repre-sentations results in an overall similar route complexity as each pair A-B occurs in each representation. However, the observed direction dependent division was also observed in previous priming, route choice and place cell firing [14–16]. Present results extend such a separation also to survey estimations.

Our results are based on one specific environment tested. It is conceivable that, for example, the observed error dissociation between forward and backward pointing is only found in environments with an overall U-shape (in which the examined systematic errors have large effects), but not so much in rather linear routes. Future experiments have to evidence whether the obtained results depend on a specific layout of our environment or also generalises to others.

3.3   Implications for Models of Spatial Memory

Returning to the three proposed models of survey estimation, the evidence would firstly not point to a read-out model, due to clear contradictions with our results. Read-out does not predict the observed distance effect, nor the familiarity or compartmental-ization effects. Mental walk model [3] can be best connected with animal literature such as pre-play [6]. Mental walk model would predict the distance effect and can account for the observed familiarity, compartmentalization and directional effects, though would require an explicit dissociation between learning (physical navigation) and estimation processes (mental walk), as latency only improves with the latter rather than the former. This is in line with findings from single cell recording, which show that in similar corridor environments, different place cells are active depending on the direction of walking [16]. Clusters of direction-specific place cells might form separate maps for forward and backward pointing. Finally, the mental model [9] is consistent with all data. It is accurate in describing the distance effect through mental model construction, and can explain performance improvement with repeated model construction through pointing that is independent from walking itself. It also assumes that the underlying representation is compartmentalised (e.g. one representation for each corridor [17–19]), thus permitting different errors resulting from unique forward and backward connections between parts. The largest downside of the mental model proposition is that it cannot be connected to animal literature, although such survey estimates might be specifically human [20, 21], with other species not possessing the cognitive capacity to build a mental model of distant locations.

In conclusion, we claim that the formation of survey estimates in humans occurs incrementally at response, rather than occurring via read-out from a cognitive map. This is suggested, first, by the increase in pointing latency with distance, and second, by decreasing latency as a function of pointing training, as opposed to familiarity with the environment. Furthermore, the bimodal distribution of pointings, suggests that human survey knowledge incorporates both quantitative errors (e.g., acquired through path integration during learning), and systematic errors (i.e., those which originate from mixing up or forgetting elements of the route walked). The error modelling provided evidence to suggest there might be no unified underlying representations for survey navigation tasks in humans. This was indicated by different model fits for forwards and backwards representations. Results are clearly inconsistent with reading out coordinates from a globally consistent survey representation. Instead, they are consistent with constructive accounts, such as mental walk and mental model.

Acknowledgements. This work was supported by the DFG grant ME 3476/2-1. We would like to thank Joachim Tesch for help with the virtual environment setup.

References

1. Poucet, B.: Spatial cognitive maps in animals: new hypotheses on their structure and neural mechanisms. Psychol. Rev. **100**, 163–182 (1993)
2. Wang, R.F.: Building a cognitive map by assembling multiple path integration systems. Psychon. Bull. Rev. **23**, 692–702 (2016)
3. Byrne, P., Becker, S., Burgess, N.: Remembering the past and imagining the future: a neural model of spatial memory and imagery. Psychol. Rev. **114**, 340–375 (2007)
4. McNaughton, B.L., Battaglia, F.P., Jensen, O., Moser, E.I., Moser, M.B.: Path integration and the neural basis of the "cognitive map". Nat. Rev. Neurosci. **7**, 663–678 (2006)
5. Sanders, H., Rennó-Costa, C., Idiart, M., Lisman, J.E.: Grid cells and place cells: an integrated view of their navigational/memory function. Trends Neurosci. **38**, 1–13 (2015)
6. Pfeiffer, B.E., Foster, D.J.: Hippocampal place-cell sequences depict future paths to remembered goals. Nature **497**, 74–79 (2013)
7. Morgan, L.K., Macevoy, S.P., Aguirre, G.K., Epstein, R.A.: Distances between real-world locations are represented in the human hippocampus. J. Neurosci. **31**, 1238–1245 (2011)

8. Howard, L.R., Javadi, A.H., Yu, Y., Mill, R.D., Morrison, L.C., Knight, R., Loftus, M.M., Staskute, L., Spiers, H.J.: The hippocampus and entorhinal cortex encode the path and euclidean distances to goals during navigation. Curr. Biol. **24**, 1331–1340 (2014)
9. Meilinger, T.: The network of reference frames theory: a synthesis of graphs and cognitive maps. In: Freksa, C., Newcombe, N.S., Gärdenfors, P., Wölfl, S. (eds.) Spatial Cognition 2008. LNCS (LNAI), vol. 5248, pp. 344–360. Springer, Heidelberg (2008). https://doi.org/10.1007/978-3-540-87601-4_25
10. Zar, J.H.: Biostatistical Analysis. Prentice Hall, Upper Saddle River (2010)
11. Thorndyke, P.W., Hayes-Roth, B.: Differences in spatial knowledge acquired from maps and navigation. Cogn. Psychol. **14**, 560–589 (1982)
12. Cheung, A., Ball, D., Milford, M., Wyeth, G., Wiles, J.: Maintaining a cognitive map in darkness: the need to fuse boundary knowledge with path integration. PLoS Comput. Biol. **8**, e1002651 (2012)
13. Tse, D., Langston, R.F., Kakeyama, M., Bethus, I., Spooner, P.A., Wood, E.R., Witter, M.P., Morris, R.G.M.: Schemas and memory consolidation. Science **316**, 76–82 (2007)
14. Janzen, G.: Memory for object location and route direction in virtual large-scale space. Q. J. Exp. Psychol. **59**, 493–508 (2006)
15. Stern, E., Leiser, D.: Levels of spatial knowledge and urban travel modeling. Geogr. Anal. **20**, 140–155 (1988)
16. Muller, R.U., Bostock, E., Taube, J.S., Kubie, J.L.: On the directional firing properties of hippocampal place cells. J. Neurosci. **14**, 7235–7251 (1994)
17. Marchette, S.A., Ryan, J., Epstein, R.A.: Schematic representations of local environmental space guide goal-directed navigation. Cognition **158**, 68–80 (2017)
18. Meilinger, T., Riecke, B.E., Bülthoff, H.H.: Local and global reference frames for environmental spaces. Q. J. Exp. Psychol. **67**, 542–569 (2014)
19. Meilinger, T., Strickrodt, M., Bülthoff, H.H.: Qualitative differences between environmental and vista space memory are caused by the separation of space, not by movement or successive perception. Cognition **155**, 77–95 (2016)
20. Bennett, A.T.: Do animals have cognitive maps? J. Exp. Biol. **199**, 219–224 (1996)
21. Grieves, R.M., Dudchenko, P.A.: Cognitive maps and spatial inference in animals: Rats fail to take a novel shortcut, but can take a previously experienced one. Learn. Motiv. **44**, 81–92 (2013)

Spatial Survey Estimation Is Incremental and Relies on Directed Memory Structures

Tobias Meilinger[(⊠)], Marianne Strickrodt, and Heinrich H. Bülthoff

Max Planck Institute for Biological Cybernetics, Tübingen, Germany
{tobias.meilinger,marianne.strickrodt,
heinrich.buelthoff}@tuebingen.mpg.de

Abstract. This study examined how navigators of large-scale environmental spaces come up with survey estimates of distant targets. Participants learned a route through a virtual city by walking it multiple times in one direction on an omnidirectional treadmill. After learning, they were teleported to intersections along the route and pointed to multiple other locations. Locations were always queried in chunks of related trials relative to a participant's current position, either to all locations route forwards or all locations route backwards. For their first pointing, participants took twice as long as for the later pointings and latency correlated with the number of intersections to the target, which was not the case for later pointings. These findings are inconsistent with reading out coordinates from a cognitive map but fit well with constructive theories which suggest that participants integrated locations between their current location and the target along the learned path. Later pointings to adjacent intersections within a chunk of trials continued this process using the previous estimation. Additionally, in first pointings participants' estimates were quicker and more accurate when targets were located route forwards than route backwards. This route direction effect shows that the long-term memory employed in generating survey estimates must be directed – either in form of a directed graph or a combination of a directed route layer and an undirected survey layer.

Keywords: Spatial memory · Survey knowledge · Environmental space
Cognitive map · Mental walk · Mental model · Virtual environment

1 Introduction

After walking through cities and buildings humans can grasp metric relationships such as distances and directions between remote landmarks. In order to do so they must integrate spatial information obtained across multiple views and places along their navigation trajectory. How do humans store the experienced information and how do they infer survey relations from them when asked to do so?

To solve a survey task, such as pointing to a distant landmark, at least one's current location and the target location must be brought into direct reference. Some theories assume that navigators form a global, world-centered reference frame within which all relevant locations are represented [1–4]. In the following a global world-centered reference frame will be called a cognitive map. Survey relations can be obtained from a

© Springer Nature Switzerland AG 2018
S. Creem-Regehr et al. (Eds.): Spatial Cognition 2018, LNAI 11034, pp. 27–42, 2018.
https://doi.org/10.1007/978-3-319-96385-3_3

cognitive map by *reading out the coordinates* of the relevant locations (e.g., the current location and the target location) and compute the difference vector between the coordinates to get the relative direction or the distance between the locations, etc. An alternative approach is taken by theories suggesting that a navigable space is not represented within a cognitive map, but by multiple local memory units which are connected in a graph structure [5–7]. For such graph structures Meilinger [7] suggested that for making survey estimates the integration of one's current position and the target within a single reference frame happens on the fly during retrieval by constructing a *mental model* of the non-visible environment (a related vector-addition model was presented for updating by Fujita et al. [8]). For example, navigators could imagine what the environment would look like if the surrounding walls were transparent. First, they imagine the adjacent street from their current position, then they add the street branching off from it, etc. In this way all locations from the current location along a route leading towards the target location are imagined step by step within the current egocentric reference frame, building a mental model of the environment. No one mentally walks through this constructed environment and the underlying memory structure is no cognitive map, but a graph consisting of local memory units of places interconnected by links.

Increasing evidence for the presence of local memory units can be found in the literature. The use of multiple, locally confined reference frames (one for each corridor) for pointing to distant targets was shown in multi-corridor environments [9–11]. Also, knowledge of spatial relations of targets within a single room seems to be partly dissociated from the knowledge about the location of the room itself [12]. Those studies clearly support graph theories [5–7]. In several studies, longer reaction times were shown for recalling a target location the more local units (e.g., individual corridors) were experienced along the path during learning between one's current location and the target [11, 13, 14]. In our study we will refer to this effect as the "distance effect", which should therefore not be understood in its Euclidean sense (i.e., straight line distance), but instead refers to the number of locations visited along a route. Such distance effects can be well explained by a mental model built from a graph-like memory structure [7]. Here, a time consuming, incremental process of activating spatial information along the learned route is underlying the estimation of the relative direction of a target. In contrast, there are other studies supporting the idea of global, cognitive maps, which could be used for a simple read out of coordinates. For example, some studies indicate that participants form reference frames (or reference directions) that are covering multiple local subspaces, such as corridors or streets [9, 11, 15]. They suggest that all spatial information gathered across multiple subspaces have been stored (also) relative to a single reference system in long-term memory. Furthermore, several models allow [6] or propose [16] the combination of local (often route related) and global (typically survey related) memory structures.

Many empirical findings suggest that human spatial memory is directed, or in other words, asymmetric. For example, people occasionally select different routes when either going from A to B compared to going from B to A [17]. Also, the error patterns that are observed when participants estimate the relative direction along a route from location A to location B do not coincide with error patterns when pointing from B to A ([14] same volume). This indicates that no coherent map was underlying survey performance. Two propositions seem eligible to account for such results. Either, one could argue that two (rather than one) coherent cognitive maps have been built, one for the forward one for the backward direction of the route, which do not need to coincide. No additional information about directed connections between locations need to be stored. Depending on the direction queried (i.e., either from A to B or from B to A), either of the two maps is selected, leading to the observed asymmetries in pointing directions. Alternatively, no global embedding took place, but a graph structure with local memory units that are connected by directed links was stored, for example, a link emphasizing the direction from A to B, but not the other way around [6, 7]. The directed links might render different paths to be preferred for forward and backward route planning and may lead to asymmetric pointing errors as link usage along the link orientation is easier than in opposite direction. For the latter the link must be inverted, which is computationally costly. Support for an embedded directedness in spatial memory comes from studies utilizing primed recognition of landmarks. Re-cognizing landmarks previously experienced along a route is faster when they are preceded by another landmark in the same order as during learning, compared to being preceded by a landmark that was succeeding the target during learning [18–20]. This route direction effect is explained by a directed encoding of connected places in the experienced direction. However, it is unclear whether findings obtained from this simple recognition task generalize to survey tasks as well. Therefore, we aimed to investigate whether directedness is a determinative part of a large-scale space representation utilized in a survey task. To exclude the possibility that navigators formed separate memory structures for route forwards and backward learning (as done by [17] same volume) we had participants learn a route only in one direction.

An interesting aspect not yet addressed in the literature is the question of how transient constructed survey estimations in working memory are and whether subsequent survey estimations can be based on them. Imagine learning landmarks A, B, C, and D along a route and being queried the bearing of D while standing at A in a first trial. Following a construction model, location B and C would be successively activated on the way of mentally walking to or constructing the relative location of D. Now, having pointed to D you are subsequently asked to point to C, the direct neighbor of D. Either this can be done by again constructing a new model from A via B to C. Alternatively, subsequent pointing to C could also be based on the previous estimation of D and calculating backwards from there to derive the location of C. In short, one could use information from the old model to compute subsequent steps from there rather than built a new model from scratch. In that case later pointings should be much quicker than first pointings if neighboring targets are queried, and their latency should not depend on the distance between pointer and target. In our study we set out to examine whether the recall of survey relations is based on all-at-once or incremental processes and whether prior recall of related locations can serve as a base for succeeding targets.

1.1 Experiment and Predictions

We had participants learn a virtual route containing a set of to-be-learned locations multiple times from start to end. Subsequently, we administered a survey task where participants were teleported to different intersections along the route and needed to face straight line direction towards several of the remaining intersections. Hereby, we manipulated multiple factors. We always queried chunks of related locations. Being teleported to an intersection, participants always had to successively recall a sequence of neighboring intersections. This was administered to examine whether later pointing was influenced by prior pointing estimates. Furthermore, targets were always selected relative to participants' current location on the route following two rules: Firstly, we varied whether the targets were lying towards the end of the route (i.e., forward, in route direction) or towards the start of the route (i.e., backwards, against route direction). Secondly, in order to balance the number of intersections between current location and target (i.e., route distance) for first and later pointings within a chunk of related trials, participants were pointing to locations in a target sequence either away from their current location (i.e., first a minimum distance to the adjacent intersection, then the second-next intersection, etc.) or participants pointed in a sequence towards their current location (i.e., first a maximum distance to the start or the end of the route, then to the second/second last intersection, etc., until ending up pointing to the neighboring intersection).

Depending on the underlying memory structure and retrieval process different predictions can be made. An all-at-once read-out process from a cognitive map would neither predict an effect of distance to the target nor an effect of route direction on the performance in the direction estimation task. In contrast, a graph representation accessed via the construction of a mental model assumes a time-consuming incremental retrieval of survey knowledge along the successively visited places towards the target, thus, taking the longer the further the target is away from the navigator along the route (distance effect). Additionally, if the graph representation consists of directed links between adjacent places faster recall of targets located towards the end of the route relative to one's current position should be shown (in learned route direction) compared to estimating direction to targets located towards the start of the route (against route direction). Regarding the interdependence between trials, later pointings within a chunk of trials may re-iterate the whole process and yield identical results as initial pointings. Alternatively, participants may build upon earlier pointing estimates and only add the difference from the previous target to the adjacent intersection. In this case later pointings should be quicker than earlier pointings, show no distance effect and route directions effects might cancel out each other as later pointings depending on the target sequence (towards or away) follow equally often a route upwards and downwards direction.

2 Methods

2.1 Participants

24 participants took part in the experiment. One participant's performance did not significantly differ from chance and was not included, leading to 23 participants (11 females and 12 males) aged between 21 and 64 ($M = 29.6$ years, $SD = 9.3$ years) used in the analysis. All participants were recruited via a subject-database, gave written

informed consent, and were paid for their participation. The procedure was approved by the ethical committee of the University Clinics Tübingen.

2.2 Material

The Virtual City. In the learning phase, participants had to learn a route through a virtual city. Figure 1 shows a snapshot of the city as seen during walking, as well as a bird's eye view of the route. The route consisted of a start, six intersections and an end, resulting in eight locations that served as targets during testing. During learning, all eight locations were marked with a white X on the floor. The type of houses changed along the route, as did street width and the heights of houses. In addition, individual houses ensured sufficient landmark information to identify each location. The eight locations were not labelled by names.

The Setup. Participants walked on a 4×4 m omnidirectional treadmill (Fig. 2 left side). It allowed them to walk for infinite distances in any direction by moving them back to the center of the treadmill. This unique interface allows for realistic proprioceptive and vestibular feedback as well as efference copies while walking in virtual environments. Participants wore a climbing harness for the unlikely event of falling and hurting themselves on the moving platform. To obtain participants' location on the treadmill we tracked their head position with 16 high-speed motion capture cameras at 120 Hz (Vicon® MX 13). This data was used both to control the treadmill and to update the visualization of the virtual environment. The visual surrounding at a location was rendered in real time (60 Hz) using a NVIDIA Quadro FX 4600 graphics card with 768 MB RAM in a standard PC. Cables connected the PC to the display via the ceiling. Participants viewed the scene in stereo using a nVisor SX60 head-mounted display that provided a field of view of $44 \times 35°$ at a resolution of 1280×1024 pixels for each eye with 100% overlap. The setup thus also provided important visual depth cues such as stereo images and motion parallax. During the test phase a circular handrail around them with 0.48 meters diameter prevented participants from leaving their location (Fig. 2 middle) and responses were given by rotating the head and pressing a button on a gamepad they were holding.

2.3 Procedure

In the learning phase, participants walked the route at least six times from start to end. They were instructed to first learn the route, and secondly be able to self-localize when teleported to an X along the route after the learning phase. Participants were free to look around as long as they wanted, however they were not allowed to look or walk back to where they came from. In their first run, they walked up to an intersection, looked around, and the experimenter pointed out the street to take when the participant looked down the correct street by stating "the route is this direction" (the experimenter was in the same room and could talk with the participant). No verbal turning information (e.g., "left", "straight on", etc.) was given. When reaching the end and having looked around participants were teleported back to the start. From the second run onwards participants were asked to approach an intersection, look into the direction the

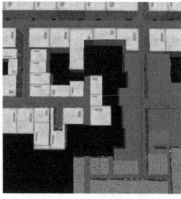

Fig. 1. The virtual city as seen from navigation perspective (left side) and from bird's eye view with the route marked in red (right side). During learning the start, the end and each of the six intersections in-between were marked with white crosses on the floor (marked by red dots in this figure). They served as locations to be teleported to and as targets during the test phase.

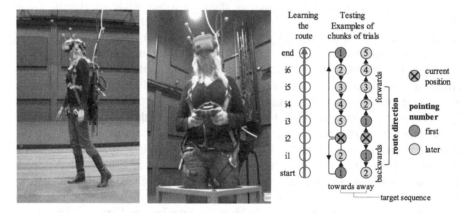

Fig. 2. Left: participant walking on the omnidirectional treadmill during learning. Middle: participant pointing to a target during testing by facing the target and pressing a button on a gamepad. Right: order of learning and examples of chunks of testing phase. The current position could be at any of the eight locations, *distance* to the targets would vary accordingly. Factors *pointing number* and *route direction* are visualized and that we varied the target sequence. (Color figure online)

route was going on and say "this way". The experimenter gave feedback whether this was right or wrong, before participants proceeded. They were not allowed to leave the route. For each new run, the virtual environment was rotated 90° clockwise relative to the lab. Sound sources within the lab could thus not be used to derive global orientation. The learning phase ended when participants walked the route at least six times and at least two runs were error-free. This criterion ensured comparable levels of route knowledge for all participants. Participants briefly trained walking on the treadmill before starting the experiment.

In the following test phase, participants were teleported to the eight locations on the route (i.e., the start, the end or i1–i6). The mark (i.e., X) for all locations was removed. For self-localization, participants could look and rotate around, but not walk around. As soon as they subjectively knew their location and orientation, they were asked to press a button on a gamepad. Then they pointed to a chunk of multiple targets. Pointing was done by turning on the spot until a vertical black line in the middle of the display matched the direction in which the participant thought the target was located. Thus, they would look directly at the target location as if the surrounding houses were transparent. When participants thought they faced the target, they pressed a button to confirm the direction and then pointed to the next target. No feedback was provided. After they had pointed to all targets within a chunk, participants pressed a second button on the gamepad and were teleported to a new position.

Figure 2 right, visualizes examples for four chunks of trials participants had to solve. The initial trial within each chunk was labelled "first" trial (dark green in figure), the remaining as "later" trials (light blue in figure), yielding the factor *pointing number*, which was introduced to examine potential dependencies between subsequent survey estimates. Four conditions determined the targets and the order in which participants were asked to point towards them within a chunk of trials. For each chunk they were instructed to point either (1) first to the start and then to all locations between start and their current location in the order of walking (i.e., start, i1, i2, etc.) (lower left example in figure), or (2) they should point to the same locations, but in reverse order (i.e., first the intersection before the current location, then the intersection before that, etc. until finally pointing to the start) (lower right example in figure). (3) They should point to the next intersection along the learned route direction after their current location, then the second next, etc. until pointing to the end (upper right example in figure). Or they should (4) point first to the end, then i6, i5, etc. until pointing to the intersection after their current location (upper left example in figure). Consequently, we varied the *route direction* (backwards to start vs. forwards to end) and target sequence (away vs. towards the current location) within a chunk of trials. *Route direction* served as a factor for analyzing potential directedness in survey estimates. Target sequence was introduced to balance average distance from the current location for first and later targets. Depending on one's current location along the route the maximum number of intersections one had to point to within a chunk of trials varied. For example, as visualized in Fig. 2 right, standing at i2 facing backwards to the start involves two targets to point to with decreasing or increasing route leg distance across a chunk depending on being queried in towards or away target sequence, while facing forward to the end involves five targets/intersections to point to. Therefore, *distance* in terms of route legs varied across the experimental trials. Please note that the adjacent, neighboring intersections were always visible during pointing.

From the eight locations on the route (including start and end) participants pointed to every other location twice (away and towards their current location). The 28 pointing chunks were presented in random order for each participant (pointing route forwards from seven locations, backwards from seven locations, both in two target sequences). This whole procedure was repeated resulting in 56 pointing chunks. After finishing a chunk participants received feedback on how many targets they missed or how many redundant targets they added. No feedback about pointing accuracy was provided.

Chunks with too few or too many responses were not analyzed as target locations could not be assigned. We recorded self-localization time (not reported), pointing latency and pointing direction for each trial. For the analysis we used latency and computed the absolute pointing error (i.e., the deviation between correct and estimated pointing direction irrespective of the direction of the error). Values deviating more than three standard deviations from the overall mean were not analyzed. Individual pointing accuracy all differed significantly from a random pointing behavior (i.e., 90°), indicating that all participants acquired some survey knowledge.

3 Results

To ascertain potential directedness in survey estimates as well as dependencies between subsequent pointings we first conducted a 2×2 ANOVA with the factors *pointing number* (first vs. later pointings) and *route direction* (pointing route forwards towards end vs. route backwards towards start). Table 1 summarizes the results for this analysis, Fig. 3 visualizes the performance patterns. Both main factors show a significant effect on latency, *pointing number* also on error. Additionally, both for error and latency, *pointing number* interacted significantly with *route direction*.[1] For first pointings participants pointed quicker ($t = 4.01$, $p < .001$) and more accurately ($t = 2.11$, $p = .042$) when the target was located route forwards towards the end than when located route backwards towards the start. This indicates a route direction effect in survey estimates predicted by directed graph models, but is not expected when reading out coordinates from a cognitive map. Interestingly, no such differences occurred in later pointings (t's < 1.2, p's $> .23$). Participants pointed slower in their first pointing than for later pointings, but also conducted less errors. The effect on latency is consistent with incremental graph theories when assuming that subsequent estimates are based on previous estimates to their direct neighbors.

For the further investigation of a potential incremental process of recalling survey knowledge we additionally considered a correlation analysis, namely, we examined whether latency and error for first and later pointings were associated with the route leg *distance* to the target. Indeed, first pointings showed a *distance* effect on latency. The further away along the route path the target was the longer participants required for pointing as indicated in a positive correlation between distance to the target and latency, with an average correlation of $r = 0.39$, $SD = 0.29$, significantly larger than zero, $t(22) = 6.55$, $p < .001$. We observed no such correlation for later pointings, $r = 0.03$, $SD = 0.12$, difference from zero $t(22) = 1.03$, $p = .31$. Errors correlated with distance both for first pointings, $r = 0.70$, $SD = .14$, $t(22) = 23.8$, p < .001, as well as for later pointings, $r = 0.45$, $SD = 0.19$, $t(22) = 11.5$, $p < .001$.

---

[1] When including target sequence (albeit not decisive on the introduced models) into the analysis all reported effects remained significant. There was no significant three-way-interaction which could have changed one of the reported effects, and no interaction with route direction. The analysis showed an effect of target sequence and its interaction with pointing number. Here participants were much quicker and accurate when their first pointing was away from their current location towards the visible neighbor intersection.

Table 1. Results of the ANOVA for latency and error. Degrees of freedom are $F(1, 22)$ for each factor(-combination). Significant effects are marked in bold.

	Latency			Error		
	F	p	η_p^2	F	p	η_p^2
Pointing number	**51.23**	**<.001**	**.70**	**34.86**	**<.001**	**.61**
Route direction	**10.04**	**.004**	**.31**	0.27	.608	.01
Number × direction	**6.50**	**.018**	**.23**	**11.79**	**.002**	**.35**

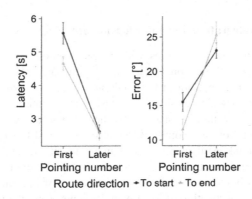

Fig. 3. Pointing performance in the form of latency (left) and absolute error (right) as a function of route direction and pointing number. Means and within-participants standard errors as estimated from the marginal means are shown.

4 Discussion

In our study we aimed to clarify whether survey estimates within navigable space are based on the incremental process of recalling target locations from a graph representation including the successive place-to-place activation of spatial information along the learned path, or whether they are based on an immediate read out of coordinates from an integrated cognitive map. More precisely, in case of reliance on a graph representation we examined whether survey estimates are based on directional encoding in long-term memory and also whether subsequent survey estimates will depend on previous estimates, thus, continuing the incremental process of recalling place-to-place information.

4.1 The Route Direction Effect in Survey Knowledge

We found a route direction effect, namely, a difference in performance for first pointing trials depending on whether participants pointed to the start or the end of the route. Participants pointed quicker and more accurate to targets located route forward towards the end of the route compared to pointing route backwards towards the start during the initial trial within a chunk. Such results support graph theories that assume route forwards encoding, as this directed encoding should speed-up integration towards the end, but slow down integration towards the start. Results for the first pointing are in line with asymmetries observed in spatial memory before in landmark recognition [18–20] and route choice [17] and extend them to survey tasks (see also [14] same volume). They suggest that participants' long-term memory consisted of a directed graph and survey estimates were directly constructed from that graph. Such a directed graph was proposed by Meilinger [7] and the undirected graph-model from Chrastil and Warren [5] is easily adjusted to it. The effect of route direction was not present in later pointings, indicating interdependence of successions of trials discussed further in the following section.

4.2   Incremental Integration and Interdependence of Survey Estimates

Contrasting incremental graph theories with simple read-out of coordinates from a cognitive map, only the former predict a route leg distance effect for latency (processing speed) in the first, but not in later pointings of a chunk of trials and interdependence between trials within a chunk (i.e., faster later pointings which profit from earlier pointings). Consistent with incremental theories participants pointed slower in their first pointing than for later pointings, but also conducted less errors. For the first pointing within a chunk participants had to integrate all intersections between the current location and the target. This time took the longer the more intersections were involved as indicated in the positive correlation of latency with route leg distance—an indicator for successive activation of local memory units along the previously learned path, rather than a read out from a cognitive map. Later pointings, successively following neighboring locations of the previous target, showed different patterns. Performance was much quicker on average and did not correlate with the target distance from the participant. This suggests that participants did not repeat the incremental process of integrating all intersections between their current location and the target again, but only added or subtracted the single segment between the old and the new target. Targets for first pointings were on average 2.5 intersections away (averaging towards and away target sequence, where initial pointings for away chunks have a route leg distance of one intersection and where initial pointings for towards chunks can vary between one and seven). In the case of interdependence between trials in a chunk later pointings are always just one intersection away from the previous estimate. Thus, the mean difficulty for estimating the direction to a new target with regards to a distance effect is lower for later pointings compared to first pointings and quicker reaction expected. Alternatively, no new estimate had to be conducted, but instead the target was already present in working memory as part of the constructed mental model and just had to be accessed from there. Neither effect on latency would be expected by read-out from a cognitive map.

For error both in first and later pointings route leg distance correlated with error. This could be due to errors encoded in long-term memory. Assuming a roughly constant random error during encoding, integration across larger distances will aggregate larger errors no matter which process is used. In fact, all models would assume such an effect. In case of integration into a cognitive map, this map would store all locations inside a single reference system, but in a distorted way. In addition to the overall distance effect, error was larger for later pointings. A simple all-at-once read-out from a cognitive map would not predict such a difference, but incremental models do so. In line with latency results, building upon first estimates, adds up the number of estimates across the chunk of trial. Higher error can be explained by assuming additional error for every mental processing step that is made.

Please note that longer latency for first pointings cannot be explained by additional processing time for self-localization as this happened before pointing. Another aspect is the required head turn. For the first pointing one can expect an average turn of 90° (from a random heading during self-localization to first target). For later pointings, participants only turned towards an adjacent intersection which required a clearly smaller average head turn. We reckon that head movement itself surely is a part of the overall performance but that the observed average latency difference of 2.6 s between first and later estimates encompasses other processes as well. Furthermore, head turning cannot explain the distance effect in our experiment (distant targets do not necessarily require larger head turns – see Fig. 1) and other experiments where no head turning was involved at all and distance effects were still observed [11, 13]. Participants took longer and were more accurate for first pointings, but quicker and more error prone for later pointings. As latency and error correlated within participants on average by $r = .04$ ($SD = 0.11$), we think that this effect is not simply be due to a speed-accuracy tradeoff.

The fact that the route direction effect disappeared for later pointings further supports the idea that later pointings build upon earlier pointings. If for every target a new incremental construction process was initiated, we should have observed a similar route direction effect as in the first pointings. Subsequent construction from the previous target was equally often along as well as against route direction: as participants pointed in target sequences towards and away from them later pointings always incorporated both route directions and any difference would average out. Therefore, no route direction effect would be expected, just as was observed in our experiment[2].

4.3   Limits and Alternative Explanations

Our results are well explained by forward directed graph models. They account for the observed effects of route direction and distance on error and latency when performing the first trial within a chunk of related trials and can explain the absence of these effects for later trials. However, there are some alternative explanations and considerations that need to be addressed before getting to the conclusion.

---

[2] If later estimates were based on estimates of previous targets, the route direction effect for later pointings should invert in the case of towards pointing (see examples in Fig. 2, right). Initially the most distant location must be constructed followed by closer targets, hence, moving along the graph structure in the opposite direction compared to the first target. This inversion for towards pointings is not reflected in participants performance (see footnote 1, no meaningful interactions with target sequence). Thus, the route direction effect does not seem to change in a meaningful way as a function of target sequence. Here participants might have also accessed previously constructed mental model parts still present in working memory. The role of route direction for later pointing thus is not yet fully clear.

The process of recalling survey estimates from a directed graph was described before by Meilinger (see introduction): constructing a mental model of the surrounding non-visible space [7]. Alternatively, navigators could *mentally walk* through a fully integrated cognitive map following the path they walked during learning. While mentally moving from one point to another, they use their path integration system to integrate the metric survey relation between their starting location and their mental position in the map until reaching the target [4, 21], resulting in a homing vector pointing back to their actual, current location. By inverting the resulting vector survey estimates from the location to the target can be derived. The activation pattern of hippocampal place cells is a plausible mediator for this process, although the conscious imagery of the mental walk might take place in posterior parietal cortex. Place cells represent locations within an environment. Even in the absence of sensory stimulation (e.g., during sleep) they can fire in an ordered fashion as they would do when walking a route [22] and such firing patterns were shown even when stationary within an environment [23]. Similar neural processes might happen during mental walks when performing a survey task. Such a mental walk process is also constructive and incremental but not based on a single graph structure.

Importantly, our findings regarding the route direction effect exclude the possibility that pointing relied exclusively on a cognitive map that abstracted from the walked direction, for example, a coordinate system. Assuming a process of mentally walking within a fully integrated cognitive map is not sufficient to explain the observed route direction effect. However, it is possible to account for this effect if survey relations are stored in such a map layer in addition to an asymmetric route knowledge layer [6, 16]. This route layer then must be involved in generating the survey estimates to introduce the observed asymmetries based on the mental walk approach.

Our study extends findings from [14] where participants learned a route in both directions and asymmetries in pointing accuracy were observed. These results could have relied on two separate and differently distorted maps for each walking direction. This is no viable explanation for the result of the present experiment. The learning experience in our study was uni-directional and effects were found both in error and latency. Thus, the asymmetry must be intrinsic to the memory of a single walked direction. Overall, the route direction effect shows that the long-term memory used for pointing must be oriented – either in form of a directed graph or a combination of a directed route layer and an undirected survey layer.

There is an important aspect inherit in the interpretation of our results of route direction as forward encoding, namely, the integration from one's current location towards the target. Such an "away" integration is assumed by both constructive positions, the mental model and the mental walk. However, our data can also be explained otherwise, namely by reversing the assumptions of forward encoding and integration away from the current location into route backward encoding and integration from the target towards the current location. While no theoretic position clearly proposes this possibility, it is still a conceivable alternative explanation that should be considered and discussed. For their first pointing participants might imagine themselves standing at the target location, mentally walk from there towards their current location while updating the vector towards the target. The resulting vector points towards their target. Importantly, to point correctly participants then must align the orientation when mentally arriving at their current location with their actual, physical orientation at that location as both will differ in most of the cases. For a backwards encoded route this process is quicker and/or more accurately for targets located towards the end (i.e., mentally walking route backwards to the current location) than for targets located towards the start when mentally walking route forwards opposite to encoding. Such a backwards route encoding might be based on spatial updating of previous locations while walking to the next location during learning, thus resulting in vectors pointing backwards. Potentially, navigators then could update not just the last visited intersection, but all previously visited locations as proposed by Wang [24]. For later pointings the previous target vector from current to the first target location first has to be inverted again, the navigator mentally teleported to the old target location which again involves an alignment of the current orientation and the mental orientation taken at the old target. Only then vector updating while mentally walking from the old target to the adjacent novel target can start. While not impossible, the required vector inversions with their associated alignment processes do seem cognitive demanding.[3]

Overall, the reverse model based on the assumption of backwards route direction encoding and integration from the target towards the current location is consistent with our data. Yet, it is disconnected with other theoretic positions, it requires the assumption of cognitive demanding inversion processes, and it is not able to incorporate findings from the literature that clearly support forward encoding. For example, the route direction effect in landmark recognition [18–20]. Furthermore, recognition triggered response models for route knowledge [6, 16] and supporting evidence from route choice [25] also are intrinsically forward oriented. Support for the mental path integration away from ones current location towards the target is given by successive activation of hippocampal place cells along a path to the goal [23]. We think that the easiest explanation and most consistent with the literature is that the route was encoded in walking forward direction and participants integrated from their current location towards the target either by constructing a mental model of the non-visible surrounding [7] or by mentally walking there and using path integration to estimate the resultant vector based on a cognitive map [4, 21] and an additional layer of directed route knowledge.

We are confident that our study provides a reliable basis for our conclusions. Participants learned a highly controlled but realistic city environment and learned from physically walking real life distances on an omnidirectional treadmill involving proprioceptive and vestibular cues. While the sample is not too large (23) it comprises of roughly 50% females and males and spans from 21 to 64 years of age showing a comparatively broad age spread. Furthermore, over 7200 data points went into our analysis which minimizes any random effects. The different comparisons and parameters such as route direction and distance effects across first vs. later pointings nicely correspond and are theoretically and empirically well connected.

---

[3] Note that the mental walk model faces similar inversion problems for later pointings. No such inversions are required when pointers construct a mental model of their non-visible surrounding based on a graph representation from their current location towards the target which then is mentally "visible" as an ego-centric vector.

We clearly cannot exclude that direction estimates sometimes relied on strategies rejected here. However, based on the strengths mentioned we think that such strategies can only comprise in a small minority of trials or persons in the present data. For generalization to other situations it is clear that different learning situations can result in different representations and estimation processes such as learning from maps vs. navigation [26, 27]. The reduced visual field and the instruction to not look back towards where participants came from during learning slightly limits generalizability of results as this restriction partly prevents natural navigation behavior. However, support for asymmetries in spatial memory were found in survey estimates despite learning the environment in route-forward and -backward direction [14]. Overall, we belief that our findings apply to real live-experiences when navigators learn a large-scale space exclusively from navigation. Based on our results we cannot exclude the possibility that global integration into a cognitive map and full abstraction from the directedness and incrementality of the learning experience might occur, for example, with extensive exposure to a sufficiently small environment. Nevertheless, one of the main insights from our study remains: to be able to make survey estimates in navigable space it is not necessary to rely on a globally consistent cognitive map. Survey estimates can and seem to be generally based on piecewise spatial knowledge connected by directed links that is used to incrementally recall target locations on the fly.

4.4   Conclusions

The most plausible interpretation of the present results in the light of previous findings and theoretic considerations is that participants encoded the environment route piece-wise in route-forward orientation and integrated this information incrementally during survey estimates from their current location towards the first target and from there onwards to later targets. Following the mental model approach, this estimation process relied on a directed graph memory of the space. When extending the mental walk approach, it can likewise explain the results by assuming that the direction estimation is based on a combination of a directed route layer and an undirected survey layer (cognitive map). Importantly, we showed that later pointings depended on earlier pointings. Overall, our results add to the growing evidence that survey estimates obtained via navigation are constructed incrementally during recall and they further show that also survey knowledge is intrinsically oriented.

Acknowledgments. This research was supported by the DFG grant ME 3476/2-1. We thank Jan Souman for help in planning the experiment and discussing the results, Nadine Simon for help in data collection, as well as Joachim Tesch, Michael Kerger, and Harald Teufel for intensive technical support.

References

1. Mou, W., McNamara, T.P., Valiquette, C.M., Rump, B.: Allocentric and egocentric updating of spatial memories. J. Exp. Psychol. Learn. Mem. Cogn. **30**, 142–157 (2004)
2. O'Keefe, J.: An allocentric spatial model for the hippocampal cognitive map. Hippocampus **1**, 230–235 (1991)

3. Gallistel, C.R.: The Organization of Learning. MIT Press, Cambridge (1990)
4. Byrne, P., Becker, S., Burgess, N.: Remembering the past and imagining the future: a neural model of spatial memory and imagery. Psychol. Rev. **114**, 340–375 (2007)
5. Chrastil, E.R., Warren, W.H.: From cognitive maps to cognitive graphs. PLoS ONE **9**, e112544 (2014)
6. Mallot, H.A., Basten, K.: Embodied spatial cognition: biological and artificial systems. Image Vis. Comput. **27**, 1658–1670 (2009)
7. Meilinger, T.: The network of reference frames theory: a synthesis of graphs and cognitive maps. In: Freksa, C., Newcombe, N.S., Gärdenfors, P., Wölfl, S. (eds.) Spatial Cognition 2008. LNCS (LNAI), vol. 5248, pp. 344–360. Springer, Heidelberg (2008). https://doi.org/10.1007/978-3-540-87601-4_25
8. Fujita, N., Klatzky, R.L., Loomis, J.M., Golledge, R.G.: The encoding-error model of pathway completion without vision. Geogr. Anal. **25**, 295–314 (1993)
9. Meilinger, T., Riecke, B.E., Bülthoff, H.H.: Local and global reference frames for environmental spaces. Q. J. Exp. Psychol. **67**, 542–569 (2014)
10. Werner, S., Schmidt, K.: Environmental reference systems for large-scale spaces. Spat. Cogn. Comput. **1**, 447–473 (1999)
11. Strickrodt, M., Bülthoff, H.H., Meilinger, T.: Memory for navigable space is flexible and not restricted to exclusive local or global memory units. J. Exp. Psychol. Learn. Mem. Cogn. (in press)
12. Marchette, S.A., Ryan, J., Epstein, R.A.: Schematic representations of local environmental space guide goal-directed navigation. Cognition **158**, 68–80 (2017)
13. Meilinger, T., Strickrodt, M., Bülthoff, H.H.: Qualitative differences between environmental and vista space memory are caused by the separation of space, not by movement or successive perception. Cognition **155**, 77–95 (2016)
14. Meilinger, T., Henson, A., Rebane, J., Bülthoff, H.H., Mallot, H.A.: Humans construct survey estimates on the fly from a compartmentalised representation of the navigated environment. In: Creem-Regehr, S., et al. (eds.) Spatial Cognition XI. LNAI, vol. 11034, pp. 15–26 (2018)
15. Wilson, P.N., Wilson, D.A., Griffiths, L., Fox, S.: First-perspective spatial alignment effects from real-world exploration. Mem. Cognit. **35**, 1432–1444 (2007)
16. Poucet, B.: Spatial cognitive maps in animals: new hypotheses on their structure and neural mechanisms. Psychol. Rev. **100**, 163–182 (1993)
17. Stern, E., Leiser, D.: Levels of spatial knowledge and urban travel modeling. Geogr. Anal. **20**, 140–155 (1988)
18. Schweizer, K., Herrmann, T., Janzen, G., Katz, S.: The route direction effect and its constraints. In: Freksa, C., Habel, C., Wender, K.F. (eds.) Spatial Cognition. LNCS (LNAI), vol. 1404, pp. 19–38. Springer, Heidelberg (1998). https://doi.org/10.1007/3-540-69342-4_2
19. Janzen, G.: Memory for object location and route direction in virtual large-scale space. Q. J. Exp. Psychol. **59**, 493–508 (2006)
20. Schinazi, V.R., Epstein, R.A.: Neural correlates of real-world route learning. Neuroimage **53**, 725–735 (2010)
21. McNaughton, B.L., Battaglia, F.P., Jensen, O., Moser, E.I., Moser, M.B.: Path integration and the neural basis of the "cognitive map". Nat. Rev. Neurosci. **7**, 663–678 (2006)
22. Skaggs, W.E., McNaughton, B.L.: Replay of neuronal firing sequences in rat hippocampus during sleep following spatial experience. Science **271**, 1870–1873 (1996)
23. Pfeiffer, B.E., Foster, D.J.: Hippocampal place-cell sequences depict future paths to remembered goals. Nature **497**, 74–79 (2013)
24. Wang, R.F.: Building a cognitive map by assembling multiple path integration systems. Psychon. Bull. Rev. **23**, 692–702 (2016)

25. Gillner, S., Weiss, A.M., Mallot, H.A.: Visual homing in the absence of feature-based landmark information. Cognition **109**, 105–122 (2008)
26. Thorndyke, P.W., Hayes-Roth, B.: Differences in spatial knowledge acquired from maps and navigation. Cogn. Psychol. **14**, 560–589 (1982)
27. Meilinger, T., Frankenstein, J., Watanabe, K., Bülthoff, H.H., Hölscher, C.: Reference frames in learning from maps and navigation. Psychol. Res. **79**, 1000–1008 (2015)

Pointing Errors in Non-metric Virtual Environments

Alexander Muryy[(✉)] and Andrew Glennerster

School of Psychology and Clinical Language Sciences, University of Reading,
Reading RG6 6AL, UK
alexander.muryy@gmail.com

Abstract. There have been suggestions that human navigation may depend on representations that have no metric, Euclidean interpretation but that hypothesis remains contentious. An alternative is that observers build a consistent 3D representation of space. Using immersive virtual reality, we measured the ability of observers to point to targets in mazes that had zero, one or three 'wormholes' – regions where the maze changed in configuration (invisibly). In one model, we allowed the configuration of the maze to vary to best explain the pointing data; in a second model we also allowed the local reference frame to be rotated through 90, 180 or 270 degrees. The latter model outperformed the former in the wormhole conditions, inconsistent with a Euclidean cognitive map.

Keywords: Human navigation · Spatial representation · Virtual reality
Metric model · Motion parallax · Binocular disparity · Topological model
Labelled graph · View-based

1 Introduction

During active exploration of a 3D scene, an observer must build up some kind of representation about the layout of objects that will be useful from a different vantage point. One hypothesis is that the representation corresponds to a type of map with metric measures such as distances and angles conforming to a Euclidean geometry, even if these are not a faithful reproduction of the environment [1–3]. Such a metric cognitive map could be constructed, for instance, on the basis of path integration. It could provide a comprehensive description of the environment and underpin a wide variety of spatial tasks such as general navigation, finding shortcuts or detours and pointing to targets. Crucially, the structure of the data stored in such a map would be independent of the task. However, while there is a predominant view that metric representations may provide an adequate description of small open environments (vista spaces), there is good evidence that this hypothesis does not hold for a global representation of large complex environments [4]. Multiple experimental studies speak against global metric representations [4–9]. For instance, Warren et al. [5] found that perceived locations of targets in a labyrinth may overlap, i.e. the perceived geometry of space is not metrically consistent (they report discontinuities in spatial representation, such as "rips" and "folds"). Typically, human participants can navigate efficiently through complicated experimental environments which supports the notion of a global

© Springer Nature Switzerland AG 2018
S. Creem-Regehr et al. (Eds.): Spatial Cognition 2018, LNAI 11034, pp. 43–57, 2018.
https://doi.org/10.1007/978-3-319-96385-3_4

spatial representation. However, their perception of metric qualities is often distorted. For instance, the perceived length of a route depends on the number of turns and junctions it contains [9, 10]. Angular and directional judgments are highly unreliable [7, 11–13] and perceived angles between junctions are biased towards 90° [9, 14].

An alternative type of representation of the environment is a topological one [5, 6, 8, 9, 15–18]. A topological graph consists of a network of nodes and edges that connect them. The exact shape of the path between nodes is not defined because the edges simply represent the connectivity of the environment, e.g. the existence of the path between two locations. Nevertheless, topological knowledge of an environment is sufficient for general navigation and allows the observer to find alternative routes and detours. This type of representation has been used to account for both human and insect navigational behaviour and has been applied in robot navigation systems [16, 19]. Arguments against topological representation for navigation have been raised [20, 21] but, at least in these cases, not convincingly so [22, 23].

Hybrid models, that include both topological information of space connectivity and metric information have also been proposed [5, 8, 15, 24, 25]. Metric information about scene layout is often assumed to be available in the region that is visible from one location, e.g. within a room, which Montello has described these as 'vista spaces' [26]. These representations are hierarchical in nature, such that metric representation is reliable locally while at the same time the global metric representation may be distorted to affect both the location of objects and the orientation of local 'vista spaces'. Evidence compatible with representations of this type has been reported on the basis of pointing, walking or other orientation judgements in environments that were known to the participant [4, 5, 9]. Another aspect of spatial behaviour that is not predicted by a metric map is that the retrieval of information may depend on the observer's location [14], so that perception of the spatial layout of the scene is different when judged from point A and point B.

In our experiments, we generated virtual environments that were impossible to recreate physically and tested participants' ability to point to targets that they had encountered previously but could not currently see. The reason that such environments are informative is that they allow predictions to be tested that could not be distinguished in a normal environment. Non-Euclidean environments of this sort were used previously to test human cognitive maps, for example [5, 27–29]. Warren et al. [5] created a virtual labyrinth with "wormholes" that teleported participants smoothly between locations. Vasylevska and Kaufmann [28] tested environments with spatially overlapping regions much like the environments in our experiments in order to simulate space compression for VR applications. Zetzsche [29] and Klus [27] developed impossible virtual environments that violate Euclidean metrics and planar topology. Surprisingly, in all these studies human participants showed remarkable insensitivity to metric inconsistencies of space. Warren [5] used 'as-the-crow-flies' walking as a measure of the perceived distance and direction of a previously-seen target. They concluded that participants in this task were using a distorted type of map which they called a 'labelled graph'. The goal of our experiment was similar but, in our case, we compared explicitly a wide range of metric configurations, with and without non-metric variations in local orientation, to see which type of representation could best explain the pointing data.

2   Methods

2.1   Participants

The 8 participants (3 male and 5 female) were students or members of the School of Psychology and Clinical Language Sciences. All participants had normal or corrected to normal vision, one participant wore glasses during experiment, and all had good stereo-acuity (TNO stereo test, 60 arcsec or better). All participants were naïve to the purpose of the study. Participants were given a one hour practice session in VR to familiarize them with our set-up in a simplified virtual environment (open room with targets in boxes, but no inner walls) and metric versions of the mazes. 6 potential participants (in addition to the 8 who took part) either experienced motion sickness during the practice session or preferred not to continue at this stage. Altogether there were 7 sessions (including the practice) roughly 1 h each, conducted on different days. Participants were advised not to stay in VR longer than 10 min between breaks. They received a reward of 12 pounds per hour. The study received approval of the Research Ethics Committee of the University of Reading.

2.2   Experimental Set-up

The experiment took place in a 3 by 3 m region of the laboratory equipped with Vicon tracking system (14 infrared cameras) that provides 6 d.o.f. information about the headset position and orientation with nominal accuracy ±0.1 mm and 0.15° respectively. We used nVis SX111 head mounted display with 111° field of view and binocular overlap of 50°. A video cable connected the HMD to a video control unit on the ceiling. The position and orientation of the HMD was tracked at 240 Hz and passed to the graphics PC with a GTX 1080 video card. The stimuli were designed using Unity 3D system and rendered online at 60fps. Participants were allowed to walk freely and explore the virtual environment in a natural way. The virtual labyrinth was originally a 5 by 5 m environment with corridors in the maze 1 m wide. In order to fit in the 3 by 3 m lab space, the labyrinth was shrunk to 0.6 scale (e.g. 60 cm wide corridors) which

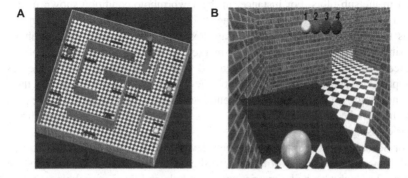

Fig. 1. Views of the labyrinth. (A) View from above. (B) First person view. The green target is visible inside a grey box. The target sequence is shown on top (Y-G-R-B) and the current target is highlighted (Yellow). (Color figure online)

meant that the floor was displayed about 1 m below eye height. Participants generally found this acceptable and did not notice that the room was not normal size, compatible with previous experiments [30]. During the experiment, participants wore a virtual wristband that provided information about the task (shown, for illustrative purposes only, at the top of Fig. 1b). Participants used a hand-held 3D tracked pointing device to point at targets during the pointing phase. In VR, the pointing device looked like as a small sphere (R = 5 cm) with an infinitely long ray emanating from it in both directions; the text was displayed next to the hand in VR providing instructions (e.g. 'point to Red').

2.3   Stimuli

We designed 2 general layouts of the virtual labyrinth. Scene 1 is shown in Figs. 1 and 2. The virtual environment could be subdivided into 25 (5 × 5) elementary squares each having a size equal to the corridor's width. A green cylinder (Fig. 1a) indicated the starting location. In order to start the experiment, the participant should stand at the start location and look along the corridor's width. In order to start the experiment, the participant stood at the start location and looked along the direction indicated by the red arrow. Then green cylinder and red arrow disappeared, so that the starting location was not marked during the exploration phase. The labyrinth contained 4 target objects (red, green, blue and yellow spheres) hidden inside open grey boxes, so that they could be seen only from a short distance. Other empty grey boxes were added as distractors. Figure 1b shows a first-person view along a virtual corridor containing the green target inside a grey box. Participants wore a virtual wristband that displayed information about the current task, namely the sequence in which targets should be collected (e.g. Yellow-Green-Red-Blue, see Fig. 1b, top) and then pointed to. See Supplementary Information for movies of the experiment and plan views of the scenes.

For each labyrinth, we increased the complexity of the environment by extending the length of the corridors with non-metric 'wormholes', see Fig. 2b and c. There were 3 conditions per scene: one metric, one containing 1-wormhole and one containing 3. Start is marked as 'S', colored circles indicate targets. The dashed lines acted as invisible triggers: when a participant crossed the trigger the environment changed as shown in the sub-plots. For instance, in the 1-wormhole condition shown in Fig. 2b, when a participant crossed the red trigger the environment changed to schematic W1 (a); as the participant continued walking down the path through the wormhole (the accessible region inside a wormhole is marked by the dashed black line) and crosses the green trigger, the environment changed again to schematic W1(b), then as the participant crossed the blue trigger he or she would exit the wormhole and the environment change back to the general layout. Participants were not aware of the presence of the triggers because the local views of the environment did not change during the trigger crossing.

For Scene 1, the same original or 'base level' layout applied in all three conditions (metric, 1-wormhole and 3-wormholes), as shown in Fig. 2a. Similar principles applied to Scene 2 (which also had a metric, one-wormhole and three-wormhole version). The corridors through the wormholes did not have junctions, thus the topological connectivity of space was the same in all 3 conditions. The only difference between metric and non-metric conditions is the length and configuration of the corridors. The wormholes extended the corridors in a way that made a global metric representation impossible. For instance, the path through the wormhole in Fig. 2b has the shape of the figure of eight, i.e. it crosses itself, although there are no visible junctions along that path, which is physically impossible.

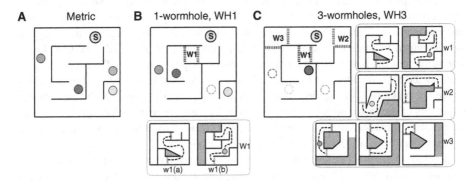

Fig. 2. Schematics of the labyrinth. (A) Metric condition. (B) Non-metric 1-wormhole condition. The green target was placed inside the wormhole. C) Non-metric 3-wormholes condition. The general layout (containing Start, which is marked as 'S') remained constant between conditions. The wormholes are marked with letters W surrounded by red and blue triggers. As the participant crossed a trigger, the environment changed as shown in the sub-schematics. Inside a wormhole, the participant could only walk along the route marked by black dashed line. These are for Scene 1. Equivalent set of maps were generated for Scene 2 (see layout in Fig. 10 and in Supplementary Information). (Color figure online)

2.4   Procedure

Participants were asked to perform a navigational and pointing tasks in a virtual labyrinth (see Fig. 1) although we report here only on the results of the pointing task. A single experimental session that took about 1 h during the three conditions were tested sequentially metric, 1-wormhole and 3-wormholes, all with the same general layout (i.e. all Scene 1 or Scene 2). This helped participants to cope with the more complex environments. The tasks and instructions were identical for all 3 conditions. For each condition, participants had to complete 8 rounds of walking and pointing. Each round started with a navigational task during which the participants were asked to collect all 4 target objects in a specified order in the most efficient way. The meaning of 'efficient' was left to participants to decide: it could mean choosing the shortest path, or the smallest number of turns or junctions (i.e. navigational decisions) but they were told not to hurry. After all targets were collected, the participants were instructed to stay at the location of the last target and to point to the Start location and then all other target locations twice, in a specified order (Start-R-G-B-Y and repeat), using a pointing device. Apart from the last sphere, the targets could not be seen from the pointing location, hence the participants had to rely on their spatial representation of the environment to complete the pointing task. Once the pointing task was complete, the next round of walking and pointing commenced. During all 8 rounds the target locations remained constant. The first 5 rounds were a 'learning' phase in which participants always began at the Start location and collected targets in the same sequence Start-Red-Green-Blue-Yellow (S-R-G-B-Y) and finally pointed to all the targets from Yellow (i.e. from the last target). After pointing, the walls of the labyrinth disappeared and the participant went to the Start location and begin the next round. The purpose of the learning phase was to allow participants to build up a spatial representation of the labyrinth gradually through multiple repetitions of the same navigational task. During the test phase (the last 3 rounds) the navigational sequences were changed to three new sequences: Y-G-B-Y-R, R-B-R-Y-G and G-Y-G-R-B, so that during test the participants had to solve novel navigational tasks. They did not have to go to the Start locations at the beginning of a round but instead started at the point where the previous round ended. Importantly, the pointing locations at the ends of the sequences of the test rounds included all target locations except for Yellow, which was the pointing location during the learning phase. Thus, during test phase we collected pointing data from all target locations, except for Yellow.

Excluding the practice session, each participant carried out 6 experimental sessions, each on a different day. We tested one Scene per session (Scene 1 or Scene 2) with three repetitions of each Scene. Across repetitions, the structure of the labyrinth and target locations were identical, but the colours of the targets were changed. This meant that while the instructions remained the same (e.g., in the learning phase, collect targets in sequence R-G-B-Y) the actual paths relating to those tasks were different on different repetitions. In the end, in Scene 1 we had 3 sets of pointing data in the test phase from the location marked as red in Fig. 2 and 2 sets of pointing data from green, blue and yellow locations (in scene 2: 3 sets from blue and 2 sets from the others). Altogether this constituted 72 pointing vectors per scene per condition per participant: 24 vectors from the red target and 16 vectors from green, blue and yellow.

3 Results

During the first couple of learning trials, while participants were not familiar with the structure of the labyrinth, their paths appeared relatively random, but closer to the end of the learning phase the participants could navigate more systematically. Here, we present the results of pointing in the test phase, after participants had completed the 5 learning trials. Figure 3 illustrates the paths that participants took through the maze during the test phase, after the learning phase of 5 rounds. In the cases shown in Fig. 3, participants were always navigating from the blue sphere to the yellow sphere, for a 'metric' (normal) maze, a maze with one wormhole and a maze with three wormholes. There are 4 possible solutions to this task, assuming that participants did not double back on themselves and avoided 'loops' in their trajectory (returning to a junction) and, in fact, by the test phase participants did not do this, demonstrating learning during the first phase. The shortest route is marked in red (in these cases, the shortest topological route is also the shortest metric route). Notice that in the 3-wormhole condition the participants' paths are significantly longer and more complex than in the metric and one-wormhole conditions even when, topologically speaking, they take the same route

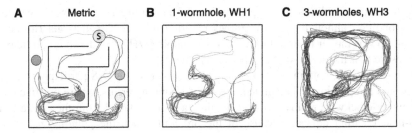

Fig. 3. Example of a participants' paths during one subset of the task, "go from B to Y". The full task for this round was: start at Yellow and go to targets in the order G-**B-Y**-R. The shortest path is marked in red, while green and blue lines represent alternative routes. Notice that in the 3-wormhole condition paths are significantly longer. (Color figure online)

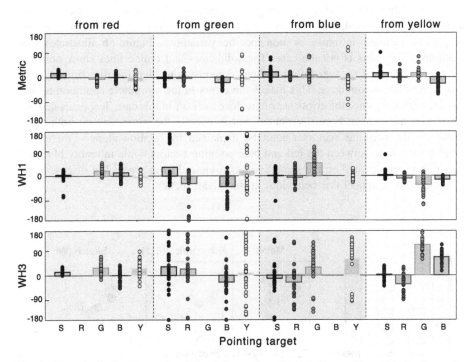

Fig. 4. Signed pointing errors for all participants (n = 8) and all repetitions (3), for Scene 1. Data for the three conditions (metric, 1-wormhole and 3-wormhole) are shown in the top, middle and bottom rows. Pointing errors are shown individually with coloured symbols indicating the pointing target (Start, Red, Green, Blue and Yellow), the bar height indicating the mean error in each case. The plot background colour indicates the location from which the participant pointed (red, green, blue and yellow columns). Very similar data were obtained for Scene 2. (Color figure online)

as in the metric condition. Participants often did not notice the non-metric nature of WH1 condition although they sometimes reported that the Green target (inside the wormhole) was harder to find. In the three-wormhole (WH3) condition all participants were aware that the scene was geometrically impossible.

Figure 4 shows pointing data for the test phase in Scene 1 (8 participants, 3 conditions and 3 repetitions). The plot shows signed pointing errors, where positive errors are counter-clockwise relative to the true direction of the target from the centre of the hand-held pointing device. Because of the order in which the pointing zones were visited, the number of 'shots' from each pointing zone was not identical: in scene 1 there were 48 pointing data-points from the red location to each of the other targets, and 32 data-points from green, blue and yellow locations while in scene 2 (see Supplementary Information): there were 48 pointing data-points from the blue location and 32 data-points from red, green and yellow locations.

Figure 4 clearly shows that the magnitude of pointing errors increases from metric to 1-wormhole to 3-wormhole conditions. This is summarized in Fig. 5a which shows the standard deviation of all the pointing errors (across all participants, repetitions and scenes) for these conditions. However, it would be misleading to describe this as simply an increase in noise or non-specific variability. Figure 5b illustrates one example of why this is not the case. The solid lines and dotted lines show pointing directions measured on two different days, demonstrating that the directions can be quite repeatable across days. This makes the errors in the wormhole condition all the more remarkable, since the errors are often close to 180°. In this case, it appears that the participant might have been disoriented, but in exactly the same way on both days. However, the pointing vectors cannot be explained by rotation alone – there is a roughly 90° angle between the red and blue pointing vectors while in reality blue and red targets were located on the same line when viewed from green. We discuss some possible ways to model this behaviour in the model section.

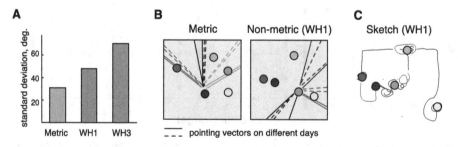

Fig. 5. Summary of pointing errors. (A) The standard deviations of signed pointing errors across all participants and all conditions for both Scenes. (B) Examples of pointing vectors in a metric (left) and non-metric condition (1-wormhole). In the non-metric case, the green target was inside the wormhole. C) A sketch drawn by a participant for the WH1 condition, scene 1. Notice that the participant is clearly much less confident about the path to the Green target, which is inside a wormhole. More sketches are included in the Supplementary Information. (Color figure online)

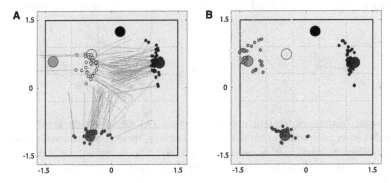

Fig. 6. Example of systematic pointing errors in a non-metric condition with one wormhole. (A) Pointing vectors to the green target from each of the other locations. The small circles show the hand location. The green target is inside the wormhole (see schematic in Fig. 10a). Most participants wrongly report that the green target is at the centre of the maze. (B) Pointing vectors to the yellow target; these are reasonably accurate from the red and blue locations but there are systematic errors from the green location. These data are from Scene 2 (Color figure online)

Such distortions are not limited to a single participant. Figure 6 shows pointing vectors of all participants to the green target from all pointing locations (left) and the same for the yellow target (right) in a one-wormhole condition (illustration from Scene 2, see Fig. 10 and Supplementary Information for schematics). Just like in Fig. 5b, the green target was inside a wormhole, while the red, blue and yellow targets and the Start location were not, and hence it is no surprise that the pointing to and from the green target shows particularly large errors. For example, pointing from the green to the yellow target and from the yellow to the green target both had errors of about 180°. Despite these large errors, participants point accurately to the yellow target from both the red and blue locations which is understandable as neither are in a wormhole and they are connected by 'metric' (physically possible) routes.

4   Model

The systematic pointing errors that participants make in non-metric environments indicate that they are not basing their responses on a correct global spatial representation of the target locations. Note that 'correct' locations of each target can still be defined according to path integration, even in the wormhole conditions. Two qualitatively different kinds of distortions are possible: structural distortion and/or local orientational distortion where the orientation of local reference frames can be misestimated (Fig. 7). In order to separate these hypotheses, we estimated the optimal

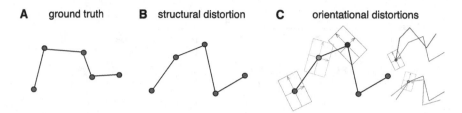

Fig. 7. Possible distortions of spatial representations. (A) Ground truth structure. (B) A structural distortion compared to (A). (C) Here, in addition, there is orientational distortion so that local reference frames are oriented inconsistently. The insets on the right show the consequences of the local reference frame having a changing orientation, e.g. on pointing responses.

configuration of targets that could best explain the pointing data in the sense that it maximizes the following likelihood function:

$$L(P_R, P_G, P_B, P_Y) = \prod_i^N \frac{1}{\sigma\sqrt{2\pi}} e^{-\frac{1}{2}\left(\frac{\alpha_i}{\sigma}\right)^2}$$

where P_R, P_G, P_B and P_Y are locations of the targets and α_i is the pointing error with respect to the actual direction of the targets; the hand location for any given trial was rigidly translated with the pointing location. This function returns the largest value when angular errors, α_i, are zero.

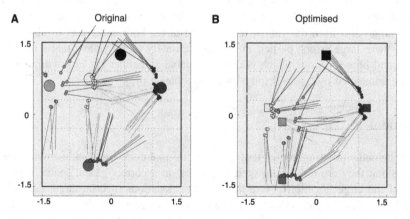

Fig. 8. Example of a distorted spatial map explaining pointing data in a 1-wormhole condition. (A) The original configuration of targets and the pointing vectors from 3 repetitions for a single participant. Taking ground truth as the 'model', the log likelihood, log(*L*), of these pointing data is −105.3 (see text). (B) The optimised (distorted) configuration of targets that best explains the pointing data. Now log(*L*) = −58.2 (see text). Notice that the locations of the green and yellow targets are swapped relative to their locations in (A). These data are for Scene 2. (Color figure online)

Altogether, there were $N = 144$ pointing vectors (48 from Blue, and 32 from Red, Green and Yellow) per participant per condition. We set the angular standard deviation, σ, as $50°$ but repeating the analysis with different values showed that the locations returned were rather insensitive to the value of σ. The Start location was treated as fixed in the optimization (it was, incidentally, always at a fixed location in the laboratory). The set of potential target locations was discrete and limited to the centers of a 5×5 grid with the same size as the labyrinth (see Fig. 8). We optimised locations of the targets (parameters $P_{R,G,B,Y}$) in order to maximize the likelihood L. The optimization was doneper condition per participant and data from the 3 repetitions were combined together i.e. we assume that on different repetitions participants develop similar representations.

Figure 8a shows the original pointing vectors from a single participant in Scene 2. The log-likelihood of the pointing data for this configuration according to our model is $\log(L) = -105$ whereas, when the configuration of the targets is optimised this improves to $\log(L) = -58$ (see Fig. 8b). Notice that the green and yellow targets have now (roughly) swapped places, consistent with the pointing directions shown in Fig. 6. Finally, in order to capture the orientational distortions illustrated in Fig. 5b, we additionally allowed a rigid rotation of the pointing vectors that a participant made from each pointing location. These rotational parameters, $\rho_r, \rho_g, \rho_b, \rho_y$, describe the orientations of the local reference frames around the red, green, blue and yellow pointing locations respectively and could only take discrete values of $0°, 90°, 180°$ and $270°$ because these were the only directions that a participant could face while looking along a corridor. The rotational parameters were optimised at the same time as the positional ones. Separate optimisations were carried out per participant (n = 8), per scene (n = 2) and per condition (metric, one-wormhole and 3-wormhole). Each of the 4 locations was encoded by 2 parameters (x, y) thus, altogether for the first model we had $8 * 2 * 4 * 2 = 128$ parameters per condition. In the second model, there were $8 * 2 * 4 * 3 = 192$ parameters per condition since each location was now encoded by 3 parameters (x, y, ρ) rather than just (x, y). The total likelihood of all the data under each of the two models was calculated by multiplying individual likelihoods per 'shot'. Adding more parameters to a model inevitably improves the likelihood of the best fit of that model, so in order to compare models with different numbers of parameters we calculate information criterion:

$$IC = -2\log(L) + kp$$

where L is the total likelihood of all data, p is the number of parameters (0 for original data, 128 for the translation model and 192 for translation and rotational model) and $k = 2$ by definition for the Akiake Information criterion (AIC) and $k = \log(n)$ for the Bayesian Information Criterion (BIC). These are shown in Fig. 9a and b for the original (ground truth) configuration and for these two optimisation two models. In the 'metric' (normal) maze, assuming the ground truth location of the targets is the best model. However, in the one-wormhole condition the pattern for AIC is reversed and for the three-wormhole condition the reversal is present for both AIC and BIC values. In this case, the best explanation of the data is one that not only allows for a distortion of the location of the targets in the participant's memory but also assumes that their reference frame for pointing may be rotated independently for different pointing locations.

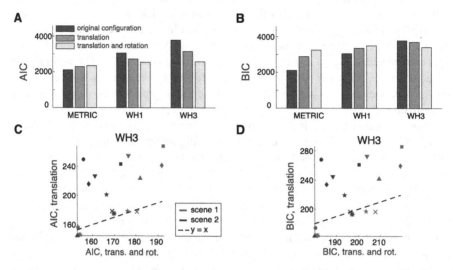

Fig. 9. (A) Akaike Information Criterion values are shown for each condition under 3 models: ground truth, optimised translation and optimised translation-and-rotation). (B) Same for Bayesian Information Criterion. (C–D) compare the AIC and BIC values for the translation and translation + rotation models. Different symbols for each participant and colours for each Scene. (Color figure online)

5 Discussion

Our results show that adding wormholes to a labyrinth environment increases pointing errors (Fig. 5a) in a way that is partly explained by assuming that observers build a distorted model of the environment (Fig. 8) but more fully explained by assuming that observers also rotate their local reference frame when they are at certain locations (Fig. 9). The latter explanation is not compatible with a single globally consistent 3D representation of the environment since that could not tolerate different rotations for different parts of the scene.

The argument that 'visual space' is distorted is a familiar one, although much of the literature on this refers to the perception of an observer that is either stationary or only moving a few centimetres [31–34]. It is more unusual to try and find a distorted map of an environment to explain an observer's behaviour when the observer is free to move around and explore all of that environment, partly because in this situation it is not immediately obvious what systematic distortions could apply. Nevertheless, in the peculiar wormhole environments that we have examined, systematic distortions of the scene layout do provide a better explanation of pointing behaviour than the ground truth layout (Fig. 9).

The modelling we have done is agnostic about the causes of the distortions. One speculation is shown in Fig. 10. This illustrates the same maze layout as is shown in Figs. 6 and 8 where participants made large errors in pointing from the green to the yellow target and vice versa. The green target is located inside a wormhole next to the left wall and hence is, in reality, to the left of the yellow target. However, as Fig. 8b shows, the best explanation of participants' pointing is that they believe the green target to be near the centre of the maze (i.e. to the right of yellow in these plan views). As Fig. 10 shows, this would be the case if participants' conception of the wormhole was that it was 'squashed' into a region between the entrance and exit of the wormhole in the rest of the maze. Participants might do this because they have learnt that the red, yellow and blue spheres are near the outer walls, forcing an interpretation in which the wormhole region is within the central part of the maze.

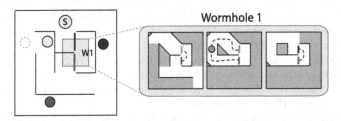

Fig. 10. A speculation about a possible cause of the bias shown in Figs. 6 and 8. The corridors making up the wormhole are shown in the green panel on the right. These are shown 'squashed' into the location where the entrance and exit to the wormhole lie (left). This process leaves the green target to the right of the yellow target in the resulting map. This example is from Scene 2. (Color figure online)

Figure 10 does not include any distortion of local orientation. When we add this in as a variable (Fig. 9), there is no longer a single, consistent metric representation that corresponds to the output of the model (i.e. x, y and ρ for each target location). This fits with the conclusion of a range of studies based on navigation or spatial knowledge of environments that find evidence against a single consistent representation of 3D space [7–9, 14, 24, 29, 35–37]. For example, Warren et al. [5] claimed that there was no consistent representation of space that could account for their data (where the task was to walk directly to targets that had been experienced in a maze with wormholes, i.e. very like our pointing measure but with an indication of perceived distance as well as direction). Our experiment and analysis build on the conclusion of Warren et al. [5] who advocate the idea of a labelled graph. In particular, we make a direct comparison between three models (ground truth, a distorted map or a translation-plus-rotation model) and find that the translation-plus-rotation model fits best. This is compatible with the idea that in the real world, especially in complex environments, observers learn a topological structure first and then a progressively more accurate labelled graph as they become more familiar with the terrain until, eventually, the information about each edge of the graph is so accurate that the result is, at least in theory, impossible to distinguish from a consistent, metric map. This putative hierarchical calibration process for representing space is similar to hypotheses about observers' representation of surface shape from binocular disparity [38–40].

Acknowledgements. This research was supported by EPSRC/Dstl grant EP/N019423/1.

Supplementary Information. Additional figures, movies and raw data are available at: http://www.glennersterlab.com/MuryyGlennerster2018_SupplementaryInfo.zip.

References

1. Gallistel, C.: The Organization of Learning. The MIT Press, Cambridge (1990)
2. O'Keefe, J., Nadel, L.: The Hippocampus as a Cognitive Map. Oxford University Press, Oxford (1978)
3. Tolman, E.C.: Cognitive maps in rats and men. Psychol. Rev. **55**, 189–208 (1948)
4. Meilinger, T., Strickrodt, M., Bülthoff, H.H.: Qualitative differences in memory for vista and environmental spaces are caused by opaque borders, not movement or successive presentation. Cognition **155**, 77–95 (2016)
5. Warren, W.H., Rothman, D.B., Schnapp, B.H., Ericson, J.D.: Wormholes in virtual space: from cognitive maps to cognitive graphs. Cognition **166**, 152–163 (2017)
6. Gillner, S., Mallot, H.A.: Navigation and acquisition of spatial knowledge in a virtual maze. J. Cogn. Neurosci. **10**, 445–463 (1998)
7. Foo, P., Warren, W.H., Duchon, A., Tarr, M.J.: Do humans integrate routes into a cognitive map? Map - versus landmark-based navigation of novel shortcuts. J. Exp. Psychol. Learn. Mem. Cogn. **31**, 195–215 (2005)
8. Chrastil, E.R., Warren, W.H.: From cognitive maps to cognitive graphs. PLoS One. **9**, e112544 (2014)
9. Byrne, R.W.: Memory for urban geography. Q. J. Exp. Psychol. **31**, 147–154 (1979)
10. Tversky, B.: Distortions in cognitive maps. Geoforum **23**, 131–138 (1992)
11. Chrastil, E.R., Warren, W.H.: Active and passive spatial learning in human navigation: acquisition of graph knowledge. J. Exp. Psychol. Learn. Mem. Cogn. **41**, 1162–1178 (2015)
12. Ishikawa, T., Montello, D.R.: Spatial knowledge acquisition from direct experience in the environment: individual differences in the development of metric knowledge and the integration of separately learned places. Cogn. Psychol. **52**, 93–129 (2006)
13. Meilinger, T., Riecke, B.E., Bülthoff, H.H.: Local and global reference frames for environmental spaces. Q. J. Exp. Psychol. **67**, 542–569 (2014)
14. Moar, I., Bower, G.H.: Inconsistency in spatial knowledge. Mem. Cognit. **11**, 107–113 (1983)
15. Poucet, B.: Spatial cognitive maps in animals: new hypotheses on their structure and neural mechanisms. Psychol. Rev. **100**, 163–182 (1993)
16. Kuipers, B., Byun, Y.-T.: A robot exploration and mapping strategy based on a semantic hierachy of spatial representations. J. Robot. Auton. Syst. **8**, 47–63 (1991)
17. Kuipers, B., Tecuci, D.G., Stankiewicz, B.J.: The skeleton in the cognitive map: a computational and empirical exploration. Environ. Behav. **35**, 81–106 (2003)
18. Schultheis, H., Bertel, S., Barkowsky, T.: Modeling mental spatial reasoning about cardinal directions. Cogn. Sci. **38**, 1521–1561 (2014)
19. Franz, M.O., Schölkopf, B., Mallot, H.A., Bülthoff, H.H.: Learning view graphs for robot navigation. Auton. Robots. **5**, 111–125 (1998)

20. Cheeseman, J.F., Millar, C.D., Greggers, U., Lehmann, K., Pawley, M.D.M., Gallistel, C.R., Warman, G.R., Menzel, R.: Way-finding in displaced clock-shifted bees proves bees use a cognitive map. Proc. Natl. Acad. Sci. **111**, 8949–8954 (2014)

21. Cheeseman, J.F., et al.: The cognitive map hypothesis remains the best interpretation of the data in honeybee navigation. Proc. Natl. Acad. Sci. **111**, E4398 (2014). Reply to Cheung et al.

22. Cheung, A., et al.: Still no convincing evidence for cognitive map use by honeybees. Proc. Natl. Acad. Sci. **111**, E4396–E4397 (2014). Fig. 1

23. Stachenfeld, K.L., Botvinick, M.M., Gershman, S.J.: The hippocampus as a predictive map. Nat. Neurosci. **20**, 1643–1653 (2017)

24. Freksa, C., Newcombe, N.S., Gärdenfors, P., Wölfl, S. (eds.): Spatial Cognition VI. LNCS (LNAI), vol. 5248. Springer, Heidelberg (2008). https://doi.org/10.1007/978-3-540-87601-4

25. Mallot, H.A., Basten, K.: Embodied spatial cognition: biological and artificial systems. Image Vis. Comput. **27**, 1658–1670 (2009)

26. Montello, D.R.: Scale and multiple psychologies of space. In: Frank, A.U., Campari, I. (eds.) COSIT 1993. LNCS, vol. 716, pp. 312–321. Springer, Heidelberg (1993). https://doi.org/10.1007/3-540-57207-4_21

27. Kluss, T., Marsh, W.E., Zetzsche, C., Schill, K.: Representation of impossible worlds in the cognitive map. Cogn. Process. **16**, 271–276 (2015)

28. Vasylevska, K., Kaufmann, H.: Towards efficient spatial compression in self-overlapping virtual environments. In: Proceedings of 2017 IEEE Symposium on 3D User Interfaces, 3DUI 2017, pp. 12–21 (2017)

29. Zetzsche, C., Wolter, J., Galbraith, C., Schill, K.: Representation of space: image-like or sensorimotor? Spat. Vis. **22**, 409–424 (2009)

30. Svarverud, E., Gilson, S., Glennerster, A.: A demonstration of "broken" visual space. PLoS One. **7**, e33782 (2012)

31. Glennerster, A.: The time course of 2-D shape discrimination in random dot stereograms. Vis. Res. **36**, 1955–1968 (1996)

32. Johnston, E.B.: Systematic distortions of shape from stereopsis. Vis. Res. **31**, 1351–1360 (1991)

33. Koenderink, J.J., van Doorn, A.J., Kappers, A.M.L., Doumen, M.J.A., Todd, J.T.: Exocentric pointing in depth. Vis. Res. **48**, 716–723 (2008)

34. Ogle, K.: Researches in Binocular Vision (1950)

35. McNamara, T.P., Diwadkar, V.A.: Symmetry and asymmetry of human spatial memory. Cogn. Psychol. **34**, 160–190 (1997)

36. McNamara, T.P.: Mental representations of spatial relations. Cogn. Psychol. **18**, 87–121 (1986)

37. Foo, P., Duchon, A., Warren, W.H., Tarr, M.J.: Humans do not switch between path knowledge and landmarks when learning a new environment. Psychol. Res. **71**, 240–251 (2007)

38. Tittle, J.S., Todd, J.T., Perotti, V.J., Norman, J.F.: Systematic distortion of perceived three-dimensional structure from motion and binocular stereopsis. J. Exp. Psychol. Hum. Percept. Perform. **21**, 663–678 (1995)

39. Koenderink, J.J., van Doorn, A.J.: Affine structure from motion. J. Opt. Soc. Am. A **8**, 377 (1991)

40. Glennerster, A., Rogers, B.J., Bradshaw, M.F.: Stereoscopic depth constancy depends on the subject's task. Vis. Res. **36**, 3441–3456 (1996)

The Effect of Locomotion Modes on Spatial Memory and Learning in Large Immersive Virtual Environments: A Comparison of Walking with Gain to Continuous Motion Control

Xianshi Xie[1], Richard A. Paris[2], Timothy P. McNamara[3], and Bobby Bodenheimer[2(✉)]

[1] Facebook Inc., 1 Facebook Way, Menlo Park, CA, USA
`xianshi.matt.xie@gmail.com`
[2] Electrical Engineering and Computer Science,
Vanderbilt University, Nashville, TN, USA
`{richard.a.paris,bobby.bodenheimer}@vanderbilt.edu`
[3] Department of Psychology, Vanderbilt University, Nashville, TN, USA
`t.mcnamara@vanderbilt.edu`

Abstract. This paper examines locomotion methods for large virtual environments presented through head-mounted displays and involving complex navigation. Our interest is on comparing methods involving bipedal locomotion to those involving motion controlled continuously through a joystick. In the first of two experiments 36 participants performed a navigational search task where they either walked, their translation/rotations were controlled by joystick, or their translations were controlled by joystick but their rotations were controlled by body-based turning. In addition, the optic flow rate, or translational gain of movement, was varied. In the second experiment, 24 participants performed a complex search involving only walking and joystick translation with body-based rotation, followed by a task in which they were asked to recall their search from novel viewpoints. Our findings suggest that for such complex tasks walking is preferable if space and equipment allow for such a locomotion mode.

1 Introduction

Large immersive virtual environments (IVEs) provide simulations that are useful in a variety of contexts and situations, such as education (Angulo and de Velasco 2014) and entertainment (Tan et al. 2015). An immediate choice confronting the designer of such large IVEs is what locomotion method to use for moving users through the environment. From the perspective of maintaining spatial orientation, bipedal locomotion is often desirable (Chance et al. 1998; Ruddle and Lessels 2009) because it is naturalistic and able to provide proprioceptive and vestibular cues that are important. However, there are situations where bipedal

© Springer Nature Switzerland AG 2018
S. Creem-Regehr et al. (Eds.): Spatial Cognition 2018, LNAI 11034, pp. 58–73, 2018.
https://doi.org/10.1007/978-3-319-96385-3_5

locomotion as a method of moving through an IVE is not viable, e.g., where the IVEs do not support a tracking interface, or where the physical space housing the IVE is so limited that it does not afford walking as a viable interface. This paper studies alternative locomotion interfaces and compares them with a bipedal locomotion interface. The goal is to have a better understanding of the trade-offs between various interfaces in different navigation scenarios. However, as there are a plethora of locomotion methods for IVEs, we limit our investigation of these interfaces. In particular, we consider locomotion with joysticks as an alternative method. Note that joysticks provide continuous translation and (potentially) rotation through a motion control device. There are many such motion control devices in the gaming community, e.g., the Oculus Touch, the Xbox controller, and the Razer Hydra (Young et al. 2014).

Many methods have been developed for navigation in large virtual environments (Bowman et al. 1997; Razzaque et al. 2001; Interrante et al. 2007; Williams et al. 2007; Engel et al. 2008; Paris et al. 2017), but the optimal method of doing so depends on many factors. These factors include the performance metric by which the method will be judged, but also such factors as room size and layout (Azmandian et al. 2017), and the virtual environment (Langbehn et al. 2017). For example, if the room size is sufficiently large, then a redirected walking technique might be employed (Steinicke et al. 2008, 2010); if the room size is small, however, some of these techniques can induce simulator sickness, and methods involving only a joystick or teleportation might be needed, e.g., Langbehn et al. (2018). If the environment is very large, then some method of locomotion beyond normal bipedal locomotion may be appropriate, e.g., the methods of Williams et al. (2007) or Interrante et al. (2007). This paper focuses its attention on metrics associated with spatial memory, as well as comparing the specific locomotion methods of bipedal locomotion to joystick-controlled movement.

2   Background

2.1   Walking in Virtual Environments

Several techniques that permit exploration of large virtual environments have been developed (Razzaque et al. 2001; Interrante et al. 2007; Williams et al. 2007; Engel et al. 2008). These techniques generally revolve around manipulating some form of visual information, which allows for a much larger virtual environment to be explored. One such technique is to add a translational gain factor (Interrante et al. 2007; Williams et al. 2006) that multiplies the virtual space by altering the optic flow experienced by users as they move through the environment. These methods have the advantage of granting proprioceptive and vestibular motion cues that are useful in integrating spatial knowledge (Ruddle 2013; Riecke et al. 2010). This result taken with prior work (Ruddle et al. 2011; Chance et al. 1998; Ruddle and Lessels 2006) suggests the benefits of walking over simple joystick motion.

2.2 Body-Based Cues

Body-based cues generated from natural walking are typically divided into two functions: these cues grant rotation information or translation information. Full rotation-based information can be provided without requiring subjects to physically translate. This allows for the separation of these two streams of information. Rotational-based cues, which provide information on the angle an individual has turned, can be useful when keeping oneself oriented in the virtual environment (Grechkin and Riecke 2014). Providing translation-based cues requires both tracking equipment and physical space. Information provided by translation-based cues are useful for estimating the distances between two objects and gauging the scale of the environment. In this work we separate these two streams of information in that we are able to provide both streams, only rotation-based information, or neither. Ruddle et al. (2011) and Riecke et al. (2010)

Development of spatial knowledge requires the integration of many smaller frames of reference (called local frames) into one larger global frame of reference (Zhang et al. 2014; Kelly et al. 2010; Greenauer and Waller 2010; Meilinger et al. 2014). The integration of these frames of reference require that there be some way of tying that information together. Mou et al. (2007) looked at using geometry as the integration point, whereas Roskos-Ewoldsen et al. (1998) looked at how orientation played a role in this combination of spatial memory. In addition to how one integrates these frames, research has been conducted into how these smaller frames are created. Prior work (McNamara et al. 2003; Marchette et al. 2011) examined the difference between egocentric and exocentric frames of reference and how they affected spatial memory. Looking further into egocentric and exocentric frames of reference, Xiao et al. (2009) analyzed how subjects built these frames relative to themselves or some external object. In the present work, subjects had to integrate spatial information after traveling from station to station. Yamamoto and Shelton (2007) also examined this type of integration and the effect of proprioceptive information.

3   Experiment 1

3.1 Materials

The experiments were conducted in a 7.3 m by 8.5 m laboratory. The virtual environment was presented by a full color stereo NVIS nVisor SX Head Mounted Display (HMD) with 1280×1024 resolution per eye, a nominal FOV of 60° diagonally, and a frame rate of 60 Hz. An interSense IS-900 precision motion tracker was used to update the participant's rotational movement around all three axes. Position was updated using four optical tracking cameras that operated with two LED lights. The virtual environment displayed in the HMD was rendered in Vizard (Worldviz, Santa Barbara, CA).

3.2 Participants

Thirty-six students from Vanderbilt University, 18 males and 18 females aged 18–32, participated in this experiment. Each was compensated $10 for participation in the experiment.

3.3 Experimental Setup and Procedure

The experimental setup was based on that of Riecke et al. (2010). We compared three locomotion modes: pure joystick (J), joystick translation with physical rotation (JR or joystick rotation condition), and free walking (W). In the joystick condition, participants used a wireless joystick to achieve translation and rotation in a virtual environment. In the JR condition, participants physically turned while using the joystick to translate in the virtual environment. In the walking condition, participants were able to freely navigate inside the virtual environment.

The task was to find eight randomly distributed targets among sixteen randomly distributed locations. In each possible location was a birdhouse, and eight red balls were used as targets and placed inside eight of the sixteen birdhouses. The environment was a featureless plane so that participants were not able to get any orienting cues from the surrounding environment (Fig. 1). The sixteen possible locations for targets were randomly distributed according to a Poisson Disk distribution (Fig. 2) so that participants were not able to get cues from intrinsic reference frames based on the layout of the targets (Mou and McNamara 2002).

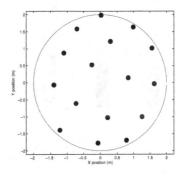

Fig. 1. Experiment 1: screen shot of the bird houses and red ball. (Color figure online)

Fig. 2. Experiment 1: example of how birdhouses were distributed in an environment—a Poisson disk distribution.

There were three different optical gains in this experiment, i.e., 1:1, 2:1, and 10:1. Therefore, the sizes of the IVEs were scaled correspondingly. For the 1:1 gain, the sixteen birdhouses were placed within a circle with radius 2m. For the 2:1 gain, the radius of the circle was 4m. For 10:1 gain, the radius of the circle was 20m. We used a mixed design: between-subjects for the different gains and within-subjects for the locomotion modes. Three groups of participants, 12 for each group, were assigned to the three different translational gain conditions. All participants performed the three locomotion methods, i.e., joystick, joystick plus rotation, and walking condition. In this experiment, each participant did one training trial before each locomotion mode condition that contained three experimental trials; in total, there were twelve trials for all three locomotion modes. The locomotion mode order was balanced; the experiment was gender balanced overall.

During the experiment, participants started in the center of the virtual space. When they approached a birdhouse, they clicked the joystick (participants carried a joystick in the Walking condition also), and the birdhouse became transparent, so that they could see whether there was a blue ball inside or not. If the birdhouse was a target birdhouse, a success audio cue would play, the ball would turn red for one second, and then return to its blue color. If the birdhouse was not a target birdhouse, then a blue ball would appear. Thus, if they revisited a birdhouse, participants could tell they were revisiting the birdhouse from the presence of the blue ball and a revisit audio cue. The task ended when all eight targets had been found or eight consecutive revisits occurred. A message in the upper right hand corner of the screen displayed the current number of targets left to find in a trial. The participants were asked to complete the task as efficiently as possible, that is to try to minimize the number of revisits and minimize the travel distance and time taken.

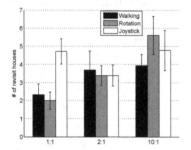

Fig. 3. Mean number of revisits across conditions. Error bars show SEs.

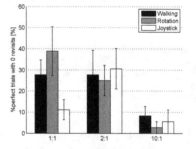

Fig. 4. Mean percentage of perfect search trials across conditions. Error bars show SEs.

3.4 Results and Discussion

We measured the number of times that participants revisited the same birdhouses that had been visited before, the number of targets found by participants, the number of targets found before a revisit, the number of targets revisited, the total time spent on the task, the accumulated turning angles, total travel distance, and number of perfect trials.

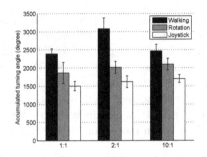
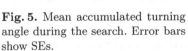
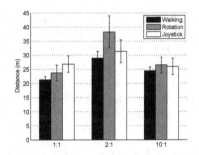

Fig. 5. Mean accumulated turning angle during the search. Error bars show SEs.

Fig. 6. Mean normalized travel distance across conditions. Error bars show SEs.

Number of Revisits. The number of revisits in the 1:1 gain condition is highest in the pure joystick condition, which is consistent with the findings of Riecke et al. (2010), while in a larger virtual space there is no difference across locomotion methods. Regarding the number of revisits, a mixed model ANOVA showed no main effect on locomotion method or gain, but an interaction between locomotion and gain conditions, $F(4,66) = 2.8$, $p = 0.03$. Examining Fig. 3 for the interaction, we can see different patterns under different translational gains. In the 1:1 gain, the joystick condition had worse performance than the walking and rotation conditions; while in the 2:1 and 10:1 gains, there was no such difference. Additionally, trials in the rotation condition seemed to have worse performance when the gain increased. Examining for simple effects, a within-subjects ANOVA on the participants who did the 1:1 gain showed a main effect of locomotion mode, $F(2,22) = 11.39$, $p < 0.001$. A post-hoc paired-sample t-test with Bonferroni correction showed difference between the JR (mean $= 2.00$, SD $= 1.65$) and J conditions (mean $= 4.72$, SD $= 2.41$), $t(11) = 4.02$, $p = 0.002$, and between the J and W conditions (mean $= 2.33$, SD $= 2.07$), $t(11) = 3.62$, $p = 0.004$, which is consistent with the findings of Riecke et al. (2010), who showed rotation may suffice for such complex spatial orientation task. However, in the 2:1 gain and 10:1 gains, a within-subjects ANOVA showed no main effect on locomotion methods. Participants performed equally well under walking, rotation, and joystick conditions.

Increasing the gain increased the number of revisits under the JR condition, but not under the walking and joystick conditions. A between-subject ANOVA for the rotation condition showed a main effect of gain, $F(2,33) = 6.129$, $p = 0.005$, but no gain effect under the J and W conditions. Under the JR condition, a post-hoc unpaired-sample t-test with Bonferroni correction showed a main effect between the 1:1 gain (mean $= 2.00$, SD $= 1.65$) and 10:1 gain conditions (mean $= 5.61$, SD $= 3.64$), $t = 3.13$, $p = 0.007$. These results indicate that the performance decreased when the gain increased under the JR condition, but the performance was not detectably changed under the J and W conditions.

Gain. The 10:1 gain condition has the worst percentage of perfect search trials. Regarding the percentage of perfect trials, a mixed model ANOVA showed a main effect of gain, $F(2,33) = 4.844$, $p = 0.01$ (see Fig. 4). A post-hoc unpaired-sample t-test with Bonferroni correction on gain showed a difference between the 1:1 gain (mean $= 25.9$, SD $= 20.4$) and 10:1 gains (mean $= 5.6$, SD $= 10.0$), $t(16.093) = 3.1169$, $p = 0.007$; and between the 2:1 gain (mean $= 27.8$, SD $= 24.9$) and 10:1 gain conditions, $t(14.506) = 2.8723$, $p = 0.01$. Therefore, the 10:1 gain reduced the number of perfect search trials which had zero revisits. A conclusion one might draw from this is that while a 50:1 translational gain is reasonable for navigation (Williams 2007), it should not be used in more challenging tasks.

Orienting Motions. Walking led to increased orienting motions. For accumulated turning angle (we measured this by recording users' real time yaw orientation and accumulating the difference of every two consecutive orientation records) during the search, a mixed model ANOVA showed a main effect on locomotion method, $F(2,66) = 36.59$, $p < 0.0001$ (see Fig. 5). A post-hoc paired-sample t-test with Bonferroni correction showed a difference between the JR (mean $= 1994°$, SD $= 726$) and W (mean $= 2646°$, SD $= 798$) conditions, $t(35) = 5.02$, $p < 0.001$, and between the J (mean $= 1609°$, SD $= 462$) and W conditions, $t(35) = 7.12$, $p < 0.0001$, and between the J and JR conditions, $t(35) = 3.93$, $p < 0.001$. The fact that participants looked around more during search under walking and joystick rotation conditions indicates that they may employ a qualitatively different navigation strategy: by looking around more participants were able to optimize the trajectory. This result is somewhat different from Riecke et al. (2010) in that participants looked around more only in the walking condition in their study.

Time and Travel Distance. There was no time difference across conditions but the 2:1 gain led to the overall highest normalized travel distance. Normalized travel distance is calculated by the accumulated optic flow distance over the translational gain. Therefore, the normalized travel distance is the physical walking distance in walking condition, and the optic flow distance over the translational gain in the two conditions involving the joystick. A mixed model ANOVA showed a main effect of gain condition, $F(2,33) = 3.556$, $p = 0.04$ (see Fig. 6). A post-hoc unpaired-sample t-test on gain showed difference between the 1:1 (mean $= 23.9$ m, SD $= 6.1$) and 2:1 (mean $= 32.9$ m, SD $= 12.1$) gains, $t(16.153) = 2.265$, $p = 0.038$, and a marginal difference between the 2:1 and 10:1 (mean $= 25.7$ m, SD $= 6.4$) gains, $t(16.59) = 1.8$, $p = 0.09$. Our best interpretation of the higher travel distance in the 2:1 gain condition is that it results from the mixture of navigation strategies being employed in solving the problem, as explained next.

Navigation Strategy. Navigation strategy may rely on the size of virtual space. According to the answers to the post-task survey, most participants typically employed two distinct navigation strategies to complete the task. In this analysis, we adopt the terminology used by Ruddle and Lessels (2009): (a) perimeter (participants initially checked the birdhouses around the perimeter, and then checked the ones in the center.); and (b) lawnmower (searching in a series of parallel lanes), although, because of the Poisson disk nature of our birdhouse distribution, a strategy only approximating this can be effected. We manually categorized participants into a perimeter or lawnmower strategy based on their travel paths. In the 1:1 gain, 58% of participants employed the perimeter strategy, and the other 42% people used the lawnmower strategy. In the 2:1 gain, 50% of people employed perimeter strategy, and 50% people used lawnmower strategy. In the 10:1 gain, 83% of people employed perimeter strategy, and 17% people used lawnmower strategy. Therefore, when the gain was increased to 10:1, there were more people using perimeter strategy. We computed the results by strategy, and found in 2:1 condition those people using the perimeter strategy had fewer visits (mean = 4.2, SD = 2.2) in the walking (mean = 2.7, SD = 2.0) and rotation (mean = 2.3, SD = 0.7) conditions compared with that of joystick condition. However, people using the lawnmower strategy had a higher number of revisits in the walking (mean = 4.7, SD = 4.7) and rotation (mean = 4.4, SD = 2.1) conditions compared with that of the joystick condition (mean = 2.6, SD = 1.5). Therefore, there is a trend that the perimeter strategy facilitated the task in the walking and rotation conditions, while the lawnmower strategy facilitated the task in the joystick condition. Unfortunately, we did not have enough power to obtain statistical significance due to the small number (around six) of participants in each group.

Interface Preference. The walking interface was preferred by most participants in all three gain conditions. According to the answers to the post-task survey, in the 1:1 gain condition, eight people liked the walking interface best, while five people preferred the joystick rotation and nobody liked the pure joystick interface; in the 2:1 gain condition, eight people preferred the walking interface, while four people liked the joystick rotation and one person liked the pure joystick; in the 10:1 gain condition, six people preferred the walking interface, while three people liked each of the joystick rotation and pure joystick interfaces, respectively. Therefore, the majority preferred the walking interface, and the fewest people liked the pure joystick interface, particularly in a room-sized virtual space with 1:1 gain.

To summarize, where participants had to find eight targets from 16 randomly placed objects, translational gain and locomotion interfaces interact; people had fewer perfect trials in 10:1 gain, which tends to indicate that for more complicated tasks higher gains are not as good; for orienting motions, walking is better than joystick rotation, and joystick rotation is better than the pure joystick, but it is not clear how this affects the task. There are suggestions that navigation strategy changes with size of environment, but nothing conclusive.

4   Experiment 2

The goal of this experiment is to investigate the relative importance of body-based rotation and translation in a more complex memory and search task scenario. Because the pure joystick (J) condition was no better in any gains in Experiment 1, we only compare the walking condition and the joystick rotation condition (joystick translation plus physical rotation) here. The scenario is similar to how people form spatial memory in complex navigation and search tasks, where it has been shown that spatial memory is more orientation dependent (Shelton and McNamara 2001; McNamara 2003).

4.1   Materials and Participants

The equipment and setting for this experiment was identical to that of Experiment 1. Eighteen subjects, nine male and nine female, aged 18–30 from Vanderbilt University, participated in this experiment and were paid $15 for their participation.

4.2   Experimental Setup and Procedure

In this experiment, participants saw a number (twenty) of trashcans scattered about a virtual plaza. Some of these trashcans contained balls. Trashcans containing balls are called "suspicious" trashcans. The task for the participants was to memorize the locations of the suspicious trashcans among all trashcans. In particular, they searched a few (eight) of the trashcans. Balls were located in some number of these. After searching all eight of the indicated trashcans, they were asked to indicate where the suspicious trashcans were. Participants searched the trashcans sequentially, that is, a trashcan to be searched was indicated to each of them, and after that trashcan was searched the next was indicated sequentially until all eight had been searched. Thus the order in which the trashcans were searched was controlled.

More specifically, participants started from home position (position 1 in Fig. 7), and the task started when they clicked the trigger of the joystick. The search was conducted in a near-to-far manner. At that time one of the trashcans would turn red. They then approached it. When they were close, participants clicked the joystick again. The trashcan would momentarily turn transparent, and they would be able to see if a ball was inside the trashcan or not. If a ball was inside, they were to note the location of that (suspicious) trashcan. When they were finished looking inside the trashcan, they looked around to find the next trashcan, which would be red and ready for searching. There were potentially a different number of target balls in the eight trash cans on each trial. The variable number of balls used we called the *set size* condition of the experiment. In this experiment we used set sizes of 3, 5, and 7 balls. The set size condition places different demands on a participant's working memory.

After the search phase was completed, participants were teleported to a new location from which they would be asked to recall the trashcans that were suspicious. The position to which they were teleported was the *viewing* position and in this experiment there were three different viewing positions. We varied the final view position because prior work has shown that spatial memory is orientation dependent (McNamara 2003; Shelton and McNamara 2001), and even view dependent under some circumstances (Diwadkar and McNamara 1997; Waller 2006). These viewing positions were a 0° view (the original start position, called the 0-view), a 90° view (orthogonal to the main direction of motion, called the

90-view), and a 135° view (at 135° to the main direction of motion, called the 135-view). These positions are illustrated in Fig. 7. Participants used the joystick to select the trashcans that they thought contained balls.

We used a within-subject design for this study. Thus, each participant completed both the walking condition and the joystick rotation condition. Before the actual experiment began, they completed a few practice trials to make sure they were familiar with the basic environment and procedures. Within either condition, they did nine trials composed of three set-sizes by the three view positions. Random configurations of trashcans and balls were generated for each trial. In the experiment, the size of the trashcan array is around 50 m by 40 m, which is much larger than the size of our physical lab. We used a translational gain of 10:1 in this experiment. We wanted to explore thoroughly how people perform in this gain condition, because prior work has shown that people can perform reasonably well in 10:1 gain (Williams 2007; Xie et al. 2010).

We measured the correct selection percentage (CSP) of the balls and the time used to make the selection. We also calculated a two dimensional similarity between the correct configurations of the suspicious trashcans and the configurations of participants' selection, using bi-dimensional regression[1] (Tobler 1994; Carbon 2013), which is suitable for a two dimensional configuration similarity comparison. Specifically, we used the Euclidean form of the regression, that transforms one configuration to another through scaling, translation, and rotation. For the correspondence of the anchor points of the two configurations, we assumed the correctly selected targets as pairs of points (e.g., we assume participants made the correct choice intentionally), iterated all possible permutations for incorrectly selected targets, and picked the configuration with highest r^2 (e.g., this measure indicates correspondence between two 2D configurations, ranging from 0 to 1; the higher, the more correspondence) among all permutations.

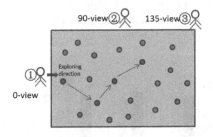

Fig. 7. Experiment 2: participants search in a near-to-far manner. Position 1, 2, and 3 indicate final viewing positions. Position 1 is the original start position.

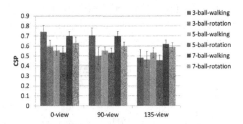

Fig. 8. Mean CSP across all conditions. Error bars show SEs.

---

[1] The bi-dimensional regression package we used is found in R.

4.3   Results and Discussion

Correct Selection Percentage. For the correct selection percentage (CSP), a three way repeated measures ANOVA shows main effects of locomotion mode ($F(1,17) = 5.6$, p = 0.03), set-size ($F(2,34) = 5.6$, p = 0.008), and view-angle ($F(2,34) = 8.6$, p = 0.001). For locomotion mode, the collapsed mean CSP is 0.62 (SD = 0.15) in the walking condition, and 0.54 (SD = 0.17) in the joystick rotation condition. For view-angle, the collapsed mean CSP is 0.62 (SD = 0.16) in the 0-view condition, 0.60 (SD = 0.15) in the 90-view condition, and 0.52 (SD = 0.16) in the 135-view condition. A post-hoc paired sample t-test with Bonferroni correction showed difference between the 0-view and 135-view, $t(17) = 3.5$, p = 0.003, and between the 90-view and 135-view, $t(17) = 3.4$, p = 0.003. For set-size, a post-hoc paired-sample t-test shows difference between the 5-ball (mean = 0.53 m SD = 0.11) and 7-ball (mean = 0.64, SD = 0.12) conditions, $t(17) = 5.7$, $p < 0.001$ (see Fig. 8).

Latency. For latency, a three way repeated measures ANOVA shows main effects of set-size, $F(2,34) = 48.9$, $p < 0.0001$, and view-angle, $F(2,34) = 8.8$, p = 0.001. The results make sense for set-size because participants have to use a longer time to choose more targets. The latency is 26.7 s, 36.2 s, and 45.4 s for the 3-ball, 5-ball, and 7-ball sets, respectively. For view-angle, the collapsed mean latency is 32.2 s (SD = 7.2) in the 0-view condition, 36.4 s (SD = 10.7) in the 90-view condition, 40.0 s (SD = 10.2) in the 135-view condition. A post-hoc paired sample t-test with Bonferroni correction shows a difference between the 0-view and 135-view, $t(17) = 6.0$, $p < 0.001$ (see Fig. 9).

Bidimensional Regression. For the Bidimensional regression (BDR) metrics, a three way repeated measures ANOVA for r^2 shows main effects of set-size ($F(2,34) = 13.5$, $p < 0.001$), and view-angle ($F(2,34) = 4.6$, p = 0.02). For view-angle, the collapsed mean r^2 is 0.82 (SD = 0.09) in the 0-view, 0.83 (SD = 0.07) in the 90-view, 0.76 (SD = 0.09) in the 135-view. A post-hoc paired sample t-test with Bonferroni correction shows a difference between the 90-view and 135-view,

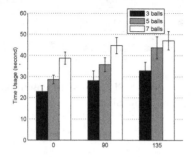

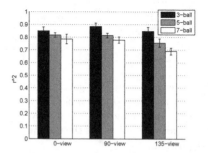

Fig. 9. Mean latency across the conditions. Error bars show SEs.

Fig. 10. Mean r^2 across the conditions. Error bars show SEs.

$t(17) = 3.5$, $p = 0.003$. For set-size, the collapsed mean r^2 is 0.86 (SD = 0.08) in the 3-ball, 0.80 (SD = 0.07) in the 5-ball, and 0.75 (SD = 0.09) in the 7-ball. A post-hoc paired sample t-test shows a difference between the 3-ball and 5-ball ($t(17) = 1.7$, $p = 0.02$), 5-ball and 7-ball ($t(17) = 2.53$, $p = 0.02$), 3-ball and 7-ball ($t(17) = 5.13$, $p < 0.001$) (see Fig. 10).

A three way ANOVA for rotation component shows main effects of locomotion mode ($F(1,17) = 7.6$, $p = 0.01$), and view-angle ($F(2,34) = 7.0$, $p = 0.003$). For locomotion mode, the collapsed mean rotation is 10.8 (SD = 4.7) in the walking, and 15.5 (SD = 7.6) in the joystick rotation. For view-angle, the collapsed mean rotation is 10.5 (SD = 6.6) in the 0-view, 11.4 (SD = 7.0) in the 90-view, 17.4 (SD = 7.7) in the 135-view. A post-hoc paired sample t-test with Bonferroni correction shows a difference between the 90-view and 135-view, $t(17) = 3.4$, $p = 0.003$, and a difference between the 0-view and 135-view, $t(17) = 3.4$, $p = 0.003$ (see Fig. 11). A three-way ANOVA for translation component shows a main effect of locomotion mode, $F(1,17) = 21.59$, $p < 0.001$. The collapsed mean translation is 3.65 (SD = 1.29) for the walking condition, and 4.87 for the joystick rotation condition (SD = 1.68).

The above BDR results show the walking condition has equivalent r^2 as the joystick rotation condition, but the former has less rotation and translation components than the latter, which indicates people were able to remember the shape of the ball configuration equally well in both conditions, but there were larger angular offsets and linear offsets of the ball configuration in the joystick rotation condition.

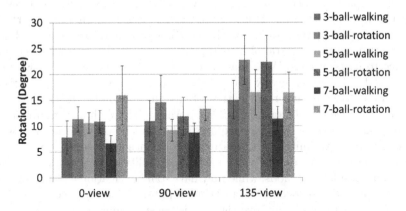

Fig. 11. Mean rotation across the conditions. Error bars show SEs.

From these results, we may conclude participants performed better with the walking interface than with the joystick interface, which indicates the importance of physical translation in spatial navigation, especially in complex memory and search tasks. Participants also performed in a view dependent way, in all measures, i.e., the CSP, latency, BDR metrics, which is consistent with previous research (Diwadkar and McNamara 1997). In terms of set-size, the 5-ball condition was worse than the 7-ball condition in the CSP measure. However, the 5-ball condition was better than the 7-ball condition in the r^2 measure, which indicates that participants did not remember the exact locations of the five balls but remembered the shape of the configuration in this configuration better than in the 7-ball condition. This pattern is strange, but was robust, as it was noticed in other pilot experiments. We hypothesize that there is interference between strategies that participants are using for remembering layouts between set sizes, but future work will be needed to verify this.

Some participants reported that they were not able to tell how far they had traveled when only using the joystick to move and thus it was hard for them to remember the path they had been through. Thus, it was harder for them to memorize the locations of the targets. Their reports are consistent with prior research that indicates physical translation is critical to path integration (Ruddle and Lessels 2009) and spatial navigation. In the first experiment, the traveled path and orientation data of participants were recorded; the data showed participants had more orienting motion and less collision with objects when they walked, consistent with both Riecke et al. (2010) and Ruddle and Lessels (2009).

5   Conclusion

This paper presented two experiments that attempted to better understand the trade-offs between a walking interface and a joystick interface as users navigated in complex task scenarios through large virtual environments. The results showed task complexity may influence the effectiveness of locomotion interfaces. Particularly, walking was significantly better than joystick translation plus body-based rotation in the scenario of Experiment 2. Therefore, our results may give guidance to users of large IVEs that there is a trade-off between the two locomotion modes. Large physically tracked spaces (e.g., room-sized), are suggested if users want to gain better navigation ability in large IVEs. In this case the physical space needs to be open for users to walk freely, with a motion tracking system. While a joystick interface requires only a small space, no need to walk, and no position tracking, users' spatial performance may suffer worse learning experiences in IVEs due to worse navigation ability. Recent work has shown that walking-in-place methods, while they have some navigational disadvantages, have some potential as locomotion methods if physical space is a concern (Paris et al. 2017). Future work will investigate this question more fully.

Acknowledgement. The authors would like to thank Qiufeng Lin for help throughout, and the reviewers for constructive comments. This material is based upon work supported by the National Science Foundation under grants 1116988 and 1526448.

References

Angulo, A., de Velasco, G.V.: Immersive simulation of architectural spatial experiences. Blucher Des. Proc. **1**(7), 495–499 (2014)

Azmandian, M., Grechkin, T., Rosenberg, E.S.: An evaluation of strategies for two-user redirected walking in shared physical spaces. In: 2017 IEEE Conference on Virtual Reality (VR), pp. 91–98. IEEE (2017)

Bowman, D.A., Koller, D., Hodges, L.F.: Travel in immersive virtual environments: an evaluation of viewpoint motion control techniques. In: 1997 IEEE Conference on Virtual Reality Annual International Symposium, pp. 45–52. IEEE (1997)

Carbon, C.-C.: BiDimRegression: bidimensional regression modeling using R. J. Stat. Softw. Code Snippets **52**(3), 1–11 (2013)

Chance, S.S., Gaunet, F., Beall, A.C., Loomis, J.M.: Locomotion mode affects updating of objects encountered during travel: the contribution of vestibular and proprioceptive inputs to path integration. Presence **7**(2), 168–178 (1998)

Diwadkar, V.A., McNamara, T.P.: Viewpoint dependence in scene recognition. Psychol. Sci. **8**(4), 302–307 (1997)

Engel, D., Curio, C., Tcheang, L., Mohler, B., Bülthoff, H.H.: A psychophysically calibrated controller for navigating through large environments in a limited free-walking space. In: VRST 2008: Proceedings of the 2008 ACM Symposium on Virtual Reality Software and Technology, pp. 157–164. ACM, New York (2008)

Grechkin, T.Y., Riecke, B.E.: Re-evaluating benefits of body-based rotational cues for maintaining orientation in virtual environments: men benefit from real rotations, women don't. In: Proceedings of the ACM Symposium on Applied Perception, SAP 2014, pp. 99–102. ACM, New York (2014)

Greenauer, N., Waller, D.: Micro-and macroreference frames: specifying the relations between spatial categories in memory. J. Exp. Psychol.: Learn. Mem. Cogn. **36**(4), 938 (2010)

Interrante, V., Ries, B., Anderson, L.: Seven league boots: a new metaphor for augmented locomotion through moderately large scale immersive virtual environments. In: IEEE Symposium on 3D User Interfaces, pp. 167–170 (2007)

Kelly, J.W., Avraamides, M.N., McNamara, T.P.: Reference frames influence spatial memory development within and across sensory modalities. In: Hölscher, C., Shipley, T.F., Olivetti Belardinelli, M., Bateman, J.A., Newcombe, N.S. (eds.) Spatial Cognition 2010. LNCS (LNAI), vol. 6222, pp. 222–233. Springer, Heidelberg (2010). https://doi.org/10.1007/978-3-642-14749-4_20

Langbehn, E., Lubos, P., Bruder, G., Steinicke, F.: Application of redirected walking in room-scale VR. In: 2017 IEEE conference on Virtual Reality (VR), pp. 449–450. IEEE (2017)

Langbehn, E., Lubos, P., Steinicke, F.: Evaluation of locomotion techniques for room-scale VR: joystick, teleportation, and redirected walking. In: Proceedings of the Virtual Reality International Conference (VRIC) (2018). (accepted)

Marchette, S.A., Yerramsetti, A., Burns, T.J., Shelton, A.L.: Spatial memory in the real world: long-term representations of everyday environments. Mem. Cogn. **39**(8), 1401–1408 (2011)

McNamara, T.P.: How are the locations of objects in the environment represented in memory? In: Freksa, C., Brauer, W., Habel, C., Wender, K.F. (eds.) Spatial Cognition 2002. LNCS, vol. 2685, pp. 174–191. Springer, Heidelberg (2003). https://doi.org/10.1007/3-540-45004-1_11

McNamara, T.P., Rump, B., Werner, S.: Egocentric and geocentric frames of reference in memory of large-scale space. Psychon. Bullet. Rev. **10**(3), 589–595 (2003)

Meilinger, T., Riecke, B.E., Bülthoff, H.H.: Local and global reference frames for environmental spaces. Q. J. Exp. Psychol. **67**(3), 542–569 (2014). PMID: 23972144

Mou, W., McNamara, T.P.: Intrinsic frames of reference in spatial memory. J. Exp. Psychol.: Learn. Mem. Cogn. **28**(1), 162–170 (2002)

Mou, W., Zhao, M., McNamara, T.P.: Layout geometry in the selection of intrinsic frames of reference from multiple viewpoints. J. Exp. Psychol.: Learn. Mem. Cogn. **33**(1), 145–154 (2007)

Paris, R., Joshi, M., He, Q., Narasimham, G., McNamara, T.P., Bodenheimer, B.: Acquisition of survey knowledge using walking in place and resetting methods in immersive virtual environments. In: Proceedings of the ACM Symposium on Applied Perception, SAP 2017, pp. 7:1–7:8. ACM, New York (2017)

Razzaque, S., Kohn, Z., Whitton, M.C.: Redirected walking. In: Eurographics Short Presentation (2001)

Riecke, B.E., Bodenheimer, B., McNamara, T.P., Williams, B., Peng, P., Feuereissen, D.: Do we need to walk for effective virtual reality navigation? Physical rotations alone may suffice. In: Spatial Cognition, pp. 234–247 (2010)

Roskos-Ewoldsen, B., McNamara, T.P., Shelton, A.L., Carr, W.: Mental representations of large and small spatial layouts are orientation dependent. J. Exp. Psychol.: Learn. Mem. Cog. **24**(1), 215–226 (1998)

Ruddle, R.A.: The effect of translational and rotational body-based information on navigation. In: Steinicke, F., Visell, Y., Campos, J., Lécuyer, A. (eds.) Human Walking in Virtual Environments, pp. 99–112. Springer, New York (2013). https://doi.org/10.1007/978-1-4419-8432-6_5

Ruddle, R.A., Lessels, S.: For efficient navigation search, humans require full physical movement but not a rich visual scene. Psychol. Sci. **17**(6), 460–465 (2006)

Ruddle, R.A., Lessels, S.: The benefits of using a walking interface to navigate virtual environments. ACM Trans. Comput.-Hum. Inter. **16**(1), 1–18 (2009)

Ruddle, R.A., Volkova, E., Bülthoff, H.H.: Walking improves your cognitive map in environments that are large-scale and large in extent. ACM Trans. Comput.-Hum. Interact. (TOCHI) **18**(2), 10 (2011)

Shelton, A.L., McNamara, T.P.: Systems of spatial reference in human memory. Cogn. Psychol. **43**(4), 274–310 (2001)

Steinicke, F., Bruder, G., Jerald, J., Frenz, H., Lappe, M.: Analyses of human sensitivity to redirected walking. In: Proceedings of the 2008 ACM symposium on Virtual Reality Software and Technology, pp. 149–156. ACM, New York (2008)

Steinicke, F., Bruder, G., Jerald, J., Frenz, H., Lappe, M.: Estimation of detection thresholds for redirected walking techniques. IEEE Trans. Vis. Comput. Graph. **16**, 17–27 (2010)

Tan, C.T., Leong, T.W., Shen, S., Dubravs, C., Si, C.: Exploring gameplay experiences on the oculus rift. In: Proceedings of the 2015 Annual Symposium on Computer-Human Interaction in Play, CHI PLAY 2015, pp. 253–263. ACM, New York (2015)

Tobler, W.R.: Bidimensional regression. Geogr. Anal. **26**(3), 187–212 (1994)

Waller, D.: Egocentric and nonegocentric coding in memory for spatial layout: evidence from scene recognition. Mem. Cogn. **34**(3), 491–504 (2006)

Williams, B., Narasimham, G., McNamara, T.P., Carr, T.H., Rieser, J.J., Bodenheimer, B.: Updating orientation in large virtual environments using scaled translational gain. In: Symposium on Applied Perception in Graphics and Visualization, Boston, MA, pp. 21–28 (2006)

Williams, B., Narasimham, G., Rump, B., McNamara, T.P., Carr, T.H., Rieser, J.J., Bodenheimer, B.: Exploring large virtual environments with an HMD when physical space is limited. In: Symposium on Applied Perception in Graphics and Visualization, Tübingen, Germany, pp. 41–48 (2007)

Williams, L.E.: Exploring large virtual environments with an hmd on foot when physical space is limited. Ph.D. thesis, Vanderbilt University, Nashville, TN (2007)

Xiao, C., Mou, W., McNamara, T.P.: Use of self-to-object and object-to-object spatial relations in locomotion. J. Exp. Psychol.: Learn. Mem. Cogn. **35**(5), 1137 (2009)

Xie, X., Lin, Q., Wu, H., Narasimham, G., McNamara, T.P., Rieser, J., Bodenheimer, B.: A system for exploring large virtual environments that combines scaled translational gain and interventions. In: Proceedings of the 7th Symposium on Applied Perception in Graphics and Visualization, APGV 2010, pp. 65–72. ACM, New York (2010)

Yamamoto, N., Shelton, A.L.: Path information effects in visual and proprioceptive spatial learning. Acta Psychol. **125**(3), 346–360 (2007)

Young, M.K., Gaylor, G.B., Andrus, S.M., Bodenheimer, B.: A comparison of two cost-differentiated virtual reality systems for perception and action tasks. In: Proceedings of the ACM Symposium on Applied Perception, pp. 83–90. ACM (2014)

Zhang, H., Mou, W., McNamara, T.P., Wang, L.: Connecting spatial memories of two nested spaces. J. Exp. Psychol.: Learn. Mem. Cogn. **40**(1), 191 (2014)

Talking About Space

A Graph Representation for Verbal Indoor Route Descriptions

Stephan Winter[1(✉)], Ehsan Hamzei[1], Nico Van de Weghe[2],
and Kristien Ooms[2]

[1] Department of Infrastructure Engineering,
The University of Melbourne, Parkville, Australia
`winter@unimelb.edu.au`
[2] Department of Geography, Ghent University, Ghent, Belgium

Abstract. Verbal indoor route descriptions contain human spatial knowledge that this paper aims to represent formally for further analysis and question-answering. Available tools – *route graphs* for route descriptions, and *place graphs* for place descriptions – both turn out to fall short on our corpus of verbal indoor route descriptions. Hence, the paper will identify the characteristics of indoor route descriptions, identify strategies for knowledge extraction, and seek a unified graph representation.

1 Introduction

Consider the following indoor *route description*[1] (taken from soleway.ugent.be):

Example 1. *Enter the hallway. Take the elevator or the stairs to the third floor. Take the double grey door between the stairs and the elevator. Turn right. Take the double brown door. My office is at the left side, a bit over halfway the corridor.*

and also this corresponding (made-up) *place description*:

Example 2. *My office is in Building S8, on the third floor, about halfway along a corridor that connects at one end to the central staircase of the building and at the other end to an emergency exit.*

Both kinds of descriptions can be mapped to graphs. Graphs contain the essence of these descriptions in a more abstract and database-accessible form. In current practice, the nodes of these graphs represent the locative noun expressions ("hallway", "double grey door"), and the edges represent the explicit relationships between these ("at the left side", "between"), or the actions to be taken to reach one from the other ("take", "turn", "enter"). Actions can also be considered as implicit relationships of connectedness.

Common language route or place descriptions are provided by people for people with certain questions ("where is", "how do I get to"). Thus, the extraction

---

[1] Terms will be defined in Sect. 3.

© Springer Nature Switzerland AG 2018
S. Creem-Regehr et al. (Eds.): Spatial Cognition 2018, LNAI 11034, pp. 77–91, 2018.
https://doi.org/10.1007/978-3-319-96385-3_6

and formal representation of human environmental knowledge aims at *automated answering* of questions of this kind, in terms close to human language. This kind of knowledge is difficult to extract from geometry-based spatial databases [11,13]. The automatic extraction from language is also challenging but not addressed in this paper (all interpretations in this paper are human-made). This paper focuses on the characteristics of human indoor route descriptions and on the capability of formal graph representations to capture the essence of the encoded human spatial knowledge.[2] It uses for its study a corpus of crowd-sourced indoor route descriptions that is investigated here for the first time.

The formalization of human route and place knowledge in graphs has been done so far for outdoor environments [2,4,36]. Hence, this paper will make the following contributions to knowledge:

1. identify deficiencies of existing route and place graph ontologies to represent spatial knowledge from indoor route descriptions;
2. identify a continuity principle in order to derive implied qualitative spatial relationships between places;
3. show that route and place graph ontologies can be integrated.

The hypothesis of this paper is that the environmental knowledge encapsulated in verbal indoor route descriptions can be extracted and represented in a graph structure for querying.

The paper starts with a review of route ontologies and graph representations for the knowledge in route and place descriptions (Sect. 2). It then explores the route graph of Brosset *et al.* [4] and the place graph of Vasardani *et al.* [36] for their respective capacity to represent indoor route descriptions, which is then also compared with the capacity of the two graphs to represent place descriptions given in route perspective (Sect. 3). From these observations, Sect. 4 seeks to integrate the two graphs. An application of graphs in query-answering is presented in Sect. 5. Conclusions are discussed in Sect. 6.

2   Literature Review

The use of graphs for spatial knowledge representation is not new. For example, all transport networks have a graph structure, but then not much semantics attached since these networks consist of geometric elements of identical semantics, such as the street segments in a road network, or the direct flight connections in an airline network. Closer to the interest of this paper are uses of graphs to represent semantically rich knowledge (of places, routes, or networks), even at the cost of geometry, since natural language descriptions are usually qualitative about places and their relationships.

Pioneering in this direction is the work of Kuipers, who made a case for qualitative spatial reasoning in robot route planning. He uses triplets of

---

[2] This paper cannot address the underlying challenge that language is only a representation of spatial knowledge, a symbolic and non-spatial encoding, while the knowledge may have been generated from perception.

'views' – sensory input that, by equivalence classes, forms a notion of place – and 'actions' – equivalent to the movement verbs in natural language descriptions [22]: (view, action, view). Later he extended this basic graph structure, which he compared with a cognitive map [23], for semantic attributes and a hierarchical structure, in order to cater for applications such as the communication of a robot (vehicle) with its passenger. The ontology developed for this purpose is the *hybrid spatial semantic hierarchy* [1,24]. Similarly, Krieg-Brückner and colleagues [21] first proposed a light-weight ontology of route graphs in an indoor environment, which then can be specialized for different user categories or travel modes, for example for people sitting in an intelligent wheelchair, and communicating with the same. Again, the application in mind is robotic route planning.

Again other route ontologies focus on multi-criteria route planning, for example for personalization purposes, or for adaptation to special circumstances or needs [5,26,29,30]. Here, an ontology-based knowledge modeling can enrich a mobility network with a range of criteria, which are then available for the route planning algorithm. Works like these aim to capture a broad range of semantics of network elements in order to enable flexible choice.

In contrast to graph representations built for route planning, the current paper is concerned with the ontology (i.e., the nature) of a route description itself. The interest of this paper is in representing the spatial knowledge from route descriptions, not the route *choice*. These ontologies are formed from studying text corpora. For [2,4], the corpus was formed of hiking or orienteering route descriptions in natural environments. Their ontology is based essentially on triplets (from location, action, to location), in our indoor context for example (from the hallway, take the elevator, to the third floor). Where the origin (from location) is missing in verbal route descriptions it can be inferred. For example, "enter the hallway" implies an origin ("from where you are", or "from outside of the building") for triplet completion.

In parallel, a similar graph model was developed to represent the knowledge in verbal *place* descriptions [36]. This model is based on triplets (locatum, spatial relation, relatum), such as in (my office, on, third floor). The spatial relation is directed from locatum to relatum. Although the triplet structure looks similar, it is worth mentioning that route descriptions refer to the location and orientation of the moving individual, while place descriptions refer to the location of places relative to each other, in varying perspectives. I.e., their reference systems are different.

A complementary approach takes a spatial knowledge representation and *generates* natural language descriptions of routes. This approach has been an active field of research particular for car navigation and web mapping services. The commercial solutions are still mostly limited to the turn-by-turn paradigm and typically hide the origin, such as "in 300 m turn right", implying a full triplet (from here, turn right, after moving for 300 m). They can afford to be stripped to the essential because they are provided in-situ, and thus do not need to be memorable. Nevertheless there have been calls to include landmarks in these descriptions in order to support people's cognitive processes of matching with the environment [7,10]. To consider landmarks, the original turn-by-turn structure requires modification for the optional inclusion of other elements. The most complete data structure in this regard has been suggested by [14].

Going one step further is generating mixed route descriptions. Provided the driver is familiar with parts of the route, natural language generation of route descriptions can start with a *place description* to identify the anchor point, before continuing with the (sequential) *route description*, such as in "Go to the post office opposite the station [you know the way], then take ..." [31]. Also a mixed form is produced by an approach to *generate* a narrative of the experience of an indoor environment from a digital geometric representation such as a CAD or BIM model [3]. The result is not necessarily a route description, but a mixture of views in the environment (a place description) and movement through the environment (a route description).

Indoor environments have some properties that make them conceptually and perceptually different from outdoor environments [28]. First and foremost, movements in indoor environments happen also across levels, a property explicitly excluded for example by the route ontology of [2,4] but adding substantially to the complexity of human wayfinding [15,16]. Indoor environments are also environments of relative short vistas and small-scale landmarks compared to outdoor environments [37], and for this reason they typically lack global landmarks and absolute spatial reference frames. Their dense structure also calls for simple route directions [34,35], among other reasons because these route directions have to be memorable in order to allow users roaming without being forced to constantly watch a smartphone screen [27]. Not only pragmatic reasons, but also linguistic research supports this aim for short descriptions [8,9]. Finally, indoor (built) environments are typically of high regularity, with narrative strategies adapted.

The current paper will extract environmental knowledge from verbal (human) indoor route descriptions. We will discover that these route descriptions are more often mixed than not, i.e., contain sequential parts (route descriptions) and configurational parts (place descriptions). Hence the paper will explore the use of the verbal route and place description ontologies, and possible combinations.

3   Exploring Graph Models for an Indoor Route Description

The hypothesis – that the environmental knowledge encapsulated in verbal indoor route descriptions can be extracted and represented in a graph structure – requires some definitions, which then can be applied to our data sets.

Definition 1. *A **route description** is a verbal instruction to follow a particular route through an environment.*

A route description answers a *how [to find]* question. The expectation is that a route description has predominantly a sequential structure (as in Example 1), although parts of the sequence can be folded [19]:

Example 3. *Go to Level 3* [you know how to], *then turn right ...*

and non-sequential forms are possible as well, for example hierarchic instructions:

Example 4. *My office? You have to get to the third floor; best to take the elevator. Just turn right behind the entrance to find the elevator.*

Definition 2. *A **place description** is a verbal explanation of a configuration of places.*

A place description answers a *where* question. Place descriptions can have a survey or a route perspective in their narrative strategy [32]. An example for a survey ('birds-eye') perspective is:

Example 5. *My office is on the third floor, in the North Wing of the building.*

An example for the route perspective is:

Example 6. *From the stairs my office is at the left side, halfway the corridor.*

Place descriptions can also have a hierarchical form, zooming in or out, like the one shown in Example 2.

Also, as mentioned before, route and place descriptions can mix, such as in Example 1, where the configurational *"My office is at the left side"*, a place description, sits at the end of a declared route description. This example also illustrates the complexity for automatic interpretation since the configurational part still carries the direction of the route as spatial reference frame for the relative direction relationship. In addition to tracking spatial reference systems, other complexities have already been mentioned above, such as the completion of triplets by inference.

Studying two corpora – one of indoor *route* descriptions[3], and one of mixed indoor-outdoor *place* descriptions of a campus [36], both manually tagged – reveals that both show substantial portions of descriptions that mix narrative structures. Of the in total 1127 indoor route descriptions 823 (73%) contain configurational parts, and of the 42 campus (place) descriptions 27 (64%) contain route perspective parts. These substantial numbers show that neither of the ontologies above will be capable to capture comprehensively the environmental knowledge expressed in verbal indoor route descriptions. In the following, we will illustrate the capacities of route graphs and place graphs, both on a route description and a place description. In addition, the applied natural language interpretation process can be stricter (allowing only for explicit relations) or more flexible (allowing also for implied relations and references across sentences). The observations will lead to a strategy for storing the collected route and place knowledge together, presented in Sect. 4.

---

[3] soleway.ugent.be.

3.1 Brosset's Route Graph Applied to Indoor Route Descriptions

We will first investigate the capability of Brosset and colleagues' route graph [2, 4] to represent the environmental knowledge in the 1127 indoor route descriptions of Soleway. The structure of this route graph is based on triplets of two places (nodes) and the action between these places (edges). The edges can have a further attribute, a qualitative spatial relation, as in "turn right", an action-relation pair. The triplets extracted from one description can be concatenated, and these *route graphs* can be further merged to *semantic networks* if different route descriptions show sufficient evidence for common places.

While there is no ontological difference between environmental knowledge extracted from outdoor descriptions (the subject of study by Brosset and colleagues) and indoor descriptions (our interest), the Soleway dataset has revealed other issues, such as:

- Indoor descriptions seem to have significantly more places characterized by their types and properties rather than by name, increasing the chance of ambiguity. Also, indoor descriptions can draw from only a small set of types due to repetitive design [18]. With higher ambiguity, indoor descriptions provide a significantly higher challenge for merging.
- Indoor descriptions seem to rely on only two types of actions (Table 1): locomotion (expressed by verbs such as *go* or *walk*) and choice (expressed by verbs such as *take* or *find*). A third group of verbs are static, relating to configurational parts.

Table 1. The frequent verbs in the soleway corpus, based on the stanford NLP toolkit.

Locomotion	*enter* (1079), *go* (953), *walk* (144), *follow* (131), *pass* (124), *reach* (65), *leave* (44), *arrive* (44), *cross* (27), *continue* (23), *climb* (19)
Choice	*take* (2657), *turn* (840), *find* (160), *use* (49), *open* (30); sometimes supported by *need* (15)
Configurational	*be* (610), *see* (105), *have* (48), *face* (11)

Choice implies a motion in order to realize the choice, hence, choice actions require a more detailed ontological commitment. A choice of a place such as "take the elevator" implies a travel on the elevator (in Example 1 from ground floor to third floor). And thus, the elevator is in this context a vehicle for motion between the two places (`elevator@GF` and `elevator@3F`), such that these triplets can be formed: (`hallway, walk, elevator@GF`), and (`elevator@GF, take_elevator, elevator@3F`). The same is true for doors: "Take the door" makes the door a passage from one space to another space. This postulate relies on an assumption of a continuous movement, independent from the actual narrative form. We call this assumption the *continuity principle*.

Figure 1 shows Example 1 in this route graph model. Nodes are the places named in the description, with those place names linked to choice actions expanded to start and end of the corresponding motion. The edges represent the actions found in the description.

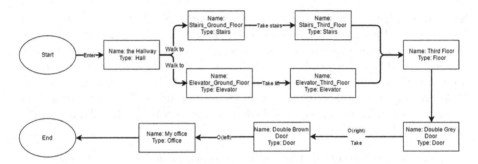

Fig. 1. Applying the route model of Brosset *et al.* to Example 1.

3.2 Vasardani's Place Graph Applied to Indoor Route Descriptions

Vasardani's place graph was formed on observations in a corpus of campus descriptions. The campus descriptions cover already indoor elements, and thus, we expected less challenges from a scale perspective, but rather from the fact that Soleway descriptions are route descriptions, not place descriptions.

Here, a now purely spatial continuity principle suggests to infer some relationships that are not explicit, forming for example triplets (elevator, in[4], hallway) and (elevator, in, third_floor). These inferred edges are included in Fig. 2.

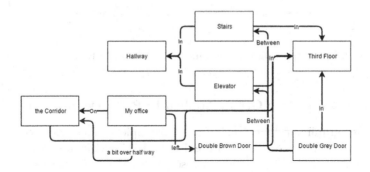

Fig. 2. Applying the place model of Vasardani *et al.* to Example 1, with inferred edges.

3.3 Brosset's Route Graph Applied to Place Descriptions

Since also verbal place descriptions can take a route perspective as narrative strategy, i.e., can contain parts that may be recognized as route descriptions, we also apply Brosset's route graph to place descriptions, for later comparison with Sect. 3.4. The common example shall be a description from the corpus of campus descriptions [36]:

---

[4] The inferred relationship is flexible; while here containment is used it could also be a topological connectedness.

Example 7. *Entering the campus from the main entrance on Grattan Street the visitor first needs to climb stairs to get onto South Lawn and on top of the carpark. Now walking towards Old Arts, the Medical School and Baillieu Library are on the left, the Geography and Architecture buildings on the right. Reaching the Old Quad, you enter the most beautiful and oldest part of the campus. Unfortunately it is not very big and soon the visitor passes University House and is again surrounded by yellow brick buildings from the 70ies. Ahead now are the sports facilities of the university.*

The place description contains references to 16 places, including "the most beautiful ... part of the campus" and "[above] the carpark", and "[a group of] yellow brick buildings". Since the graph is formed from triplets only, Fig. 3 shows in particular that only a subset of these places (11) are connected by an action.

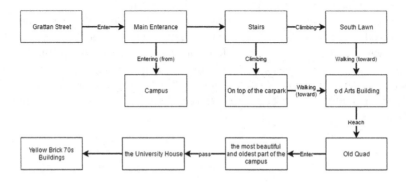

Fig. 3. Applying the route model of Brosset to Example 7.

3.4   Vasardani's Place Graph Applied to Place Description

Also a place graph can be extracted from Example 7. This graph contains all named places that are connected in the description by a qualitative spatial relationship (Fig. 4), which is a different subset than before, of 7 places.

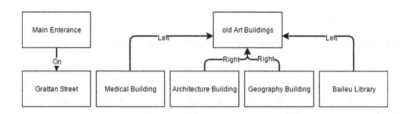

Fig. 4. Applying the place model of Vasardani to Example 7.

3.5   Observations on Environmental Knowledge Capture

Based on the experiments above, place and route information coexist in both place and route descriptions, and can be disambiguated by the verbs (Table 1). Their coexistence could have multiple reasons, beyond individual preference for a particular narrative strategy. In particular, configurational elements may occur in route descriptions for the conversational context (e.g., assumed familiarity of the recipient with the environment) or for environmental context (e.g., a need for disambiguation) [12]. The speaker of Example 1 sees a need to disambiguate "the door between stair and elevator" from other doors, and is using relations instead of actions. In addition, observations show a strategic use of switching between route and place elements to provide a spatial reference frame – the heading of the route – for relative directions in the configurational part of the description. For example, in "Take the double brown door. My office is at the left" (Example 1) the *left* in the configurational part refers to the walking direction.

The coexistence of place and route information in route as well as place descriptions [33] is a compelling motivation for reconciling the current graph representation models for places and routes, despite their ontological differences in nodes, edges, and reference frames. Relying on one model only, even if it is the one that fits best in a current situation, will lose some of the environmental knowledge encapsulated in the verbal description. This reconciliation will be investigated in the next section.

4   Integrating the Graphs

Here, a strategy is proposed for storing extracted place and route knowledge in an integrated graph representation.

4.1   Reconciling the Edges

An integrated graph has to address the different semantics of edges in route and place graphs. While in route graphs the edges are representing actions, possibly enriched by (mostly) directions, in place graphs the edges represent qualitative spatial relationships (often topological ones) without a link to an action.

The way to integrate edges of different types in an ontology is by abstraction. The integrated edge represents (just) a *relation* between two places, which can be further established by attributes:

(1) `relation:: {action, qsrelation}`
`    action :: Walk | Take | NoAction`
`    qsrelation :: Near | Left | Right | In | ...| NoQSRelation`

For example, `relation = {Walk, NoQSRelation}` reverts to a route graph edge, and `relation = {NoAction, Near}` reverts to a place graph edge. Since all considered graphs are multi-graphs, both edges can co-exist between two nodes. Thus, this abstraction allows to merge the basic route and place graphs into one graph.

4.2   Inferences

The unified graph representation can be enriched by inferred relationships.

Locomotion verbs can induce a topological relationship of *path-connectedness*.

(2) (action = Walk) → (qsrelation = path-connected)

This inference can either be made explicit as a relation, or set up as a database constraint. Qualitative reasoning on this relationship is possible: If A is path-connected with B, and B with C, then it is possible to reach C from A.

Choice verbs led previously to a split of nodes in the route graph, while the nodes were preserved in place graphs. The two different needs can be reconciled by maintaining the semantics and granularity of place graphs – describing the locations of places in relation to each other – and adding a new element to the integrated graph: A loop. A loop is an edge that connects a node to itself, and thus a loop can describe a movement with a place ("take the elevator"), on a place ("take the stairs"), or through a place ("take the door"). The loop has two attributes: A from and a to, where the places are inferred from path continuity. The action of a loop is by default Take, and the spatial relationship is by default NoQSRelation.

(3) looprelation :: {from, to}
      from :: place
      to :: place

For example, "take the elevator to the third floor" would be represented by a loop:
      l1 = elevator, (from: hallway, to: third floor), elevator
And the "take the [double grey] door" would be represented by a loop:
      l2 = door, (from: elevator, to: corridor), door

Qualitative spatial relations and static verbs allow a default assumption of path-connectedness, and thus reachability, in another inferred edge. In some sense this inference is the inverse to Specification (2):

(4) (qsrelation = In ∨ Next ∨ Near) → (action = Walk)

Similarly, the static verb *see* suggests to add a relation viewrelation :: InView | NotInView to Specification (1). A viewrelation is neither about reachability, nor is it a canonized qualitative spatial relation [6,25] since any reasoning with it requires geometry. However, it can be derived directly ("from … you see …") or implied by common sense for many expressed actions (for example, "take the elevator" implies that I perceive the elevator by some environmental cues when I consume this instruction) and spatial relationships (for example, "the door between elevator and stairs" implies that I see all three places). Such common sense (default) reasoning is part of the strategy of a recipient of such descriptions [20]. Even if this relationship is not about reachability *per se*, in indoor space it often (and thus by default assumption) is the case, as another facet of the spatial continuity assumption.

Such inferences from default reasoning allow a natural language parser to translate some configurational statements into actionable statements. For example, if "the door between elevator and stairs" in Example 1 implies that I see all three places when I consume this description (and that is when I have reached Level 3 either by elevator or stairs), then the following triplets can be added:

```
t1 = (elevator at Level 3, walk, door)
t2 = (landing at Level 3, walk, door)
```

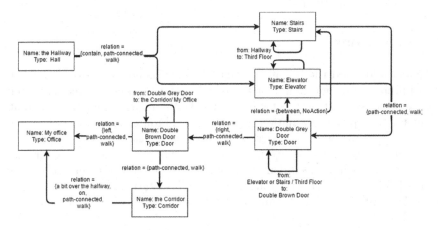

Fig. 5. Integrating place and route graph by abstracting edges in Example 1.

5   Application

If integrated route graphs contain the knowledge of human route descriptions, then it should be possible to generate route descriptions from the graphs again. This is a relevant thought, enabling to use a few collected route descriptions to prepare many more route descriptions by recombination. In this regard, the merging of graphs from different route descriptions is a process functionally equivalent to the cognitive process of integrating route knowledge into survey knowledge, which also enables the recombination of segments to routes from anywhere to anywhere [32].

Querying the integrated indoor route graph for paths relies on the connectedness (reachability) provided by action terms. Route planning can happen on any edge with a positive action attribute (i.e., not `NoAction`). Then, natural language generation can apply the well-known paradigm of (`from loc`, `action`, `to loc`). The example below guides from the elevator at Level 3 to "my office", using the knowledge of the integrated graph in Fig. 5.

From elevator (walk to/take) double grey door;
from grey double door (walk to/take) brown double door;
from brown double door (walk to/take) corridor;
from corridor (walk to/take) my office.

or simply, with implied origins:

(walk to/take) grey double door;
(walk to/take) brown double door;
(walk to/take) corridor;
(walk to/take) my office.

Configurational edges (`qsrelation`) are not yet included. They may be used to add landmarks along the route.

6   Conclusions

The paper addressed the hypothesis that the environmental knowledge encapsulated in natural language indoor route descriptions can be extracted and represented in a graph structure for querying. As the experiments showed, route information and place information coexist in verbal route descriptions. The complementary role of route and place information were discussed using examples.

Existing route and place graph ontologies were compared, and their individual limitations have been demonstrated. The observations helped to identify four mechanisms to develop a stronger graph representation of the environmental knowledge contained in verbal indoor descriptions, based on the verb classification of Table 1:

1. Locomotion verbs can induce an edge for *connectedness*.
2. Choice verbs can induce a loop in the graph representing a movement (change of location) while being in, on, or at a place.
3. Static, configurational verbs in conjunction with spatial prepositions (characterizing qualitative spatial relationships between places) are only one kind of relation – the integrated graph uses a generalized concept of *relation*.
4. Applying a continuity principle (in space and time), first, missing origins of movements can be inferred, and secondly, some configurational descriptions can be converted into locomotion actions.

The integrated graph demonstrably contains more of the environmental knowledge: While Fig. 1 has 9 places (but two duplicated by splitting) and 7 labelled relations, and Fig. 2 has 8 places and 10 labelled relations, the integrated graph in Fig. 5 has 8 places and 24 labelled relations. Thus, there is strong evidence supporting the hypothesis: that the environmental knowledge can be represented in one integrated graph, and with more detail than either in the route or place graph, by mechanisms of inference. Also, the same inferences made to add to the integrated graph can be used to answer questions. Thus, the paper also demonstrated ways of using the integrated route graph ontology for query-answering.

The principles identified leave a number of questions for future work. First, the specifications are conceptual so far, and neither implemented nor comprehensive. For example, other modes of mobility in indoor environments than walking (wheelchair), or walking with certain constraints, are not yet considered. Secondly, the specifications have to be implemented in natural language parsers in order to extract not only explicit triplets [17], but also those that can be inferred from the verbs. And thirdly, the integration of graphs from multiple verbal indoor route descriptions (of the same building) requires new attention, since the intersecting elements are not always explicit [2].

Acknowledgements. This work has been supported by the European Commission's ERASMUS + program and by the Australian Research Council, DP170100109. Anonymous reviewers gave feedback pointing far beyond this page-limited paper.

References

1. Beeson, P., MacMahon, M., Modayil, J., Murarka, A., Kuipers, B.J., Stankiewicz, B.J.: Integrating multiple representations of spatial knowledge for mapping, navigation, and communication. In: AAAI Spring Symposium on Interaction Challenges for Intelligent Assistants, vol. SS-07-04. AAAI Technical Report (2007)
2. Belouaer, L., Brosset, D., Claramunt, C.: Modeling spatial knowledge from verbal descriptions. In: Tenbrink, T., Stell, J., Galton, A., Wood, Z. (eds.) COSIT 2013. LNCS, vol. 8116, pp. 338–357. Springer, Cham (2013). https://doi.org/10.1007/978-3-319-01790-7_19
3. Bhatt, M., Schultz, C., Thosar, M.: Computing narratives of cognitive user experience for building design analysis: KR for industry scale computer-aided architecture design. In: 14th International Conference on Principles of Knowledge Representation and Reasoning. AAAI (2014). https://www.aaai.org/ocs/index.php/KR/KR14/paper/view/7978/7964
4. Brosset, D., Claramunt, C., Saux, E.: A location and action-based model for route descriptions. In: Fonseca, F., Rodríguez, M.A., Levashkin, S. (eds.) GeoS 2007. LNCS, vol. 4853, pp. 146–159. Springer, Heidelberg (2007). https://doi.org/10.1007/978-3-540-76876-0_10
5. Codescu, M., Vale, D.C., Kutz, O., Mossakowski, T.: Ontology-based route planning for OpenStreetMap. In: Kolas, D., Perry, M., Grütter, R., Koubarakis, M. (eds.) Terra Cognita Workshop on Foundations, Technologies and Applications of the Geospatial Web, vol. 901, Paper 6. CEUR-WS (2012)
6. Cohn, A.G., Renz, J.: Qualitative spatial representation and reasoning. In: van Harmelen, F., Lifschitz, V., Porter, B. (eds.) Handbook of Knowledge Representation, pp. 551–596. Elsevier, Amsterdam (2008)
7. Dale, R., Geldof, S., Prost, J.P.: Using natural language generation in automatic route description. J. Res. Pract. Inf. Technol. **37**(1), 89–105 (2005)
8. Denis, M.: The description of routes: a cognitive approach to the production of spatial discourse. Curr. Psychol. Cogn. **16**(4), 409–458 (1997)
9. Denis, M., Pazzaglia, F., Cornoldi, C., Bertolo, L.: Spatial discourse and navigation: an analysis of route directions in the city of venice. Appl. Cogn. Psychol. **13**(2), 145–174 (1999)
10. Duckham, M., Winter, S., Robinson, M.: Including landmarks in routing instructions. J. Locat.-Based Serv. **4**(1), 28–52 (2010)

11. Goodchild, M.F.: Formalizing place in geographical information systems. In: Burton, L.M., Kemp, S.P., Leung, M.C., Matthews, S.A., Takeuchi, D.T. (eds.) Communities, Neighborhoods, and Health: Expanding the Boundaries of Place. SDHHC, vol. 1, pp. 21–35. Springer, New York (2011). https://doi.org/10.1007/978-1-4419-7482-2_2

12. Grice, P.: Logic and conversation. In: Syntax and Semantics, vol. 3, 41–58 (1975)

13. Hamzei, E., Chen, H., Hua, H., Tomko, M., Vasardani, M., Winter, S.: Deriving place graphs from spatial databases. In: Peters, S., Khoshelham, K. (eds.) Research at Locate. CEUR (2018)

14. Hansen, S., Richter, K.F., Klippel, A.: Landmarks in OpenLS: a data structure for cognitive ergonomic route directions. In: Raubal, M., Miller, H.J., Frank, A.U., Goodchild, M.F. (eds.) Geographic Information Science. LNCS, vol. 4197, pp. 128–144. Springer, Heidelberg (2006). https://doi.org/10.1007/11863939_9

15. Hölscher, C., Brösamle, M., Vrachliotis, G.: Challenges in multi-level wayfinding: a case-study with space syntax technique. Environ. Plann. B **39**(1), 63–82 (2012)

16. Hölscher, C., Meilinger, T., Vrachliotis, G., Brösamle, M., Knauff, M.: Up the down staircase: wayfinding strategies in multi-level buildings. J. Environ. Psychol. **26**(4), 284–299 (2006)

17. Khan, A., Vasardani, M., Winter, S.: Extracting spatial information from place descriptions. In: Scheider, S., Adams, B., Janowicz, K., Vasardani, M., Winter, S. (eds.) ACM SIGSPATIAL Workshop on Computational Models of Place, pp. 62–69. ACM Press (2013)

18. Khoshelham, K., Diaz-Vilarino, L.: 3D modelling of interior spaces: Learning the language of indoor architecture. In: The International Archives of the Photogrammetry, Remote Sensing and Spatial Information Sciences, vol. XL-5, pp. 321–326 (2014)

19. Klippel, A., Tappe, H., Habel, C.: Pictorial representations of routes: chunking route segments during comprehension. In: Freksa, C., Brauer, W., Habel, C., Wender, K.F. (eds.) Spatial Cognition 2002. LNCS, vol. 2685, pp. 11–33. Springer, Heidelberg (2003). https://doi.org/10.1007/3-540-45004-1_2

20. Knauff, M.: Space to Reason: A Spatial Theory of Human Thought. MIT Press, Cambridge (2013)

21. Krieg-Brückner, B., Frese, U., Lüttich, K., Mandel, C., Mossakowski, T., Ross, R.J.: Specification of an ontology for route graphs. In: Freksa, C., Knauff, M., Krieg-Brückner, B., Nebel, B., Barkowsky, T. (eds.) Spatial Cognition 2004. LNCS (LNAI), vol. 3343, pp. 390–412. Springer, Heidelberg (2005). https://doi.org/10.1007/978-3-540-32255-9_22

22. Kuipers, B.J.: The 'map in the head' metaphor. Environ. Behav. **14**(2), 202–220 (1982)

23. Kuipers, B.J.: The cognitive map: could it have been any other way? In: Pick, H., Acredolo, L. (eds.) Spatial Orientation: Theory, Research, and Application, pp. 345–359. Plenum Press, New York (1983)

24. Kuipers, B.J., Levitt, T.S.: Navigation and mapping in large-scale space. AI Magazine **9**(2), 25–43 (1988)

25. Ligozat, G.: Qualitative Spatial and Temporal Reasoning. Wiley, Hoboken (2013)

26. Malizia, A., Onorati, T., Diaz, P., Aedo, I., Astorga-Paliza, F.: SEMA4A: an ontology for emergency notification systems accessibility. Expert Syst. Appl. **37**(4), 3380–3391 (2010)

27. Miller, G.A.: The magical number seven, plus or minus two: some limits on our capacity for processing information. Psychol. Rev. **63**, 81–97 (1956)

28. Montello, D.R.: Scale and multiple psychologies of space. In: Frank, A.U., Campari, I. (eds.) COSIT 1993. LNCS, vol. 716, pp. 312–321. Springer, Heidelberg (1993). https://doi.org/10.1007/3-540-57207-4_21
29. Niaraki, A.S., Kim, K.: Ontology based personalized route planning system using a multi-criteria decision making approach. Expert Syst. Appl. **36**(2), 2250–2259 (2009)
30. Onorati, T., Malizia, A., Diaz, P., Aedo, I.: Modeling an ontology on accessible evacuation routes for emergencies. Expert Syst. Appl. **41**(16), 7124–7134 (2014)
31. Richter, K.F., Tomko, M., Winter, S.: A dialog-driven process of generating route directions. Comput. Environ. Urban Syst. **32**(3), 233–245 (2008). https://doi.org/10.1016/j.compenvurbsys.2008.02.002
32. Siegel, A.W., White, S.H.: The development of spatial representations of large-scale environments. In: Reese, H.W. (ed.) Advances in Child Development and Behavior, vol. 10, pp. 9–55. Academic Press, New York (1975)
33. Tversky, B., Lee, P., Mainwaring, S.: Why do speakers mix perspectives? Spat. Cogn. Comput. **1**(4), 399–412 (1999). https://doi.org/10.1023/A:1010091730257
34. Vanclooster, A., Ooms, K., Viaene, P., Fack, V., Van de Weghe, N., De Maeyer, P.: Evaluating suitability of the least risk path algorithm to support cognitive wayfinding in indoor spaces: an empirical study. Appl. Geogr. **53**, 128–140 (2014). http://www.sciencedirect.com/science/article/pii/S0143622814001258
35. Vanclooster, A., Van de Weghe, N., Fack, V., De Maeyer, P.: Comparing indoor and outdoor network models for automatically calculating turns. J. Locat. Based Serv. **8**(3), 148–165 (2014). https://doi.org/10.1080/17489725.2014.975289
36. Vasardani, M., Timpf, S., Winter, S., Tomko, M.: From descriptions to depictions: a conceptual framework. In: Tenbrink, T., Stell, J., Galton, A., Wood, Z. (eds.) COSIT 2013. LNCS, vol. 8116, pp. 299–319. Springer, Cham (2013). https://doi.org/10.1007/978-3-319-01790-7_17
37. Viaene, P., Vanclooster, A., Ooms, K., De Maeyer, P.: Thinking aloud in search of landmark characteristics in an indoor environment. In: Ubiquitous Positioning Indoor Navigation and Location Based Service (UPINLBS), pp. 103–110. IEEE (2014)

Object Orientation in Dialogue: A Case Study of Spatial Inference Processes

Gesa Schole[1], Thora Tenbrink[2(✉)], Elena Andonova[3], and Kenny Coventry[4]

[1] University of Tuebingen, GRK 1808 Ambiguity, Tuebingen, Germany
`gesa.schole@uni-tuebingen.de`
[2] Bangor University, Bangor, Wales, UK
`t.tenbrink@bangor.ac.uk`
[3] New Bulgarian University, Sofia, Bulgaria
`eandonova@nbu.bg`
[4] University of East Anglia, Norwich, UK
`K.Coventry@uea.ac.uk`

Abstract. Most research on spatial communication focuses either on route instructions or on object reference, detailing how places and objects are referred to and where they are located. In this paper, we address object *orientation* in a spatial dialogue situation involving the placement of dollhouse furniture, and explore the role of canonical orientation for the amount of details provided and success of communication. Our results show that speakers are extremely creative when referring to and inferring object orientation information. They achieve communicative success in spite of leaving decisive aspects implicit, drawing on common sense. Where objects are oriented in a non-canonical way, references become more explicit, allowing for a similar level of success.

1 Introduction

Imagine you are moving house, and a friend is helping you place furniture into the various rooms. Because you can't be everywhere at once, you describe to her how chairs and tables should be placed. You might say things like *This one goes into the living room, on the wall to your left as you walk in* or *Put the chairs around the dining room table.* But would you also explain how the furniture items should be oriented? Would you add *All chairs must face the table*? Most likely, you would take this aspect of the object placement for granted - you have good reason to assume that your friend knows very well how chairs are normally oriented, relative to a table. Perhaps you would mention it if the chairs should be oriented in a *different,* unexpected way. Or if you didn't, the result might not be as desired.

In this paper, we address this kind of scenario by drawing on a dialogue corpus collected to explore spatial object reference in a referential communication task, where a *Director* explains to a *Matcher* how objects should be placed in order to match a given dollhouse configuration. We investigate the role of canonical orientation in such a situation. If objects are not oriented in the way they

© Springer Nature Switzerland AG 2018
S. Creem-Regehr et al. (Eds.): Spatial Cognition 2018, LNAI 11034, pp. 92–106, 2018.
https://doi.org/10.1007/978-3-319-96385-3_7

functionally relate to each other, will Directors become more explicit in their instructions, so as to compensate where common sense fails - or will communicative success be hampered?

For illustration, consider the following examples (adapted from our data, described below). Example 1 contains no orientation information, whereas the Director in Example 2 makes several attempts to clarify how the object's back side relates to the addressee's current position. Both objects were oriented correctly by the addressee, using common sense along with explicit information.

1. Put the couch at some distance to the longer side of the table, namely to the left.
2. In the front, there is a double armchair. Put it with its backside towards you so to speak with its back to you. So that the backside points to you.

To see more generally how dialogue partners manage to understand each other in the face of incomplete information (as in Example 1), we first take a look at communicative principles and then turn to spatial descriptions in particular.

2   Communicative Principles

One main goal underlying all conversation is to establish and expand common ground [4]. This is defined as the knowledge, beliefs, and suppositions that dialogue partners believe to be shared between them. Within a given dialogue, further common ground is accumulated based on the verbal exchange as well as contextual and non-verbal information (e.g. gestures and facial expressions).

Whenever dialogue partners do not share some information, the speaker expects the addressee to point this out [5], or to draw inferences from common ground. Conversational success, therefore, depends on the coordinated actions between the speaker and the addressee [6]. According to the *principle of least collaborative effort* [7], both dialogue partners try to minimize the conversational effort both for themselves and for their partner. While this can involve the risk of miscommunication [2], repairing failures typically involves less effort than anticipating information needs by the addressee, or spelling everything out in meticulous detail. In effect, this means that a larger portion of everyday discourse relies on inferences. In our initial example, your friend will probably assume that all chairs should be facing the table even if you don't tell her so. Neither of you may be aware of the fact that the given information is incomplete – that alternatives are possible. Since chairs in our everyday experience normally face tables, the inference is natural that they should do so in this case also.

Levinson [16] distinguishes between three types of heuristics or implicatures that license inferences. The Q-heuristic 'What isn't said, isn't' [16, p. 31] relates to the *Maxim of Quantity* according to Grice [11], which states that speakers normally aim to be as informative as required in the dialogue context. As a result, whatever information a speaker does not express is not evoked by the discourse. Using an example by Levinson [16], if the speaker refers to a *pyramid*, he or she is not talking about a *cone* although the forms are similar.

The M-heuristic 'What's said in an abnormal way, isn't normal; or Marked message indicates marked situation' [16, p. 33] relates to Grice's *Maxim of Manner* [11], which state that speakers normally aim to represent situations in a clear and orderly way. The M-heuristic takes this idea further by stating that abnormal situations are typically represented in language in some way. Thus, when referring to an object as a *cuboid block*, the addressee may infer that the object is not a stereotypical *cube* but similar to one [16].

The I-heuristic 'What is simply described is stereotypically exemplified' [16, p. 32] draws on a different aspect of Grice's *Maxim of Quantity* [11]. It states that a contribution is normally not more informative than is required in a context, because minimal descriptions may already evoke fairly rich interpretations of the situation, based on everyday knowledge. The I-heuristic therefore allows for very efficient communication. If the speaker refers to a pyramid simply as a *pyramid*, the addressee may draw the conclusion that it is a stereotypical one.

Although dialogue partners aim to achieve maximal understanding using principles such as these, they will never reach identical mental states [10]. Mostly this is unproblematic; speakers will be happy with a mutual belief that they have understood each other 'well enough for current purposes' [4, p. 221]. A dialogue involving specific goals, such as a referential communication task, allows for assessing if this belief is correct. If a Director believes to have understood the Matcher's instructions, they will act accordingly, and the result can be evaluated for accuracy. Spatial reference is a particularly well suited domain in this respect, since communicative success can be derived from clearly specifiable aspects. We will now briefly summarize some main findings in this domain.

3   Reference to Objects in Space

Placing objects in a referential communication task involves three main aspects [22]: the identification, the localization, and the orientation of the object in question. Each of these aspects makes different features of the spatial scene relevant. While identifying an object can be achieved either by reference to the object's features as such or by contrasting it with other candidate objects, location and orientation information always involve some kind of reference to spatial entities in the context. In the following we use the terms *locatum* and *relatum* to refer to two entities that are relevant for descriptions of spatial relations.

Locatum: The locatum is the object in question, which is to be located or oriented.[1]

Relatum: The relatum is an entity that serves to specify the locatum's position or orientation.[2] The relatum may remain linguistically implicit even if conceptually present [24].

While the identification and localization of objects in space have been extensively debated in the relevant literature, the orientation of objects in space has

---

[1] Talmy [20] refers to this entity as *Figure*, and Langacker [14] as *trajector*.

[2] Synonyms for relatum are *reference object*, *Ground* [20], and *landmark* [14].

been mostly taken for granted (again indicating the intuitive nature of everyday inferences when placing objects). It is therefore one of the goals of this paper to specify in more detail what it means to verbalize object orientation in an unambiguous way. This will involve a clear distinction of explicit information (given by a speaker) as opposed to inferences made on the basis of common ground or world knowledge. To establish a firm basis for this specification, we will now take a closer look at the two better explored aspects - object identification and object localization.

3.1   Object Identification

The identification of a particular object to be placed, the locatum, may be as simple as calling it by its conventional name, e.g. *the vase*. However, if there is more than one object available that looks like a vase, further information is necessary. Speakers then either refer to salient object features such as size, colour, shape etc., or to their spatial location (if available). Recognizing suitable discriminating features and using them to identify objects is not hard; speakers do it all the time, and they adapt flexibly to changes in the situation that require them to switch to a different reference strategy [12]. References to the locatum are often over-specified, i.e. they involve more features of the locatum than necessary for identification [9]. This redundancy facilitates ruling out competing objects quickly. In contrast, *underspecification* occurs mainly when the object has already been identified in the current context and is still accessible in the dialogue partners' common ground [18].

3.2   Object Localization

Reference to the location of an object involves a spatial term that describes the relationship of the locatum to a *relatum*. Depending on the type of spatial term, the location description may be based on an underlying *perspective*.

Relatum Choice. Relata are often larger and more stationary compared to locata [20]. Normally, the sentence *The vase is on the table* would therefore be preferred to its converse *The table is under the vase* [19]. If the table's location is to be described, speakers would choose another similar-sized object as relatum, or a room area as in *The table is in the middle of the room*. Furthermore, according to the *Spatial Term First Hypothesis* [3], speakers prefer relata with a simple spatial relation to the locatum. If the spatial scene does not offer simple relations between the locatum and other entities in the surrounding, speakers might have a weak preference to choose relata due to their salient features. Here are some examples of frequent choices of relata in an object placement task [24].

3. The table is at the back wall. (environment)
4. The chair is behind the table. (object)
5. The table is in front of me. (observer)
6. The couch is to the left. (implicit)

Environmental relata as in Example 3 are very common [3]. References to the speaker's position as in Example 5 are similar to references to the addressee's position (*in front of you*) (hence *observer*). Speakers may also describe objects relative to more than one relatum, or they leave the relatum implicit as in Example 6, where the relatum is available conceptually (e.g. to *my* left) but not expressed in language [24]. In extended descriptions of spatial arrays, it is common to describe sequences of objects in an orderly manner [1,25].

Spatial Terms. Coventry and Garrod [8] distinguish between locative and directional prepositions, where directional prepositions are related to movement (*across, through, along*, etc.), whereas locative prepositions are static. Static prepositions include projective terms (*to the left/right of, in front of, behind, above, below*, etc.) and topological terms (*in, on, at*, etc., involving coincidence, contact, containment, contiguity, or proximity [17]), plus a few others such as *between* and *opposite* that express further types of spatial relationships [21]. Topological terms in particular are known to be sensitive to functional object relationships: for instance, a flower is *in the vase* not because it's geometrically enclosed but because the vase exerts location control [8]. Related effects can also be found for other kinds of spatial prepositions used to describe spatial location.

Projective terms depend on an underlying perspective, based on an *origin* that may be made explicit or remain implicit in the context. The terms *above* and *below* are usually implicitly interpreted relative to the earth's gravity [15], whereas terms such as *left, right, front, behind* normally relate to people or objects in the context: e.g., *my* left or *your* left, using either the speaker's or the addressee's perspective if nothing else is clear from the context.

Based on cross-cultural studies, Levinson [17] found that languages mainly use three types of spatial reference frames. *Absolute* reference frames use environmental information such as cardinal directions (*north, west, south, east* etc.). With an *intrinsic* frame, the relatum must have some kind of asymmetry so that its intrinsic sides can serve as origin (e.g., *to your left* or *in front of the car*). *Relative* frames, in contrast, require another entity that provides a perspective on the scene (e.g., *to the left of the chair from my/your/her point of view*).

3.3   Reference to Object Orientation

According to the Oxford English dictionary, to *orient* an object means specifying it relative to cardinal directions or other positions identified in the context. Consider Examples 7 to 10, where various kinds of directional information specify how the chair's back is oriented.

7. The chair's back points north.
8. The chair's back points to the right.
9. The chair's back is along the left wall.
10. The chair's back is towards the table.

The examples highlight some observations concerning orientation descriptions. Example 7 suggests that the notion of an absolute reference frame is readily applicable to orientation descriptions, with the compass providing an available system for directionality. Example 8 illustrates the use of projective terms for orientation descriptions. In contrast to location descriptions, an intrinsic reference frame does not seem to be available, and a relatum is not required. All that is needed to make sense of the description in Example 8 is a perspective, based on an *origin*, for instance the speaker looking at the scene. In contrast, Examples 9 and 10 demonstrate that some directions encoded by spatial terms (such as *along* and *towards*) do require a relatum (*left wall* and *table*, respectively). Finally, to align the locatum with a particular direction, it is necessary to specify at least one of its axes (such as the chair's *back*). We will now take a closer look at some of these issues.

Features of the Locatum. An object's orientation is based on its geometric properties like axes or parts. Landau and Jackendoff [13] distinguish between three different axes and two forms, based on the human body. The principal axis is the vertical one that due to the earth's gravity is usually considered a directed axis (i.e. top-bottom). The secondary axes are orthogonal to the principal axis, and may either be directed (e.g. differentiating between *front* and *back*), or regarded as symmetric (e.g., not differentiating in a directional sense between *left* and *right*). Whether an object has directed or symmetric axes depends on its features and the way humans use it. For instance, speakers may project the differentiation of *left* and *right* onto objects like chairs and wardrobes, whereas other objects have no directed axis at all (e.g., dinner tables).

Direction via Spatial Term and Relatum. In contrast to the common sequential order of object location descriptions where previously located objects serve as relata for the following ones, *orientation* descriptions do not seem to follow this principle [24]. Instead, speakers seem to prefer relata depending on where the locatum *points towards*, among the available objects and entities. Paralleling the Spatial Term First Hypothesis for object location described above [3], a potential relatum for object orientation might, therefore, be chosen for its simple relation to one of the locatum's axes - disregarding any other factors that have been found to influence the choice of relatum in *location* descriptions, such as size, movability, sequential order, and so on.

Parameters for Object Orientation. Following the observations so far, we can conclude that being explicit about object orientation differs from object location in some respects. Locating an object requires the parameters of *locatum, relatum, spatial term*, and (with projective terms) a *reference frame* based on an *origin*. Orienting an object by an explicit spatial description requires specifying the *locatum* and its *axis* (which can be *directed* or not), and a *direction parameter* that encodes how this axis is oriented. The direction parameter may be filled by a *directional term* (e.g., *to, towards, along*) together with a *relatum*, or via an *absolute frame of reference* (e.g., compass direction terms like *north, south*). Alternatively, the direction may be expressed by a projective term (*left, right*), whose directionality is determined by an available perspective (based on an *origin*). Spatial terms differ with respect to whether they presuppose a directed axis or not. While the common expression *points to* presupposes a directed axis, a directional term like *along* does not.

In [23], we observed that functional object relationships affected whether speakers provided orientation information, but the relationship to task success remained inconclusive. Here we take this line of research further by examining the extent to which parameters are specified for object orientation, whether further strategies for orienting objects can be identified, and under what circumstances addressees may fail to interpret orientation descriptions correctly.

4   Empirical Study

Our study uses data from a dialogue corpus previously published in [23], in which participants negotiated spatial configurations in a dollhouse.

29 pieces of dollhouse furniture were placed in one of two identical dollhouses (two-storied, measuring $71 \times 38 \times 53$ cm, and comprising four same-sized rooms). One participant (henceforth called *Director*) was placed in front of it, and was asked to describe for a dialogue partner (henceforth called *Matcher*) how to furnish their version of the dollhouse, which was empty, with an identical set of 29 furniture items placed aside. No further information was provided (e.g., as to how precisely the objects should be placed). A screen separated the participants, so that they could not see each other nor the interior of their partner's dollhouse.

There were two within-participants conditions, designed to explore the effects of everyday knowledge on spatial dialogue. In the *functional* condition (henceforth abbreviated as F), the furniture items were arranged conventionally so that the rooms could be identified as kitchen, living-room, bedroom, and bathroom. In the *non-functional* condition (henceforth abbreviated as NF), the furniture arrangement did not correspond to any specific room functions (see Fig. 1). All participants did both conditions, in balanced order and with switched *Director* and *Matcher* roles. Here, we focus on the first run for each dyad only (resulting in a between-participants design for the current analysis).

The study was conducted in German (our examples in this paper are translated from the original). Before beginning, the participants were allowed to have a look at the furniture which was loosely set aside of the unfurnished house, but they were not allowed to talk to each other. The study was audio and video recorded and the Matcher's finished dollhouse was photographed.

Participants were 34 females (16 F-NF; 18 NF-F) and 14 males (10 F-NF; 4 NF-F) with an age range of 16–26 (mean age: 20 years). Participants were assigned in pairs of same gender and similar age; none of them was familiar with the background of the study. 13 pairs started with the functional condition, and 11 pairs started with the non-functional condition.

Objects were coded as oriented wrongly when their orientation differed from the model at 45° or more. Error scores were coded for object location and orientation by two independent raters who agreed in 96.77% of the cases.[3] A third coder resolved coding disagreements.

---

[3] The number is based on the annotation for the entire study reported in [23].

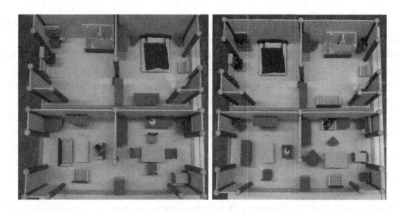

Fig. 1. The model houses of the functional (F) (left) and the non-functional (NF) condition (right).

The utterances were analysed with respect to completeness of object orientation information, based on the parameters outlined in Sect. 3.3. This included reference to the locatum's (directed) axes (*yes, no, undirected*), relata, and spatial terms; projective terms were specified as such (*yes, no, projective*). If objects were positioned diagonally, this would have to be mentioned in complete orientation descriptions (*yes, no*); however, if objects were parallel to the walls, this parameter was coded as *not applicable*.

Based on this annotation, references to object orientation were coded as *complete, incomplete*, or *missing* (see Table 1). A description of object orientation was regarded as *complete* if it involved an explicit reference to (i) one of its

Table 1. Examples of annotated orientation descriptions in the functional and non-functional condition.

Cond.	Speaker	Orientation Description	Locatum	Locatum's Axes	Direction	Diagonal	Extent Explicitness
F	Director	uh the toilet is uh parallel to the shower practically placed at the back wall	A02	undirected	yes	n.a.	incomplete
F	Director	and the opening points toward the bed, yes	B08	yes	yes	n.a.	complete
F	Director	yes, well, diagonally opposite the wardrobe so beside the armchair there in the corner	B07	no	yes	yes	incomplete
NF	Director	with the blue thing at the wall, right	B05	yes	yes	n.a.	complete
NF	Matcher	so uhm with the back towards me with the	B01	no	yes	n.a.	incomplete
NF	Director	n+ n+ no with the side towards you, and the side towards you	B01	undirected	yes	n.a.	incomplete

axes and the axes' directedness if applicable, and (ii) a fully specified direction. Direction was regarded as incomplete if one of the required parameters was missing, such as the underlying perspective for a projective term. The orientation of diagonal objects was considered as completely described only when (iii) diagonality was made explicit. If object orientation was not communicated at all the description was annotated as *missing*. Where speakers used alternative ways of communicating object orientation, decisions about completeness were made on a case by case basis. We will discuss some of these cases in Sect. 5.2.

5   Results

Figure 2 (left) summarizes the extent to which orientation information was made explicit during successful object placement (the breakdown for failed placements is shown on the right). While error scores did not diverge much between conditions, the amount of information given by Directors did:[4] In the functional condition (F), nearly half of the descriptions were *missing* (i.e., orientation was taken for granted), whereas in the non-functional condition (NF), nearly half of the descriptions were *complete*, i.e. fully specified. About 1/4 of descriptions in F and 1/3 in NF included incomplete orientation (i.e., descriptions with a missing parameter, or alternative descriptions as discussed in Sect. 5.2 below).

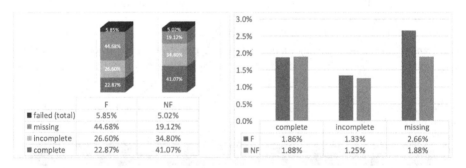

	F	NF
■ failed (total)	5.85%	5.02%
■ missing	44.68%	19.12%
■ incomplete	26.60%	34.80%
■ complete	22.87%	41.07%

	complete	incomplete	missing
■ F	1.86%	1.33%	2.66%
■ NF	1.88%	1.25%	1.88%

Fig. 2. Left: orientation information given in the functional (F) and non-functional (NF) condition. Right: breakdown of information given in cases of failed orientation.

The error rate for object orientation was generally low: 5.85% (22 out of 377 objects) in F, and 5.02% (16 out of 319 objects) in NF. Figure 2 (right) reveals that objects were sometimes wrongly oriented even with full information provided. We will now take a closer look at orientation failures (Sect. 5.1) and at alternative ways of conveying orientation information (Sect. 5.2).

---

[4] In [23] we noted inclusion of object orientation in any given utterance. Here we provide a far more detailed breakdown based on our operationalization of orientation parameters presented in Sect. 3.3.

5.1   Exploring Error Cases

7 errors occurred with complete orientation information in F, and 6 in NF. Sometimes the Matcher simply ignored relevant information, as in Example 11:

11. Director: So, first the upper floor in the left half, there is uh the shower. The shower is placed at the middle wall.
    Matcher: Yes wait a minute, uhm middle wall right or left?
    Director: uhm yes well uh
    Matcher: oh I see at the middle
    Director: the left side at the middle wall
    Matcher: ah okay yes alright.

The video recording for this dialogue extract reveals that the Matcher places the shower with its back axis pointing to the middle wall, ignoring the reference to the object's left side. This corresponds to the conventional practice of placing objects with their back towards a wall that is indicated during the location process (*at wall x*). This kind of location information does not include orientation information, but it seems very natural to infer in such cases that the back axis should point to the wall in question. The general acceptance of this inferential preference appears to have led to the error in Example 11.

In F, errors with *complete* information reveal some problems of understanding either the orientation information in general, or references to a specific directed axis in particular. In NF, errors in this category occur mainly with a specific object type, a triangular bedside table which repeatedly caused problems for orientation description. Speakers would often refer to its orientation as follows:

12. The round side points to the shower, triangle points to the wardrobe.

Although complete, the orientation information provided in this example can easily misunderstood, as illustrated in Fig. 3.

Fig. 3. The orientation of the bedside table in the model dollhouse (left) and as a possible interpretation of Example 12 (right).

In F, errors related to *incomplete* orientation information (5 cases) were due to problems caused by the bedside table, a failure to refer to the locatum's directed axis, and by incorrect orientation information. The 4 errors in NF in this category were caused by miscommunication, ignoring the information that had been given, and by different interpretations of the term *längs* (*along*) in two cases where the locatum was symmetric and the relatum was the room.

Errors based on *missing* orientation information occur most often in F (10 cases, 2.66%; 6 in NF, 1.88%). These errors occurred mainly with objects for which no stereotypical orientation was available, and for diagonally oriented objects. However, even in the complete absence of any orientation information, the error rate is strikingly low. It seems that in most of these cases orientation was inferable from the identification and location process. For instance, the location description *at wall x* allows for reasonable inferences about orientation.

5.2 Alternative Ways of Communicating Object Orientation

Even though alternative ways of communicating object orientation were rarely unambiguous and therefore coded as *incomplete*, they typically allowed for object orientation to be inferred correctly. One frequent method (across both conditions) was to mention the object's function as in Example 13:

13. The wardrobe is at the back wall (...) so that one can use it, of course.

By indicating the usage of the wardrobe, the Director hints at its frontal axis, the only object side with a usage function. In addition to this information, orientation is further constrained by placing it at a wall, supporting the common *at wall x* inference. The marker *of course* reveals how obvious this is felt to be.

Secondly, the objects' front or back axis was frequently hinted at (but not mentioned explicitly) using verbs such as *gucken* (*look*) and *zeigen* (*show*) or nouns such as *Blick* (*view*), *Gesicht* (*face*), and *Rücken* (*back*). Here the direction of an axis is projected onto the locatum via analogy to the human body. This kind of projection was never questioned by the dialogue partners.

Thirdly, axes could be projected onto the locatum by establishing symmetry between the locatum and the relatum. If the relatum was another object, this would usually be expressed by spatial terms such as *(so) wie (the same as)*, *andersrum (the other way round), parallel (parallel), symmetrisch (symmetrical), spiegelverkehrt/gespiegelt (mirror-inverted), im rechten Winkel (perpendicular), waagerecht (level)*, and *senkrecht (vertical)*. This description type is risky if no additional orientation information is given, as in Example 14. The descriptions are incomplete because a reference to the locatum's directed axis is missing.

14. Director: uhm now in the other slanted corner there is the toilet placed at the back wall as well
    Matcher: uh again
    Director: uh the toilet is uh parallel to the shower practically placed at the back wall. Can you imagine?
    Matcher: Parallel to the shower
    Director: Well it is at the roof of the house pra+ well at the roof yes. The shower is at the middle wall and the toilet is at the roof.

In this example, the toilet's orientation is described as parallel to the shower's, which had been placed incorrectly (cf. our Example 11 above). The present description specifies that the toilet is placed at the back wall but it does not involve a reference to the toilet's directed axis. Therefore, the Matcher is unable to disambiguate the description, and subsequently orients the toilet incorrectly but symmetrically to the shower.

If the relatum was the room (or a part of it), symmetry was mainly indicated by spatial terms such as *längs (alongside), quer (crosswise), seitlich (sideways), waagerecht (level), vertikal (vertical), im rechten Winkel (perpendicular)*, and *parallel (parallel)*. This type of symmetry was mainly used for objects with undirected axes (like tables). Since the dollhouse rooms were actually square, references to the symmetry of the room as a whole (e.g. *the table is alongside the room*) are not quite precise, leading to a need for further negotiation by reference to other available relata.

6   Discussion

In the present study, we asked how speakers negotiate object orientation information and to what extent this leads to success in orienting objects correctly, based on a corpus involving object placements in functional and non-functional dollhouse furniture arrangements. Results reveal that dialogue partners achieved a similarly high success rate across the different spatial configurations, but the extent to which explicit information was given differed widely between the conditions. We started our analysis of orientation information by identifying explicit spatial descriptions of a similar type as object location descriptions, based on a set of parameters derived from the literature and available examples. In our corpus, it turned out that this type of explicit spatial orientation information was not provided or incomplete in the majority of cases. Instead, speakers were creative in suggesting object orientation in a number of other ways, or they assumed that the addressee would be able to draw relevant inferences based on world knowledge. Although this was risky, the low error rate for object orientation suggests that this strategy of minimal or inference-based information was overall successful.

In general, it can be assumed that people within a society share knowledge about how furniture items are typically arranged in a house. This allows dialogue partners to draw on Levinson's I-heuristic 'What is simply described is stereotypically exemplified' [16, p. 32]: if minimal descriptions (such as the location description *at wall x*) already evoke rich interpretations of the situation, no further specific information is required. In our data, it appears that the Directors and Matchers mostly relied on the I-heuristic for objects where the spatial array was stereotypical (in our *functional* condition). Clearly, functional arrangements in general support and simplify communication, adding to previous findings on effects of functional relationships [8]. When objects relate to each other in a functional way or are arranged ready to be used based on their function, the I-heuristic is licensed and the potential interpretations are limited to the functionally adequate orientation of the locatum. Monologue studies show that typical arrangements may license stereotypical interpretations irrespective of further contextual information [1, 24].

In atypical spatial configurations, addressees are still able to draw inferences based on cultural knowledge to a limited extent. Our data show that dialogue partners far less often relied on this kind of common ground, and instead negotiated object orientation explicitly. This happened even in cases where the locatum was, in fact, oriented in a typical way. In this way, the use of the I-heuristic appeared to be mediated by the typicality of the object arrangement. With a non-typical arrangement, the need for object orientation information was enhanced, leading to less *simple* descriptions (in Levinson's terms [16]) and, accordingly, less stereotypical interpretations. By being more informative than might arguably be required concerning *typical* spatial aspects, speakers accounted for the *atypicality* of the entire spatial array.

This also supports Clark's [5] suggestion that information is frequently communicated when perceived as necessary. However, this perception is not always valid – incorrect inferences are possible. In the functional condition, the higher error score within the category of *missing* orientation information suggests that speakers sometimes take a high risk when relying on the *principle of least collaborative effort*, rather than avoiding underspecification and ambiguity. The nature of the risk was, of course, negligible in our scenario as there was no penalty for incorrect object placements; dialogue partners were simply motivated by the playful challenge of the situation itself.

Our data clearly demonstrate that both dialogue partners were sensitive to the availability of cultural knowledge. Directors (and sometimes Matchers[5], in their creative contributions to the joint effort) adjusted their descriptions of orientation information to context-specific conditions, and Matchers reacted by regularly making correct inferences based on incomplete or missing orientation information, using their cultural knowledge to fill in the gaps. While dialogue partners tended to negotiate orientation information explicitly for atypical spatial arrangements, with typical object arrangements they tended to rely on inferences drawn from cultural knowledge. Based on this adaptation to the availability of cultural knowledge, errors occurred rarely and to a similar extent in both conditions - irrespective of the typicality of the spatial situation.

Cultural background knowledge was invoked, for instance, when axes were projected onto the locatum via analogy to the human body. These strategies to imply object orientation were successful as long as the verbal information was in line with general inference preferences (such as placing objects with their back to the wall). When the locatum was described based on symmetry to another available entity, the axes of the two entities involved needed to be compared to each other and adjusted accordingly. This task often appeared difficult to resolve, and was often accompanied by further negotiation of orientation.

---

[5] In [22] we found that although Matchers in our dialogue corpus often provided suggestions to specify object location (adding to the Director's instructions), they did so less often concerning orientation.

In contrast, leaving the perspective on the scene implicit when using projective terms did not cause problems for interpretation, as all of the Matchers simply used their own perspective, matching the Director's in this scenario. It remains to be investigated how dialogue partners treat diverging perspectives when talking about object orientation, and whether any further spatial frames of reference may be available, paralleling the complexity of references to object location.

7   Conclusion

In dialogue, speakers pursue different strategies to refer to object orientation. They provide explicit and implicit information about how the object in focus is directed towards a particular reference entity, partially requiring the addressee to draw inferences based on knowledge about typical furniture arrangements and the projection of the human body's axes, or they refer to how the object can be used, licensing inferences of typical object utilization. The way information was negotiated by our participants, along with their conversational success, suggests a high degree of sensitivity for specific contextual needs, relative to the functionality of the array. We conclude that speakers heavily rely on common ground when determining the extent to which explicit information is required to enable successful communication. This same source is also the main basis for inferring or interpreting information about object orientation across situation contexts.

References

1. Andonova, E., Tenbrink, T., Coventry, K.R.: Function and context affect spatial information packaging at multiple levels. Psychon. Bull. Rev. **17**(4), 575–580 (2010)
2. Carletta, J.: Planning to fail, not failing to plan: risk-taking and recovery in task-oriented dialogue. In: Proceedings of the 14th International Conference on Computational Linguistics, pp. 896–900 (1992)
3. Carlson, L.A., Hill, P.L.: Formulating spatial descriptions across various dialogue contexts. In: Coventry, K.R., Tenbrink, T., Bateman, J.A. (eds.) Spatial Language and Dialogue: Explorations in Language and Space, pp. 89–103. Oxford University Press, Oxford (2009)
4. Clark, H.H.: Using Language. Cambridge University Press, Cambridge, New York (1996)
5. Clark, H.H., Brennan, S.E.: Grounding in communication. In: Baecker, R.M. (ed.) Readings in Group-Ware and Computer-Supported Cooperative Work: Assisting Human-Human Collaboration. Morgan Kaufman, San Mateo, CA (1991)
6. Clark, H.H., Schaefer, E.F.: Contributing to discourse. Cogn. Sci. **13**, 259–294 (1989)
7. Clark, H.H., Wilkes-Gibbs, D.: Referring as a collaborative process. Cognition **22**(1), 1–39 (1986)
8. Coventry, K.R., Garrod, S.C.: Saying, Seeing, and Acting: The Psychological Semantics of Spatial Prepositions. Psychology Press, Hove, New York (2004)
9. Deutsch, W.: Sprachliche Redundanz und Objektidentifikation: Inauguraldissertation. Philippsuniversität Marburg/Lahn, Marburg/Lahn (1976)

10. Garrod, S.C., Pickering, M.J.: Alignment in dialogue. In: Gaskell, M.G. (ed.) The Oxford Handbook of Psycholinguistics. Oxford University Press, Oxford (2009)
11. Grice, H.P.: Logic and conversation. In: Cole, P., Morgan, J.L. (eds.) Syntax and Semantics, pp. 41–58. Academic Press, New York (1975)
12. Guhe, M., Bard, E.G.: Adapting referring expressions to the task environment. In: Proceedings of the Annual Conference of the Cognitive Science Society, pp. 2404–2409 (2008)
13. Landau, B., Jackendoff, R.: "What" and "where" in spatial language and spatial cognition. Behav. Brain Sci. **16**, 217–265 (1993)
14. Langacker, R.W.: Foundations of Cognitive Grammar. Stanford University Press, Stanford (1987–1991)
15. Levelt, W.J.M.: Some perceptual limitations on talking about space. In: Doorn, A.J., van Grind, W.A., van de Koenderink, J.J. (eds.) Limits in Perception, pp. 323–358. VNU, Utrecht (1984)
16. Levinson, S.C.: Presumptive Meanings: The Theory of Generalized Conversational Implicature. MIT Press, Cambridge, Mass (2000)
17. Levinson, S.C.: Space in Language and Cognition: Explorations in Cognitive Diversity. Cambridge University Press, Cambridge, New York (2003)
18. Mangold-Allwinn, R., Barattelli, S., Kiefer, M., Koelbing, H.G.: Wörter für Dinge: Von flexiblen Konzepten zu variablen Benennungen. Westdeutscher Verlag, Opladen (1995)
19. Shanon, B.: Room descriptions. Discourse Process. **7**, 225–255 (1984)
20. Talmy, L.: How language structures space. In: Pick Jr., H.L., Acredolo, L.P. (eds.) Spatial Orientation: Theory, Research, and Application, pp. 225–282. Plenum Press, New York, London (1983)
21. Tenbrink, T.: Space, Time, and the use of Language: An Investigation of Relationships. Mouton de Gruyter, Berlin, New York (2007)
22. Tenbrink, T., Andonova, E., Coventry, K.R.: Negotiating spatial relationships in dialogue: the role of the addressee. In: Ginzburg, J., Healey, P.G.T., Sato, Y. (eds.) Proceedings of the 12th Workshop of the Semantics and Pragmatics of Dialogue, pp. 201–208 (2008)
23. Tenbrink, T., Andonova, E., Schole, G., Coventry, K.R.: Communicative success in spatial dialogue: the impact of functional features and dialogue strategies. Lang. Speech **59**(3), 1–12 (2016)
24. Tenbrink, T., Coventry, K.R., Andonova, E.: Spatial strategies in the description of complex configurations. Discourse Process. **48**(4), 237–266 (2011)
25. Ullmer-Ehrich, V.: The structure of living space descriptions. In: Jarvella, R.J., Klein, W. (eds.) Speech, Place, and Action, pp. 219–249. Wiley, Chichester (1982)

Spatial Distribution of Local Landmarks in Route-Based Sketch Maps

Vanessa Joy A. Anacta[1]([envelope]), Rui Li[2], Heinrich Löwen[1],
Marcelo De Lima Galvao[1], and Angela Schwering[1]

[1] Institute for Geoinformatics, University of Muenster, Münster, Germany
{v_anac02, loewen.heinrich, galvao.marcelo,
schwering}@uni-muenster.de
[2] Department of Geography and Planning, University of Albany,
SUNY, Albany, NY, USA
rli4@albany.edu

Abstract. Landmarks are important elements in route instructions communicated for wayfinding in unfamiliar environments. This paper aims to investigate the distribution of local landmarks in human sketch maps provided for wayfinding purpose. We investigated sets of route instructions given by student participants who were asked to give directions in environments that they are very familiar with to someone unfamiliar. These environments differ in size as well as their relation to city centers. In particular, one route goes into the city, one route goes through the city center, and the third route ranges between two cities. The results show that local landmarks are distributed differently in each route and showing high density of landmarks at some portions of the route. The study further clarifies the distribution of landmarks along routes with relation to the length of the route. It also contributes to the work concerning the cognitive aspects of wayfinding with a specific focus on the distribution of landmarks in route instructions.

Keywords: Local landmarks · Route instructions · Sketch maps
Wayfinding

1 Introduction

Assume that someone asks you for directions at the train station or in a supermarket for going to a place that you are familiar with. Which types of information would you provide to help the person reach his/her destination and at the same time learn about this area? Allen [1] emphasizes that there are principles behind how people provide wayfinding instructions. People's knowledge corresponds to the physical environment such that they are capable of producing 'cognitive spatial descriptions' [2]. Differences in route descriptions depend on several factors such as the mode of used transportation, the distance, and the time it takes to arrive at the destination. It is important that a 'common ground' is established [1] for the direction provider and the recipient. This common knowledge serves as a basis for effective understanding of the instructions for the wayfinder. In this paper, we investigate local landmarks oftentimes mentioned in three routes using different mode of transportation regardless of the route choices of participants and where the landmarks are concentrated in the entire route.

© Springer Nature Switzerland AG 2018
S. Creem-Regehr et al. (Eds.): Spatial Cognition 2018, LNAI 11034, pp. 107–118, 2018.
https://doi.org/10.1007/978-3-319-96385-3_8

1.1   Importance and Characteristics of Landmarks

Landmarks are important elements for acquiring spatial knowledge in an unfamiliar environment. Most people rely on landmark information when asking for giving route directions as this makes it easier for them to remember. In wayfinding-related studies, many researchers from the fields of cognitive science, geography, computer science, psychology, and linguistics have developed systematic methods for analyzing verbal descriptions. For example, these methods include analyzing landmark characteristics [3], propositions of spatial descriptions [4] to understanding ontologies [5] and building up a taxonomy of a wayfinding task [6].

Studies on analyzing landmark characteristics range from different types of spaces. This includes investigating saliency of landmarks in indoor space such as airports [7] and outdoor space analyzing buildings in a city [8]. A formal model of salience was developed focusing on visual, semantic and structural properties of landmarks [9]. This framework then further investigates structural salience of landmarks regarding where they are located along the route [10]. For instance, it was suggested that the saliency of landmarks at decision points [11] depends on the direction of travel. Sorrows and Hirtle [3] identified certain characteristics that make landmarks stand out in the environment for real and virtual space. These are cognitive, structural, and visual elements. The authors emphasized that when navigating in a familiar environment, there are more visual and cognitive types of landmarks used. But in unfamiliar environment, it calls for more visual and structural forms to help maintain orientation and form a cognitive map. Cognitive landmarks are suggested to play an essential role in orientation for a familiar environment. We aim to evaluate this aspect in this paper in order to specify where specific landmarks are mostly mentioned in the instruction of someone familiar with the environment to a complete stranger. Schroder et al. [11] emphasized that visibility of features should be taken into consideration in route instructions. Since Dale et al. [12] pointed out that people tend to use visible features for turning action, we will further evaluate this aspect in the route instructions provided in this study.

1.2   Location of Landmarks

Human-generated route instructions consist of mostly local landmarks [13]. They are suggested to be included in route guidance as it is a natural way of how people provide instructions [12, 14, 15]. In addition to the importance of landmarks in route instructions, location of landmarks has been extensively studied in order to know which landmark should be included in the route instructions. Should it be located along the route, at decision points, or distant from the route? The role of landmarks at decision points has been addressed specifically regarding where turning action is needed [16, 17]. The combination of having action with a landmark, as suggested in the skeletal description developed by Denis [4], has been extensively used and tested successfully in experiments regarding its efficiency was in wayfinding tasks [18, 19]. While many studies have considered landmarks at decision points essential in wayfinding studies [14, 20, 21], landmarks along the route are also mentioned when giving verbal instructions [22]. Its importance and usefulness in wayfinding, however, are not extensively investigated.

Sadalla [23] investigated the importance of reference points in establishing spatial relationship within the environment. Reference points refer to places whose locations are well known which are referred to other adjacent places. These can be used in organizing spatial features in space as it is said to be easier to orient a specific place to a reference point than to a non-reference point. These reference points are already stored in a person's mind and usually retrieved when relating to a non-reference point.

Regarding concentration of landmarks, more landmarks are mentioned at the end of a route [24]. That is to say, there is an increase of landmarks when going towards the end such that the person is able to fix his location during wayfinding. Brosset et al. [25] investigated wayfinding in a natural environment and showed that there were more landmarks mentioned at the end of the route. However, Lovelace et al. [22] showed a different result stating that there is no evidence that more landmarks should be mentioned at the end of the route. It showed in the experiment that no landmark was mentioned at the end of the route in their cases. Consequently, this claim relies on the availability of landmarks or the type of environment. With these factors in mind, we further investigate in this study if the use of landmarks at the end of the route is based on factors such as the type of environment and the mode of transportation. It is important to point out that the previous studies on the use of landmark are based on collected verbal descriptions. Although we consider using the similar method to collect wayfinding directions in an earlier study [26], the authors suggested that in general sketched maps consist of more landmarks than verbal descriptions. Therefore we aim to use the method of using sketch maps as the way of collecting wayfinding instructions to collect as many landmarks as possible for our investigation. The extracted landmarks from sketch maps will become the main database in this study.

1.3 Landmarks in Sketch Maps

There are many ways for communicating route instructions. Human generated instructions are qualitative. It involves extensive use of landmarks to enable one to put oneself of the receiver's perspective [27] and select a route with fewer number of turns [28]. But, it is difficult to teach the computer how to communicate space like humans do [27]. There have been several attempts to computationally extract landmarks from spatial databases [29] or web harvested data [30, 31]. All approaches rely on the salience categories by Sorrows and Hirtle [3]. They first extract potential landmark candidates before refining the selection to the most salient landmarks in terms of visual, structural and semantic salience. Furthermore, there are approaches to automatically include landmarks in wayfinding instructions [13, 30–32]. For this study, we focus on the use and distribution of local landmarks in sketch maps for routing irrespective of the route choice.

The goal of this paper is to determine where local landmarks are situated in the entire route in human sketch maps. We hypothesize that the composition of landmarks varies with the type of route and a certain portion of the route shows higher density of landmarks. The paper is structured as follows: Sect. 2 explains the experiment design. Section 3 discusses the results. Section 4 provides the discussion and Sect. 5 gives the conclusion and outlook.

2 Methods

2.1 Participants

There were a total of 20 university students (10 M, 10 F) with a mean age of 22.9 years (SD = 2.93) who participated in the experiment. They were all German native speakers who have been residing in the student dormitory for at least six months and claimed to be familiar with the study area. The participants were from various disciplines. They were paid 10€ per hour for their participation.

2.2 Materials and Methods

Each route was drawn on an A4 paper. We collected a total of 60 sketch maps. Each participant had to describe three routes in the experiment. The study area was in the city of Muenster, Germany. The first route, about 1.2 km (going to city center), was from a train station (Hbf) to the cathedral (Dom). The second route (passing the city center) was a longer route approximately 5.2 km, which was from a supermarket (Lidl) in Gievenbeck neighborhood to the train station (Hbf). The third route (intercity route) was from the dormitory to their hometown in Germany; hence, different routes were taken among participants. In particular, we asked participants who are familiar with the environment to give route descriptions to someone new in the area using bike for the Route 1 and 2 because this is the frequent mode of transportation in Muenster and using car for Route 3 as this is a longer route connecting different cities. All participants drew the routes in similar order.

German students living in a dormitory were invited to participate in this experiment. A questionnaire was given to evaluate their familiarity. They were asked to draw a sketch map of three different routes. They were given a paper and a pen to draw each map. No additional information was given to them on how to draw a sketch map, for as long as they describe a comprehensible route to someone who is new in the area.

Regardless of the route described, we went through sets of sketch maps and analyzed all the local landmarks that people include in the instructions. The analysis was focused on *local landmarks*, meaning those landmarks situated along the route both at decision points and non-decision points.

In the analysis, we divided the route into segments. For the purpose of this study, route segmentation refers to (a) nodes where a decision is made and (b) route segments between two decision points. The road network is represented as a graph $G = (V, E)$ consisting of a set of nodes (V) and edges (E), and a route as a directed graph $G'(V', E') \subseteq G$ from origin $o \in V$ to destination $d \in V$. Each route consists of a set of decision points $D \subseteq V'$. Decision points are defined by a set C of decision point classes, represented by a function $class : D \rightarrow C$, such that for every $d \in D, class(d) = c, c \in C$ (see Table 1). The "straight on" decision point determines to only add a decision point of this type when there is an intersection with a street of the same or higher class. The "exit" decision point specifically refers to highways, as there are no junctions on highways, but highways are only connected via exits. The location of a $d \in D$ is represented by the distance from the origin: dist(d) = $d(o, d)$.

We normalize the distribution of $d \in D$ along the route by a normalization function:

$$normdist : D \to [0, 1000]$$

such that

$$nordist(d) = \frac{dist(d) * 1000}{\max(\{dist(d')|d' \in D\})}$$

3   Results

It showed that participants provided different route choices from the origin to the destination. Although participants included global landmarks (off-route) in their sketch maps, only local landmarks are considered as points were analyzed in this study (see Figs. 2, 4 and 6). Global landmarks are included only for visualization purpose. The total number of local landmarks provided for each route are 64 (Route 1), 105 (Route 2) and 63 (Route 3).

Among all participants, more than half of them described the same route for sketch maps for Routes 1 and 2. Figures 1 and 3 show the different routes participants described and highlights the frequently taken route in Route 1 and Route 2.

Figure 2 shows the distribution of landmarks on Route 1 at a normalized distance scale from 1 to 1000. For the largest part of the route, there is a low frequency of local landmarks of maximum five landmarks per range. However, the histogram clearly shows that there are a lot more local landmarks towards the end of the route. With regard to the decision point distribution, there are more landmarks drawn when the type is 'straight on' and when turning action is required. The colors relate to the classification of decision points, as presented in Table 1.

Table 1. Classification of decision points along a route.

Decision point (DP) class	Type of decision point
0	Start/destination
1	Straight on (same class or higher)
2	Turn not at a junction
3	Turn at T-junction
4	Turn at junction
5	Turn at roundabout
6	Exit (only for motorways and trunks)

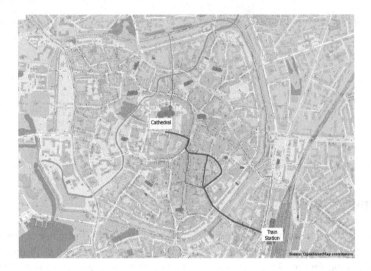

Fig. 1. Route choices for Route 1 (Hbf-Dom). The thick line represents the most frequently referred route. Source: OpenStreetMap contributors

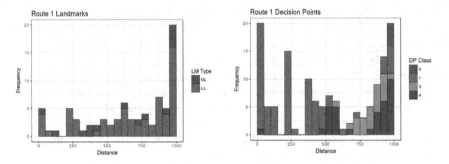

Fig. 2. Histogram of distribution of landmark and decision points (Route 1).

In the case of Route 2, Fig. 3 shows the most preferred route by the participants from a supermarket (Point A) to the central train station (Point B).The thick line shows the most frequent route used by participants.

Figure 4 shows the distribution of landmarks on Route 2 considering the different routes taken. It is again plotted onto a normalized distance scale from 1 to 1000. The peak of more local landmarks mentioned was in both start and end part of the route. But, there are also many landmarks drawn in between the whole route. Participants drew landmarks at almost all decision point classes with more landmarks were drawn in class 'straight on'. When there is a presence of roundabout, participants oftentimes include this in their sketch map.

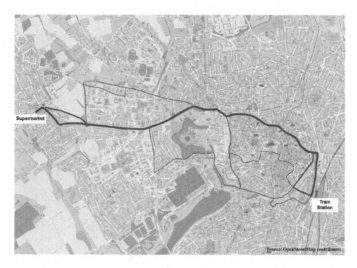

Fig. 3. Route choices Route 2 (Supermarket-Hbf) and the most frequent route is in thick line.

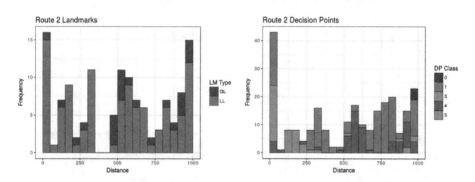

Fig. 4. Histogram of distribution of landmarks and decision points (Route 2).

Figure 5 shows the different routes of participants from the dormitory to their hometown in Germany. The route length ranges from approximately 45 km to 550 km. The longest route was a route from the dormitory in Muenster to the participant's home in Dresden.

Figure 6 shows the distribution of landmarks on Route 3 on a normalized scale considering the different routes taken. We can again see peaks of more landmarks at the start and at the end of the route. The histogram also shows the distribution of decision points, normalized to a distance scale from 1 to 1000 m. This reveals that landmarks are found in all types of decision point classes with more on 'straight on' class.

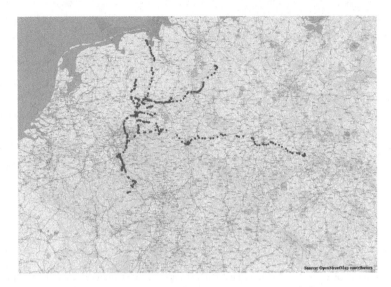

Fig. 5. Route 3 (Dormitory-Hometown) Route choices

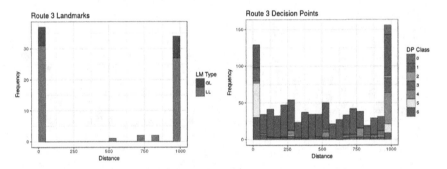

Fig. 6. Histogram of distribution of landmarks and Decision points (Route 3).

4 Discussion

Local landmarks, either situated along the route or at decision points, have been commonly used in giving route instructions. It further confirms what Raubal and Winter [13] highlighted in their study on the importance of providing local landmarks in wayfinding instructions that these should be included in route instructions focusing on the visual, sematic and structural elements.

Where are landmarks concentrated in wayfinding instructions? Many studies have investigated the importance of landmarks at decision points where an action is taken [4, 19, 20]. This was evident in the data as in the different classes of decision points showing concentration of landmarks. In Allen's [1] study, it showed that more landmarks should be mentioned at the end of the verbal route instructions. Also, Brosset et al.'s [25] study suggested that the distribution of landmarks increases when getting near the end of the route as well as with reference to metrics in natural environment. This is also evident in our study. But it should be considered that there are differences of the overall distribution of landmarks for the three routes. The structure of the city or the environment could play a role in the differences of placement of landmarks. In natural environments as what Brosset et al. [25] indicated, there are more landmarks mentioned at the end portion of the route for confirmation purposes. However, within the city where there is more presence of landmarks, there is unvarying distribution of landmarks in all parts of the route. Based on what Lovelace et al. [22] emphasized in their study, there could be more landmarks in the beginning or at the end part of the route which depends on the type of the environment. Hence, it is not always the case that more landmarks are located at the end part of the route.

The study shows that the intercity route does not result in the use of many landmarks compared to the other shorter routes. This suggests that the number of landmarks to be included does not depend on the route length. It is possible that when routes involve crossing many cities where there are not a lot of decision points and when not many things are happening along the way, there are not many landmarks included in the sketch maps unless the class 'straight on'. In this case, highway exits are the most important features that participants highlighted. This is mostly evident in longer route. When the route is nearing the destination, more landmarks are drawn. Route 2 showed more landmarks drawn compared to other routes. This route is from one district passing through the city center. This might be that since many shops can be considered landmarks here, participants try to select those that they think are more prominent when a change of action is required. Landmarks were well distributed with beginning and end having the highest concentration. Interestingly, there is also much concentration of landmarks in the middle part of the route, where the city center with many possible landmarks is. This suggests that when crossing the region, participants tend to recognize the importance of including landmarks for orientation purposes. Similar to Route 3, there are many landmarks also drawn when nearing the goal which is to also orient the person. But also participants have frequently included landmarks at the beginning of the route. Route 1, although short route, also showed a similar pattern with the other routes with more landmarks indicated at the end part of the route. Similar to Route 2, as this route goes inside the city center, participants drew many landmarks along the way especially when an action is indicated. Route2 and Route 3 tend to orient the participant at the beginning of the route by always referring to landmarks which guides the wayfinder of the route direction to take.

Regarding the characteristics of the routes, the most common routes for Route 1 and Route 2 followed are one with less number of turns. The route frequently chosen by participants supports Dalton's [28] study that people follow a straight route with less angular deviations. The data also show the presence of global (off-route and distant) landmarks for orientation purposes referring to a prominent feature as a reference point [23] which serve as confirming information that the person is travelling on the right path.

5 Conclusion and Outlook

Human-generated instructions contain many landmarks. Several studies have been conducted to analyze the different landmarks mentioned in spatial descriptions mostly focusing on local landmarks. The placement of landmarks in the route instruction is also worth investigating. Reasons could be that of confirmation information, orientation and reorientation, or directional purpose. It shows that the longer the route segment does not necessarily mean more landmarks to be mentioned, although it showed more landmarks near the end portion of the route. This depends also on the availability of landmarks and when there is presence of decision points. It is important to point out that we only considered landmarks mentioned in the form of sketch map. To provide a more comprehensive understanding, the results of landmarks used in sketch map should be cross-evaluated with those used in verbal descriptions. Furthermore, we have identified the use of global landmarks in the collected data. To adhere to the theoretical framework in our analyses, we only examined the local landmarks. For future work, we will look at both local and global landmarks in the route instructions in both forms of cognitive maps and verbal descriptions. This outcome can benefit researchers who work on automatic generation of landmarks for a specific route which will be useful for navigation.

Acknowledgements. We acknowledge the support of the German Research Foundation (DFG) with project number SCHW 1372/15-1 and the European Research Council (ERC Starting Grant No. 637645).

References

1. Allen, G.: Principles and practices for communicating route knowledge. Appl. Cognit. Psychol. **14**(4), 333–359 (2000)
2. Kuipers, B.: The "map in the head" metaphor. Environ. Behav. **14**(2), 202–220 (1982)
3. Sorrows, M.E., Hirtle, S.C.: The nature of landmarks for real and electronic spaces. In: Freksa, C., Mark, D.M. (eds.) COSIT 1999. LNCS, vol. 1661, pp. 37–50. Springer, Heidelberg (1999). https://doi.org/10.1007/3-540-48384-5_3
4. Denis, M.: The description of routes: a cognitive approach to the production of spatial discourse. Cahiers de psychol. cognit. **16**(4), 409–458 (1997)
5. Timpf, S.: Ontologies of wayfinding: a traveler's perspective. Netw. Spat. Econ. **2**(1), 9–33 (2002)
6. Wiener, J., Büchner, S., Hölscher, C.: Towards a taxonomy of wayfinding tasks: a knowledge-based approach. Spat. Cognit. Comput. Interdiscip. J. **9**, 152–165 (2009)
7. Raubal, M., Egenhofer, M.: Comparing the complexity of wayfinding tasks in built environments. Environ. Plann. B **25**, 895–914 (1998)
8. Nothegger, C., Winter, S., Raubal, M.: Selection of salient features for route directions. Spat. Cognit. Comput. Interdiscip. J. **4**(2), 113–136 (2009)
9. Winter, S.: Route adaptive selection of salient features. In: Kuhn, W., Worboys, M.F., Timpf, S. (eds.) COSIT 2003. LNCS, vol. 2825, pp. 349–361. Springer, Heidelberg (2003). https://doi.org/10.1007/978-3-540-39923-0_23

10. Klippel, A., Winter, S.: Structural salience of landmarks for route directions. In: Cohn, A.G., Mark, D.M. (eds.) COSIT 2005. LNCS, vol. 3693, pp. 347–362. Springer, Heidelberg (2005). https://doi.org/10.1007/11556114_22

11. Schroder, C., Mackaness, W., Gittings, B.: Giving the 'right' route directions: the requirements for pedestrian navigation systems. Trans. GIS **15**(3), 419–438 (2011)

12. Dale, R., Geldof, S., Prost, J.-P.: Generating more natural route descriptions. In: Proceedings of the 2002 Australasian, pp. 41–48 (2002)

13. Raubal, M., Winter, S.: Enriching wayfinding instructions with local landmarks. In: Egenhofer, M.J., Mark, D.M. (eds.) GIScience 2002. LNCS, vol. 2478, pp. 243–259. Springer, Heidelberg (2002). https://doi.org/10.1007/3-540-45799-2_17

14. Elias, B.: Determination of landmarks and reliability criteria for landmarks (2003)

15. Tom, A., Denis, M.: Referring to landmark or street information in route directions: what difference does it make? In: Kuhn, W., Worboys, M.F., Timpf, S. (eds.) COSIT 2003. LNCS, vol. 2825, pp. 362–374. Springer, Heidelberg (2003). https://doi.org/10.1007/978-3-540-39923-0_24

16. Rehrl, K., Leitinger, S., Gartner, G., Ortag, F.: An analysis of direction and motion concepts in verbal descriptions of route choices. In: Hornsby, K.S., Claramunt, C., Denis, M., Ligozat, G. (eds.) COSIT 2009. LNCS, vol. 5756, pp. 471–488. Springer, Heidelberg (2009). https://doi.org/10.1007/978-3-642-03832-7_29

17. Jackson, P.: In search of better route guidance instructions. Ergonomics **41**(7), 1000–1013 (1998)

18. Meilinger, T., Knauff, M.: Ask for directions or use a map: a field experiment on spatial orientation and wayfinding in an urban environment. Spat. Sci. **53**(2), 13–23 (2008)

19. Denis, M., Pazzaglia, F., Cornoldi, C., Bertolo, L.: Spatial discourse and navigation: an analysis of route directions in the city of Venice. Appl. Cognit. Psychol. **13**(2), 145–174 (1999)

20. Michon, P.-E., Denis, M.: When and why are visual landmarks used in giving directions? In: Montello, D.R. (ed.) COSIT 2001. LNCS, vol. 2205, pp. 292–305. Springer, Heidelberg (2001). https://doi.org/10.1007/3-540-45424-1_20

21. Brosset, D., Claramunt, C., Saux, E.: A location and action-based model for route descriptions. In: Fonseca, F., Rodríguez, M.A., Levashkin, S. (eds.) GeoS 2007. LNCS, vol. 4853, pp. 146–159. Springer, Heidelberg (2007). https://doi.org/10.1007/978-3-540-76876-0_10

22. Lovelace, K.L., Hegarty, M., Montello, D.R.: Elements of good route directions in familiar and unfamiliar environments. In: Freksa, C., Mark, D.M. (eds.) COSIT 1999. LNCS, vol. 1661, pp. 65–82. Springer, Heidelberg (1999). https://doi.org/10.1007/3-540-48384-5_5

23. Sadalla, E., Burroughs, W., Staplin, L.: Reference points in spatial cognition. J. Exp. Psychol. Hum.Learn. Mem. **6**(5), 516–528 (1980)

24. Allen, G.L.: From knowledge to words to wayfinding: issues in the production and comprehension of route directions. In: Hirtle, S.C., Frank, A.U. (eds.) COSIT 1997. LNCS, vol. 1329, pp. 363–372. Springer, Heidelberg (1997). https://doi.org/10.1007/3-540-63623-4_61

25. Brosset, D., Claramunt, C., Saux, E.: Wayfinding in natural and urban environments: a comparative study. Cartographica **43**(1), 21–30 (2008)

26. Schwering, A., Li, R., Anacta, V.: orientation information in different forms of route instructions. In: Danny Vandenbroucke, B. (ed.) Proceedings on The 16th AGILE International Conference on Geographic Information Science (2013)

27. Winter, S.: Communication about space. Trans. GIS, Guest Editor. **8**(3), 291–296 (2004)

28. Dalton, R.: The secret is to follow your nose: route path selection and angularity. Environ. Behav. **35**(1), 107–131 (2003)

29. Elias, B.: Extracting landmarks with data mining methods. In: Kuhn, W., Worboys, M.F., Timpf, S. (eds.) COSIT 2003. LNCS, vol. 2825, pp. 375–389. Springer, Heidelberg (2003). https://doi.org/10.1007/978-3-540-39923-0_25
30. Dräger, M., Koller, A.: Generation of landmark-based navigation instructions from open-source data. In: Proceedings of the 13th Conference of the European Chapter of the Association for Computational Linguistics, Stroudsburg, PA, USA, pp. 757–766 (2012)
31. Rousell, A., Hahmann, S., Bakillah, M., Mobasheri, A.: Extraction of landmarks from OpenStreetMap for use in navigational instructions. In: Proceedings of the 18th AGILE Conference on Geographic Information Science, Lisbon, Portugal (2015)
32. Duckham, M., Winter, S., Robinson, M.: Including landmarks in routing instructions. J. Locat. Based Serv. 4(1), 28–52 (2010)

The Influence of Animacy and Spatial Relation Complexity on the Choice of Frame of Reference in German

Katarzyna Stoltmann[1,2(✉)], Susanne Fuchs[2], and Manfred Krifka[1,2]

[1] Humboldt-University, 10099 Berlin, Germany
[2] Leibniz-Center General Linguistics (ZAS),
Schützenstr. 18, 10117 Berlin, Germany
{stoltmann, fuchs, krifka}@leibniz-zas.de

Abstract. Robotics and automatization have become a part of our everyday life. This often involves locating and moving objects in space, hence spatial expressions are of great importance for any human-machine interface. Improper interpretation of spatial terms, for instance in medicine, can have enormous consequences. Thus, it is important to understand how humans perceive and describe spatial relations. This article discusses the impact of animacy of reference objects. We test whether animacy of the reference object itself, or in the presence of an animate agent, influences the way participants interpret spatial relations. Our experimental results (mouse tracking, 46 German speakers) show that participants interpret spatial relations with a localized object in front of or behind an animate reference object more frequently with respect to the intrinsic frame of reference than with an inanimate reference object. In contrast, in spatial relations of the second horizontal axis (left versus right), participants interpreted the situations more frequently using the intrinsic frame of reference with an inanimate reference object. When another agent is present, we observe a perspective shift from intrinsic to relative. We conclude that the animacy of an intrinsic reference object as well as the introduction of an agent lead to perspective changes.

Keywords: Spatial cognition · Frames of reference · Mouse tracking

1 Introduction

Describing the location of an object with respect to a reference object can be tricky. While the vertical axis (above/below) is uncontroversial in everyday situations where this axis is defined by gravity, different options arise with the first horizontal axis (in front of/behind) and the second horizontal axis (to the right of/to the left of) (e.g. [1–4]). This depends on whether the reference object has an intrinsic reference frame that distinguishes between a front and a back side, and a right and a left side. This is the case with many everyday reference objects, such as cupboards, and is particularly relevant for higher animate objects, like dogs or people. An entity can be described by a speaker as being located in front of a cupboard, because it is in between the speaker and the cupboard, or as being located behind the cupboard if it is closer to the intrinsically

© Springer Nature Switzerland AG 2018
S. Creem-Regehr et al. (Eds.): Spatial Cognition 2018, LNAI 11034, pp. 119–133, 2018.
https://doi.org/10.1007/978-3-319-96385-3_9

defined back side of the cupboard. This has been established in previous research; it is also well-known that speakers of different languages may have different preferences (e.g. [4–6]).

The present study deals with two questions: First, we investigate whether the location strategies are influenced by the animacy of the reference object. With reference objects that have a front/back asymmetry, we hypothesize that animate reference objects more easily evoke an intrinsic frame of reference, as speakers more easily assume the perspective of the reference object. Second, we investigate the question as to whether the mere presence of another person whose perspective is not aligned with that of the speaker has an influence on the location strategies. We hypothesize that the presence of another person leads to identification with the perspective of that other person, and hence allows a location strategy that is relative to that person.

As for their ability to serve as reference objects, entities can be divided into those without intrinsic orientation, like balls, which are symmetric with respect to all axes, and others that have an intrinsic orientation, which are characterized by asymmetries with respect to some or all axes. There are objects that show an asymmetry with the vertical axis (above-below, e.g. tables), with the first horizontal axis (front-back, e.g. cupboard) or the second horizontal axis (left-right, e.g. cars). In his groundbreaking work on the linguistics of spatial reference, Hill proposes a rule that if an object possesses an orientation towards the first horizontal axis, it also does so along the vertical axis, that is, that the vertical axis is most prominent (e.g. [5, 7]). It is possible to spontaneously assign sides to objects which are symmetrical relative to all spatial axes (e.g. [5, 8, 9]). Animate objects, like persons, have a vertical and a first and second horizontal axis specified. This is in spite of the fact that most animates appear symmetric in the second horizontal axis (exceptional cases are, for example, lobsters with claws of different sizes).

Humans can allocate sides to intrinsic objects using one of two strategies: first, the intrinsic perspective (e.g. in the case of vehicles that are driven by a person and get their intrinsic orientation from the speaker's imagination of sitting in the car) and second, the relative perspective for other objects. One important subclass comprises so-called vis-à-vis objects that are typically faced from a particular side when used, such as cupboards (e.g. [10–12]). If the reference object is animate, speakers can identify with them and take on their perspective, a phenomenon of Theory of Mind (e.g. [13]).

In previous research, scientists have shown that animacy is important for the description of several spatial relations in different languages. Feist [14] as well as Feist and Gentner (s. [15, 16]) suggest that animacy of the reference and the localized object affects the choice of the preposition in the particular spatial relation. Specifically, Feist [14] points out that spatial relations with animate reference objects are described more frequently with the preposition *in* than spatial relations with inanimate reference objects, because the animate reference object better serves as a container. Similarly, Bowerman [17] observes that the animacy of localized objects influences the use of spatial prepositions such as *aan* in Dutch.

Baltaretu et al. [18] conducted an acceptability rating experiment in which the authors explored participants' preferences for specific reference objects. The results of their study provide evidence that the participants preferred spatial relations in which an animate reference object was mentioned first. In contrast, the production study of

Baltaretu and colleagues does not indicate any effects of animacy on spatial relation description [18], suggesting differences between production and perception.

Hüther et al. [19] investigated the influence of animacy in generic and medical (animate) contexts, testing students of medicine and law in different semesters. In an online survey, participants were asked to select which of the situations best fit the description. The results show that the medical students interpreted the medical situation with humans as reference objects more frequently with respect to the intrinsic frame of reference than law students did. Given the importance of spatial descriptions in medicine, it is surprising that only 44.2% of the beginners and 49.8% of the advanced medical students chose the intrinsic perspective. The rest used one of the strategies of relative perspective. Furthermore, the results show that on average only 26% of all law students interpreted the spatial relations with a human as reference object along the intrinsic frame of reference.

The current study investigates the influence of animacy in spatial relations in two aspects: First, we investigated the influence of inanimate and animate reference objects on the interpretation of spatial terms. Second, we investigated the interpretation of terms attributed to an (animate) person. The originality of our approach lies in the exploration of the interpretation of the dimensional spatial expressions pertaining to the first horizontal axis 'in front of'/'behind' as well as the second horizontal axis 'to the right/left of' in German using mouse tracking as an experimental method. We hypothesized that animacy of the reference object (dog vs. cupboard) does influence the choice of the frame of reference for interpreting spatial relations in German native speakers (first hypothesis). Furthermore we also investigated the stability of the participants regarding the intrinsic perspective choice in more complex intrinsic relations with a cupboard as a reference object (supplemented by a person vs. without a person). Complex situations are those with the inclusion of an agent *Hans* in the scenario; simple situations do not include the agent. We hypothesize that this scenario influences the choice of reference, even though the attribution to the agent is by indirect speech (second hypothesis). The motivation is again that speakers take on the perspective of other animate agents. Note that the current study does not deal with the possible influence on the choice of reference by the position and orientation of an addressee.

This study serves as further evidence for the influence of language and culture on the conceptualization of spatial relations and cognition in general (e.g. [1, 4, 20, 21]). To examine these issues, we conducted a survey in which we investigated the assignment of sides to the canonically and non-canonically positioned cupboard (Sect. 2). The results of the survey serve as a baseline for the data analysis of the mouse tracking experiment (Sect. 3). Within the results, we defined an interpretation hierarchy for the dimensional spatial expressions of German, depending on the situation (Sect. 3.2).

2 Preliminary Study: Identifying Sides

2.1 Motivation and Experimental Design

In a preliminary study, we sought to obtain a general baseline for the assignment of spatial locations to an intrinsic reference object. Participants were asked to identify the four sides to a cupboard on a simple drawing. The drawing matched the reference object and the general situation in the later experiment. There were two conditions in which the cupboard was placed. In the first, the cupboard was placed canonically, i.e. with the front side towards the participants, and in the second, it was placed non-canonically, i.e. with the back side towards the participants (see Fig. 1). 30 German native speakers participated in the survey: 23 women and 7 men, with a mean age of 30.7 years. All of them also took part in the mouse tracking experiment.

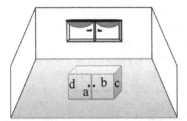 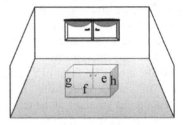

Fig. 1. The figures visualize the illustrations of the cupboards with the front side (left image) and the back side (right image) towards the viewer.

It was expected that in the spatial relations with canonical positioned cupboard, the participants would assign the following sides to the cupboard with respect to the outside perspective of the intrinsic frame of references (s. [10, 11, 22] later on, we will use only outside perspective): (a) front side, (b) back side, (c) right side, (d) left side (Fig. 1, left). Transferred to the non-canonical positioned cupboard (Fig. 1, right), (e) would be associated with the front side, (f) the back side, (g) the right side and (h) the left side.

The survey was designed to provide evidence as to whether participants recognize a cupboard as a *vis-à-vis* or *vehicle* intrinsic object or rather as an *extrinsic* object by assigning the sides along the *align*, *reflection* or *rotation* strategy (e.g. [1, 19]. Furthermore, it provides a baseline for the question whether participants conduct a mental rotation (e.g. [23]) for the assignment of the front and back sides as well as whether they assign the positive (right) and negative (left) sides of the second horizontal axis egocentrically.

2.2 Results

We found that participants almost exclusively assign *front* and *back* in the expected direction. If the cupboard was placed in the *canonical position*, all participants (100%) chose (a) (see Fig. 1) for the front side, and (b) for the back side. If the cupboard was placed in the *non-canonical position*, 97.7% of the participants selected (e) for the front side and (f) for the back side.

Participants differed in their use of the second horizontal dimension, *left* and *right*. When the cupboard was positioned *canonically*, 13% of the participants assigned *left* to (c) and *right* to (d), conducting a mental rotation of 180°. If the cupboard was located *non-canonically*, even more participants, 33.3%, deviated from the expected strategy ad assigned *left* to (g) and *right* to (h).

These results serve as a baseline. In the next section, we will show to what extent these answers also match up with the simple and complex situations in the mouse tracking experiment.

3   Mouse Tracking Experiment

3.1   Methodology

Participants. The experiment was conducted at the Leibniz-Center General Linguistics (ZAS) in Berlin. 46 native speakers of German (33 females and 13 males) took part in the experiment. Participants were between 19 and 60 years old, with a mean of 28.9 years.

Experimental Procedures and Tasks. The study consisted of a mouse tracking experiment. The data were recorded with MouseTracker (Freeman and Ambady [24]). This technique records and visualizes the participants' hand movements while choosing one of the multiple response possibilities in a lexical decision task. It reflects aspects of the cognitive processes that influence the decision between stimulus and completed action (e.g. [25, 26]). Generally, the movement trajectories are used to compute the Maximum Absolute Deviation (MAD) and the Area under the Curve (AUC) with respect to the straight movement from the base position to the target. The greater the MAD and AUC values are, the more uncertain a person is about her answer.

To familiarize the participants with the task, three different trials with a lexical classification task were shown. These trials were not related to the topic of space and language. The practice trials were carried out without time constraints and the participants had the opportunity to ask questions regarding the methodology. After these practice trials, the actual experiment started. Participants were asked to interpret spatial expressions which they may face in everyday situations.

For the experiment, a within-subject design was used as displayed in Fig. 2. Figure 2 displays two parts of the experiment, separated by the two frames. To investigate the first hypothesis, a simple situation was used with an *inanimate* reference object (cupboard) and an *animate* one (dog). Both references could be visible viewed from either the front or the back side (shown only from the front side in Fig. 2). Participants had the task of answering the simple interrogative sentence: „Wo steht die Flasche? "(*Where is the bottle standing?*). The response alternatives were the same, but their order on the computer screen was randomized.

In the simple spatial relations, participants saw the following four response alternatives:

- in front of/behind/to the right of/to the left of the **cupboard**
- in front of/behind/to the right of/to the left of the **dog.**

The presentation of each trial began with showing a START button in the center of the screen and four responses in the four corners of the screen. After pressing the button the interrogative sentence was presented on the computer screen followed by the picture. This setup is similar to the experiment in Stainfeld and Zwaan [27]. After every 20 trials, an additional sign for a break appeared. During this period, participants were asked to take a short break if needed and press enter when they were ready to continue.

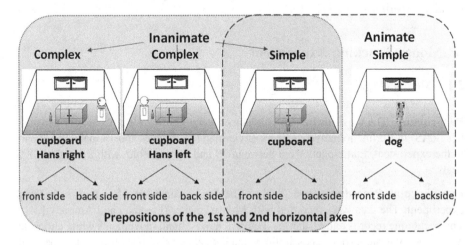

Fig. 2. Mouse tracking: experimental design

To investigate the second hypothesis, a cupboard was used as an inanimate reference object, but the situational complexity varied (see Fig. 2). The simple situations were as described earlier, while in the complex situations an additional agent called *Hans* was introduced. Hans was placed on either the left or the right side of the reference object. Participants had to react to the sentence *Hans sagt, dass die Flasche steht* ... 'Hans says that the bottle is standing ...'. In the complex situations, participants saw four response alternatives:

- in front of/behind/to the right of/to the left of the **cupboard**.

The experiment included 248 sentences in total. Additionally, 113 sentences (≈31%) were added as filler items.

The technique of mouse tracking, in contrast to a simple questionnaire study or a reaction time experiment, allows us to observe complex decision processes. Note, for example, that in the case of Hans and bottle standing on the left (see Fig. 2), four responses are possible:

- *"behind"* the cupboard (corresponding to the interpretation with respect to the align strategy of the relative frame of reference)
- "in front of" the cupboard (corresponding to the reflection strategy of the relative frame of reference)

- "to the left of" the cupboard (corresponding to the interpretation with respect to the intrinsic frame of reference)
- "to the right of" the cupboard (corresponding to the interpretation with respect to the inside perspective of the intrinsic frame of references).

Data Preprocessing and Statistical Analyses. The data were preprocessed with mousetrap, an integrated, open-source mouse tracking package [28] that allows the data from all participants to be merged and several parameters to be calculated while providing the source code. Three different variables were calculated: the *response* (left, right, in front of, behind), the *Maximum Absolute Deviation* (MAD), and the *Area under the Curve* (AUC) of the hand trajectories. All statistical analyses were carried out in R (version 3.4.2 [29]) using the packages lme4 [30] and ggplot2 [31].

First Hypothesis. Animacy of the reference object affects the interpretation of spatial relations between the localized and reference objects.

We will first report the categorical answers and then describe the results for the continuous measures of the mouse trajectories. The categorical answers are given in the upper bar plots in Fig. 3 (canonical positioning) and Fig. 4 (non-canonical positioning).

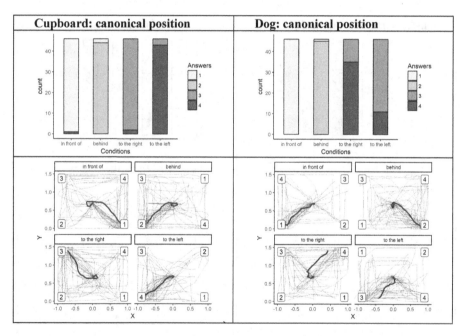

Fig. 3. Answers for the simple intrinsic relation with cupboard and dog viewed from the front side: upper plots: bar plots with counts of answers; lower plots: mouse trajectories during the response with the mean trajectories in bold. The numbers correspond to the following: 1 = in front of, 2 = behind, 3 = to the right of, 4 = to the left of.

The bar plots for the categorical response selection show some differences in animacy regarding the intrinsic frame of reference (Fig. 3). The largest differences are visible for the interpretation of the bottle to the right and left regarding the canonical positioned reference objects. A Fisher's exact test revealed highly significant differences between both reference objects and positions (p < 0.001). No significant differences were found in categorical judgements of the other cases.

Several linear mixed effects models were run using one of the continuous factors MAD or AUC. The final model (with the lowest AIC value which was significantly better than the others) consisted of *animacy* (animate versus inanimate), *side* (canonical versus non-canonical), and *position of the localized object* (bottle in front of, behind, to the right of, to the left of the reference object) as independent factors, the interactions (animacy * side, animacy * bottle, side * bottle), and participant as random effect. Two significant effects were found for the MAD, a main effect for the position of the bottle (behind versus in front of t = 2.614, p = 0.009), and an interaction between the side and the position of the bottle (t = −2.91, p = 0.004). Participants were more uncertain (showed greater MAD values) when they saw the reference objects in the canonical position than in the non-canonical one and the bottle was placed behind vs. in front of the reference object. No effect of animacy was found.

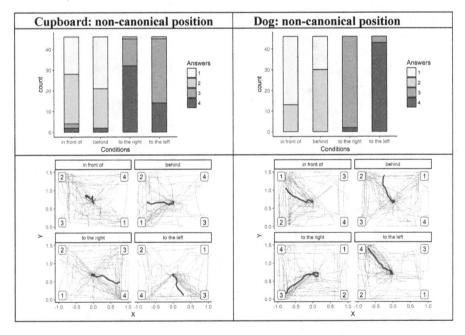

Fig. 4. Answers for the simple intrinsic relation with cupboard viewed from the back side: bar plots with answer counts (above) and trajectories during the response with the mean trajectories in bold (below). The numbers correspond to the following: 1 = in front of, 2 = behind, 3 = to the right of, 4 = to the left of.

For the non-canonical position (Fig. 4), it is evident that, overall, participants show more variable responses when interpreting spatial relations with the inanimate object. This result differs from the animate reference object, where participants decided more consistently that the bottle was *to the right of* and *to the left of* the dog. A Fisher's exact test revealed significant differences for animacy and both positions with $p < 0.001$. This also applies to the first horizontal dimension (in front of vs. behind) and the both reference objects.

Each of the investigated spatial relations elicited a variety of responses. This is supported by the selected answers as well as by the trajectories leading to the responses. The mean trajectories appear between different responses. This is most striking for the spatial relation with the bottle behind the cupboard. Larger MAD values, i.e. more uncertainty, were found when the bottle was placed in front of the reference object than when it was behind the reference object. Animacy did not affect the MAD values and no significant differences were found for AUC.

Second Hypothesis. The presence of an agent in a spatial relation causes a perspective shift from the intrinsic to the relative. More specifically, in our spatial relations we hypothesize a shift from outside perspective of the intrinsic frame of references to reflection strategy of the relative frame of references. Later on, we will use only reflection strategy.

To test this hypothesis, different situations with more (an additional agent Hans, a reference and a localized object) or less complex (a reference and a localized object only) scenarios were compared. For the complex situations, all spatial relations between the localized and reference object were the same, except for an additional agent placed either on the left or right side of the cupboard. The aim of this part was to determine whether or not the participants change the perspective from intrinsic to relative. As above, we will first report the categorical responses and then the outcomes for the continuous measures of the mouse trajectories.

For the simple situation, it was found that German native speakers consistently interpreted the canonically positioned cupboard with respect to the outside perspective. In contrast, if the cupboard was placed non-canonically, participants had problems in all spatial relations and frequently used the reflection strategy.

The statistical results of the Fisher's exact test show highly significant effects for complexity ($p < 0.001$). This result indicates that the German native speakers selected the outside perspective more frequently in the simple spatial relations than in the complex one. In the latter situations, participants shifted the perspective to the agent and interpreted the constellations from his point of view with respect to the reflection strategy. Furthermore, a detailed analysis has shown that significant differences were found in all spatial relations with canonical but not with non-canonical positions. The Fisher's exact test revealed for all canonical relations (*in front of, behind, to the right of, to the left of*) with respect to complexity ($p < 0.001$). However, for the non-canonical spatial relations, the Fisher's exact tests indicated no significant differences for complexity, i.e. a similar number of participants chose the same answers in simple and complex conditions. This is also visible on the bar plots in Figs. 4 and 5.

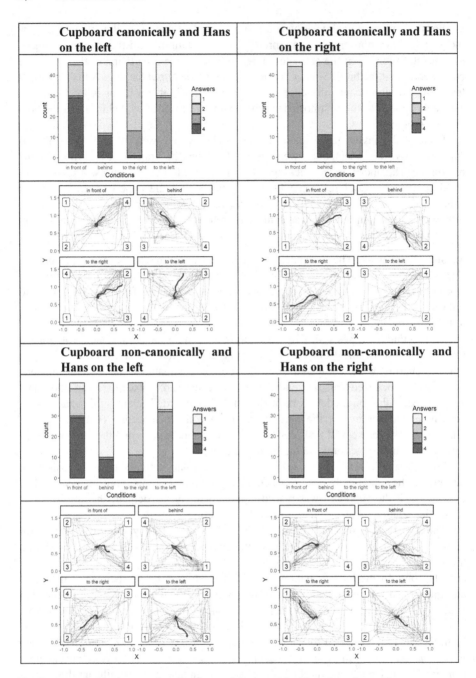

Fig. 5. Answers for the complex situation supplemented by Hans: bar plots with answer counts (above) and trajectories during the response with mean trajectories (below). The numbers correspond to the following: 1 = in front of, 2 = behind, 3 = to the right of, 4 = to the left of.

Several linear mixed effect models were run with either MAD or AUC as the dependent variable and *situation* (*s*imple vs. complex & Hans on the left, complex & Hans on the right), *side* (reference object with canonical versus non-canonical side to the participants), and *position of the localized object* (bottle in front of, behind, to the right of, to the left of the reference object) as independent factors as well as two-way interactions and subject as a random effect. For the MAD values, an interaction between situational complexity and side was found (t = 2.322, p = 0.020). In the simple situation, mouse trajectories deviated more when the cupboard was presented canonically rather than non-canonically. In the complex situation, the effect of side changed, i.e. more deviations were visible when the cupboard was presented non-canonically. The AUC values showed no significant differences.

To sum up, up to 83% of participants chose the reflection strategy from Hans' point of view. That means that in these situations participants shifted the origo from the cupboard to Hans' viewing direction. Moreover, it also means that these participants shifted the perspective, and therefore the second hypothesis should be accepted: The presence of an agent in a spatial relation causes a perspective shift from the intrinsic to the relative.

3.2   Discussion

Does animacy influence the choice of frame of reference in German?

In our mouse tracking study, we investigated whether the animacy of a reference object influences the choice of the reference frame. Additionally, we explored the process which occurred while selecting the answer. For this, we compared spatial relations with a cupboard as a representative of inanimate entities and with a dog as an animate entity. A bottle served as a localized object, which was positioned either *in front of*, *behind*, *to the right of*, or *to the left of* the reference object individually. The results of our study clearly show that the reference object's animacy significantly affects the perspective choice regarding the responses of the first horizontal axis. For the animate object, 74% of the participants selected an answer from the intrinsic perspective (in front vs. behind) and only 41% chose the respective spatial relations with the inanimate object. However, we did not find any significant differences for spatial relations of the second horizontal axis in general, only for the canonical position. Moreover, participants interpreted the situations more frequently in terms of the intrinsic frame of reference when the object was inanimate. This result is surprising due to the fact that a dog possesses clear sides of the second horizontal axis while a cupboard does not.

The results of our study support and expand upon the assumption of Bowerman [17] (for the preposition *aan*), Feist and Gentner [15] (for *in*), Feist [14], Hüther et al. [19], and Baltaretu et al. [18] that the animacy influences the choice of the spatial expression. However, this is true only with respect to the choice of spatial expressions of the first horizontal axis *in front of* and *behind* and not of the second horizontal axis in the case of German.

Results also reveal that categorical answers provide different results than online measures of decision making. In particular, the hypothesized effect of animacy of the reference object was only present in the responses, but not in the parameters reflecting the decision making process.

However, analyzing the trajectory plots in detail, we were able to recognize some trends with respect to animacy. For the canonically positioned reference objects, German native speakers did not show any doubts interpreting the bottle in front of the dog, whereas their trajectory deviated from the ideal line in the spatial relations with the cupboard. A trend is also indicated by the mean trajectory for the bottle *to the left* and *right of* one of the reference objects. Here, the German native speakers showed more problems with interpretation of the spatial relations with the dog due to the fact that, for the intrinsic left and right sides of the dog, participants had to conduct a mental rotation while for the cupboard, this was not the case.

For the non-canonical positions of the reference objects, the situation changes, because the view directions of the dog and the participants match. Therefore, it is less complicate for the participant to take on the perspective of the dog. The right and left sides of the dog coincide with the right and left sides of the participants and no mental rotation is needed for the interpretation. This does not apply to the cupboard. The mean trajectories to the responses "to the right of the dog" and "to the left of the dog" are almost ideal, whereas this is not the case for the cupboard.

The parameter Area Under the Curve (AUC) did not reveal any differences in comparison to Maximum Absolute Distance (MAD). This may be due to the fact that four answers were possible and participants can in principle move the mouse in a circle during their decision making.

Furthermore, we investigated whether German native speakers assign sides to cupboards and how they interpret spatial relations with cupboards as a reference object with and without the presence of an additional agent. The results showed that significantly more participants assigned the sides to the cupboard (62%) with respect to the outside perspective in the survey than in the mouse tracking experiment (max. $\approx$28.3%). The finding may also be affected by the nature of the task. In contrast to the mouse tracking experiment, in the survey, no bottle was present. In the survey, participants were asked to assign the sides to the cupboard directly and in the mouse tracking to interpret a spatial relation between a cupboard as a reference object and a bottle as a localized object using the dimensional spatial expressions. These results can be compared to a previous survey study on 75 German speakers [4]. In this experiment, the task was "Put the bottle in front of/behind/to the right of/to the left of the cupboard". Pursuant to Wunderlich [32], spatial relations of the first horizontal axis are described with dynamic verbs with respect to the relative perspective and with static verbs using the intrinsic perspective. Results of the study show that almost all participants interpreted situations of the first and second horizontal axis and a canonically positioned cupboard as a reference object using the outside perspective. When the cupboard was placed non-canonically, far fewer participants chose the outside perspective (only 48% for *to the right of* and $\approx$41% for *to the left of*).

Looking at these results in total, an interpretation hierarchy can be determined: Most participants selected the outside perspective in the survey of the current study ($\approx$62%), where the participants were asked to assign the sides to the cupboard and not to interpret a spatial relation with the object. This point arises as an important factor.

The results of the survey [4] appear in second position (≈41%) regarding the intrinsic spatial interpretations.

Only 28% of the participants in the mouse tracking study opted for the outside perspective. In contrast to the survey, the participants were asked to interpret a situation with a bottle and a cupboard directly. This means they saw the localized as well as the reference object and were asked to interpret a static relation.

Furthermore, our mouse tracking results provide evidence for a perspective shift when an additional agent is present. In the complex situation, the selection rate of the intrinsic reference frame decreased significantly with respect to the simple situation. Most participants shifted the origo to Hans' point of view and interpreted the spatial relations using the reflection strategy (up to 76.1%). Our results also show that the perspective shift depends on the spatial relations. Participants selected the outside perspective more frequently when the bottle was positioned along the first horizontal axis than along the second one.

In a next step, this study will be extended to additional languages to find the similarities and differences among languages and cultures.

Acknowledgment. This work was supported by a grant from the BMBF (Ministry of Education and Research, 01UG1411) as well as Leibniz Association to all authors. We would like to thank Olivia Maky for proof reading and Luke Tudge for statistical advice and our participants.

References

1. Levinson, S.C.: Space in Language and Cognition. Cambridge University Press, Cambridge (2003)
2. Tenbrink, T.: Reference frames of space and time in language. J. Pragmat. **43**(3), 704–722 (2011)
3. Tenbrink, T., Dylla, F.: Sailing: cognition, action, communication. J. Spat. Inf. Sci. **15**, 3–33 (2017). http://www.josis.org/index.php/josis/article/viewFile/350/189
4. Stoltmann, K.: Stelle die Flasche vor den Tisch! Interpretation von dimensionalen Lokalisationsausdrücken im DE, EN, IT und PL. In: Raumlinguistik und Sprachkontrast. Neue Beiträge zu spatialen Relationen im Deutschen, Englischen und Spanischen, pp. 251–267 (2014)
5. Hill, C.: Up/down, front/back, left/right. A contrastive study of Hausa and English. In: Here and There. Cross-linguistic Studies on Deixis and Demonstration, pp. 13–42, Amsterdam, Philadelphia, Benjamins (1982)
6. Levinson, S.C.: Grammars of Space. Cambridge University Press, Cambridge (2006)
7. Wunderlich, D.: Raum und die Strunktur des Lexikons. In: Perspektiven auf Sprache, pp. 212–231. De Gruyter, Berlin (1986)
8. Herrmann, T., Miller, G.A.: Vor, hinter, rechts und links: das 6H-Modell. Psychologische Studien zum sprachlichen Lokalisieren/In front of, behind, left and right: the 6H-model. Psychological studies in verbal localisation. LiLi.Zeitschrift fürr Literaturwissenschaft und Linguistik **78**(20), 117–140 (1990)
9. Levelt, W.: Zur sprachlichen Abbildung des Raumes: Deiktische und intrinsische Perspektive. In: Perspektiven auf Sprache. Interdisziplinäre Beiträge zum Gedenken an Hans Hörmann, pp. 187–211. De Gruyter, Berlin (1986)

10. Grabowski, J.: Raumrelationen: Kognitive Auffassung und Sprachlicher Ausduck. West-deutscher Velag, Opladen (1999)

11. Grabowski, J., Miller, G.A.: Factors affecting the use of dimensional prepositions in German and American english: object orientation, social context, and prepositional pattern. J. Psycholinguist. Res. **29**, 517–553 (2000)

12. Grabowski, J., Weiß, P.: Das Präpositioneninventar als Determinante des Verstehens von Raumpräpositionen: vor und hinter in fünf Sprachen. In: Deutsch-Typologisch, pp. 289–311 (1996)

13. Perner, J.: Theory of mind. In: Developmental Psychology: Achievements and Prospects, pp. 205–230 (1999)

14. Feist, M.: On in and on: an investigation into the linguistic encoding of spatial scenes (Doctoral dissertation). Northwestern University, Evanston (2000)

15. Feist, M., Gentner, D.: Animacy, control, and the IN/ON distinction. In: Fourteenth National Conference on Artificial Intelligence, Workshop on Language and Space, Providence, RI (1997)

16. Feist, M., Gentner, D.: On plates, bowls, and dishes: factors in the use of English IN and ON. In: Proceedings of the Twentieth Annual meeting of the Cognitive Science Society (1998)

17. Bowerman, M.: The origins of children's spatial semantic categories: cognitive versus linguistic determinants. In: Rethinking Linguistic Relativity, pp. 145–176 (1996)

18. Baltaretu, A., Krahmer, E.J., van Wijk, C., Maes, A.: Talking about relations: factors influencing the production of relational descriptions. Front. Psychol. **7**, 103 (2016)

19. Hüther, L., Müller, T., Spada, H.: Professional experience and referencing context explain variance in use of spatial frames of reference. Appl. Cogn. Psychol. **30**, 580–590 (2016)

20. Boroditsky, L.: Does language shape thought?: Mandarin and English speakers' conceptions of time. Cogn. Psychol. **43**(1), 1–22 (2001)

21. Klippel, A., Wallgrün, J.O., Yang, J., Mason, Jennifer S., Kim, E.-K., Mark, David M.: Fundamental cognitive concepts of space (and time): using cross-linguistic, crowdsourced data to cognitively calibrate modes of overlap. In: Tenbrink, T., Stell, J., Galton, A., Wood, Z. (eds.) COSIT 2013. LNCS, vol. 8116, pp. 377–396. Springer, Cham (2013). https://doi.org/10.1007/978-3-319-01790-7_21

22. Herrmann, T., Grabowski, J.: The dimensional conception of space and the use of dimensional prepositions in different languages. In: Syntax and Semantics, pp. 265–292 (1998)

23. Shepard, R., Metzler, J.: Mental rotation of three-dimensional objects. Science **171**(3972), 701–703 (1971)

24. Freeman, J.B., Ambady, N.: Mousetracker: software for studying real-time mental processing using a computer mouse-tracking method. Behav. Res. Methods **42**(1), 226–241 (2010)

25. Spivey, M.J., Grosjean, M., Knoblich, G.: Continuous attraction toward phonological competitors. In: Proceedings of the National Academy of Sciences of the United States of America, vol. 102, no. 29, pp. 10393–10398 (2005)

26. Tomlinson, J.J.M., Gotzner, N., Bott, L.: Intonation and pragmatic enrichment: how intonation constrains Ad Hoc scalar inferences. Lang. Speech **60**(2), 200–223 (2017)

27. Stanfield, R.A., Zwaan, R.A.: The effect of implied orientation derived from verbal context on picture recognition. Psychol. Sci. **12**(2), 153–156 (2001)

28. Kieslich, P., Wulff, D., Henninger, F., Brockhaus, S.: Mousetrap: an R package for processing and analyzing mouse-tracking data (2016)

29. Team, R.C.: R: a language and environment for statistical computing (computer program). Version 3.4.2. Citeseer 2017. Accessed Oct 2017

30. Bates, D., Maechler, M., Bolker, B., Walker, S., Christensen, R., Singmann, H., Dai, B., Grothendieck, G., Green, P.: Package 'lme4'. R Foundation for Statistical Computing (2017)
31. Wickham, H., Chang, W., Wickham, M.H.: Package 'ggplot2' (2016)
32. Wunderlich, D.: Linguistic strategies. In: Festschrift for Native Speaker, pp. 279–296, Paris, Mouton (1981)

Spatial Discourse Production: Applying Denis's Framework to Non-urban Context

Ekaterina Egorova[✉]

University of Zurich, 8057 Zurich, Switzerland
ekaterina.egorova@geo.uzh.ch

Abstract. This study applies the framework proposed by Denis [5] to analyze the structure and content of online alpine route directions. It first describes methodological challenges associated with the process of generation and classification of propositions in the context of rich spatial discourse. Further, it compares results to previous studies, suggesting that the discourse structure reflects the role of locomotion in mountaineering. In conclusion, the study emphasizes the importance of applying the framework to domains and discourses that go beyond urban route directions.

Keywords: Spatial discourse · Route descriptions
Propositional classes · Non-urban space

1 Introduction

Mountaineering is a unique type of navigation in a structurally specific environment. From the perspective of wayfinding, it is affected by the space structure: natural environments are characterized by curved, irregular and asymmetric shapes. This results in visual diversity, complexity and homogeneity of the environment at the same time [19]. Further, while in urban space one can find the way by matching the symbolic information from the map with the same symbolic information in the "real world", this is hardly possible in natural environments. Borrowing the example of Whitaker and Cuqlock-Knopp, the label Mt. Shasta found on the map will not be displayed in neon letters on top of the actual mountain [29]. From the perspective of locomotion, mountaineering involves multiple sensory (e.g. vision, touch, hearing, vestibular sensing) and motor systems (e.g. climbing). As a result, the spatial properties of the environment are not just seen, but sensed multimodally [20].

Studying mental representations of space resulting from direct environmental experience in the context of mountaineering is important for several reasons. First, it enhances our understanding of how lay people navigate in and communicate about space, adding to the body of knowledge known as Naive Geography [7]. Second, examining activities in settings that go beyond urban and campus-like environments – e.g. orienteering [1] or sailing [26] – has been shown to unveil the role of context in spatial reasoning. Finally, the findings can be incorporated

S. Creem-Regehr et al. (Eds.): Spatial Cognition 2018, LNAI 11034, pp. 134–148, 2018.
https://doi.org/10.1007/978-3-319-96385-3_10

in context-aware assistance services [16,22] and, given the increasing amount of people choosing mountains as a destination for leisure activities [13], can have important practical applications.

However, as with many other types of natural environments, controlled participant experiments in situ would put participants' safety at stake and would most likely be impacted by a large variation of environmental conditions [25]. In this light, online platforms where people share reports of ascents and describe routes represent a wealth of data that can offer an alternative to participant experiments for some research questions. Moreover, as pointed out by Hirtle et al. [11], such data represents natural discourse with a "real-life" communicative goal and thus possesses external validity. Yet, the opportunities and challenges of compiling a corpus based on the type of *space* and using it to examine spatial language (and thus, some aspects of thinking) have so far been largely overlooked.

Egorova et al. [8] analysed alpine route directions and reported how some key elements – decision points and segments, actions and landmarks – are encoded linguistically. This study uses the same corpus to systematically examine the structure of spatial discourse in the same corpus by applying the framework suggested by Denis [5]. The framework is grounded in a proposition (i.e. a minimal information unit) as a unit of analysis and includes five classes of propositions (e.g. "Introducing landmark"). It thus allows for the comparison of the distribution of classes and is widely used to investigate the impact of a variety of conditions on the structure of spatial discourse [1,4,9,21,23]. However, few studies describe methodological steps in detail [5,16] and our first aim is to address this gap by documenting challenges arising from the semantic richness of spatial discourse related to non-urban settings [8]. Our second aim is to investigate aspects of spatial thinking and discourse production in the context of mountaineering through the analysis of the structure of alpine route directions (i.e. distribution of classes of propositions). The two research questions are thus of both methodological and conceptual nature:

1. What are the methodological challenges of applying the framework of Denis [5] to semantically rich alpine route directions? What are the additional challenges arising from the absence of knowledge of routes described?
2. How does the distribution of propositional classes in alpine route directions compare to the findings of previous studies?

2   Related Work

Route directions are widely accepted as an excellent data for studying how people conceptualize space [27] and can be collected "en route" or "not en route" (e.g. in laboratory settings). The two ways involve different cognitive processes [23]. The production of "en route" – or, situational – route directions is rooted in perception and working memory [21]. A "not en route" description process relies on long-term memory, since the speaker has to activate the internal representation of the environment in question in order to plan the route [5,27].

To explore the structure and content of route directions, Denis [5] proposed a framework that provides first general characteristics of this type of spatial discourse. The unit of analysis is a propositional expression[1] – a minimal information unit that includes a predicate and one or two arguments. Route descriptions are thus first transformed into propositions – e.g. "You will arrive at a bridge" is represented by a proposition ARRIVE AT (YOU, BRIDGE). Further, propositions are classified according to the five classes' scheme, grounded in the combination and presence/absence of two main elements of route directions – landmarks and action prescriptions:

Class 1: Prescribing Action Without Reference to Landmark. Propositions in this class contain action prescriptions (e.g. "Turn left")[2].

Class 2: Prescribing Action with Reference to Landmark. Here, propositions contain an action prescription in relation to a landmark (e.g. "Cross the river").

Class 3: Introducing Landmark. In this class, propositions refer to a new landmark without mentioning any action to be executed. Linguistically, they are marked by expressions of the type "There is X", "One finds X", "You will see X".

Class 4: Describing Landmark. Propositions in this class describe non-spatial properties of landmarks and can represent denominations (e.g. "This building is Building 300"), describe visual features (e.g. "It is a big pink colored building"), specify the information content (e.g. "The signpost indicates the campus"), attract attention to landmarks (e.g. "The path is difficult to see").

Class 5: Commentaries. These are statements providing overall summaries of routes (e.g. "Follow the main roads of the campus") and can include metric (e.g. "The route is about 2 km") and pseudo-metric evaluations (e.g. "It will not take long").

This framework has been widely accepted and used in a number of comparative studies of route directions collected under varied conditions (summarized in Fig. 1).

In the first study describing the framework, Denis [5] involved 20 participants to collect oral "not en route" directions for two routes on a university campus in Paris. Apart from establishing the classification scheme, the study demonstrated the central role of landmarks and associated actions. The three related classes (Class 2, 3, 4) accounted together for 86.4% of all propositions. Relatively few instances of Class 1 in comparison to Class 3 and 4 further revealed the cognitive prominence of landmarks. According to Denis, this correlates with the fact that only 1.1% of propositions contained some metric information, reflecting the mainly qualitative reasoning involved in route directions spatial discourse.

---

[1] We will refer to propositional expressions as "propositions" through the paper for convenience.

[2] Definitions and examples of propositional classes are borrowed from Denis [5].

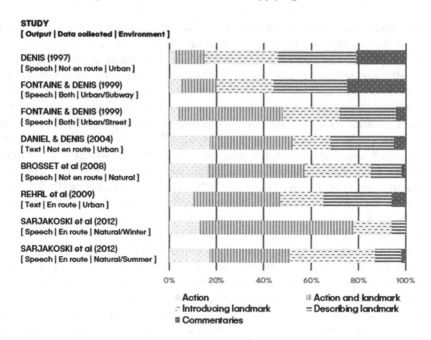

STUDY
[Output | Data collected | Environment]

DENIS (1997)
[Speech | Not en route | Urban]

FONTAINE & DENIS (1999)
[Speech | Both | Urban/Subway]

FONTAINE & DENIS (1999)
[Speech | Both | Urban/Street]

DANIEL & DENIS (2004)
[Text | Not en route | Urban]

BROSSET et al (2008)
[Speech | Not en route | Natural]

REHRL et al (2009)
[Text | En route | Urban]

SARJAKOSKI et al (2012)
[Speech | En route | Natural/Winter]

SARJAKOSKI et al (2012)
[Speech | En route | Natural/Summer]

0%   20%   40%   60%   80%   100%

Action   Action and landmark
Introducing landmark   Describing landmark
Commentaries

Fig. 1. Distribution of five Denis's propositional classes in comparable studies of route directions.

In [9], Fontaine and Denis applied the framework to investigate route directions in a specific "transitional" – urban/underground – context. 48 participants were asked to describe a route from a subway station to a nearby building in Paris. The findings revealed that participants relied heavily on signs as landmarks when providing directions for the underground parts of the route; further, the necessity to describe them resulted in the dominance of Class 2. In parts of directions referring to the outside segments of the route, the distribution of classes was more regular and, in general, more information was provided. Daniel and Denis [4] compared "not en route" directions for a university campus in Paris produced by 40 participants, where one group received standard instructions without any constraints, while the other group was explicitly instructed to provide utmost concise yet informative directions. The authors observe that Class 1 and Class 2 remained least affected, while the proportion of the other three classes was considerably reduced, which confirms the crucial importance of action prescriptions and landmarks in the structure of route directions. Rehrl et al. [21] applied the framework to the data from two "en route" experiments in Vienna and Salzburg, where 20 participants described route choices along four routes directly at decision points. Two noticeable peculiarities in the findings – an increase in the proportion of Class 2 and Class 4 in comparison to previous studies – are explained by the authors as a result of the "en route" nature of experiment.

Two studies have focused on non-urban settings. Brosset et al. [1] examined "not en route" directions provided by 15 orienteers, who were asked to remember and communicate their route at the end of the run. The significant role of Class 4– 27% of all propositions – is interpreted by the authors as a result of simultaneous diversity and "cyclical" nature of environment. Since "many natural entities are frequently present in several places", a detailed description is needed for a correct identification of a particular landscape feature [1, p. 28]. In another study of non-urban settings, Sarjakoski et al. [23] involved 20 participant in an "en route" experiment in a national park in Finland in summer and winter conditions. Class 4 in particular accounted for large proportions – 31% and 33% for summer and winter respectively – which echoes the findings of [1]. Further, the authors highlight the relatively large proportion of Class 5 – 25% for summer and 21% for winter, which differs drastically from all other previous studies.

The framework has thus originated in and been mostly applied to route directions in urban settings. At the same time, expanding the types of investigated settings to include non-urban environments could reveal whether and how previous findings are sensitive to more specific contexts. Indeed, the analysis of spatial discourse related to natural settings has been shown to be semantically very rich [8]. A systematic documentation of challenges and ambiguities associated with the analysis of non-urban discourse is the first step towards the examination of the transferability of the framework (and thus concepts embedded into it) in other contexts.

3   Data and Methodology

The data represents a corpus of alpine route directions compiled manually from a US-based online platform www.summitpost.org. The site's content is created and maintained by its members, who have profiles with basic personal information (e.g. location, age, gender). One section of the website ("Routes") is dedicated to the descriptions of routes, which usually include the following sections: "Getting There", "Route Description", "Essential Gear", "Commentary", "When to Climb", and "Images". The type of the route (i.e. the type of space it runs through) can be selected through an advanced search with search parameters including location (country), route type (e.g., mountaineering, bouldering, scrambling, etc.), rock difficulty, and grade.

We set the route type (mountaineering) and grade (IV and above) as search parameters and thus collected descriptions of routes running on mixed types of terrain (rock, snow, ice) that require certain skills and equipment from a mountaineer. We only included the "Route Description" sections with a length between 350 and 400 words. Referring to the authors' profiles, we ensured that only one text by each author appeared in the corpus, and that the USA was indicated as the author's home country (assuming that would signal a probability of a native speaker of the American English). Data collection and analysis (in particular, generating propositions) were conducted in parallel, and the data collection was stopped the moment the number of propositions was comparable to the average in previous studies, resulting in a corpus of 19 route directions.

The workflow included the following steps: **Step 1** – operationalizing and identifying landmarks in route directions; **Step 2** – rewriting route directions into the canonical imperative form; **Step 3** – generating propositions; **Step 4** – classifying propositions. In general, the procedure as described by Denis [5] was followed closely; ambiguous cases and suggested ways of dealing with them were documented. In what follows, each of the steps is described in detail.

3.1   Step I. Operationalizing Landmarks

In previous studies applying the framework, a landmark is defined as any geographic entity [1,5,16] – that is, "any observed physical, clearly distinguishable permanent feature in the environment" [16, p. 43]. The definition is necessarily inoperative in the context of online alpine route directions. First, in the lack of knowledge of actual spatial layouts being described, it is utterly impossible to judge how *clearly distinguishable* the feature is, although some linguistic markers can provide hints (e.g. "obvious chute", "prominent hill"). Second, in the context of alpine space, the concept *permanent* becomes highly problematic. Snow, seen as a temporal feature in the analysis of protocols collected in the natural park in [15], is quite permanent above certain height in the mountains. Clearly, the way *permanence* has been defined in an urban context – the likelihood of the landmark being present either in form (shape/size etc.) or in label (name, logo, etc.) [2] – cannot be applied to features such as crevasses that constantly change their shape (and thus exact location), unless the fact that they usually have a "general location", as seen in (1a), could be considered as a sign of permanence.

(1)   a.   There are <u>quite a few small, and possibly bigger crevasses</u> on the saddle and also on the way up towards the summit.

A hybrid linguistic approach was developed for identifying landmarks in text for the purpose of this study. On the one hand, all geographic entities (e.g. as represented by landscape terms) are annotated as landmarks based on their semantics alone unless there is a linguistic marker hinting at temporality – e.g. "usually", "in summer", "may", as in (2a–2b). On the other hand, we annotate as landmarks linguistic structures representing the STARTING POINT, TRAJECTOR and GOAL of a MOTION EVENT, as in (2c), or a GROUND in location descriptions, as in (2d).

(2)   a.   <u>At times</u> an ice flow forms up the main gully.

b.   You <u>may</u> hit a buried patch of water ice, rock, or slab.

c.   Drop down into the <u>notch</u>, then climb steep exposed <u>snow</u>. (GOAL, TRAJECTOR)

d.   Above the <u>crater</u> (9,800 feet) the grade becomes steeper. (GROUND)

3.2   Step II. Rewriting Route Directions into the Canonical Imperative Form

In this step, route directions are rewritten into the canonical – imperative – form of an action prescription [5]. Among previous studies, only Denis himself reports on "expressions using the third person" used (in French) for action prescriptions and found in route directions [5, p. 425].

In our study, a wide variety of linguistic structures encode action prescriptions: recommendations starting with "It is important", "It is advisable" (3a), sentences using the indefinite "one" as a subject (3b), passive voice (3c), noun phrases (3d). Rewritten, such prescriptions take the form of imperatives:

(3)   a.   It's a good idea to rope up. – Rope up.

  b.   From the hut one walks... – From the hut walk...

  c.   The ridge crest is followed for 100 m. – Follow the ridge crest for 100 m.

  d.   ...before a detour on to (sic!) the east face. – ...make a detour onto the east face.

While the linguistic structures exemplified above can be easily transformed into the imperative form, two particular phenomena – past tense and fictive motion – prove to be less straightforward to deal with.

Past Tense. Alpine route directions often contain sections written in the past tense, where the route giver switches from providing future-oriented instructions to describing *his or her actions* at a certain route segment *in the past*, when he or she was there. The vague conceptual boundary between the description of the route giver's own action and action prescription is clearly seen in (4a), where the route giver switches from "I" to "you" within one clause. In this study, such instances are treated as implicit action prescriptions (and are rewritten correspondingly) if the spatial information (sequence of route segments) is incomplete without them. For example, if the second sentence referring to the past experience in (4b) is removed, part of the spatial information is lost – namely, the route segment represented by "several hundred feet of 40° snow and neve". The spatial puzzle is then incomplete – where does the "pitch" come from in the third sentence? Hence, the second sentence represents an implicit action prescription.

(4)   a.   I went straight towards the highest point you can see above you.

  b.   Do not traverse out to the right here. Above this we simulclimbed several hundred feet of 40° snow and neve to reach a steep chimney pitch with ice in it. Belay this pitch, then simulclimb several hundred more feet.

Fictive Motion. This phenomenon is quite pervasive in alpine route directions – moreover, it can both imply an action prescription or provide a description of a static scene. The general guiding principle for dealing with this ambiguity is the same as in case with past tense – relying on the wider context to identify if the sequence of route segments is incomplete without this structure. In (5a), fictive motion in the first clause implies the action prescription and is rewritten into the imperative form "Traverse left...". The clause in brackets describes a static spatial layout of a scene and remains in the original form.

(5)   a.   The <u>route traverses</u> left and up below the rock formations to the obvious open chute on your right (also where the <u>West Crater Rim Route joins</u> to the summit).

Clauses Describing Completed Action. These mostly start with "once" or "after" and can be followed by a gerund (6a), a spatial preposition (6b), a goal-oriented path verb (6c), or a verb in the present perfect tense (6d). Such clauses do not prescribe any action, although they do describe a completed action. Essentially, they indicate the STARTING POINT of a new route segment by focusing on reaching the GOAL of the previous segment, usually construing the latter as difficult [8]. Such instances are rewritten into noun phrases starting with the spatial preposition "from", representing the STARTING POINT of a MOTION EVENT:

(6)   a.   After cresting the ridge... – From the ridge...
       b.   Once past the bergschrund... – From the bergschrund...
       c.   Once you top out in the Chute... – From the Chute...
       d.   Once you have crossed the tricky crevassed section... – From the tricky crevassed section...

3.3   Step III. Generating Propositions

In the next step, route directions are rewritten into a standard proposition-like format. Propositions are "minimal information units combining a predicate and one or two arguments" [5, p. 426]. Thus, the above-listed examples (3a–3d) are transferred into the propositions (7a–7d).

(7)   a.   ROPE UP
       b.   WALK (HÖRNLI HUT, HORIZONTALLY)
       c.   FOLLOW (RIDGE CREST, 100 METERS)
       d.   MAKE A DETOUR ONTO (EAST FACE, LEDGE)

However, the process of proposition generation can quickly become less straightforward in instances such as "From this step traverse left to a shoulder", which should theoretically be transformed into two propositions to follow the rule of two arguments maximum: TRAVERSE (STEP, SHOULDER), TRAVERSE (LEFT)[3]. This duplicates the action prescription and potentially affects the class of the proposition – TRAVERSE (LEFT) then belongs to Class 1 (Action without landmark), despite the fact that the action prescription is actually given in relation to two landmarks. None of the previous studies comment on such cases. In this study, such units are rewritten into propositions with three (or, though very rare, four) arguments.

---

[3] Even the chosen combination of arguments can be different.

Furthermore, previous studies do not report on ways of dealing with set expressions (e.g. "weather conditions"), verb phrases of the type "make a traverse", noun phrases indicating parts of entities (e.g. "base of the couloir", "edge of the ledge"). In this study, these were treated as one argument (or predicate, in the case of verb phrases).

3.4   Step IV. Classifying Propositions

A number of ambiguous cases were encountered in the process of classification. First, the definition of Class 4 (Describing landmark) proved to be vague: does "non-spatial" exclude descriptions of spatial properties or spatial relations? Since Denis appears to use the term "non-spatial" [5, p. 427] interchangeably with "non-locating" [5, p. 429], we assumed that Class 4 excludes spatial relations, but allows for *spatial properties* (e.g. "narrow couloir", "30° slopes"). Second, the framework does not provide for *safety- and locomotion-related* propositions (e.g. "This section of the route is exposed to rock fall"). We annotated such propositions as Class 5 (Commentaries), although in Denis's definition Class 5 includes overall summaries of routes, not comments on particular segments.

Two other examples of ambiguous cases encountered in alpine route directions are *description of the landmark's location*, as in (8a)[4], and *description of the observer's location*, as in (8b). Both cases are annotated as Class 3 (Introducing landmark), since the description of their location signals that they are introduced for the first time.

(8)   a.   Set your first belay once past the rock gulley that lies along the main glacier.

   b.   You're now on the famous West Ridge of Forbidden Peak,   one   of the 50 Classic Climbs in North America.

Finally, we also encountered ambiguous cases that were described by Kettunen [16] – in particular, *introducing a route alternative*, as in (9a), and *introducing a landmark with two or more descriptive modifiers*, as in (9b). The same principles of classification were followed in this study.

(9)   a.   ...traverse west...or head up the steep gully...(Class 1: Action without landmark), (Class 1: Action with landmark)

   b.   ...climb steep exposed snow to reach the middle (highest) summit. (Class 3: Introducing landmark), (Class 4: Describing landmark)

An interesting case of ambiguity described by Kettunen is *introducing a fuzzy feature*, e.g. "The forest is dense here", "The path begins to rise steeply" [16].

---

[4] Following Denis [5], examples are expressed in natural language for the sake of readability.

According to the author's rationale, "the feature is boundless" – hence, the proposition represents a landmark description (Class 4), not a landmark introduction. "Feature" refers here not to the forest or the path (these are landmarks in Kettunen's classification), but to their properties in a specific location – the density of the forest and the increasing gradient of the path. There is one major reason for questioning belonging of such propositions to Class 4 (Describing landmark)[5]. Essentially, they do not describe the forest (or the path) as one whole – instead, they refer to its particular *spatial part*, and can be interpreted as an introduction of a landmark of its own on a finer level of granularity. Furthermore, it appears that the key question that one has to ask when allocating such cases to a class relates to the communicative goal. Is the information provided for the purpose of wayfinding or locomotion? In the first scenario (if the forest gets dense, you are on the right way), it can be interpreted as Class 3 (Introducing landmark). In the second scenario (the forest is dense here, it might be more difficult to walk), it should be allocated to Class 5 (Commentaries).

4   Results

The 19 route directions were rewritten into the total of 1165 propositional phrases. Let us have a close look at the propositional classes.

Class 1: Prescribing Action Without Reference to Landmark. This class represents the smallest group (**3.6%**). Not surprisingly, there is only one item referring to reorientation ("Turn right"), which is typical for this class in urban route directions [5]. Most propositions refer to direction or distance associated with a particular route segment. Direction is represented by two types of reference frames: absolute (e.g. "Walk east") and relative (e.g. "Head left") [17]. Relative frame of reference is also used to specify the spatial region within the path (e.g. "Keep to the left"). Distance can be encoded both qualitatively (e.g. "Do not go too far") and by referring to distance units (e.g. "Climb several hundred more feet"). Another frequent type of action prescriptions refers to safe locomotion. These propositions call either for a particular way of locomotion (e.g. "Do not glissade", "Move quickly") or the use of particular equipment (e.g. "Rope up", "Strap up crampons"). Few interesting cases related to wayfinding offer the route recipients to make their own decision concerning the next action (e.g. "Check options") or call for remembering certain places (e.g. "Make a mental note").

Class 2: Prescribing Action with Reference to Landmark. This class constitutes **20.5%** of all propositions. The latter are diverse in terms of the amount and combination of arguments – e.g. they can include multiple landmarks or landmarks along with references to direction or distance. Most of the action prescriptions are represented by verbs of motion. Semantically reach path verbs reflect various conceptualisations of spatial relations between the moving

---

[5] We are setting aside the ontological question of what is not boundless in natural settings [24].

observer and the environment, as well as the spatial properties of the latter: e.g. *ascend, veer, follow, traverse, approach, get closer, attain, obtain, arrive, enter, top out, detour, avoid*. Manner verbs range from general verbs (e.g. *move, go*) to more specific mountaineering jargon, representing certain ways of locomotion (e.g. *downclimb, glissade*). Finally, as in Class 1, one finds action prescriptions related to wayfinding (e.g. "Ignore this valley")[6].

Class 3: Introducing Landmark. Linguistic structures introducing landmarks go beyond the prototypical cases mentioned by Denis [5]: "There is", "One finds", "You will see". On the one hand, landmarks can be introduced by goal-oriented path verbs and verb phrases such as *come across, arrive at, encounter, reach*, as in (10a). On the other hand, adjectives such as *obvious, salient, prominent* strongly mark the introduction of a landmark, as in (10b). However, new landmarks are often not marked in any particular way, which requires following closely the discourse, in order to be able to identify newly introduced discourse entities. Peculiarly, newly introduced landmarks are not necessarily marked by indefinite articles (which is usually the case of new information in discourse), as in case with "ridge" in (10c).

(10) a. Around 6,000 feet you encounter the beginning of the glacier.

   b. From Iceberg Lake ascend the obvious gully to the west.

   c. From this saddle, go south to the narrow ridge that climbs steeply eastward.

This class makes up only **4.5%** of all propositions and is represented by two types, as in case with urban route directions [5]. In the first type, the landmark is introduced without further specification of its location, as in (11a) – such cases are relatively rare. More frequent is the second type where an explicit reference to the landmark's location is provided. The two variants of this type found in urban route directions [5] are also present in alpine route directions. The location of a landmark can be specified through another landmark or a frame of reference (relative or absolute); both are exemplified in (11b). Further, the specification of location in alpine route directions can be done quantitatively – through the reference to the height above the sea level, as in (10a).

(11) a. Once you are on sight of the round shaped turquoise lake...

   b. On your left you can see the end of small valleys/gullies in between sharp rock towers.

Class 4: Describing Landmark. Non-locating landmark descriptions account for **24.5%** of all propositions and refer to the type of surface or terrain (e.g. "icy couloir", "grassy slopes", "snow saddle", "rock gully"), dimension (e.g. "sharp ridge", "narrow couloir", "deep notch"), steepness (e.g. "exposed ridge", "30° slope"), colour (e.g. "red colored peak", "white slabs", "turquoise lake"). Finally,

---

[6] Detailed information on the ways spatial information is encoded in alpine route directions is provided by Egorova et al. [8].

a locomotion-related property – difficulty – is encoded by adjectives and noun phrases such as *moderate, serious, difficult, nasty, easy, awkward, tricky, 4th class.*

Class 5: Commentaries. This class represents almost half of all propositions (**47%**) and includes a wide scope of information relevant in alpine route directions: general spatial layout of the route (12a); experience of previous parties or common practices on the route (12b); type of terrain and technical difficulty of particular route segments, references to potential obstacles and hazards and ways of securing locomotion (12c); descriptions of spots for camping, availability of water and traffic on the route, as well as recommendations on the best season for the route.

(12) a. There's only one straightforward route to the summit.

   b. Most parties belay this part of the climb.

   c. This section of the route is exposed to rock fall.

5   Discussion and Conclusion

This study examined 19 alpine route directions to address two goals: to explore the methodological challenges of applying the framework of Denis [5] to the natural discourse and to compare results to previous findings.

Methodological challenges are of three types – on the level of analytical concepts, on the level of discourse and on the level of content. A good example of the former is the identification of references to landmarks in text – as we have seen, concepts such as *permanent, salient,* and *boundless* become problematic in the context of natural space and in the absence of knowledge of the spatial layouts being described. Previous studies applying the framework examine descriptions of particular known routes. Thus, the coding of data in the study by Sarjakoski et al. [23] is rooted in the team's thorough knowledge of the test area. For example, propositions about forest type are classified as Class 3 or Class 4 depending on how distinct the forest type is[7]. In this study, we had to adopt a linguistically-grounded approach, based on the variety of markers related to the elements of a MOTION EVENT and FIGURE–GROUND relations. Applying this approach, it is still important to be aware of the discrepancy between the system of concepts coming from *spatial semantics* (e.g. TRAJECTOR) and those coming from *spatial cognition* (e.g. landmark).

The second methodological challenge is found on the level of discourse and pertains to the semantic ambiguity inherent to language. Rewriting route directions in the imperative form has unveiled a number of peculiarities – e.g. the use of fictive motion and past tense, both of which can implicitly encode future-oriented instructions. Such cases have not been described in previous work and required a solution (we suggested following the *spatial puzzle* of the route). At

---

[7] It is important to note that this approach also has its limitations, including ignoring potential individual differences in the perception of saliency.

the same time, these discourse peculiarities reveal particular cognitive aspects of spatial discourse production. Thus, the use of fictive motion reflects the conceptual primacy of the spatial entity and its configuration in space, while also influencing the recipient's mental representation of space [18]. Cases where route providers describe their own actions at certain route segments in the past bear strong resemblance to *deictic switches* known in cognitive narratology [6,10]. In alpine route directions, route givers alternate between "was" and "is", "you" and "I", shifting from the deictic center of past events (own experience) to the center of the future act of wayfinding (by the route recipient). This suggests a hybrid nature of alpine route directions which peculiarly blend instructions for the future and a narrative about the past, representing a mental *re-experiencing* [3]. These phenomena require further investigation.

Finally, alpine route directions contain multiple comments related to safety and locomotion. Denis's framework, grounded in discourse related to wayfinding in urban settings, does not provide for such cases. In this study, we allocated such propositions to Class 5 (Commentaries), although the latter includes overall descriptions of the route in Denis's definition [5]. In future studies, it is important to consider if the framework should be expanded to be effectively applied in settings where the role of locomotion is as prominent as the role of wayfinding.

Comparing the distribution of propositional classes to previous studies, three observations should be made. First, the distribution of classes is remarkably irregular: Class 5 represents almost half of propositions, while Class 1 and Class 3 constitute only 2.6% and 4.4%, respectively. At the same time, the ratio between action- and landmark-related propositions is rather close to one-to-one, which echoes previous findings [1,5,21] and confirms the key importance of these two elements. Second, the prevalence of Class 5 (47%) stands in striking contrast to previous studies where it fluctuated between 2% and 5% [4,5,21]. A high proportion of Class 5 is only found in the "en route" study in a national park, where the authors report 25% for summer and 21% for winter conditions [23]. The nature of information in this class is not disclosed, which excludes the possibility for a comparison. Yet in another study of natural settings – that of orienteering [1] – Class 5 constitutes only 5% of the propositions. This suggests that the experimental settings and the activity that wayfinding is embedded into are as important as the type of environment [12,21]. Thus, in [23], the high proportion of Class 5 might relate to the "en route" character of the experiment, while in [1] its low proportion might be explained by the role of wayfinding in orienteering (hence, importance of landmarks and actions). In alpine route directions, the prevalence of Class 5 relates to the role of locomotion in mountaineering (hence, importance of locomotion-related information). Third, the proportion of Class 4 (24.5%) is rather similar to the 27% reported for orienteering, where it is explained by the simultaneous diversity and "cyclical" nature of environment [1]). In alpine route directions, the landmarks' descriptions are provided not only for the purpose of wayfinding (e.g. items related to colour), but also (and predominantly) for the purpose of locomotion (e.g. items related to difficulty, type of terrain, gradient).

Interpreting these results, it is important to remember the existing vagueness of definitions (e.g. Class 4), scheme relaxations that were adopted in this study (e.g. number of arguments in propositions, definition of Class 5), as well as the remaining subjectivity in dealing with some cases. Furthermore, given the nature of the data used in this study, it is important to find a way of verifying the findings in more controlled conditions.

To summarize, Denis's framework [5] provides a widely accepted reference point for comparative analyses of route directions. So far, it has mostly been applied in urban environments. Exploring the transferability of the framework to other settings (but also types of spatial discourse – e.g. [28]) can not only reveal aspects of spatial thinking in various contexts, but also contribute to the refinement of analytical concepts used in this line of research at a meta level [14].

References

1. Brosset, D., Claramunt, C., Saux, E.: Wayfinding in natural and urban environments: a comparative study. Cartograph. Int. J. Geograph. Inf. Geovis. **43**(1), 21–30 (2008)
2. Burnett, G., Smith, D., May, A.: Supporting the navigation task: characteristics of 'good' landmarks. Contemp. Ergon. **1**, 441–446 (2001)
3. Couclelis, H.: Verbal directions for way-finding: space, cognition, and language. In: Portugali, J. (ed.) The Construction of Cognitive Maps. GEJL, vol. 32, pp. 133–153. Springer, Dordrecht (1996). https://doi.org/10.1007/978-0-585-33485-1_7
4. Daniel, M., Denis, M.: The production of route directions: investigating conditions that favour conciseness in spatial discourse. Appl. Cogn. Psychol. **18**(1), 57–75 (2004)
5. Denis, M.: The description of routes: a cognitive approach to the production of spatial discourse. Cahiers de Psychol. Cogn. **16**(4), 409–458 (1997)
6. Duchan, J.F., Bruder, G.A., Hewitt, L.E.: Deixis in Narrative: A Cognitive Science Perspective. Routledge, New York (2012)
7. Egenhofer, M.J., Mark, D.M.: Naive geography. In: Frank, A.U., Kuhn, W. (eds.) COSIT 1995. LNCS, vol. 988, pp. 1–15. Springer, Heidelberg (1995). https://doi.org/10.1007/3-540-60392-1_1
8. Egorova, E., Tenbrink, T., Purves, R.S.: Where snow is a landmark: route direction elements in alpine contexts. In: Fabrikant, S.I., Raubal, M., Bertolotto, M., Davies, C., Freundschuh, S., Bell, S. (eds.) COSIT 2015. LNCS, vol. 9368, pp. 175–195. Springer, Cham (2015). https://doi.org/10.1007/978-3-319-23374-1_9
9. Fontaine, S., Denis, M.: The production of route instructions in underground and urban environments. In: Freksa, C., Mark, D.M. (eds.) COSIT 1999. LNCS, vol. 1661, pp. 83–94. Springer, Heidelberg (1999). https://doi.org/10.1007/3-540-48384-5_6
10. Herman, D.: Spatial cognition in natural-language narratives. In: Proceedings of the AAAI Fall Symposium on Narrative Intelligence, pp. 21–25 (1999)
11. Hirtle, S., Richter, K., Srinivas, S., Firth, R.: This is the tricky part: when directions become difficult. J. Spat. Inf. Sci. **1**, 53–73 (2010)

12. Hirtle, S.C., Timpf, S., Tenbrink, T.: The effect of activity on relevance and granularity for navigation. In: Egenhofer, M., Giudice, N., Moratz, R., Worboys, M. (eds.) COSIT 2011. LNCS, vol. 6899, pp. 73–89. Springer, Heidelberg (2011). https://doi.org/10.1007/978-3-642-23196-4_5

13. Johnston, B.R., Edwards, T.: The commodification of mountaineering. Ann. Tour. Res. **21**(3), 459–478 (1994)

14. Kavouras, M.: Geonoemata elicited: concepts, objects, and other uncertain geographic things. In: Navratil, G. (ed.) Research Trends in Geographic Information Science. LNGC, pp. 17–25. Springer, Heidelberg (2009). https://doi.org/10.1007/978-3-540-88244-2_2

15. Kettunen, P., Irvankoski, K., Krause, C.M., Sarjakoski, T.L.: Landmarks in nature to support wayfinding: the effects of seasons and experimental methods. Cogn. Process. **14**(3), 245–253 (2013)

16. Kettunen, P.: Analysing landmarks in nature and elements of geospatial images to support wayfinding. Finnish Geodetic Institute (2014)

17. Levinson, S.C.: Frames of reference and Molyneux's question: crosslinguistic evidence. In: Bloom, P., Peterson, M.A., Nadel, L., Garrett, M.F. (eds.) Language and Space, pp. 109–169. MIT press, Cambridge (1999)

18. Matlock, T.: Abstract motion is no longer abstract. Lang. Cogn. **2**(2), 243–260 (2010)

19. Montello, D.R.: Navigation. In: Shah, P., Miyake, A. (eds.) The Cambridge Handbook of Visuospatial Thinking, pp. 257–294. Cambridge University Press, Cambridge (2005)

20. Montello, D.R., Freundschuh, S.M.: Sources of spatial knowledge and their implications for GIS: an introduction. Geograph. Syst. **2**(1), 169–176 (1995)

21. Rehrl, K., Leitinger, S., Gartner, G., Ortag, F.: An analysis of direction and motion concepts in verbal descriptions of route choices. In: Hornsby, K.S., Claramunt, C., Denis, M., Ligozat, G. (eds.) COSIT 2009. LNCS, vol. 5756, pp. 471–488. Springer, Heidelberg (2009). https://doi.org/10.1007/978-3-642-03832-7_29

22. Richter, K.: Context-Specific Route Directions: Generation of Cognitively Motivated Wayfinding Instructions. Akademische Verlagsgesellschaft Aka GmbH, Berlin (2008)

23. Sarjakoski, T.L., Kettunen, P., Flink, H., Laakso, M., Rönneberg, M., Sarjakoski, T.: Analysis of verbal route descriptions and landmarks for hiking. Pers. Ubiquit. Comput. **16**(8), 1001–1011 (2012)

24. Smith, B., Mark, D.M.: Do mountains exist? Towards an ontology of landforms. Environ. Plann. B: Plann. Des. **30**(3), 411–427 (2003)

25. Snowdon, C., Kray, C.: Exploring the use of landmarks for mobile navigation support in natural environments. In: Proceedings of the 11th International Conference on Human-Computer Interaction with Mobile Devices and Services (2009)

26. Tenbrink, T., Dylla, F.: Sailing: cognition, action, communication. J. Spat. Inf. Sci. **15**, 3–33 (2017)

27. Tversky, B., Lee, P.U.: How space structures language. In: Freksa, C., Habel, C., Wender, K.F. (eds.) Spatial Cognition. LNCS (LNAI), vol. 1404, pp. 157–175. Springer, Heidelberg (1998). https://doi.org/10.1007/3-540-69342-4_8

28. Vasardani, M., Timpf, S., Winter, S., Tomko, M.: From descriptions to depictions: a conceptual framework. In: Tenbrink, T., Stell, J., Galton, A., Wood, Z. (eds.) COSIT 2013. LNCS, vol. 8116, pp. 299–319. Springer, Cham (2013). https://doi.org/10.1007/978-3-319-01790-7_17

29. Whitaker, L.A., Cuqlock-Knopp, G.: Navigation in off-road environments: orienteering interviews. Sci. J. Orienteer. **8**(2), 55–71 (1992)

Agents, Actions, and Space

Differences and Commonalities in Self-localization Accuracy of Humans and Robots in a Complex Building

Rul von Stülpnagel[1(✉)], Vincent Langenfeld[2],
and Christoph Hölscher[3]

[1] Center for Cognitive Science, Freiburg University,
Hebelstr. 10, 79104 Freiburg, Germany
`rul.von.stuelpnagel@cognition.uni-freiburg.de`
[2] Department of Computer Science, Freiburg University,
Georges-Köhler-Allee 52, 79110 Freiburg, Germany
`langenfv@informatik.uni-freiburg.de`
[3] Chair of Cognitive Science, ETH Zürich,
Clausiusstrasse 59, 8092 Zurich, Switzerland
`choelsch@ethz.ch`

Abstract. We investigated robot and human self-localization abilities in a simulated building with and without landmarks, optimized for humans and robots, respectively. Robot self-localization accuracy was determined by the uniqueness of the current location's spatial properties, as operationalized by simulated laser scans and quantified in isovist analyses. Humans exposed to a virtual simulation relied on qualitative configurational information to localize themselves rather than isovist properties reflecting the local vistas. Landmarks enhanced the self-localization accuracy of both robots and humans, and especially when optimized to the respective needs. Our research highlights challenges for scenarios that encompass robot-human cooperation in regard to spatial orientation and navigation.

Keywords: Self-localization · Spatial ambiguity · Landmarks
Isovist analysis

1 Introduction

Large and architecturally complex buildings (e.g., airports or museums) represent a challenge for both robot and human orientation and navigation. However, the sensor apparatus of humans and robots differs as much as their means to process spatial information. For example, the memory system of robots allows for a precise comparison of the current vista space with all other known vista spaces, whereas the human cognitive system has been found to limit such comparisons [24]. The growing number of human-robot interactions ranging from search & rescue missions [e.g., 18] to navigation assistance [e.g., 28] requires a better understanding of commonalities and differences of humans and robots concerning their representation and processing of spatial information [35].

© Springer Nature Switzerland AG 2018
S. Creem-Regehr et al. (Eds.): Spatial Cognition 2018, LNAI 11034, pp. 151–166, 2018.
https://doi.org/10.1007/978-3-319-96385-3_11

At the core of successful orientation and navigation, self-localization is an essential element of the wayfinding process [6]. "Self-localization" has been addressed (with sometimes differing connotations) in research on robot navigation [e.g., 35] as well as in the context of human spatial cognition [e.g., 24]. We consider self-localization as the ability to correctly identify the own position within a given environment, by linking the spatial information available from the current position to already existing internal or external spatial knowledge. Considering differing sensor systems and processing capacities, focusing on the particular element of self-localization allows a more systematic comparison of humans and robots as compared to testing higher-level wayfinding tasks. An important distinction can be made between indoor and outdoor spaces. However, the availability of GPS has solved most challenges for the outdoor self-localization of robots (but not necessarily for humans), whereas there are several aspects that make indoor navigation particularly challenging, including a higher degree of verticality as well as more narrow and segmented spaces [22, and see 9 for a discussion of this matter]. One of the sensors typically used by robots for indoor navigation are 2D laser scanners, which we therefore set as a representative sensor input in this research.

Taken together, our first aim is to compare human and robot self-localization accuracy at isolated locations within a familiar indoor environment. Furthermore, there have been approaches in both fields to enhance self-localization by enabling the ad-hoc installment of landmarks [2, 4]. Thus, our second goal concerns the question how and where landmarks must be placed to reduce spatial ambiguity (and thus enhance self-localization accuracy) of robots and humans, and to what extent these placements align.

1.1 Robot Self-localization

A robot needs to identify its pose in an environment before any route planning can take place. This task is particularly challenging with incomplete information about the environment's configuration and missing access to external positional (e.g., a GPS signal). Robot navigation research often utilizes the *SLAM* (simultaneous localization and mapping) approach, where a robot navigates an unknown environment while keeping track of its current position. The sensor input (e.g., laser scans) are continuously merged into a metric map of all encountered parts of the environment [8]. Depending on the building's uniformity and size, this process becomes computationally expensive and error-prone. Several researchers enhanced SLAM through the ad-hoc installment of RFID chips at locations identified as ambiguous by the robot [2], or by identifying existing landmarks [13].

Another instance of robot self-localization is the "kidnapped robot scenario", where a robot is in possession of a map of the environment, but has no knowledge about its current location in this environment. The difficulties of restoring orientation after getting lost can be quantified through an algorithm [as introduced by 17]. This algorithm computes the level of uncertainty (or robot U) that a (simulated) laser scan at the current location is confused with a (simulated) laser scans at other locations in the environment.

There have also been approaches to integrate human concepts to the spatial representation of robots. [23] transferred findings on human spatial reasoning to robot self-localization by incorporating information about object occlusion. [35] described a multi-layered process in which the raw sensor data of a robot is transferred into a topological or even conceptual map of an environment suited to human terms of spatial entities [also see 1, 7]. One core element of the approach described in [35] is the identification of doorways as dividers of topological units. Although this approach appears suitable for domestic uses, a potential limitation may be imposed by large-scale buildings with open spaces and relatively few distinctive and small doorways (e.g., airports).

1.2 Human Self-localization

In an early approach of investigating human self-localization in a real-world setting, [31] showed images of buildings from different perspectives to participants, who were instructed to indicate their position on a floor plan outlining the buildings. Correctness of self-localization depended strongly on the orientation of the floorplan [also see 32] included a self-localization task in an indoor wayfinding study featuring different kinds of maps, and found some advantages of schematized maps over floor plans. One conclusion was that self-localization was mainly based on the network structure of the building. This contrasts studies on reorientation, which highlight the relevance of geometric features [e.g., 11]. [24] examined participants' uncertainty about their current location (and thus their ability for self-localization) in a number of virtual mazes. With increasing size of the mazes, participants became unable to update and maintain the set of previous actions and observations due to their limited cognitive resources.

Several studies addressed the relation of self-localization and landmarks. [14] used mobile eye tracking to demonstrate the importance of landmarks referred on a map when attempting self-localization in the real world. In [30], participants were required to return to a specific virtual location after repeatedly studying the location's relation to three landmarks. The authors' findings imply that distance information exceeded angular information. In [25], participants' uncertainty about their current location in a grid-like virtual environment was evaluated in dependency on structural landmarks (i.e., the local environmental layout) and object landmarks (i.e., pictures on the wall). The authors report a bias toward encoding the environmental layout over object landmarks, thus highlighting the importance of an environment's configurational properties for self-localization. In [4], one group of participants installed landmarks at their own discretion for the facilitation of an anticipated search task in a sparse, virtual environment. It can be reasoned these landmarks indicate areas the participants perceived as particularly ambiguous. However, the locations of these landmark were not further investigated in this study. In a very similar setup, the distribution of the individually placed landmarks revealed strong consistencies across all participants [26]. These consistencies imply that there is a supra-individual perception of a location's spatial relevance for the disambiguation of one's location during a wayfinding task.

An approach promising to shed light on human self-localization is the so-called *Space Syntax* method, which transfers an environment' configurational properties into a graph, with the aim of linking the properties of this graph to human perception and behavior [12]. In a *Visibility Graph Analysis* [VGA, 29], an even grid of cells is applied to all accessible spaces of an environment. The area visible from one specific cell forms a so-called *isovist* [3], which can be analyzed for its various metric properties (e.g., the number of other visible cells, or its jaggedness or "spikiness"). These properties have been linked to spatial decision making [34] or stopping behavior during exploration [5]. It appears plausible that some of these features may be relevant during human during self-localization [but see 19]. The concept of isovists also shows a strong resemblance to a robot's sensor input derived from a 2D laser scan. Whereas an isovist quantifies the spatial properties of the local vista, *integration* takes the global relation of a cell to all other cells in the environment into account. Integration has been repeatedly found to be a strong predictor of human navigation [e.g., 20]. Furthermore, both global [10] and local [27] Space Syntax measures appear to be good predictors for the inclusion of landmarks in sketch maps. Thus, we hypothesize that the spatial properties of a specific location as captured by a VGA may affect human self-localization accuracy. It remains to be tested to what extent humans also account for local and global spatial properties when placing landmarks for a disambiguation of this environment [26].

It is frequently assumed that humans prefer topological over metric information for wayfinding and spatial representation [e.g., 10, 21]. This is also reflected in approaches on robot mapping and navigation [15, 35]. The only attempt to quantify topological information and link this information to self-localization we are aware of was reported in [31], who showed that the visibility of corners or unique features allowed predictions about participants' ability to pinpoint their position in relation to a single schematized building. It thus appears plausible that very distinct topological and configurational information is more accessible to human spatial perception than pure metric informa- tion, and may also facilitate self-localization accuracy in a complex indoor environment.

1.3   Aims of This Research

We aim at comparing the commonalities and differences of human and robot self- localization, and at identifying the spatial properties that determine self-localization accuracy. However, sensor apparatus and processing capacities of humans and robots create very different requirements and performances in navigation task including locomotion and wayfinding. Thus, we constrained our investigation to a spatial task allowing a comparison as clear and systematic as possible. More specifically, we compared robots and human ability to localize themselves on a map in a scenario where they possess a generally complete representation of the building, but no knowledge of their current position (resembling to the attempt to restore orientation after getting lost). In order to increase the comparability of robot and human performance, we refrained from using a visually rich environment featuring distinctive landmarks.

In *Stage 1 (No LMs)*, we tested self-localization accuracy of robots and humans without distinctive landmarks. This allowed us to investigate to which extent robots and humans can make use of metric information (based on isovist properties of the current location) and qualitative configurational information (based on attributes of a given room in the environment) for this purpose. Whereas robot self-localization should be tightly linked to isovist properties, we hypothesize that human self- localization might depend more on qualitative configurational information. However, we speculate that if humans take the overall structure of an environment into account, integration as a global measure of centrality could be relevant for human self-localization (but less so for robot self-localization).

There has been converging research how landmarks can facilitate spatial orientation of humans and robots. Thus, the results of Stage 1 were used to determine positions of five landmarks optimizing robot and human self-localization, respectively. The spatial properties of these landmarks may already allow inferences on the specific challenges for robot and human self-localization. Additionally, we tested the self-localization accuracies of robots and humans within the same environment including landmarks optimized for robots in *Stage 2 (Robot LMs)*. *Stage 3 (Human LMs)* corresponded to Stage 2, but featured landmarks optimized for humans. It can be expected that distinctive landmarks in an otherwise visually sparse environment enhance self-localization accuracy in general. It remains to be tested to what extent this enhancement depends on the specific requirements of robots and humans, respectively.

2 Method

2.1 Test Environment

We based our investigation on the layout of a museum (the Tate Gallery London, see Fig. 1). For all following computations, we applied a regular grid of 1×1 m cells on this layout, resulting in a total of 3,101 accessible cells. Robot self-localization accuracy was evaluated on the basis of this 2D floorplan (see *Procedure* for details).

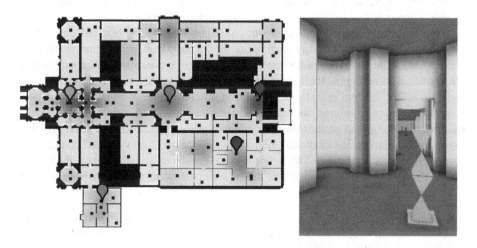

Fig. 1. Left panel: plan of the test environment. Black dots indicate cells used for the evaluation of human self-localization accuracy. The heat map indicates the frequency cells were chosen by participants during the (subjective) landmark placement task in Stage 1 (with darker coloration indicating more placements). Tear-shaped markers indicate the five landmark position optimized for humans used in Stage 3, based on the (objective) self-localization accuracy in Stage 1. Right panel: Illustration of the virtual environment and landmarks used in Stages 2 & 3.

2.2   Procedure

In *Stage 1 (No LMs)*, the layout contained no distinctive landmarks other than provided by the layout itself. We applied robot U [see 17] to quantify robot pose discrimination ability. This measure assumes that a robot's sensor observations (i.e., simulated 2D laser scans) are subject to stochastic errors. It defines the uniqueness of a pose x by the probability of obtaining the same sensor observation as in x from any other pose in the environment, averaged over all other poses. In other words, given a sensor model $p(z|x)$ stating the probability of making observation z when at pose x for every possible observation z and every pose $\bar{x} \in X$ in the environment X, the uniqueness of pose x can be approximated by

$$U(x) = \frac{1}{\int_{\bar{x} \in X} p(z^{x*}|\bar{x})d\bar{x}} \tag{1}$$

with z^{x*} being the most likely observation at pose x. The resulting distribution of robot self-localization accuracy for all 3,101 cells is illustrated in the top left of Fig. 2.

For the evaluation of human self-localization accuracy, participants were to study first-person views in a desktop VR, which featured ambient lighting to support the perception of borders and edges (see Fig. 1), but contained no visually distinctive elements other than provided by the spatial layout itself (with the exception of landmarks in Stages 2 & 3)[1]. Testing localization accuracy for all 3,101 cells was not feasible. In order to account for a wide spectrum of spatial properties, we selected a subset of 100 cells based on maxima and minima of integration, isovist area, isovist jaggedness, and robot U (see Fig. 1). We decided against randomly choosing cells to avoid highly particular locations (e.g., directly in a corner) or an odd distribution (with a large number of test locations being situated in a single room).

Fifteen undergraduates with an about equal gender ratio familiarized themselves with the building's layout in a *training phase*. In the *test phase*, participants studied the 100 selected locations. They were instructed to memorize their surroundings until they felt confident to recognize their location on the floor plan, before being exposed to a location with a random initial orientation and no time limit. Viewing direction was controlled with a computer mouse. The study time until participants pressed the spacebar was logged as an indicator of cognitive processing demands[2]. After pressing the spacebar, participants estimated the location of the previously studied position via mouse click on a floor plan of the environment. Participants could correct their mark before finalizing their decision. Participants' estimates were counted as successful if

---

[1] This displays a change from 2D sensor information for robots to (very basic) 3D information for humans. However, we reasoned that for humans, 2D isovists represent a highly unusual perspective of their surroundings, thus severely impairing their self-localization abilities. Nevertheless, we presented ten pure 2D isovists extracted from the floorplan to participants (thus closely matching the information provided by a simulated laser scan) at the end of Study 1, and asked them to estimate their location within the environment. A qualitative analysis confirmed our initial concerns, with participants choosing basically random locations.

[2] Study times were log-transformed to achieve a better distribution of the data for all statistical analyses, but are reported in seconds below to enhance readability.

they were located within a radius of 15 m (reflecting the limit of clearly distinguishability on the computer screen) and within line of sight of the original location. Next, participants were asked to rate the confidence in their estimate on a 7-point scale (1 = very unsure to 7 = very sure). This procedure was repeated for all 100 locations in random order. After 25 test locations each, participants worked on a landmark placement task where they marked five locations on the floor plan they considered to be most helpful for the self-localization tasks. Participants were informed that these markers were not visible during the following self-localization tasks. The experiment lasted about one hour. Participants received course credit or €7.50.

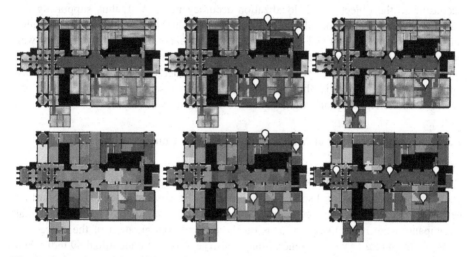

Fig. 2. Robot (top row) and human (bottom row) self-localization accuracy in Stage 1 'No LMs' (left), in Stage 2 'Robot LMs' (center), and Stage 3 'Human LMs' (right). Darker coloration indicates higher self-localization accuracy. Landmarks (white markers) are portrayed uniformly for clarity, but were individually identifiable for both robots and humans (see Fig. 1).

In *Stage 2 (Robot LMs)*, we identified the five cells that had to contain a landmark to maximize robot self-localization accuracy, assuming that a detected landmark enables perfect self-localization. Running a brute force approach taking all cells into account turned out to be too costly to process within reasonable time constraints. Thus, we limited this computation to the subset of 100 cells humans were tested at in Stage 1. The position of the five landmarks optimized for robot self-localization accuracy and the resulting distribution of robot self-localization accuracy is depicted in Fig. 2, top center. Human self-localization accuracy (supported by landmarks optimized for robots) was assessed by testing sixteen new undergraduates with an about equal gender distribution. Materials and procedure resembled to Stage 1 with the exception that the five landmarks were visible both from the first-person perspective (see Fig. 1) and on the floorplan used for the localization estimate. The resulting distribution of human self-localization accuracy is depicted in the bottom center of Fig. 2.

In *Stage 3 (Human LMs)*, we identified the five landmark positions maximizing human self-localization accuracy, based on the probability of successful human self-localization at each location in Stage 1 and the assumption that a visible landmark always enables successful self-localization based on the criteria defined above. However, it was unclear whether this computation reflected the subjective requirements of the participants. Thus, we resorted to the landmark placement tasks intermitting the self-localization tasks in Stage 1. We generated a heat map of the landmark positions participants considered most beneficial for self-localization (see Fig. 1). There was a high level of consistency across all participants with several distinct clusters [similar to 26]. These clusters closely matched the landmark positions we identified to be optimal according to the objective self-localization accuracy in Stage 1, thus supporting the validity of our computation of landmark positions optimized for humans. The evaluation of robot and human self-localization with landmarks optimized for humans was equivalent to Stage 2, with the adjusted landmark positions and the data collection of sixteen new undergraduates with an about equal gender distribution being the only difference. The resulting distributions of robot and human self-localization accuracy are depicted on the right top and right bottom of Fig. 2, respectively.

2.3 Operationalization of Metric and Qualitative Configurational Properties

We computed isovist area and isovist jaggedness of all cells as two frequently used geometric indicators of local spatial properties. We also computed the integration of all cells as a measure of their centrality within the entire building. We reasoned that participants were more likely to focus on the general configuration of the space surrounding them (e.g., a room's general shape; also see [31]). We identified 59 individual room segments in the Tate Gallery (with some areas such as the central corridor consisting of several distinctive segments). These rooms were categorized into eleven distinctive room shapes (e.g., resembling a square or an octagon). Based on the number of rooms in one category, we computed the probability a location would be correctly chosen in the self-localization task if participants based their estimate solely on the factor room shape[3] (see Table 1). Next, we counted each room's number of connections (e.g., doors, corridors) to its surrounding rooms as another qualitative configurational feature [35]. Again, we computed the probability of marking the correct room

Table 1. Descriptive data of the configurational categorization of the environment's 59 rooms.

	Room shape	Number of connections	Arrangement of connections
Number of categories	11	6	17
Mean probability (*SD*)	.21 (.29)	.13 (.18)	.36 (.31)

---

[3] For example, there are two octagonal rooms, thus belonging to one room shape category. If participants studied a location in one of these rooms and based their subsequent estimate solely on the octagonal shape, their probability to choose the correct room was $p = .5$.

purely based on the number of connections. However, we found that both categorizations showed a predominance of some features (e.g., 30 rectangular rooms, equaling about 50% of all rooms), resulting in very low probabilities that the correct room would be chosen based on one of these categories. Thus, we considered a third factor, namely the specific arrangement of connections in a room. This categorization accounted for the fact that two individual rooms with two doors each can be distinguished by the two doors facing each other in one room, but laying orthogonal to each other in the other room. With 17 categories, the granularity of this factor was distinctively higher than those of the other two factors.

3 Results

Values of robot U were scaled to range from 0 to 1 (representing the lowest and highest value across all experiment stages) to enhance clarity. As we were not interested in individual performances, we collapsed the data across participants and used the means of localization accuracy, study time, and confidence per location for all analyses below.

3.1 Self-localization Accuracy with and Without Landmarks

Across the three experimental stages for robots (see Table 2), we found the lowest robot U in Stage 1 (No LMs), an enhanced robot U in Stage 3 (Human LMs), and the highest robot U in Stage 2 (Robot LMs). A repeated measures ANOVA with experiment stage as independent variable revealed a significant main effect, $F(2, 6200) = 829, 12$, $\eta_p^2 = .21$, $p < .001$. Post-hoc paired sample t-tests indicated significant differences in self-localization between all experimental stages, all $p < .001$. Analogously, human self-localization accuracy increased from Stage 1 (No LMs) over Stage 2 (Robot LMs) to Stage 3 (Human LMs; also see Table 2). A corresponding ANOVA revealed a significant effect, $F(2, 198) = 58.57$, $\eta_p^2 = .37$, $p < .001$. Post-hoc paired sample t-tests significant differences between all experimental stages, all $p < .001$. As expected, landmarks enhanced self-localization accuracy of both robots and humans. The significantly higher localization accuracies of robots supported by Robot LMs and of humans supported by Human LMs point towards different challenges in the localization process.

Table 2. Mean robot U, human self-localization accuracy, human confidence, and human study time, separately for all experiment stages. Values in brackets indicate standard deviations.

		Stage 1 (No LMs)	Stage 2 (Robot LMs)	Stage 3 (Human LMs)
Robots	Robot U	.55 (.31)	.75 (.25)	.66 (.29)
Humans	Accuracy (proportion)	.57 (.20)	.68 (.22)	.80 (.18)
	Confidence (1–5 scale)	3.17 (.72)	3.87 (1.25)	4.48 (.93)
	Study time (in seconds)	18.30 s (4.36)	15.89 s (4.29)	18.84 s (5.23)

We refrained from a statistical comparison of robots and humans, as the data resulted from very different approaches and computational processes. However, we ran Spearman correlations for the 100 cells where data on both human and robot self-localization accuracy were available, separately for all three stages. We found no correlations at all (Stage 1: $r = .02$, $p > .81$; Stage 2: $r = -.14$, $p > .17$; Stage 3: $r = .02$, all $p > .83$). In other words: locations that allowed easy self-localization for humans were highly ambiguous for robots, and vice versa.

In order to shed further light on the factors underlying the apparently divergent self-localization processes, we focused our analyses on Stage 1 (No LMs). Using a forward selection method, we ran two multiple linear regression models with predictors derived from isovist analysis as well as by a location's qualitative configurational distinctiveness with the criterion of robot and human self-localization accuracy, respectively (see Table 3). For robots, both isovist jaggedness and isovist area proved to be significant predictors of self-localization accuracy, $F(2, 89) = 91.96$, $p < .001$. This finding reflects the conceptual closeness of isovist properties and 2D laser scans. In contrast, the arrangement of corridors remained as the only significant factor of human self-localization accuracy, $F(1, 90) = 5.00$, $p < .03$. Thus, humans were apparently unable to process the metric information of the visible space (i.e., the isovist), and relied more on qualitative configurational properties of the current room. Taken together, both robots and humans were able to solve a self-localization task in a complex environment even without distinctive landmarks. However, we found drastic differences in the spatial information that was considered for this task.

Table 3. Forward multiple linear regression models testing isovist area, isovist jaggedness, integration, room shape, number of connections, and arrangement of connections as predictors for robot self-localization accuracy (left panel, $R^2 = .67$ for step 1; $\Delta R^2 = .12$, $p < .001$, for step 2) and human self-localization accuracy (right panel, $R^2 = .05$). $* = p < .05$.

Robot self-localization accuracy				Human self-localization accuracy			
	B	SE B	β		B	SE B	β
Step 1				**Step 1**			
Constant	1.92	.15		Constant	.52	.03	
Isovist jaggedness	-.36	.03	-.74*	Arrangement of corridors	.15	.07	.23*
Step 2				**Step 2**			
Constant	1.63	.14					
Isovist jaggedness	-.25	.04	-.52*				
Isovist area	-.001	.00	-.41*				

3.2 Spatial Properties of the Optimized Landmark Positions

Spatial properties of Robot LMs resembled to the average values across the whole environment (see Table 4). In contrast, Human LMs were positioned at more integrated

Table 4. Median (and range) of isovist size, jaggedness, and integration, separately for the whole environment, for cells containing Robot LMs, and for cells containing Human LMs.

	Whole Env.	Robot LMs	Human LMs
Isovist size	89.69 (9–526)	138.67 (120–220)	401.00 (86–516)
Isovist jaggedness	3.99 (2.72–6.01)	4.15 (3.94–5.06)	4.57 (4.10–5.26)
Integration	.75 (.39–.86)	.74 (.64–.80)	.85 (.65–85)

spaces and more connected locations as compared to the whole environment. These observations must be considered preliminary due to the low number of landmarks. However, they contrast the findings from the previous section: Whereas the viewpoint's isovist properties were strong predictors of robot, but not of human self-localization accuracy, isovist properties of the landmarks' locations optimized for humans were more distinct than those optimized for robots.

3.3 Cognitive Correlates of Human Self-localization Accuracy

Next to the self-localization accuracy, we measured confidence and study time of our participants (see Table 2). A repeated measures ANOVA revealed a significant effect of participants' confidence, $F(2, 198) = 59.84$, $\eta_p^2 = .38$, $p < .001$. Post-hoc paired sample t-tests indicated that confidence increased significantly from Stage 1 (No LMs) to Stage 2 (Robot LMs), and again to Stage 3 (Human LMs), all $p < .001$. Thus, the presence of landmarks improved participants' confidence in their self-localization estimate, especially if they were optimized for humans. A corresponding ANOVA revealed a significant effect for study time, $F(2, 198) = 20.48$, $\eta_p^2 = .17$, $p < .001$. Post-hoc paired sample t-tests indicated that participants spent less time studying the locations in Stage 2 (Robot LMs) as compared to Stage 1 (No LMs) and Stage 3 (Human LMs), both $p < .001$, whereas there was no difference between the latter two conditions ($p > .52$). We refrain from further interpretation of this unexpected finding.

Subsequently, we correlated self-localization accuracy, confidence, and decision time for all test locations, separately for all experiment stages. The results are depicted in Table 5. Throughout all experiment stages, we found significant correlations between localization accuracy and confidence: Participants were surprisingly good at judging the accuracy of their self-localization. At the same time, higher confidence went along with shorter study times: Participants assumed to know their position right away rather than becoming more confident over time. The correlation between accuracy and study time was not significant in Stage 1, but increased in Stage 2 and further

Table 5. Correlation coefficients of human self-localization accuracy, confidence, and study time, separately for all experiment stages. * = p < .05; ** = p < .01; *** = p < .001.

	Stage 1 (No LMs)		Stage 2 (Robot LMs)		Stage 3 (Human LMs)	
	Accuracy	Study time	Accuracy	Study time	Accuracy	Study time
Confidence	.63***	−.36***	.72***	−.49***	.74***	−.65***
Study time	−.10		−.25*		−.35***	

so in Stage 3. We explain this pattern by the availability of landmarks, which did support human self-localization not only in regard to accuracy, but also in regard to swiftness.

4 Discussion

The present research aimed at comparing differences and commonalities in self-localization accuracies of robots and humans in a complex building, and how spatial ambiguity can be overcome by installing landmarks at crucial locations. On the first glance, our research highlights the differences between robots and humans: The analysis of spatial properties determining self-localization success in Stage 1 (No LMs) indicated that isovist properties are good predictors of robot, but not of human self-localization accuracy. This finding reflects that laser scans resemble closely to the concept of isovists. It follows that robots can deal best with highly complex locations featuring a large number of irregularities, but struggle with comparatively uniform areas. In line with previous findings [19], humans do apparently not possess the required processing and storage capacities to successfully use this kind of information. This interpretation was further corroborated by the null-correlation between robot U and human self-localization accuracy throughout all experiment stages. In contrast, the human participants relied on qualitative configurational information [31]. More specifically, the specific arrangement of doors in a room within the whole environment was the only significant predictor of human self-localization accuracy: Similar to a jigsaw puzzle, only a limited number of variables and places must be scrutinized for a particularly shaped piece. Furthermore, our analyses imply that self-localization is not a bottom-up process, where confidence and accuracy increase over time spent processing a location's spatial configuration. Instead, humans apparently believe to know their position right away, and tend to become less confident over time. However, considering the cognitive demands of transferring the egocentric study perspective to the allocentric localization perspective, humans performed surprisingly well even without landmarks [16].

As one of the few commonalities, unique landmarks in the environment fostered the localization process of both robots and humans, in line with previous research from both fields [2, 4]. This finding is not particularly surprising. However, the more relevant finding is that landmarks geared towards the requirements of robots were significantly less suited for humans, and vice versa. Landmarks optimized for robots were located in segregated areas where high ambiguity was measured, as robots are more unlikely to make errors in the uniquely shaped central areas of the building. However, the spatial properties of the landmark positions were inconspicuous. In contrast, landmarks optimized for humans were tightly linked to a high visibility as well as their integration in the general layout of the building. Thus, landmarks served the human participants to eliminate residual ambiguity for a large part of the building (e.g., the main hall) rather than to disambiguate specific areas [26]. Thus, although humans are apparently unable to process the spatial properties of their own location for the purpose of self-localization, they do take the global structure of the environment into account when facilitating self-localization with external spatial information such as landmarks.

4.1   Limitations and Future Directions

Based on our findings, we argue that one major difference between self-localization of humans and robots is the level of granularity. More specifically, it is of little interest for humans to determine the very exact spot in a room they are standing at, as long as they are confident about the room's general location in the entire building. They are unlikely to mix up a highly unique configurational space (e.g., an octagonal room with three doorways) with a similar space (e.g., a quadratic room with three doorways). In contrast, frequently used approaches on robot navigation such as SLAM do not explicitly take such qualitative configurational information into account. Several studies addressed this issue by incorporating heuristics for the identification of doorways [35] or landmark information [1]. Given that information about configurational properties is to some extent implicitly available from the current laser scan, a robot might be enabled to make additional use of spatial information that so far has been limited to humans [7]. Furthermore, we can conclude that robot orientation is impeded by architectural designs geared towards human needs, with a small number of highly distinctive and central locations, but a large number of uniform functional rooms. Thus, future research should further test this hypothesis by taking the underlying structure of building types and their different legibility into account (see for example [33]).

Our research can be extended in several directions. Our qualitative operationalization of the environment's configuration implies that humans do take configurational information into account. However, our categorization of configurational features might not have been exhaustive enough: For example, the surrounding rooms could provide additional information useful for human self-localization which we did not consider (such as unique features, see [31]). Also, we deliberately limited our paradigm to static self-localization within a completely explored building in order to increase the comparability of human and robot performance. Even for this rather particular task, several additional concessions concerning the presentation format were necessary: robot sensor input were simulated 2D laser scans, humans studied 3D scenes at their own discretion. However, the virtual model consisted of straight walls and a completely plain ceiling. Thus, simulating 3D laser scans would have provided no additional information for robots, whereas the human participants could gain little additional information from the visually sparse virtual model. Furthermore, we did not control how participants studied the scenes. Thus, it is possible that they did not study the full isovist. We decided against a forced presentation of a 360° turn in order to keep the participants involved and active. Finally, we had to limit the evaluation of human self-localization to a subset of cells. It is possible (but highly unlikely) that the selected locations are confounded in a specific but unknown way. In this regard, our research must be seen as a first step towards a systematic comparison of spatial processing of humans and robots. Extending our approach to a scenario featuring additional aspects such as SLAM abilities, locomotion and wayfinding tasks or visually more distinct environment represents a worthwhile, but due to the fundamental differences between robots and humans also a highly complex challenge.

4.2   Conclusion

Our research represents one of the first attempts for a systematic comparison of robot and human self-localization. We demonstrate that the specific means to process spatial information lead to very different challenges. Consequently, the requirements of information supporting self-localization (e.g., landmarks) differ as well. Thus, our findings highlight some of the challenges that need to be addressed for any scenario that encompasses robot-human cooperation in regard to spatial orientation and navigation.

Acknowledgments. This research was granted by the SFB/TR8—Spatial Cognition. We thank Wolfgang Burgard, Ruth Conroy-Dalton, Freya Fleckenstein, Saskia Kuliga, Laura Wächter, and Flora Wenczel for their support at various stages of this research.

References

1. Bastianelli, E., et al.: On-line semantic mapping. In: 2013 16th International Conference on Advanced Robotics (ICAR), pp. 1–6. IEEE (2013)
2. Beinhofer, M., et al.: Deploying artificial landmarks to foster data association in simultaneous localization and mapping. In: ICRA, pp. 5235–5240. IEEE (2013)
3. Benedikt, M.L.: To take hold of space: isovists and isovist fields. Environ. Plan. B Plan. Des. **6**(1), 47–65 (1979)
4. Cliburn, D., et al.: Dynamic landmark placement as a navigation aid in virtual worlds. In: Proceedings of the 2007 ACM Symposium on Virtual Reality Software and Technology, pp. 211–214. ACM (2007)
5. Conroy-Dalton, R.: Spatial Navigation in Immersive Virtual Environments. University of London, London (2001)
6. Downs, R.M., Stea, D.: Image and Environment: Cognitive Mapping and Spatial Behavior. Edward Arnold, London (1973)
7. Epstein, S.L., et al.: Spatial abstraction for autonomous robot navigation. Cogn. Process. **16** (S1), 215–219 (2015)
8. Folkesson, J., et al.: Vision SLAM in the measurement subspace. In: Proceedings of the 2005 IEEE International Conference on Robotics and Automation, pp. 30–35. IEEE (2005)
9. Giudice, N.A., et al.: The informatics of indoor and outdoor space: a research agenda. Presented at the Second ACM SIGSPATIAL International Workshop on Indoor Spatial Awareness (2010)
10. Haq, S., Girotto, S.: Ability and intelligibility: wayfinding and environmental cognition in the designed. Presented at the 4th International Space Syntax Symposium, London (2003)
11. Hermer-Vazquez, L., et al.: Sources of flexibility in human cognition: dual-task studies of space and language. Cognit. Psychol. **39**(1), 3–36 (1999)
12. Hillier, B.: The Social Logic of Space. Cambridge University Press, Cambridge (2008)
13. Jefferies, M.E., Cree, M., Mayo, M., Baker, J.T.: Using 2D and 3D landmarks to solve the correspondence problem in cognitive robot mapping. In: Freksa, C., Knauff, M., Krieg-Brückner, B., Nebel, B., Barkowsky, T. (eds.) Spatial Cognition 2004. LNCS (LNAI), vol. 3343, pp. 434–454. Springer, Heidelberg (2005). https://doi.org/10.1007/978-3-540-32255-9_24

14. Kiefer, P., et al.: Where am I? Investigating map matching during self-localization with mobile eye tracking in an urban environment. Trans. GIS **18**(5), 660–686 (2014)

15. Kuipers, B., Byun, Y.-T.: A robot exploration and mapping strategy based on a semantic hierarchy of spatial representations. Robot. Auton. Syst. **8**(1), 47–63 (1991)

16. Meilinger, T., Hölscher, C., Büchner, S.J., Brösamle, M.: How much information do you need? Schematic maps in wayfinding and self localisation. In: Barkowsky, T., Knauff, M., Ligozat, G., Montello, D.R. (eds.) Spatial Cognition 2006. LNCS (LNAI), vol. 4387, pp. 381–400. Springer, Heidelberg (2007). https://doi.org/10.1007/978-3-540-75666-8_22

17. Meyer-Delius, D., et al.: Using artificial landmarks to reduce the ambiguity in the environment of a mobile robot. In: 2011 IEEE International Conference on Robotics and Automation (ICRA), pp. 5173–5178. IEEE (2011)

18. Nourbakhsh, I.R., et al.: Human-robot teaming for search and rescue. IEEE Pervasive Comput. **4**(1), 72–79 (2005)

19. Peebles, D., Davies, C., Mora, R.: Effects of geometry, landmarks and orientation strategies in the 'drop-off' orientation task. In: Winter, S., Duckham, M., Kulik, L., Kuipers, B. (eds.) COSIT 2007. LNCS, vol. 4736, pp. 390–405. Springer, Heidelberg (2007). https://doi.org/10.1007/978-3-540-74788-8_24

20. Peponis, J., et al.: Finding the building in wayfinding. Environ. Behav. **22**(5), 555–590 (1990)

21. Raubal, M., Worboys, M.: A formal model of the process of wayfinding in built environments. In: Freksa, C., Mark, D.M. (eds.) COSIT 1999. LNCS, vol. 1661, pp. 381–399. Springer, Heidelberg (1999). https://doi.org/10.1007/3-540-48384-5_25

22. Richter, K.-F.: Indoor wayfinding tools. In: Shekhar, S., et al. (eds.) Encyclopedia of GIS, pp. 1–8. Springer, Cham (2015). https://doi.org/10.1007/978-3-319-17885-1_1622

23. Santos, P.E., et al.: Probabilistic self-localisation on a qualitative map based on occlusions. J. Exp. Theor. Artif. Intell. **28**(5), 781–799 (2016)

24. Stankiewicz, B.J., et al.: Lost in virtual space: studies in human and ideal spatial navigation. J. Exp. Psychol. Hum. Percept. Perform. **32**(3), 688–704 (2006)

25. Stankiewicz, B.J., Kalia, A.A.: Acquisition of structural versus object landmark knowledge. J. Exp. Psychol. Hum. Percept. Perform. **33**(2), 378–390 (2007)

26. von Stülpnagel, R., et al.: Supra-individual consistencies in navigator-driven landmark placement for spatial learning. In: Bello, P., Guarini, M., McShane, M., Scassellati, B. (eds.) Proceedings of the 36th Annual Conference of the Cognitive Science Society, pp. 1706–1711. Cognitive Science Society, Austin (2014)

27. von Stülpnagel, R., Frankenstein, J.: Configurational salience of landmarks: an analysis of sketch maps using space syntax. Cogn. Process. **16**(S1), 437–441 (2015)

28. Triebel, R., et al.: SPENCER: a socially aware service robot for passenger guidance and help in busy airports. In: Wettergreen, D.S., Barfoot, T.D. (eds.) Field and Service Robotics. STAR, vol. 113, pp. 607–622. Springer, Cham (2016). https://doi.org/10.1007/978-3-319-27702-8_40

29. Turner, A., et al.: From isovists to visibility graphs: a methodology for the analysis of architectural space. Environ. Plan. B Plan. Des. **28**(1), 103–121 (2001)

30. Waller, D., et al.: Place learning in humans: the role of distance and direction information. Spat. Cogn. Comput. **2**(4), 333–354 (2000)

31. Warren, D.H., et al.: Perception of map-environment correspondence: the roles of features and alignment. Ecol. Psychol. **2**(2), 131–150 (1990)

32. Warren, D.H.: Self-localization on plan and oblique maps. Environ. Behav. Beverly Hills Calif. **26**, 1 (1994)

33. Weisman, J.: Evaluating architectural legibility: way-finding in the built environment. Environ. Behav. **13**(2), 189–204 (1981)
34. Wiener, J.M., et al.: Gaze behaviour during space perception and spatial decision making. Psychol. Res. **76**(6), 713–729 (2012)
35. Zender, H., et al.: Conceptual spatial representations for indoor mobile robots. Robot. Auton. Syst. **56**(6), 493–502 (2008)

A Comparison of Mental and Physical Rotation Using Gaze-Based Measures

Stefanie Wetzel$^{(\boxtimes)}$ and Sven Bertel

Usability Research Group, Flensburg University of Applied Sciences,
Kanzleistraße 91-93, 24943 Flensburg, Germany
{stefanie.wetzel,sven.bertel}@hs-flensburg.de

Abstract. Over the past few years, a number of studies have reported on procedural similarities and differences between mental rotation and physical (i.e., manual) rotation of Shepard and Metzler-type stimuli. These similarities include comparable angular disparity effects and comparable final angular offsets in problem solving. This paper presents results from further comparisons based on gazed-derived measures obtained across the course of trials. In a within-subject design, participants solved the same tasks as mental and as physical rotation problems. We compare time courses of mean fixation duration and of saccade amplitude, and interpret these with respect to underlying mental processes and loads. The results point to additional specific procedural similarities and differences, which nicely complement the previous findings. The results are of additional, practical use for establishing how and when physical rotation can provide a useful proxy for mental rotation for purposes of process analysis, of ability assessment, and of training.

Keywords: Mental rotation · Physical rotation
Comparison of mental processes · Gaze-based measures

1 Introduction

Good spatial skill have been found to be an indicator for success in STEM domains [18]. Studies have shown that spatial skills can be improved by training (e.g., [17]). One of the key spatial abilities is the ability to mentally rotate two- and three-dimensional objects. Not surprisingly, mental rotation training improves mental rotation skills, however, mental rotation skills also benefit from physical (i.e., manual) rotation training [1,19]. Although specific similarities between mental and physical rotation have been discovered (see e.g. [6]), it is still unclear how similar or different the specific cognitive processes are that respectively underlie mental and physical rotation. Finding out more about how exactly processes in mental and physical rotation are related is not just academically interesting: On a practical level, procedural similarities might be usefully exploited for training and assessing mental rotation skills by using physical rotation as a proxy.

© Springer Nature Switzerland AG 2018
S. Creem-Regehr et al. (Eds.): Spatial Cognition 2018, LNAI 11034, pp. 167–179, 2018.
https://doi.org/10.1007/978-3-319-96385-3_12

We report on results of a study in which we logged subjects' eye movements during the solving of mental and physical rotation problems. We analyze time courses of fixation duration and saccade amplitude as gaze-derived measures to compare mental and physical rotation processes. The aim is to increase our knowledge about specific similarities and differences between the two.

1.1   Mental Rotation

The ability to mentally rotate two- and three-dimensional objects has been intensively studied over the years. Shepard and Metzler [13] were the first to study mental rotation using two 3D cube figures placed side by side in different orientations. Subjects had to judge whether the figures showed the same or different objects. Shepard and Metzler found that response times were linearly related to the initial angular disparity between the figures. Larger initial disparities revealed longer response times (angular disparity effect; ADE). They concluded that their subjects were mentally rotating one of the objects into or near the orientation of the other object, thereby aligning them and making the decision easier. Importantly, such linear relationship holds only for tasks in which the two figures are the same. For *different* figures, an orientation alignment is not possible and a meaningful angular disparity can, thus, not be calculated by some general method.

1.2   Eye Movements During Mental Rotation

Just and Carpenter [4] were the first to study eye movements during mental rotation as an indicator for cognitive processes. Based on an analysis of the subjects' scan path they identified three phases: At the beginning of the task, subjects will search for corresponding segments between the figures (1). These segments will then be mentally transformed to decrease the angular disparity between them (2). This process comes to a halt when the angular disparity falls below a 50° threshold. The figures can then be compared for concordance (3). Especially the last phase is supposed to be cognitively demanding since it consists of mental transformations of segments and comparing them between the figures. Besides the linear relationship between response time and initial angular disparity for *same* task, Just and Carpenter reported on a comparable relationship between the mean fixation duration per task and the initial angular disparity.

1.3   Physical Rotation

As mentioned above, mental rotation skills can also be improved through physical rotation training [1,19]. Wiedenbauer et al. [19] reported on an experiment in which subjects used a joystick to rotate 3D cube figures to decrease the angular disparity. The training resulted in lower response times for mental rotation tasks, but was limited to trained objects. This raises the question if such kind of training is process- or rather memory-based. Gardony et al. [6] compared mental and physical rotation based on recorded physical rotation trajectories. In their study, subjects were able to rotate 3D cube figures using a ball in hand. They found that participants decreased the angular disparity between the two figures ending with a characteristic angular difference between 30° and 60°. Bertel et al. [2] found similar physical rotation trajectories and similar characteristic final angular offsets for primary school students using a touch-based input metaphor on an iPad. This suggests that such characteristics are unlikely to originate from properties of a specific input control, but are general and likely reflect on underlying mental processes. Also, the final angular disparity found by Bertel et al. is similar to the final angular disparity of 50° during mental rotation postulated by Just and Carpenter [4].

1.4   Time Course of Eye Movements

For this contribution we decided to focus on time series of fixation duration and saccade amplitude as gazed-based measures since they are relatively easy to process using an mobile eye tracker and are common measures to infer properties of cognitive processes for various tasks. Fixation duration has been found to be related with mental workload in a variety of studies (e.g., during real life tasks such as driving [10,16] or for scene perception [15]). Fixation duration increases when the workload increases. Importantly, this only holds for situations during which subjects complete the tasks successfully. If subjects struggle to engage with a task and experience high levels of stress they will produce shorter fixations [7].

Saccade amplitudes can serve as an additional measure for task difficulty and mental load (e.g., for search tasks [21], tone counting [8], or while driving [12]). Studies found that mean saccade amplitude decreases when the mental workload increases. These finding could be explained by a sort of 'tunnel vision' [20] where subjects rather focus on nearby areas than produce longer saccades during cognitive processing.

Various studies analyzed the time course of fixation duration and saccade amplitude (e.g., for scene perception [3,15]). Mills et al. [9] compared fixation duration and saccade amplitude over time between different task types, such as visual search, memory tasks and free-viewing. They found that the task type has an effect on fixation duration and saccade amplitude over the whole course of time. While the overall shapes of the time course plots were similar for saccade amplitude, the shapes differed for fixation duration. The process of mental rotation involves various cognitive sub-processes, such as visual search and object perception. We therefore assume that if processes that occur during mental rotation also occur during physical rotation, they should produce similar patterns of fixation duration and saccade amplitudes over time.

2   Method

Thirty-two university students from STEM fields participated in our user study (9 of which identified as female; mean age: 24.8 years). They were paid 10 € as compensation for participating.

2.1   Conditions

To allow us to compare mental and physical rotation, each subject had to solve 96 tasks in a *mental* condition and 96 tasks in a *physical* condition. Following the classical mental rotation tasks introduced by Shepard and Metzler [13] subjects had to decide whether two 3D figures showed the same figure or not. The tasks were presented in German language on an iPad and subjects provided answers by either tapping on a "Ja" (=*same*) or "Nein" (=*different*) button (cf. Fig. 1). In the *mental* condition, subjects had no opportunity to interact with the presented 3D figures. In contrast, in the *physical* condition subjects were able to rotate the right-hand 3D figure using an Arcball interaction technique [14]. This technique enables the subjects to rotate the figures around all axis using 2D touch input on the iPad.

   Each condition consisted of two levels containing 48 tasks each. The order of the conditions was randomized between subjects. Each subject started with the first condition solving the tasks of level 1. After a short break, the tasks from level 2 were presented. After another short break the second condition with the respective two levels started. Within a level, tasks were presented in randomized order. There was no time limit for the solving of the tasks but subjects were instructed to solve tasks as correctly and as fast as possible.

2.2   Tasks

For the construction of the tasks, we used cube figures consisting of ten cubes each from a mental rotation stimulus library provided by Peters and Batista [11] (level 1), as well as self-constructed extensions of this set with 15 cubes each (level 2; see Fig. 1). The newly constructed figures were visually more complex and were intended to increase task difficulty to reduce possible ceiling effects for task performance. Mirrored figures were used for *different* tasks. Initial angular disparities were equally distributed across all tasks, ranging from 0 to 180°.

2.3   Apparatus

Subjects' eye movements were recorded during the solving of the tasks using a pair of SMI Glasses 2.0 at 60 Hz. Subjects were placed approximately 60 cm in front of an iPad (iPad Air, 9.7″ with 2048 × 1536 pixels) on which the tasks were presented and through which interactions were logged using our own app *Rotate it!*. They were instructed to sit comfortably, yet try not to move much. A three-point calibration was conducted before the start of each level. Fixations and saccades were determined using the event detection algorithm provided by SMI's BeGaze software. Since we were only interested in fixation duration and saccade amplitude we omitted the mapping of the fixations onto a reference image.

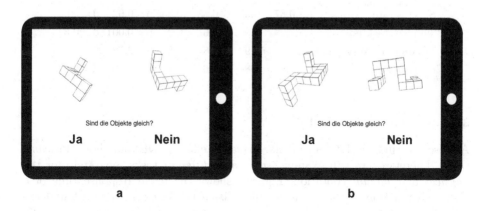

Fig. 1. Sample tasks used in the study from (a) level 1 with 10 cubes and (b) level 2 with 15 cubes.

3   Results

On average, subjects needed 30 min to solve all tasks. One physical and three mental rotation tasks needed to be excluded from the analyzed because of missing eye tracking data. This resulted in 3069 remaining mental and 3071 remaining physical rotation tasks for the analysis. Because of these large sample sizes, we also computed effect size using Cohen's d (interpreted after Cohen [5]: 0.2 small effect, 0.5 medium effect, 0.8 large effect) and r (interpreted after Cohen [5]: 0.1 small effect, 0.3 medium effect, 0.5 large effect) to interpret magnitudes of significant differences.

Before we will look at time courses of gaze-derived measure to compare processes underlying mental and physical rotation, we will present results from analyses of general aspects, such as of the ADE and rotation trajectories, that will enable us to compare our study with previous work.

3.1   Comparability of Levels

We started with comparing the tasks of level 1 and 2. Table 1 shows the means of the performance measures and overall eye movements parameters. We found no significant differences for the mean fixation duration per task. For success, time on task and saccade amplitude significant differences were revealed. However, the highest magnitude of $d = 0.34$ is still a small effect, meaning that, on a practical level, our newly constructed tasks were hardly more difficult to solve than tasks from level 1. Thus, we decided to pool tasks from level 1 and 2 for further analyses.

Table 1. Means and standard deviations for performance and averaged eye movement measures per task level.

Measure	Level 1		Level 2		Statistics
	M	SD	M	SD	
Success rate	0.87	0.33	0.85	0.35	p = 0.026, d = 0.05
Time on task (s)	7.7	4.8	9.6	6.3	p < 0.001, d = 0.34
Fixation duration (ms)	239.5	57.9	239.8	51.8	p = 0.788
Saccade amplitude (°)	7.9	1.8	7.6	1.7	p < 0.001, d = 0.17

3.2 Angular Disparity Effect

As described in Sect. 1.1, the angular disparity effect (ADE) only holds for *same* tasks. Therefore, we will examine *same* and *different* tasks separately for the *physical* and *mental* condition. Figure 2 shows the mean response time of a task as a function of the initial angular disparity. As expected, we found the ADE for *mental* and *physical same* tasks (*mental*: $r = 0.48$, $p < 0.001$, $N = 1535$; *physical*: $r = 0.44$, $p < 0.001$, $N = 1536$). For the *different* tasks we found significant, though very small linear relationships between time and initial disparity (*mental*: $r = 0.09$, $p < 0.001$, $N = 1534$; *physical*: $r = 0.07$, $p = 0.002$, $N = 1535$). The findings for the *mental* tasks are in line with findings from other mental rotation studies (e.g., [4]). Findings for the ADE during physical rotation are similar to findings of Bertel et al. [2] and Gardony et al. [6]. To better appreciate the robust nature of these effects, it is important to realize that Bertel et al. tested secondary school children but used the same physical interaction metaphor as we used here, while Gardony et al. used a comparable sample of participants, but employed a different physical interaction metaphor. Based on the established differences between *same* and *different* tasks, we will analyze these separately for the *mental* and *physical* condition in the following analyses.

3.3 Task Performance

Table 2 gives an overview about success rates and times on task for all tasks. Success rates for *same* tasks show no significant differences between the *mental* and *physical* condition. Only, for *different* tasks, significantly higher scores are revealed for the *physical* condition, with a small effect. Mean times on task for both task types are comparable between the *mental* and *physical* condition. However, since we set no time limit during the study we still have different times for each task. As a consequence, we will compare the gaze-based measures over the course of time based on relative time steps. This allows us to compare tasks with different task lengths.

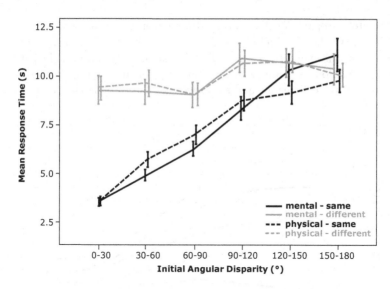

Fig. 2. Mean response time as a function of initial angular disparity for mental and physical rotation. Error bars indicate the 95% confidence interval.

Table 2. Means and standard deviations for performance per condition and task type, with t-test comparisons.

Measure	Mental		Physical		Statistics
	M	SD	M	SD	
Success rate - *same*	0.85	0.35	0.85	0.35	p = 0.833
Success rate - *different*	0.81	0.39	0.92	0.26	p < 0.001, d = 0.33
Time on task (s) - *same*	7.4	5.7	7.3	4.7	p = 0.598
Time on task (s) - *different*	9.8	6.3	9.9	5.4	p = 0.912

3.4 Physical Rotation Trajectories

As a last step before comparing gaze-derived parameters of mental and physical rotation, we analyzed the physical rotation trajectories. Since we used the same interaction metaphor and presentation device as Bertel et al. [2] but targeted a different age group we wanted to see if we could replicate the angular disparity patterns. This was the case: Fig. 3 shows the physical rotation trajectories for *same* tasks pooled by their initial angular disparity range (in 30° steps). We found that the angular disparity was decreased until a range between 20° and 70° was reached.

3.5 Time Courses of Eye Movements

For the analysis of fixation duration and saccade amplitude gathered across tasks, we sampled and averaged values for these measures at equal relative times of task (in 10% steps). We thus obtained nine averaged fixation duration values for each task. We chose to excluded the last 10% average of each task from further analyses, as, at those points in time, subjects had already completed their mental or physical rotation task and were now looking for and at the answer buttons. We also all excluded fixations and saccades that fell outside the iPad.

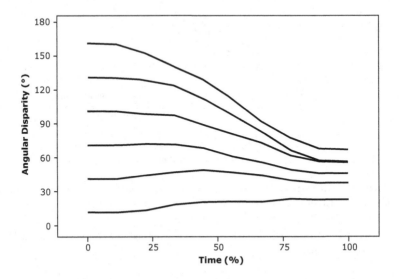

Fig. 3. Course of angular disparity over time for *same physical* tasks.

Fixation Duration. Figure 4 shows mean fixation duration for *same* and *different* tasks in both conditions. The two trajectories for the *mental* condition show similar trends: Both curves start at a comparable level of approximately 195 ms. For *same* tasks in the *mental* condition, the fixation duration increases over the course of time with a small slope ending around 240 ms. For *different* tasks, the curve increases with a relatively greater slope resulting in higher fixation durations and reaching a level of 250 ms after half of the task time. From this point on, the curve remains on a relative constant level until the end. The confidence intervals of both *mental* trajectories largely overlap at the beginning and show only small overlapping at the end. In-between, they do not overlap at all.

In comparison, the two fixation duration trajectories for the *physical* condition show greater positive slopes at the beginning, but the trajectories decrease after half of the task time. For *physical same* tasks, the curve shows a similar course of time as the curve for *mental different* task until 50% of task time. Both curves start at 195 ms and increase to a level of 250 ms. Within this period of time the confidence intervals of both curves show large overlaps at respective points of time. The curve for *physical same* tasks then decreases until the end of the task, ending with a fixation duration of around 230 ms. For *physical different* tasks, the curve shows the largest increase of all curves starting at 200 ms and reaching its maximum at around 60% of task time at 270 ms. As for the *physical same* tasks, the fixation duration then drops until the end to a level of 250 ms. Confidence intervals overlap at the beginning and at the end of the task. Overall fixation duration trajectories show comparable patterns within each condition but they vary regarding slopes and the maximum values reached.

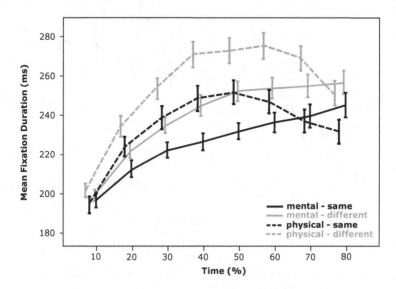

Fig. 4. Fixation duration as a function of time for mental and physical rotation. Error bars indicate the 95% confidence interval.

Saccade Amplitude. Figure 5 shows the mean saccade amplitude for *same* and *different* trials for both conditions. All four curves follow a similar general trend starting with a steep increase within the first 20% of the time, which is followed by a smaller increase. *Same mental* tasks start with the lowest saccade amplitude of 6°. After the initial increase to 8.5° the saccade amplitude remains on a constant level until about the 50% time mark. After this, saccade amplitude increases again but with a smaller positive slope ending at 8°. In contrast, the curve for *different mental* tasks remains nearly constant after the initial increase and shows a small increase within the last 10% of time to 7.5°. Especially, within the first 50% of time, confidence intervals of both curves show large overlaps. Over the course of time *different mental* tasks show the shortest saccade amplitudes.

For *same* trials in the *physical* condition, the curve has the steepest slope within the first 30% of time starting at 7.5°. It then remains on a constant level until half of the time and shows an increase to approximately 9° until the end. The curve for *different physical* trials shows a similar progress until the 50% time mark but then remains for longer on the constant level of 8° until the increase at the end. Both curves of the *physical* condition show a lot of concordance and overlapping confidence intervals within the first half of the time but run apart later. Overall curves for the *mental* conditions show lower values for saccade amplitude over the course of time.

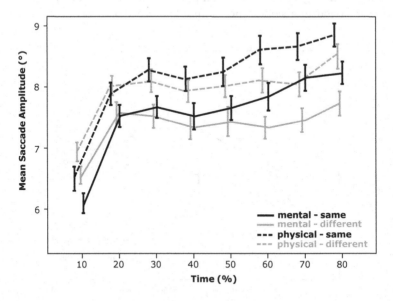

Fig. 5. Saccade amplitude as a function of time for mental and physical rotation. Error bars indicate the 95% confidence interval.

4   Discussion

Our analysis revealed different fixation duration patterns over time for *mental* and *physical* rotation tasks. While fixation duration increases over the whole course of time for *mental* tasks, it decreases within the last 20% to 30% for *physical* tasks. For saccade amplitude, our analysis revealed similar patterns for mental and physical rotation. Beginning with an increase within the first 20% of time saccade amplitudes remained on a constant level and showed a small increase at the end of the tasks. The measures can be interpreted in the context of mental load and help us draw inferences on the underlying cognitive processes.

Mental Load. The drop of the fixation duration for the *physical* condition could be explained with changing levels of mental load across the course tasks. Assuming that higher fixation duration indicates higher levels of mental load, we can conclude that load in mental rotation increases during the task and reaches the highest level within the last 20% to 30% of time. The graphs also show that fixation duration for *different mental* tasks are consistently higher than for *same mental* tasks, again pointing to differences of mental load. This difference is also reflected by the lower success rate for *different mental* tasks than for *same mental* tasks, indicating that these tasks were indeed more difficult to solve.

According to the literature, lower saccade amplitudes often indicate higher levels of mental load. Following this interpretation, *mental* rotation tasks in our study would induce consistently higher mental loads than *physical* rotation tasks. However, this contradicts interpretations based on fixation duration. The figures that had to be compared during the tasks are approximately 18 cm (visual angle of 17.5°) away from each other and had an extension of 10 to 12 cm (visual angle of 10°). Shorter saccades at the beginning of a task may reflect the search phase during which figures were inspected closely to select segments for transformation and comparison. The increase of saccade amplitude over time may reflect an increase of transitions between both figures indicating comparison and transformation processes. According to our data, it might be not appropriate to use saccade amplitude as a reliable measure for mental load.

Cognitive Processes. Considering the mental rotation phases described by Just and Carpenter [4], roughly the last 30% of the task time would fall into phase 3. Within this confirmation phase, mental transformations as well as comparisons between the transformations take place. The data for angular disparity changes gathered during *physical* rotation suggests that many participants physically decreased the offset between the two figures for *same* tasks. In combination, this means that, compared to *mental* rotation, the last phase during *physical* rotation may likely just be a simple visual comparison between the two figures where no additional mental transformations needed to be executed. This involves more transitions between both figures which results in consistently higher saccade amplitudes.

For *same* and *different* tasks, respective fixation duration within the first half of the time is higher for the *physical* condition. Before actually rotating the figures during physical rotation subjects need to plan how to rotate and in which direction. Additionally, subjects need to activate motor processes to move their hand. These processes might induce additional small amounts of mental load compared to the *mental* condition in the first half of trials.

Conclusion. Based on our findings of success and our gaze-based measures, we can conclude that the underlying processes of mental and physical rotation seem to be different to some extent. Especially in the last phase of the *physical* tasks, we found evidence for differences in cognitive load and underlying processes. The offloading of the intermediate transformations and the physical rotation of the 3D figures seem to trigger other processes, such as potentially visual comparison. This finding could be of practical importance for a training of mental rotation skills using physical rotation. It could mean that physical rotation can be used to train some aspects of mental rotation, such as determining the correct direction of rotation or the speed of rotation, but may not serve to train all sub-processes needed in mental rotation. If this is the case, mental rotation success would not necessarily increase after receiving a physical training but the time on task would decrease as a result of the accelerated sub-processes.

Further research is needed to examine whether additional gaze-derived measures, such as scanpaths or transitions between areas of interest, can give further insight into the comparison of mental and physical rotation processes. Also, it may be worthwhile to investigate hybrid versions of mental and physical rotation, for instance, versions in which stimuli may only be physically rotated by a fraction of what would be necessary to achieve an alignment of both objects. In such a setting, mental rotation training may well benefit from jump-starting solution processes physically and by visual comparison, but require *proper* mental rotation to complete the process. Last, as our results point to some characteristic differences between mental and physical rotation processes especially at the end of trials, it may be profitable to re-investigate the question of which tasks train which (does mental rotation train physical rotation?, does physical rotation train mental rotation?, similar to [1]), only this time with a focus on sub-processes respectively employed in mental and physical rotation.

References

1. Adams, D.M., Stull, A.T., Hegarty, M.: Effects of mental and manual rotation training on mental and manual rotation performance. Spat. Cogn. Comput. **14**(3), 169–198 (2014). https://doi.org/10.1080/13875868.2014.913050
2. Bertel, S., Wetzel, S., Zander, S.: Physical touch-based rotation processes of primary school students. In: Barkowsky, T., Burte, H., Hölscher, C., Schultheis, H. (eds.) Spatial Cognition/KogWis - 2016. LNCS (LNAI), vol. 10523, pp. 19–37. Springer, Cham (2017). https://doi.org/10.1007/978-3-319-68189-4_2
3. Buswell, G.T.: How People Look at Pictures (1935)
4. Carpenter, P.A., Just, M.A.: Eye fixations and cognitive processes. Cogn. Psychol. **8**(4), 441–480 (1976). https://doi.org/10.1016/0010-0285(76)90015-3
5. Cohen, J.: Statistical Power Analysis for the Behavioral Sciences, 2nd edn. (1988)
6. Gardony, A.L., Taylor, H.A., Brunyé, T.T.: What does physical rotation reveal about mental rotation? Psychol. Sci. **25**(2), 605–612 (2014). https://doi.org/10.1177/0956797613503174
7. Holmqvist, K., Nyström, M., Andersson, R., Dewhurst, R., Jarodzka, H., Van de Weijer, J.: Eye Tracking: A Comprehensive Guide to Methods and Measures. Oxford University Press, Oxford (2010)
8. May, J.G., Kennedy, R.S., Williams, M.C., Dunlap, W.P., Brannan, J.R.: Eye movement indices of mental workload. Acta Psychologica **75**, 75–89 (1990)
9. Mills, M., Hollingworth, A., Van der Stigchel, S., Hoffman, L., Dodd, M.D.: Examining the influence of task set on eye movements and fixations. J. Vis. **11**(8), 17 (2011). https://doi.org/10.1167/11.8.17
10. Miura, T.: Active function of eye movement and useful field of view in a realistic setting (1990)
11. Peters, M., Battista, C.: Applications of mental rotation figures of the Shepard and Metzler type and description of a mental rotation stimulus library. Brain Cogn. **66**(3), 260–264 (2008). https://doi.org/10.1016/j.bandc.2007.09.003
12. Recarte, M.A., Nunes, L.M.: Mental workload while driving: effects on visual search, discrimination, and decision making. J. Exp. Psychol. Appl. **9**(2), 119–137 (2003). https://doi.org/10.1037/1076-898X.9.2.119

13. Shepard, R.N., Metzler, J.: Mental rotation of three-dimentional objects. Science **171**(3972), 701–703 (1971). https://doi.org/10.1126/science.171.3972.701
14. Shoemake, K.: ARCBALL: a user interface for specifying three-dimensional orientation using a mouse. Graph. Interface **92**, 151–156 (1992)
15. Unema, P.J.A., Pannasch, S., Joos, M., Velichkovsky, B.M.: Time course of information processing during scene perception: the relationship between saccade amplitude and fixation duration. Vis. Cogn. **12**(3), 473–494 (2005). https://doi.org/10.1080/13506280444000409
16. Unema, P.J.A., Rötting, M.: Differences in eye movements and mental workload between experienced and inexperienced motor-vehicle drivers. In: Brogan, D. (ed.) Visual Search, pp. 193–202. Taylor & Francis, Abingdon (1990)
17. Uttal, D.H., Meadow, N.G., Tipton, E., Hand, L.L., Alden, A.R., Warren, C., Newcombe, N.S.: The malleability of spatial skills: a meta-analysis of training studies. Psychol. Bull. **139**(2), 352–402 (2013). https://doi.org/10.1037/a0028446
18. Wai, J., Lubinski, D., Benbow, C.P.: Spatial ability for STEM domains: aligning over 50 years of cumulative psychological knowledge solidifies its importance. J. Educ. Psychol. **101**(4), 817–835 (2009). https://doi.org/10.1037/a0016127
19. Wiedenbauer, G., Schmid, J., Jansen-Osmann, P.: Manual training of mental rotation. Eur. J. Cogn. Psychol. **19**(1), 17–36 (2007). https://doi.org/10.1080/09541440600709906
20. Williams, L.J.: Tunnel vision or general interference? Cognitive load and attentional bias are both important. Am. J. Psychol. **101**(2), 171 (1988). https://doi.org/10.2307/1422833
21. Zelinsky, G.J., Sheinberg, D.L.: Eye movements during parallel-serial visual search. J. Exp. Psychol.: Hum. Percept. Perform. **23**(1), 244–262 (1997)

Deictic Adaptation in a Virtual Environment

Nikhil Krishnaswamy[✉] and James Pustejovsky

Department of Computer Science, Brandeis University,
415 South Street, Waltham, MA 02453, USA
{nkrishna,jamesp}@brandeis.edu
http://www.voxicon.net/

Abstract. As human-computer interfaces become more sophisticated, people expect computational agents to behave more like humans. However, humans interacting make assumptions about mutual conceptual understanding that they may not make when interacting with a computational agent, where spatial cues in the environment affect their assumptions about the agent's knowledge. In this paper, we examine an interaction between human subjects and a virtual embodied avatar displayed on a screen, wherein a surface displayed on the screen is either "continued" in the real world by a physical surface or not. Subjects are, with minimal instruction, asked to indicate objects displayed in the shared environment to the agent in the course of a collaborative task. We then examine the subjects' adaptations, in aggregate, to the different configurations.

Keywords: Spatial cognition · Deixis · Virtual agent
Embodiment · Spatial reasoning

1 Introduction

In person-to-person interactions, assumptions about the interlocutor and the world influence everything from communication style or "message design" [13] to available concept vocabulary and modalities [4]. If two people jointly experience a localized event, they can be said to be *co-situated* and *co-perceptive*. Additionally, if engaged in a collaborative task, they *co-intend* to complete the task and must *co-attend* to the situation. Coordination between multiple agents becomes particularly advantageous when each agent may have incomplete knowledge of the situation, but can rely on their interlocutor(s) to clarify or provide instructions, which is facilitated by imagining the situation from a different perspective [8], or at a deeper level by neural structures like mirror neurons [3]. These parameters come together in a theory of *common ground* [5,11,36,41]. A rich, diverse literature exists on assumptions and presuppositions underlying human communication (e.g., [10,41,42]), and we have previously examined these factors from a computational perspective continued in this line of research [38].

© Springer Nature Switzerland AG 2018
S. Creem-Regehr et al. (Eds.): Spatial Cognition 2018, LNAI 11034, pp. 180–196, 2018.
https://doi.org/10.1007/978-3-319-96385-3_13

Some problems in a strictly presuppositional view of common ground have been raised by Abbott [2], which can be mitigated by the introduction of such mechanisms as "accommodation" of non-controversial information (a la Lewis [28]), or reminding the interlocutor of known but non-forefronted information.

At least some of the assumptions underlying common ground are not in force when a human interacts with a non-human. Just as the common ground between a human and an animal is limited [23], so too is it between a human and a robot or virtual agent, as no mechanism for accommodation or reminding exists in a computer system unless put there by the developers. However, unlike an animal, a robot or embodied agent is often created with the intent to approximate human behavior, and as they become more sophisticated, humans come to see them as human-analogue and expect them to behave as such [12,16]. How, then, do these conflicting cues—a perhaps subconscious expectation of an embodied agent's human or near-human capability, plus the agent's lack of some of the more sophisticated mechanisms to communicate its own situational perception— manifest in an interaction where some understanding of common ground is both present and required to complete a shared task?

This paper examines one such angle, using a platform which integrates a multimodal model of semantics (Multimodal Semantic Simulations, *MSS*) [25,37] with a realtime vision system for recognizing human gestures [45]. The result [24,33] creates an environment where a human interacts with a virtual agent to communicate spatially-grounded instructions in a collaborative task, and we examine how human users adapt their deictic techniques based on variant spatial cues in the experimental setup, as a proxy for the underlying assumptions they make about their virtual interlocutor, her embodiment, and understanding.

1.1 Deixis in Virtual Environments

Humans do intuitively understand virtual worlds to be different from the real one, particularly if said virtual world appears on a screen while the spatial cues of the real world remain visible [40]. This presents an interesting problem for the transfer of spatial cognitive tasks between the virtual space and real space. Many virtual interaction systems integrate the virtual space with the real space in order to make the transition as natural as possible. This inclination of course presages virtual reality (VR) and augmented reality (AR) systems, and thus we end up with tables and walls that act as tablet surfaces [22,39] or for content-sharing [21], and computer vision-tracked interaction with surfaces using gestures [29].

One of the most basic spatially-grounded gestures is deixis. Many (e.g., Hostetter [20]) argue that gestures are simulated action, but Clark [11], Volterra [43] and others view gesture as a more general mode of reference. While our multimodal semantic modeling language, VoxML, treats gestures as a special case of action programs for generating MSS, gestures may also simulate *objects* by decoupling object attributes (e.g., size, shape, relative location) from the object itself, and binding them to some denotational aspect of the gesture. In the case of deixis by pointing, this aspect is the location of the object as interpreted by the pointing agent. The pointing gesture binds a location—in most cases, the location denoted by the vector of the pointer (e.g., the finger) intersecting some salient area (e.g., a real or imagined surface plane). The pointing gesture might then refer to a location, or to objects occupying it (cf. [6]).

Using an utterance S and a corresponding gesture G there are three ways for an agent a to perform a communicative act C [36]:

$$\text{a. } C_a = (G) \qquad \text{b. } C_a = (S) \qquad \text{c. } C_a = (S, G)$$

If gesture and speech are temporally aligned, the agent may point to an object and say "that one" or to a location and say "there," and the utterance may select for an object versus a location, while the gesture can be formally realized as a snippet of a context-free grammar, e.g., $Point_G \rightarrow Loc \mid Obj$.

Deixis serves as a method of directing attention. Being temporally aligned with speech, the object indicated by deixis is usually also the current topic of discussion or conversation [9]. This expectation is also in effect in a virtual world, or co-situated worlds mediated by virtualization technology, such as video conferencing. Therefore a disconnect between agents due to a misalignment in their respective frames of reference, or information available to one agent that is invisible to the other, makes it difficult to agree on or to communicate which object or coordinate is being indicated by deixis [18]. Research in both kinematics [34] and human-computer interaction tasks [49] points to speed of pointing as an inverse correlate of the difficulty of the pointing task being performed.

Pointing is one of the most basic communicative gestures, as demonstrated by various studies [31,32,46]. The gesture set used in this line of research comes from studies by Wang et al. [44], wherein one human, the *builder*, has a table with blocks on it, and another human, the *signaler*, is given a pattern of blocks to build, invisible to the builder. As only the builder can move the blocks, the signaler must instruct the builder on how to construct the target pattern. Further details about these elicitation studies in particular are given in [44].

Because in the elicitation studies, the subjects were standing before tables, the gestures elicited naturally used the table as a reference point. A subject might first indicate a spot on the table and then another to indicate a relative location. Because the subjects were physically separated from each other, the signalers naturally fell into a pattern of using points on their own table surface to indicate blocks or positions on the builder's table surface. This turns the $Point_G \rightarrow Loc \mid Obj$ interpretation into a mirroring exercise where $Point_G \rightarrow Loc\prime \mid Obj\prime$, and the location indicated on the signaler's table space is translated into the builder's table space. In less-constrained situations, without the presence of a common reference point such as a table, many studies have shown that subjects naturally default to pointing relative to another context. This might be a free-floating point situated within an immersive virtual reality environment [47], or, when relevant information is displayed on a screen, the screen [19,30].

This setup, where the system requirements for accurate/fluent deixis conflict with users' documented tendencies when interacting with technology, creates an opportunity to study if and how users adapt their use of deixis to the system.

2   Experimental Design

2.1   Scenario and Data Capture

In our experimental scenario, users collaborated with an avatar to build a test pattern. All users were asked to build a six-block, three-stepped staircase using the blocks available. The definition of "success" was left up to the user, as far as placement of specifically colored blocks, orientation of the staircase, exactness of the blocks' alignment, etc. Users were told to use gesture and speech to achieve the goal but were not given the vocabulary of gestures and words understood by the avatar.

The purpose of the previously-mentioned elicitation studies was to observe and catalog the use of naturalistic gestures in the given task. Thus the gesture set in use is adapted to the environment in which the task is conducted, and it is these uses that were used to develop the avatar-interaction system (hereafter referred to as HAB, or "human-avatar-blocks world"). The data evaluated hereafter was gathered as part of a larger study evaluating the coverage of the HAB system [27]. Focusing specifically on the pointing data here allows us to use the results of this larger evaluation study to examine the particularities of deixis in a virtual environment with a virtual interlocutor.

Our experiment recreates the experimental setup from the aforementioned elicitation studies, except the builder is not a human in a physical room but an embodied avatar in a 3D world rendered on a monitor. This creates a parallel to the original elicitation study, where the human and the avatar are "separated" by the computer screen, and only the avatar can access the blocks.

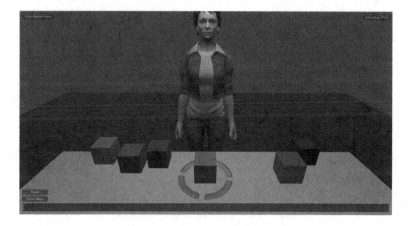

Fig. 1. Scene with embodied avatar.

This virtual world is created using VoxSim [25, 26], a semantically-informed 3D event simulator used for experiments in communicating with computational agents. VoxSim is built on the Unity game engine and contains a sophisticated model of object and event semantics based on VoxML and dynamic logic which allows the agent to access existing context to interpret input from a human user in multiple modalities. Here we focus on natural language and gesture.

Gestures are recognized in real time using depth data from a Microsoft Kinect® [50] which is classified using ResNet-style deep convolutional neural networks (DCNNs) [17] implemented in TensorFlow [1]. The system recognizes 35 independent gestures that represent attributes or programs with semantics encoded in VoxML [37]. The HAB avatar's contextual interpretations of each gesture type are enumerated in [24,33]. Here we focus primarily on pointing, with supplemental gestures to communicate affirmation or negation. Figure 2 shows the VoxML semantics for a pointing gesture.

$$
\begin{bmatrix}
\textbf{point} \\[2pt]
\text{LEX} = \begin{bmatrix} \text{PRED} = \textbf{point} \\ \text{TYPE} = \textbf{assignment} \end{bmatrix} \\[12pt]
\text{TYPE} = \begin{bmatrix}
\text{HEAD} = \textbf{assignment} \\
\text{ARGS} = \begin{bmatrix}
\text{A}_1 = \textbf{x:agent} \\
\text{A}_2 = \textbf{y:finger} \\
\text{A}_3 = \textbf{z:location} \\
\text{A}_4 = \textbf{w:physobj} \bullet \textbf{location}
\end{bmatrix} \\
\text{BODY} = \begin{bmatrix}
\text{E}_1 = extend(x, y) \\
\text{E}_2 = def(vec(x \rightarrow y \times z), as(w))
\end{bmatrix}
\end{bmatrix}
\end{bmatrix}
$$

Fig. 2. VoxML semantics for a [[POINT]] gesture. A_4, w, shows the compound typing (a la Generative Lexicon [35]) of the indicated region and objects within that region.

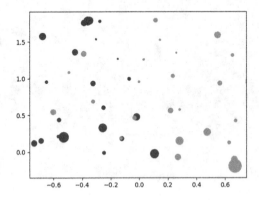

Fig. 3. The variance when a user points at a set of sampled points, using blue for left hand, red for right hand, and circle size proportionate to variance. The top edge of the figure represents space closer to the Kinect® while bottom edge represents space closer to the user. (Color figure online)

The HAB system uses a Kinect® positioned above and slightly behind the monitor displaying the avatar and the virtual world. Coordinates indicated on the user's table space are calculated relative to the Kinect® and then transposed into the virtual world. Therefore, if the user points at the coordinate represented in Fig. 3 as (0.0, 1.6), which approximately represents the point directly beneath the Kinect® on the table, this appears in the virtual world as the coordinate at the center of the table's "far" edge relative to the user (i.e., the edge closest to the avatar). The point represented in the figure as (0.6, 0.0) would appear in the virtual world as the point at the right-hand corner of the table closer to the human (rendered at the bottom of the screen). Coordinates were calculated by intersecting the vector extending through the forearm and extended finger with an infinite plane situated at the height of the physical table's surface. These coordinates were transposed into equivalent coordinates in the virtual world and visualized as a rotating purple target (as shown in Fig. 1). As the user moved their arm, this target also moved in real time, which allowed the user to situate the coordinate at which they were pointing in the virtual world. When the user was pointing at a coordinate interpreted as being on the surface of the virtual table, the target was displayed at full opacity, while if it wandered off the table's surface, the target decreased in opacity proportional to the distance of the interpreted coordinate to the table's surface. This cue allowed the user to see the target while they attempted to move it back onto the table.

We logged all interactions in the following format: INDEX, SYMBOL, CONTENT, TIMESTAMP. SYMBOL is a two letter code consisting of H (human) or A (avatar) followed by S (speech/utterance), G (non-pointing gesture), P (pointing) or A (action). CONTENT is the shallow semantic content of the move, including coordinates where applicable. TIMESTAMP is the time in seconds after the beginning of the interaction. Further details of logging and evaluation scheme may be found in [27]. For this study we focus only the circumstances surrounding human pointing gestures (prefixed HP). Table 1 shows an example snippet of a log file captured during the user studies.

Table 1. Sample trial log (abbreviated)

```
1 HG engage start 1.145281
2 AS "Hello." 1.145281
3 HP r,-0.25,-0.87 4.889832
4 HP r,-0.16,-1.21 4.928307
5 HP r,-0.07,-1.18 4.960413
6 HP r,-0.03,-1.06 5.040221
7 HP r,-0.09,-0.95 5.072867
8 HP r,-0.07,-0.27 5.15642
...
73 HP r,-0.08,11.69 8.552608
74 HG right point high,-0.02,5.45 8.588802
75 AS "Are you pointing here?" 8.588802
```

2.2 Experimentation and Evaluation

We ran user trials on 20 subjects taken from the university graduate student population. All subjects were computer-literate but had no knowledge of the particulars of interaction and had no prior experience using this integrated gesture system. Subjects were divided evenly in one of two environments, shown in Fig. 4. Kinects were placed at the same height in both setups and centered above and slightly behind the widescreen monitor. The test pattern was displayed on an iPad to the left of the screen for the subject's reference. In the setup with the table (**Environment A**), users stepped up to the table's edge to begin the interaction. In the setup without the table (**Environment B**), they stepped up to the blue tape line on the floor.

Fig. 4. Variant conditions with table, and monitor placed at the rear of the table (left) and without table, with monitor placed at the front edge of the supporting desk (right). The lines on the floor in the right-hand image demarcate the bounds (projected downward) of the imaginary table used for calculating pointing coordinates.

The 10 subjects in each environment were also divided into two conditions: half those in Environment A were explicitly told to consider the real table as an extension of the virtual table into the real world, as if the avatar were another person standing behind a glass screen or window, and half those in Environment B were explicitly told to imagine that the virtual table extended out of the screen into the real world, as if the avatar were another person standing behind a glass screen or window. This drew attention to the table or imagined table space and served as an implicit "hint" that it had some role to play in the interaction. The remaining subjects in each environment were not given any extra cues on considering the virtual table. This allowed us two small samples to examine how this extra information affected the users' pointing strategies, and we end up with 4 distinct experimental conditions (Table 2).

Interactions were logged from start to finish, defined as the point at which the user decided that the test pattern was built to their satisfaction, and stepped away from the table's edge/demarcated line.

Table 2. 5 subjects were placed in each experimental condition.

Condition	Physical table	Supplemental information
1	Present (**A**)	None
2	Absent (**B**)	None
3	Present (**A**)	Physical table extends virtual table
4	Absent (**B**)	Virtual table extends into real world

In evaluating the data, we were interested in the time it takes a user in a given condition to settle on a particular position on the table after beginning their pointing gesture. As discussed in Sect. 1.1, deixis may either refer to a location or be coerced to a reference to objects that occupy that location. So, once the system has recognized that the subject has stopped moving their finger and is pointing at a specific location, the system then asks for a confirmation of the location. This question can take many forms based on context, e.g., "Are you pointing here/at this?" (if the user is just starting the interaction), "The <color> block?" (if deixis lands in an area containing one or more blocks), "Should I place something here?" (if deixis lands in a region empty of blocks but a block has been previously indicated), among others. No matter what the question or the context that prompted it, the user must answer it with a *positive acknowledgment* (the word "yes" or a thumbs-up gesture) or a *negative acknowledgment* (the word "no" or a thumbs-down). We define a *successful pointing* as a pointing followed by a positive acknowledgment (that is, the user pointed to a spot that the system recognized and the user confirmed), and a *failed pointing* as a pointing followed by a negative acknowledgment (the user pointed to a spot, the system recognized a different spot, and the user denied that this was correct). The time taken to successfully point is extracted from the log file as the time from the commencement of pointing (e.g., move 3 in Table 1) to the recognition of the location (move 74 in Table 1), but only in those blocks where the pointing event is succeeded by a positive acknowledgment. If a user adapts their deictic strategy to the system, intuitively these times to complete a successful pointing should decrease as the user proceeds further into the interaction. We can model the adaptation in pointing times as a *learning rate* and examine in which conditions users adapt a strategy more quickly.

3   Results and Discussion

We aggregated the data from all sessions of all users in a single condition, and removed outliers, defined as those times lying outside the interquartile range (IQR), for the distribution of all times logged, independent of experimental condition. Since each session may span a different length of time from start to finish, we cannot use the raw duration of an interaction as the independent variable when plotting results, so we normalized by plotting a user's pointing times against the *percentage* of the total interaction completed to that point. We plotted the postprocessed data in two ways:

(1) The raw times taken to complete successful pointing events against the percentage of interaction completed. This allows us to assess a learning curve (see below) for an average user in a given condition and see if the raw time to successfully complete a pointing declines over the course of an interaction, stays flat, or increases.

   – According to Wright's cumulative average model [48], a *learning curve* is modeled as a power law: $y_n = ax^b$. y_n is the average time to "produce the first n units" (in this context, the average time to successfully point to a location on the table the first n times for each trial subject in a given condition). Therefore a is the time to successfully point the first time, and b is the natural slope of the learning curve (over raw times we will denote this b_ρ), which reflects whether learning proceeds rapidly or slowly. A percentage, $s = 2^b$, can be used to express how much the time to point in that environment can be expected to increase or decrease each time the number of pointing events doubles. $s < 1$ (negative b_ρ) indicates increasing adaptation as the interaction proceeds in the condition under examination, as successive points take less time overall. $s > 1$ (positive b_ρ) indicates increasing confusion or difficulty in successfully pointing.

(2) The *ratio* between the time to complete a logged successful pointing event and the *geometric mean* time to complete a successful pointing in that condition, against the percentage of interaction completed.

   – Since we aggregate all data, and since individual users might take longer or shorter on average to indicate a location than others, taking the difference from the mean allows us to normalize some of the variation due to a given subject's natural level of aptitude with the system. Using a ratio rather than a difference allows us to use the geometric mean of the recorded values and thereafter plot the line of best fit using a linear regression, which represents a more intuitive analogue of the learning curve achieved by taking the log of both sides: $log\ y_n = log\ a + b\ log\ x$. The slope of the line, b_μ, reflects changes in a user's ability to successfully point relative to their normalized mean pointing time—regarded as a proxy for the user's natural "set point" ability to successfully indicate a location to the system—in the condition under examination. As above, negative b_μ indicates adaptation to the system and positive b_μ indicates increasing confusion over time.

The Figs. 5 and 6 below show the aggregate data plotted for each experimental condition (see Table 2). In all graphs the X-axis displays the users' progress through their interaction trials, represented as a percentage. In the graphs on the left, the Y-axis shows the time to complete a successful pointing event. On the right, the Y-axis shows the time to complete a successful pointing event, as a ratio to the geometric mean of all recorded pointing times for the user whose time is plotted. Line of best fit is shown as a least-squares fitted power law (left), and a linear regression (right), with b for each curve displayed in the caption.

Overall, the data tends to be dispersed when plotted against best-fit lines, even when removing IQR outliers. Nevertheless, most points tend to cluster near the bottom of the plotted distributions, between 0–2 s for the raw pointing times, and close to a 1:1 ratio of individual pointing times to geometric mean. We can observe a few trends that contrast between experimental conditions, and we expect these trends, where they appear, would be more pronounced with larger sample size, possibly with a higher r^2 value.

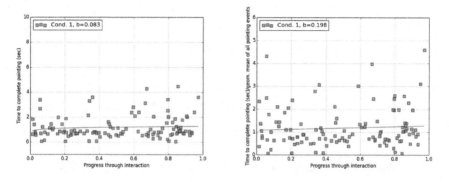

Fig. 5. Results in condition 1. $b_\rho \approx 0.083$, $s \approx 1.059$; $b_\mu \approx 0.198$

In Condition 1, both lines are almost flat, with a very slight upward curve ($b_\rho \approx 0.083$, $s \approx 1.059$; $b_\mu \approx 0.198$), suggesting that users did not adapt a more

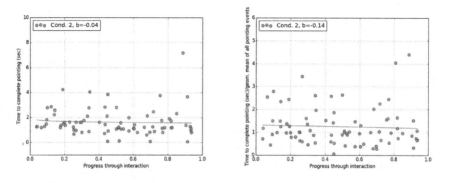

Fig. 6. Results in condition 2. $b_\rho \approx -0.044$, $s \approx 0.970$; $b_\mu \approx -0.144$

efficient pointing strategy by the end of an interaction when compared to the start. The positive b values suggest that users in this condition became slightly *less* efficient at pointing, and although the values are not large enough to be very significant, it does suggest that using the system in this condition (in the presence of the physical table, with no additional information about its role in the setup) may create some confusion for the user.

In Condition 2, both lines are about as flat the best-fit lines in Condition 1, trending very slightly downward ($b_\rho \approx -0.044$, $s \approx 0.970$; $b_\mu \approx -0.144$), but also not enough to draw a firm conclusion. Users appear not to adapt a significantly more efficient pointing strategy in this condition (without the physical table, with no additional information about the table's role), or if so, the learning rate was not fast enough to make an apparent difference over a single interaction (Fig. 7).

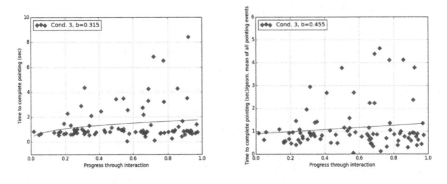

Fig. 7. Results in condition 3. $b_\rho \approx 0.315$, $s \approx 1.245$; $b_\mu \approx 0.455$

Condition 3 demonstrates a negative learning rate (increasing time to point successfully as the interaction goes on). As the interactions proceed, the pointing times get notably more dispersed and the divergent values trend away from the

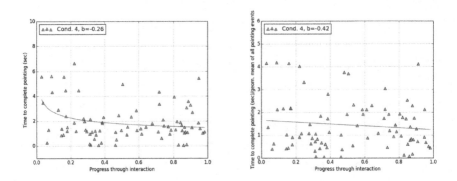

Fig. 8. Results in condition 4. $b_\rho \approx -0.265$, $s \approx 0.832$; $b_\mu \approx -0.427$

geometric mean of users' pointing times ($b_\rho \approx 0.315$, $s \approx 1.245$; $b_\mu \approx 0.455$). Users in this condition (with the physical table, told to regard it and the virtual table as extensions of each other) appear to display increasing difficulty in indicating a location successfully (Fig. 8).

Condition 4 is the only condition in which users display a marked ability to adapt a more efficient pointing strategy over the course of the interaction ($b_\rho \approx -0.265$, $s \approx 0.832$; $b_\mu \approx -0.427$). Users in this condition (without the physical table, told to imagine that the virtual table extends into the real world) appear, in aggregate, to be able to successfully point about 17% faster by each point at which their cumulative number of successful pointing events has doubled (i.e., from 1 to 2 or from 2 to 4, etc.).

4 Conclusion

When we examine the minimal pair of conditions 1/3 vs. 2/4 (that is, the conditions with the physical table and the conditions without the physical table, regardless of users' knowledge of the table's role), we see a trend of increasing difficulty in successfully pointing in conditions with the table, and a trend of more efficient pointing in conditions without the table. This is actually the opposite of what we expected, in that the presence of the table did not seem to provide the users with a reference point with which to ground their deictic gestures and in fact seemed to make pointing more difficult, indicating that it introduced a measure of confusion to the interaction, perhaps causing them uncertainty about which was the valid reference point, the table or the screen.

In Conditions 3 and 4, the difference between the "table" condition and "tableless" condition is more pronounced than in Conditions 1 and 2. The nearly flat lines in Conditions 1 and 2 suggest that users barely changed their pointing strategies in reaction to the system at all. We can speculate that in both conditions they tended to settle on a particular strategy (most likely pointing at the monitor screen/toward the avatar, as suggested by the literature, which was also anecdotally observed during the trials[1]), and persisted with it through the trials, making minimal changes despite difficulties encountered. Presented with no suggestion about how the table might be used in the interaction, subjects adhered to their initial pointing strategies.

Meanwhile, subjects in Conditions 3 and 4, where they are given a prompt about the table's role, display either marked adaptation or marked confusion. Subjects in Condition 4 typically demonstrate appreciable adaptation in pointing strategies over the course of their interactions, while in Condition 3 the time subjects took to successfully point *increased* regularly as the interactions went on. We can hypothesize that, when their attention was drawn to the (physically present) table, users set about trying to use it in the interaction, and if they did not meet with initial success (e.g., were unable to quickly figure out that they should use it to mirror positions on the virtual table), grew confused. In Condition 4, without the physical table present, users could perhaps more

---

[1] No personal information or video of the subjects was captured.

easily imagine the virtual table extended into a space in their world and point to coordinates relative to their own bodies (and body-centered coordinate systems do seem to be natural and ingrained in spatial representation [15]) without the distraction of another object filling the space between themselves and the virtual world. Put simply, it's possible that the presence of the physical table imposed extra cognitive load on the task of trying to imagine the virtual table extending out of the monitor. All this points to difficulties in situating oneself in "mixed-reality" environments [7,14], perhaps due to the cognitive load involved in transforming one's embodied coordinate system to that of the virtual world. Further research would be needed to examine whether the precise phrasing of the relationship between the physical and virtual tables might that have any influence in the results, such as on the mental transformations being performed.

Due to the nature of the experimental setup (e.g., distractors not accounted for in the surrounding environment or that emerge during the course of the interaction), we should forward some caveats and possible alternate explanations for some phenomena. In some conditions, pointing became more difficult in the later stages of the trial. It may be that in some cases, as the target structure emerged, it became more difficult to accurately point at the desired location with the greater need for precision and increased density of blocks. However, this increasing difficulty only emerges in some conditions, so in the others, it may be overridden by the learning adaptation. In addition, the test subjects were allowed free reign to adapt their overall strategy for the building task (i.e., for actions supervenient on the individual vocabulary items and gestures such as pointing), so if pointing at a particular location proved difficult, they adapted their overall plan by (for example), moving objects to new locations entirely (by pointing) or by loosening the constraints on what they determined to be successful actions (e.g., allowing spaces between the blocks so that block location could be easier to indicate by pointing).

In both physical conditions, providing explicit instructions on how to conceive of the task led to more marked results than not providing any guidance. This suggests that the person's model of the situation matters, as well as the physical situation itself.

Due to the partition of subjects into four conditions, we were only able to run five subjects in each condition. As such, these results should be considered tentative. Nonetheless, the conclusions suggested by the results are intriguing, worth further examination, and may become more pronounced in studies with more subjects.

The data we have gathered suggests that when interacting with a virtual environment on a screen, humans have a strong preference for indicating positions relative to that screen, even when physical cues are present that imply that the displayed scene is not the entirety of the environment involved. When these factors are merely implicit, they seem to have little effect on subjects' behavior, but when more attention is drawn to them, subjects are either able to adapt their behavior or the environment, or find the physical cues in conflict with their assumptions about the virtual world. Although deixis is just one part of interacting with a virtual world, it is an important one, and this insight into how humans treat deixis in a virtual environment should be useful to developers seeking to build intelligent systems capable of interacting fluently with humans.

Acknowledgments. The authors would like to thank the reviewers for their helpful comments. We would also like to thank our colleagues at Colorado State University and the University of Florida for developing the gesture recognition systems: Prof. Bruce Draper, Prof. Jaime Ruiz, Prof. Ross Beveridge, Pradyumna Narayana, Isaac Wang, Rahul Bangar, Dhruva Patil, Gururaj Mulay, Jason Yu, and Jesse Smith; and our Brandeis University colleagues, Tuan Do and Kyeongmin Rim, for their work on VoxSim. Additional thanks to Jason for providing Fig. 3. This work is supported by a contract with the US Defense Advanced Research Projects Agency (DARPA), Contract W911NF-15-C-0238. Approved for Public Release, Distribution Unlimited. The views expressed are those of the authors and do not reflect the official policy or position of the Department of Defense or the U.S. Government.

References

1. Abadi, M., Barham, P., Chen, J., Chen, Z., Davis, A., Dean, J., Devin, M., Ghemawat, S., Irving, G., Isard, M., et al.: TensorFlow: a system for large-scale machine learning. In: Proceedings of the 12th USENIX Symposium on Operating Systems Design and Implementation (OSDI), Savannah, Georgia, USA (2016)
2. Abbott, B.: Presuppositions and common ground. Linguist. Philos. **31**(5), 523–538 (2008)
3. Arbib, M., Rizzolatti, G.: Neural expectations: a possible evolutionary path from manual skills to language. Commun. Cogn. **29**, 393–424 (1996)
4. Arbib, M.A.: From grasp to language: embodied concepts and the challenge of abstraction. J. Physiol. Paris **102**(1), 4–20 (2008)
5. Asher, N., Gillies, A.: Common ground, corrections, and coordination. Argumentation **17**(4), 481–512 (2003)
6. Ballard, D.H., Hayhoe, M.M., Pook, P.K., Rao, R.P.: Deictic codes for the embodiment of cognition. Behav. Brain Sci. **20**(4), 723–742 (1997)
7. Benford, S., Greenhalgh, C., Reynard, G., Brown, C., Koleva, B.: Understanding and constructing shared spaces with mixed-reality boundaries. ACM Trans. Comput.-Hum. Interact. (TOCHI) **5**(3), 185–223 (1998)
8. Bergen, B.K.: Louder than Words: The New Science of How the Mind Makes Meaning. Basic Books, New York (2012)
9. Brooks, A.G., Breazeal, C.: Working with robots and objects: Revisiting deictic reference for achieving spatial common ground. In: Proceedings of the 1st ACM SIGCHI/SIGART Conference on Human-Robot Interaction, pp. 297–304. ACM (2006)
10. Clark, H.H., Brennan, S.E.: Grounding in communication. In: Resnick, L., Levine, B., John, M., Teasley, S.D. (eds.) Perspectives on Socially Shared Cognition, pp. 13–1991. American Psychological Association (1991)
11. Clark, H.H., Schreuder, R., Buttrick, S.: Common ground at the understanding of demonstrative reference. J. Verbal Learn. Verbal Behav. **22**(2), 245–258 (1983)

12. David, N., Bewernick, B.H., Cohen, M.X., Newen, A., Lux, S., Fink, G.R., Shah, N.J., Vogeley, K.: Neural representations of self versus other: visual-spatial perspective taking and agency in a virtual ball-tossing game. J. Cogn. Neurosci. **18**(6), 898–910 (2006)
13. Edwards, A., Shepherd, G.J.: Theories of communication, human nature, and the world: associations and implications. Commun. Stud. **55**(2), 197–208 (2004)
14. Flintham, M., Benford, S., Anastasi, R., Hemmings, T., Crabtree, A., Greenhalgh, C., Tandavanitj, N., Adams, M., Row-Farr, J.: Where on-line meets on the streets: experiences with mobile mixed reality games. In: Proceedings of the SIGCHI Conference on Human Factors in Computing Systems, pp. 569–576. ACM (2003)
15. Fogassi, L., Gallese, V., Di Pellegrino, G., Fadiga, L., Gentilucci, M., Luppino, G., Matelli, M., Pedotti, A., Rizzolatti, G.: Space coding by premotor cortex. Exp. Brain Res. **89**(3), 686–690 (1992)
16. Fussell, S.R., Kiesler, S., Setlock, L.D., Yew, V.: How people anthropomorphize robots. In: Proceedings of the 3rd ACM/IEEE International Conference on Human Robot Interaction, pp. 145–152. ACM (2008)
17. He, K., Zhang, X., Ren, S., Sun, J.: Deep residual learning for image recognition. In: Proceedings of the IEEE Conference on Computer Vision and Pattern Recognition, pp. 770–778 (2016)
18. Hindmarsh, J., Fraser, M., Heath, C., Benford, S., Greenhalgh, C.: Object-focused interaction in collaborative virtual environments. ACM Trans. Comput. Hum. Interact. (TOCHI) **7**(4), 477–509 (2000)
19. Hindmarsh, J., Heath, C.: Embodied reference: a study of deixis in workplace interaction. J. Pragmatics **32**(12), 1855–1878 (2000)
20. Hostetter, A.B., Alibali, M.W.: Visible embodiment: gestures as simulated action. Psychon. Bull. Rev. **15**(3), 495–514 (2008)
21. Izadi, S., Brignull, H., Rodden, T., Rogers, Y., Underwood, M.: Dynamo: a public interactive surface supporting the cooperative sharing and exchange of media. In: Proceedings of the 16th Annual ACM Symposium on User Interface Software and Technology, pp. 159–168. ACM (2003)
22. Johanson, B., Hutchins, G., Winograd, T., Stone, M.: PointRight: experience with flexible input redirection in interactive workspaces. In: Proceedings of the 15th Annual ACM Symposium on User Interface Software and Technology, pp. 227–234. ACM (2002)
23. Kirchhofer, K.C., Zimmermann, F., Kaminski, J., Tomasello, M.: Dogs (canis familiaris), but not chimpanzees (pan troglodytes), understand imperative pointing. PLoS ONE **7**(2), e30913 (2012)
24. Krishnaswamy, N., Narayana, P., Wang, I., Rim, K., Bangar, R., Patil, D., Mulay, G., Ruiz, J., Beveridge, R., Draper, B., Pustejovsky, J.: Communicating and acting: understanding gesture in simulation semantics. In: 12th International Workshop on Computational Semantics (2017)
25. Krishnaswamy, N., Pustejovsky, J.: Multimodal semantic simulations of linguistically underspecified motion events. In: Barkowsky, T., Burte, H., Hölscher, C., Schultheis, H. (eds.) Spatial Cognition/KogWis - 2016. LNCS (LNAI), vol. 10523, pp. 177–197. Springer, Cham (2017). https://doi.org/10.1007/978-3-319-68189-4_11
26. Krishnaswamy, N., Pustejovsky, J.: VoxSim: a visual platform for modeling motion language. In: Proceedings of COLING 2016, the 26th International Conference on Computational Linguistics: Technical Papers. ACL (2016)
27. Krishnaswamy, N., Pustejovsky, J.: An evaluation framework for multimodal interaction. In: Proceedings of LREC (2018, forthcoming)

28. Lewis, D.: Scorekeeping in a language game. J. Philos. Logic **8**(1), 339–359 (1979)
29. Malik, S., Ranjan, A., Balakrishnan, R.: Interacting with large displays from a distance with vision-tracked multi-finger gestural input. In: Proceedings of the 18th Annual ACM Symposium on User Interface Software and Technology, pp. 43–52. ACM (2005)
30. Moeslund, T.B., Störring, M., Granum, E.: A natural interface to a virtual environment through computer vision-estimated pointing gestures. In: Wachsmuth, I., Sowa, T. (eds.) GW 2001. LNCS (LNAI), vol. 2298, pp. 59–63. Springer, Heidelberg (2002). https://doi.org/10.1007/3-540-47873-6_6
31. Morris, M.R., Huang, A., Paepcke, A., Winograd, T.: Cooperative gestures: multi-user gestural interactions for co-located groupware. In: Proceedings of the SIGCHI Conference on Human Factors in Computing Systems, pp. 1201–1210. ACM (2006)
32. Morris, M.R., Wobbrock, J.O., Wilson, A.D.: Understanding users' preferences for surface gestures. In: Proceedings of Graphics Interface 2010, pp. 261–268. Canadian Information Processing Society (2010)
33. Narayana, P., Krishnaswamy, N., Wang, I., Bangar, R., Patil, D., Mulay, G., Rim, K., Beveridge, R., Ruiz, J., Pustejovsky, J., Draper, B.: Cooperating with avatars through gesture, language and action. In: Intelligent Systems Conference (IntelliSys) (2018, forthcoming)
34. Papaxanthis, C., Pozzo, T., Schieppati, M.: Trajectories of arm pointing movements on the sagittal plane vary with both direction and speed. Exp. Brain Res. **148**(4), 498–503 (2003)
35. Pustejovsky, J.: The Generative Lexicon. MIT Press, Cambridge (1995)
36. Pustejovsky, J.: From actions to events: communicating through language and gesture. Interact. Stud. **19**(1) (2018)
37. Pustejovsky, J., Krishnaswamy, N.: VoxML: a visualization modeling language. In: Calzolari, N., Choukri, K., Declerck, T., Goggi, S., Grobelnik, M., Maegaard, B., Mariani, J., Mazo, H., Moreno, A., Odijk, J., Piperidis, S. (eds.) Proceedings of the Tenth International Conference on Language Resources and Evaluation (LREC 2016). European Language Resources Association (ELRA), Paris, May 2016
38. Pustejovsky, J., Krishnaswamy, N., Draper, B., Narayana, P., Bangar, R.: Creating common ground through multimodal simulations. In: Proceedings of the IWCS Workshop on Foundations of Situated and Multimodal Communication (2017)
39. Scott, S.D., Grant, K.D., Mandryk, R.L.: System guidelines for co-located, collaborative work on a tabletop display. In: Kuutti, K., Karsten, E.H., Fitzpatrick, G., Dourish, P., Schmidt, K. (eds.) ECSCW 2003, pp. 159–178. Springer, Heidelberg (2003). https://doi.org/10.1007/978-94-010-0068-0_9
40. Spence, I., Feng, J.: Video games and spatial cognition. Rev. Gen. Psychol. **14**(2), 92 (2010)
41. Stalnaker, R.: Common ground. Linguist. Philos. **25**(5–6), 701–721 (2002)
42. Tomasello, M., Carpenter, M.: Shared intentionality. Dev. Sci. **10**(1), 121–125 (2007)
43. Volterra, V., Caselli, M.C., Capirci, O., Pizzuto, E.: Gesture and the emergence and development of language. Beyond nature-nurture: Essays in honor of Elizabeth Bates, pp. 3–40 (2005)
44. Wang, I., Narayana, P., Patil, D., Mulay, G., Bangar, R., Draper, B., Beveridge, R., Ruiz, J.: EGGNOG: a continuous, multi-modal data set of naturally occurring gestures with ground truth labels. In: To appear in the Proceedings of the 12th IEEE International Conference on Automatic Face & Gesture Recognition (2017)

45. Wang, I., Narayana, P., Patil, D., Mulay, G., Bangar, R., Draper, B., Beveridge, R., Ruiz, J.: Exploring the use of gesture in collaborative tasks. In: Proceedings of the 2017 CHI Conference Extended Abstracts on Human Factors in Computing Systems, CHI EA 2017, pp. 2990–2997. ACM, New York (2017). https://doi.org/10.1145/3027063.3053239

46. Wobbrock, J.O., Morris, M.R., Wilson, A.D.: User-defined gestures for surface computing. In: Proceedings of the SIGCHI Conference on Human Factors in Computing Systems, pp. 1083–1092. ACM (2009)

47. Wraga, M., Creem-Regehr, S.H., Proffitt, D.R.: Spatial updating of virtual displays. Mem. Cogn. **32**(3), 399–415 (2004)

48. Wright, T.P.: Learning curve. J. Aeronaut. Sci. **3**(1), 122–128 (1936)

49. Zhai, S., Kong, J., Ren, X.: Speed-accuracy tradeoff in fitts' law tasks-on the equivalency of actual and nominal pointing precision. Int. J. Hum. Comput. Stud. **61**(6), 823–856 (2004)

50. Zhang, Z.: Microsoft kinect sensor and its effect. IEEE MultiMedia **19**, 4–10 (2012)

Analyzing Strong Spatial Cognition:
A Modeling Approach

Jasper van de Ven[1(✉)], Munehiro Fukuda[2], Holger Schultheis[1],
Christian Freksa[1], and Thomas Barkowsky[1]

[1] Bremen Spatial Cognition Center, University of Bremen, Bremen, Germany
{vandeven,schulth,freksa,barkowsky}@uni-bremen.de
[2] Computing and Software Systems Division, University of Washington Bothell,
Bothell, USA
mfukuda@u.washington.edu

Abstract. Natural cognitive agents such as humans and animals may
frequently solve spatial problems in their environment by manipulating
their environment instead of doing all the computation in their head (e.g.,
untangling a power cable by inspection and direct interaction: pull here,
push there). We call this replacement of computational effort from the
central processor by direct manipulation *strong spatial cognition*. Artificial cognitive agents are currently lacking a comparable ability to exploit
their spatio-physical environment for efficient problem solving. One main
issue with equipping artificial cognitive agents with strong spatial cognition is that the constraints and properties of this type of problem
solving are still insufficiently understood. Being tightly embedded in the
spatio-physical and temporal surrounding renders strong spatial cognition difficult to assess by traditional methods. This makes it hard to
gain an explicit understanding of its nature and to compare it to existing
computational approaches. In this paper, we propose to employ *models*
of strong spatial cognition to gain a deeper understanding of this phenomenon and its nature. We created models of an example application
of strong spatial cognition to solve the shortest path problem. By considering different approaches for a computational simulation model, our
modeling work revealed that (instantaneous) information propagation
constitutes a core characteristic of strong spatial cognition. Moreover,
modeling facilitated identifying those questions, which seem of major
importance for further deepening our understanding of strong spatial
cognition.

1 Introduction

Solving spatial tasks is an important part of everyday activity in the lives of animals, humans, and cognitive agents, in general. Examples include chores such
as setting the table and orientation while moving through the world. Humans
seem to often solve these problems with more ease, if they can be visualized or
are available as concrete instances in their environment, which can be manipulated. In [1] the idea of *strong spatial cognition* is presented to investigate and

© Springer Nature Switzerland AG 2018
S. Creem-Regehr et al. (Eds.): Spatial Cognition 2018, LNAI 11034, pp. 197–208, 2018.
https://doi.org/10.1007/978-3-319-96385-3_14

exploit this kind of spatial action- and perception-based problem solving. That is, humans solve spatial problems not only by generating symbolic representations and applying reasoning to compute solutions, but by invoking actions, perceiving their effects, and adapting the action. For example, if one has to untangle two cables, the common approach is to pick them up and start pushing and pulling on cable parts and see where a cable end can be pulled out of a loop in order to reduce the degree of entanglement.

This basic ability to utilize space and change to directly solve problems seems to be an essential part of our cognitive abilities. Therefore a cognitive agent, be it living or artificial, must have not only internal perception and reasoning functions, but also an understanding or at least an assumption of the affordances of the environment. Figure 1 illustrates this view on a full cognitive system including internal knowledge representation and reasoning, perception and action options, physical capabilities, and the inhabited environment.

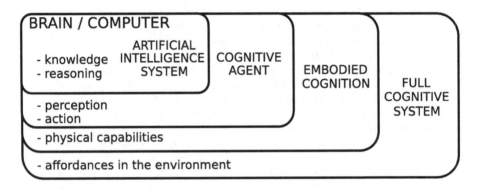

Fig. 1. Structure of a full cognitive system [1, 2]

Artificial cognitive agents are currently lacking a comparable ability to exploit their spatio-physical environment for efficient problem solving. One main issue with equipping artificial cognitive agents with strong spatial cognition is that the constraints and properties of this type of problem solving are still insufficiently understood. Being tightly embedded in the environment it is difficult to assess strong spatial cognition by traditional methods. This makes it hard to gain an explicit understanding of strong spatial cognition or to compare it to traditional computing approaches. In order to approach this, we propose to employ *models* of strong spatial cognition to gain a deeper understanding of this phenomenon, its properties, and its nature.

In the remainder of this paper, we discuss the concept of strong spatial cognition in more detail, address model design and instances, and introduce and discuss observations made during model creation and evaluation. In order to have a practical application for illustration, we utilize the shortest path search as a running example.

2 Strong Spatial Cognition

Strong spatial cognition [1,2] aims at preserving spatial structure and directly exploits features and properties of spatial transformations and affordances. In the structure presented in Fig. 1, strong spatial cognition methods are found at the border between embodied cognition to a full cognitive system. That is, a cognitive agent utilizes its spatio-physical capabilities to invoke actions in and on spatial objects and configurations in the environment and perceives their effects. It is important to note that these actions are not necessarily performed by the agent, but can be inherent within the environment. Spatial objects and configurations are represented by themselves or by mild abstraction [2], rather than by symbolic representations. This avoids information loss due to early representational commitments, i.e., it is not necessary to decide beforehand which aspects to abstract away and which spatial reference frame to use. The advantage is that at a later point in time more information may be available to make a better-informed decision about which specific (mild) abstraction and frame of reference to apply.

The strong spatial cognition approach is to concentrate on the specific spatial problem to be solved by creating an appropriate object or spatial configuration, e.g., by removing task-irrelevant entities and features or by reconstructing the essence of the object or spatial configuration through mild abstraction, e.g., scaling, rotation, or translation. It is hard to predict the optimal object or spatial configuration to create. However, spatial problems pose a special case as natural agents have enough meta-knowledge, i.e., experiences with affordances and physical effects, about the environment to apply useful heuristics for supporting object or spatial configuration creation. The created entities are then exposed to the environment and the result either presents a direct solution or a configuration that may be more suitable for a knowledge-based approach to solve the original problem.

The insight that spatial relations and physical operations are strongly connected to cognitive processing may lead to a different division of labor between the perceptual, representational, computational, and locomotive parts of cognitive interaction than the one pursued in classical AI systems. That is, rather than putting all the configurational reasoning into the computer or agent, the strong spatial cognition approach employs (physical) spatial reconfiguration by the environment in order to simplify or nullify the problem to be solved. The approach uses structural and procedural 'knowledge in the world' [3], i.e., physics and affordances, to solve spatial problems by exploiting intrinsic structures of space and time. To do this successfully, the computer or agent must be equipped with meta-knowledge and respective reasoning abilities in order to identify and perform useful actions and to perceive significant effects.

Our hypothesis is that a flexible assignment of physical and computational resources for cognitive problem solving is closer to natural cognitive systems than the current purely computational approaches. For example, when cognitive agents search for a certain object in the environment, they have at least two strategies at their disposal: they can represent the object in their mind and try to imagine and mentally reconstruct where the object should or could be located, i.e., the classical AI approach, or they can visually search for the object in the physical environment. Which is better (or more promising) depends on a variety of factors including memory and physical effort and the environment. We think that most often a clever combination of both approaches will be best.

To illustrate the concept of strong spatial cognition, we use shortest path search as a running example throughout this paper. Figure 2 presents a physical network of connected nodes and the task is to identify the shortest path between two specific nodes. In order to create the network, a map is used as basis and roads are (3D) printed as strings and each intersection or location of interest is printed as a circular node. By applying a physical force/action we can pull the two specific nodes apart until the connections between them form a straight line (see Fig. 3), which explicates the shortest path. Furthermore, applying the same force/action we would also directly explicate, if there is one or more shortest paths (see Fig. 4).

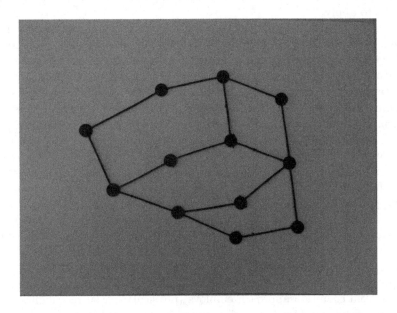

Fig. 2. Strong spatial cognition shortest path object

This example illustrates several important aspects of strong spatial cognition, e.g., mild abstraction, exploiting spatial constraints and continuity, and perception and action apparatus of the involved cognitive agent and thus provides an instance of problem solving by a full cognitive system. It also highlights a number of prerequisites for successfully applying strong spatial cognition such as (I) that mild abstraction preserves required environmental properties and (II) that the perception of and actions within the environment are (mostly) cheap.

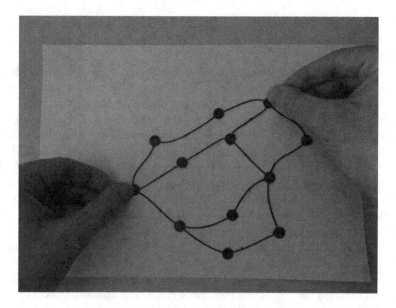

Fig. 3. Strong spatial cognition shortest path

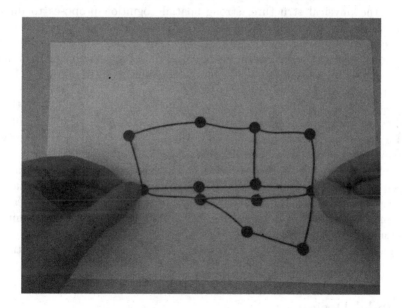

Fig. 4. Strong spatial cognition shortest paths

Thus, strong spatial cognition is based on the following basic assumptions: (1) mild abstraction allows to create objects and spatial configurations within the environment that preserve specific properties, (2) there exists a cognitive agent within the environment, and (3) the cognitive agent can perceive and interpret as well as act on the environment to interact with the objects or spatial configuration.

As such, strong spatial cognition has a number of relations to but also sets itself apart from contemporary approaches to analyzing and building cognitive agents. Strong spatial cognition builds on arguments of Norman [3], who argues for the importance of distinguishing "knowledge in the head" from "knowledge in the world" and Kirsh [4], who highlights the importance of physical interactions for (human) problem solving. Strong spatial cognition can also be seen in the tradition of biology-inspired approaches as pioneered by [5,6] and Gibson's [7] idea of affordances. However, in contrast to these biology-inspired approaches, strong spatial cognition goes beyond strictly reactive behavior, but includes physical interactions that are deliberately used to solve problems. Furthermore, strong spatial cognition interprets affordances as conditions that permit actions in spatial environments and not exclusively as conditions that can be perceptually identified [8]. Strong spatial cognition also bears resemblance to the notion of analogical representations [9,10] and diagrammatic reasoning [11,12] in the sense that all three stress the importance of (preserving) the spatio-physical structure of the problem (environment). While analogical representations and diagrammatic reasoning work towards representation structures that mirror important parts of the physical structure, strong spatial cognition proposes to directly exploit the spatial structure. This direct exploitation is also what sets strong spatial cognition apart from traditional knowledge-based approaches, in which facts and relations about space in general and about specific problem domains are encoded as knowledge that describes the domain (e.g., in ontologies [13] or in qualitative spatial representations [14,15]).

A use of ambient properties comparable to strong spatial cognition is exploited in morphological computation [16,17]. Morphological computation exploits the properties of an agent's body (its morphology) in interactions with its environment. That is, we can perceive morphological computation as a real subset of strong spatial cognition, as it is restricted to exploiting interactions between the agents morphology and the environment while strong spatial cognition takes a more general approach in including any interaction between the agent and the environment as well as interaction occurring purely within the environment.

A more in-depth discussion of the relation of strong spatial cognition to previous approaches can be found in [2].

3   Model Design

Figures 2, 3 and 4 present how we envision the actual use of strong spatial cognition for the example of the shortest path search. By investigating this example, we identified different approaches to use forces/actions to explicate the shortest path between two nodes. That is, we apply a strong force to the start node (grasping or pinning down action) to fix it in position. Then a force (pull action) is applied to the goal node explicating the shortest path. Here, it also occurred to us that we could apply the force to all nodes, like gravity applies to all objects in our world (see Fig. 5). This simultaneously explicates all shortest paths outgoing of the start node. That is, the force works simultaneously on all nodes, i.e., the 'computation' and information propagation of positions happens in parallel in either case.

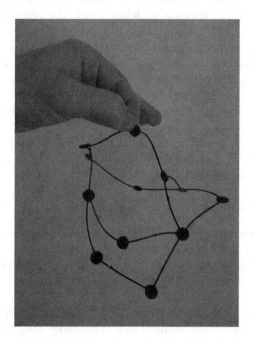

Fig. 5. Strong spatial cognition with gravity

In essence, we identified two types of forces applicable:

- *individual force*, i.e., a force that is directly applied to one specific node, and
- *ambient force*, i.e., a force that is applied to all nodes (e.g., gravity).

These forces can also be present simultaneously in the environment.

However, the problem remains that this embedded approach is very hard to analyze. How do objects or spatial configurations interact with the environment? Why does this interaction seem so effective? What are the 'computational' properties, i.e., what properties explicate the solution? How does this 'computation' unfold?

To address and, ultimately, answer these questions we need a way to investigate strong spatial cognition. As argued above, a direct investigation by well known means does not seem feasible. Against this background, we argue that an appropriate way to make strong spatial cognition amenable to thorough analyses is by building and analyzing computational models of it. Such a computational modeling approach shares a number of advantages with modeling in other domains (e.g., [18]): First and foremost, a computational realization afford ways of analyses that are unfeasible for the entity that is modeled. Second, building computational models forces theoretical explicitness and precision. Third, because a computational model has to be explicit and precise, it facilitates pinpointing those aspects of the to-be-modeled entity that are still insufficiently understood, that is, modeling draws the attention to the crucial open questions.

Specifically, we propose to generate and investigate models of specific strong spatial cognition instances. These models map a spatio-physical environment to computational simulation approaches. We build on computational approaches as there exist standardized and well understood methods for the analysis of computational models. Note, however, that these models of strong spatial cognition are not actual strong spatial cognition instances or possibilities how we propose to utilize strong spatial cognition. That is, they are meant to help analyze and understand the strong spatial cognition idea and not as an implementation pattern for strong spatial cognition programs.

4   (Computational) Model Instances

In order to get a better understanding of the inner workings of strong spatial cognition, i.e., what properties or aspects are crucial, we decided to implement computational models of the shortest path search that imitate the use of gravity. For this, we assumed, that the central property of 'environmental computation' is parallelism.

Based on this, we decided to use the MASS (Multi-Agent Spatial Simulation) library [19,20] for our implementation as it is specially designed to build spatial simulations with a parallel programming paradigm. The MASS library allows implementing parallel multi-agent systems by implementing the two concepts of *Places* and *Agents*. This fits very well with the internal structure of strong spatial cognition as we see it at the moment. That is, we are able to model individual agents and space they inhabit as well as other objects in space in a clear way. *Places* are represented as a multi-dimensional array of elements that are dynamically allocated over a cluster of multi-core computing nodes. Each *Place* is capable to make parallel function calls with all neighboring *Places* to exchange information. *Agents* are actors that can reside in *Places* and autonomously migrate to any other *Place* and synchronize with all other *Agents* according to function calls. Thus, *Agents* can interact with one another through setting and perceiving information within the *Place* they inhabit. Parallelization is realized through a set of multi-core computing nodes connected through a secure network layer. This left us with two implementation options to be considered for using MASS:

- *Place-only implementation:* Each *Place* represents a different node. *Places* forward gravity as a message through a repetition of their exchange of information with their neighbors. A limitation of such a MASS implementation is to force all *Places* to exchange messages with their neighbors regardless of an arrival of gravity, which results in having all *Places* keep forwarding null messages to their neighbors.

- *Agent-based implementation:* Similar to the first option, each *Place* represents a different node. We introduce an *Agent* as gravity that travels from the source node (i.e., *Place*) to the destination by cloning itself along all neighbors. Although an *Agent* is a larger object than a message, the number of *Agents* spawned over a simulation is much lower than the number of messages to be exchanged among *Places* in the first implementation.

As MASS only provides us with a fully distributed model, i.e., computations and storage are distributed, we decided to also implement a model that uses a centralized storage. The idea being that in the real world, all information is also stored in one entity, i.e., the spatio-physical environment. The computations are again set to be conducted distributively in parallel. That is, each node is realized as an individual thread and a central storage contains information regarding the position of each node as well as a set of constraints (maximal distances) between specific nodes. In an iterative approach, each node gets the instruction to drop (change its position). It checks and makes sure that the changed position does not violate any constraint and updates the position information in the central storage. If a constraint violation would happen due to a position change, the position update is restricted to the maximal change that does not violate any constraint.

All three implementations model the shortest path search using an ambient force (gravity) while applying a very strong force keeping the start node fixed in its original location. During execution, the models only simulate selected physical properties, i.e., gravitation, which moves all nodes until they are fully constrained. That is, each simulation propagates position information updates for all nodes throughout the model until no further changes are possible.

5   Model Discussion

The design and implementation of these computational models to simulate strong spatial cognition led to a couple of observations. To us the two most noteworthy are: (1) information propagation seems the most crucial aspect of the solution generation and (2) that all implementations required a representation of the object or spatial configuration as well as a definition of at least selected properties of the environment as functionality, i.e., simulations like physics.

Regarding information propagation, the strength of the strong spatial cognition approach is that the actual work of updating, synchronizing, and consistency checking of information is provided by the environment and does not require additional work from the 'computational' side. It is also important to note, that this data management is not only provided, but is also instantaneous (one could call it *ambient*), i.e., we cannot get into a world state where data is inconsistent due to some form of reader-writer problem. This also indicates a concept of parallelism in the real world and as a consequence in strong spatial cognition that is rather different from the concept of parallelism in computer science. Where parallelism in traditional computer science addresses mainly the execution, in strong spatial cognition it addresses always all aspects, i.e., execution, knowledge exchange, and knowledge storage.

Regarding the design and implementation of computational models of strong spatial cognition, it seems that strong spatial cognition approaches only explicate the knowledge representation, while in the computational approach we also have to explicate the functionality to compute the solution. Thus, the amount of representational work in strong spatial cognition seems to be more streamlined and there is a clearer distinction between information representation (i.e., the object or spatial configuration) and the possibilities for change (i.e., the environmental properties). In computational implementations both of these aspects have to be explicitly represented in a program.

Next to these two major observations, building and running the models also helped to identify the following research questions that are central for gaining a more comprehensive understanding of strong spatial cognition:

(Q1) What is complexity in the context of strong spatial cognition?
(Q2) How does strong spatial cognition relate to traditional computing?
(Q3) Which axioms and properties are crucial for strong spatial cognition and its definition?
(Q4) What are design patterns to 'implement' strong spatial cognition?
(Q5) What is the relation between object or spatial configuration and environment in strong spatial cognition?
(Q6) Which heuristics are optimal for the creation of objects or spatial configurations in given contexts?
(Q7) To what extent and how is strong spatial cognition learned?
(Q8) Is strong spatial cognition only available to individuals that are or were able to actively manipulate the environment or may it also derive from (passive) perception of the environment?

Question Q1 was already raised by [21]. The other questions basically address the internal workings of strong spatial cognition (Q3 and Q5), how we can utilize strong spatial cognition (Q2, Q4, and Q6), or how we develop the capability of strong spatial cognition (Q7 and Q8).

6   Conclusion

Strong spatial cognition aims at moving the computational effort from the central processor to the environment. In this paper we presented a first step towards analyzing strong spatial cognition by designing and implementing computational simulation models. The results show that especially the properties of the environmental memory in terms of instantaneous synchronization and ambient accessibility are key aspects of this approach. Furthermore, these properties seem to be strongly linked to the special form of parallelism exploited by strong spatial cognition.

As next steps we will investigate in more detail the information propagation in strong spatial cognition and computational simulation models. We intend to focus on the amount of information propagated as well as how the information flow is restricted. The idea being that this might lead to an initial comparable measure of complexity for strong spatial cognition and traditional computer science.

In addition, we will further investigate the general properties of strong spatial cognition by creating further computational simulation models of different strong spatial cognition approaches. We will also investigate the use of physics- and other simulation engines in order to generate models with environments that implicitly provide action capabilities, i.e., affordances. We believe that this is the way forward to develop a better definition of strong spatial cognition and to shed light on the question on how to connect or combine it with computational approaches.

Acknowledgements. We thank the anonymous reviewers for their valuable comments and feedback. The research reported in this paper has been partially supported by the German Research Foundation DFG, as part of Collaborative Research Center (Sonderforschungsbereich) 1320 'EASE - Everyday Activity Science and Engineering', University of Bremen (http://www.ease-crc.org/). Research was conducted in subproject P3 - Spatial reasoning in everyday activity.

References

1. Freksa, C.: Strong spatial cognition. In: Fabrikant, S.I., Raubal, M., Bertolotto, M., Davies, C., Freundschuh, S., Bell, S. (eds.) COSIT 2015. LNCS, vol. 9368, pp. 65–86. Springer, Cham (2015). https://doi.org/10.1007/978-3-319-23374-1_4
2. Freksa, C., Olteţeanu, A.-M., Barkowsky, T., van de Ven, J., Schultheis, H.: Spatial problem solving in spatial structures. In: Phon-Amnuaisuk, S., Ang, S.-P., Lee, S.-Y. (eds.) MIWAI 2017. LNCS (LNAI), vol. 10607, pp. 18–29. Springer, Cham (2017). https://doi.org/10.1007/978-3-319-69456-6_2
3. Norman, D.: The Design of Everyday Things. Verlag Franz Vahlen GmbH, München (2016)
4. Kirsh, D.: Embodied cognition and the magical future of interaction design. ACM Trans. Comput. Hum. Interact. (TOCHI) **20**(1), 3 (2013)
5. Braitenberg, V.: Vehicles: Experiments in Synthetic Psychology. MIT Press, Cambridge (1986)
6. Pfeifer, R., Scheier, C.: Understanding Intelligence. MIT Press, Cambridge (2001)
7. Gibson, J.: The Ecological Approach to Visual Perception. Lawrence Erlbaum, New Jersey (1979)
8. Raubal, M., Moratz, R.: A functional model for affordance-based agents. In: Rome, E., Hertzberg, J., Dorffner, G. (eds.) Towards Affordance-Based Robot Control. LNCS (LNAI), vol. 4760, pp. 91–105. Springer, Heidelberg (2008). https://doi.org/10.1007/978-3-540-77915-5_7
9. Sloman, A.: Interactions between philosophy and artificial intelligence: the role of intuition and non-logical reasoning in intelligence. Artif. Intell. **2**(3–4), 209–225 (1971)

10. Sloman, A.: Afterthoughts on analogical representations. In: Proceedings of the 1975 Workshop on Theoretical Issues in Natural Language Processing, pp. 164–168. Association for Computational Linguistics (1975)
11. Glasgow, J., Narayanan, N.H., Chandrasekaran, B.: Diagrammatic Reasoning: Cognitive and Computational perspectives. MIT Press, Cambridge (1995)
12. Goel, A.K., Jamnik, M., Narayanan, N.H. (eds.): Diagrammatic Representation and Inference. LNCS (LNAI), vol. 6170. Springer, Heidelberg (2010). https://doi.org/10.1007/978-3-642-14600-8
13. Bateman, J.A., Hois, J., Ross, R., Tenbrink, T.: A linguistic ontology of space for natural language processing. Artif. Intell. **174**(14), 1027–1071 (2010)
14. Cohn, A.G., Renz, J.: Qualitative spatial representation and reasoning. Found. Artif. Intell. **3**, 551–596 (2008)
15. Dylla, F., et al.: A survey of qualitative spatial and temporal calculi: algebraic and computational properties. ACM Comput. Surv. (CSUR) **50**(1), 7 (2017)
16. Ghazi-Zahedi, K., Langer, C., Ay, N.: Morphological computation: synergy of body and brain. Entropy **19**(9), 456 (2017)
17. Ghazi-Zahedi, K., Deimel, R., Montúfar, G., Wall, V., Brock, O.: Morphological computation: the good, the bad, and the ugly. In: 2017 IEEE/RSJ International Conference on Intelligent Robots and Systems, IROS 2017, Vancouver, BC, Canada, 24–28 September 2017, pp. 464–469 (2017)
18. Cooper, R.P.: Modelling High-Level Cognitive Processes. Psychology Press, London (2002). (Contributions: Yule, P.G., Fox, J., Glasspool, D.W. and Cooper, R.P.)
19. Chuang, T., Fukuda, M.: A parallel multi-agent spatial simulation environment for cluster systems. In: 2013 IEEE 16th International Conference on Computational Science and Engineering. IEEE, December 2013
20. Ma, Z., Fukuda, M.: A multi-agent spatial simulation library for parallelizing transport simulations. In: 2015 Winter Simulation Conference, WSC. IEEE, December 2015
21. Furbach, U., Furbach, F., Freksa, C.: Relating strong spatial cognition to symbolic problem solving—an example. arXiv preprint arXiv:1606.04397 (2016)

Individuals in Space

Do Spatial Abilities Have an Impact on Route Learning in Hypertexts?

Markus Kattenbeck[1]([envelope]), Thomas Jänich[1], and Ludwig Kreuzpointner[2]

[1] Chair for Information Science, University of Regensburg,
93053 Regensburg, Germany
`markus.kattenbeck@ur.de, thomas@jaenich.de`
[2] Chair for Medical Psychology, Psychological Diagnostics and Research
Methodology, University of Regensburg, 93053 Regensburg, Germany
`ludwig.kreuzpointner@ur.de`

Abstract. Metaphors of navigation have been widely used to describe the behaviour of users surfing the World Wide Web. We present the results of a web-based experiment ($N = 85$ participants) on route learning in Wikipedia. As spatial abilities and sense of direction are known to be important for real-world wayfinding abilities, we examine the extent to which the participants are able to retrace a learned route on their own and the time taken to do this can be predicted using these variables. The tested (G)LMM models, however, show a lower than expected relevance of spatial abilities and sense of direction. The results suggest that both personal factors (such as age and gender) and task are important for the duration of tasks.

1 Introduction

Human spatial abilities and sense of direction are known to be of major importance for the navigational abilities humans show in real-world environments (see e.g. [9,20,65]). While this effect has been repeatedly analyzed, both in real-world (see e.g. [24]) and virtual environments (see e.g. [32] for a very recent study), it has been of less interest in hypertext environments. Metaphors of navigation have been used to describe user behaviour in large hypertexts from the beginning of the concept (see e.g. [16] for a very early account). This metaphor is useful (see [23] for a discussion) due to, in addition to other reasons, the pervasiveness of navigation in everyday life (see e.g. [18, pp. 68–69] and [35, p. 264] for a review of this argument). To date, however, little is known about how factors such as sense of direction and spatial abilities impact on navigational abilities on the web. This is of general interest because of the empirical evidence on users' preferences for navigation over search in digital filing systems (see e.g. [4]) and when trying to re-find mails (see e.g. [8]). Empirical findings suggest, moreover,

---

We would like to thank 85 persons willing to participate. We are grateful to David Elsweiler for his valuable comments to a draft version of this paper and to 4 anonymous reviewers for their feedback regarding possible improvements.

S. Creem-Regehr et al. (Eds.): Spatial Cognition 2018, LNAI 11034, pp. 211–227, 2018.
https://doi.org/10.1007/978-3-319-96385-3_15

that navigation in folder structures and physical environments use similar brain regions (see [6]). The work presented here, which is exploratory in nature, investigates this aspect by focusing on a specific task on the web: We analyze whether self-reported sense of direction and spatial mental abilities can be used to predict a person's ability to remember a sequence of links in Wikipedia. Choosing route learning is reasonable because it is commonly thought of as the first step of developing a cognitive map (see [49]). Using Wikipedia ensures ecological validity because it is a real-world hypertext system which has successfully been used in other navigation studies.

2   Related Work

Given the goal of this study, we examine two bodies of related work. The first deals with experiments on route learning under different conditions, whereas the second reviews studies dedicated to navigation involving Wikipedia.

Route learning has recently been studied from diverse perspectives. One aspect researchers are interested in is how body movement influences route-learning. Ruddle and colleagues [46,47] provide a strong argument for the importance of body-based information for both navigation tasks and the development of cognitive maps. Other studies examine the importance of gestures for memory recall (see [54,55]) and find evidences that gestures will increase recall across different levels of spatial abilities. A second aspect deals with the influence of age. O'Malley and colleagues [40] find differences with respects to route knowledge (older participants acquire less route knowledge). Lingwood et al. [32] compare the learning and recall capabilities of children of different ages with adults in a virtual environment. They find that even young children can learn routes very quickly in a non-repetitive manner. Similarly, Hartmeyer et al. [22] presents findings suggesting that older adults learn routes more slowly than younger adults. A third aspect of interest is the effect of different environments. Lloyd and colleagues [33] report on a pilot study regarding the equivalence of route learning in real and virtual reality environments. They find evidence indicating that results in terms of error rates and strategies applied by participants are very similar across different environments. This fits with the finding that the mode (treadmill w/o rotation vs. joystick) of conducting experiments on spatial learning has a major impact on landmark, route and survey knowledge acquisition [11,12]. More specifically, decision making fosters graph knowledge whereas idiothetic knowledge increases survey knowledge. Larrue et al. [29] draw the conclusion that "body-centred informations [sic] are more involved in allocentric (distance estimates) than egocentric navigational strategies". This aligns with the findings of van der Ham et al. [21] who compare abilities for learning routes in diverse real and virtual environments, concluding that a combination of walking a route, which is displayed on a mobile device, in an open field yields survey knowledge effects very close to real-world experiments while virtual environment experiments do not. The second body of research, relevant to our work, relates to Wikipedia, where interest in hypertext navigation has increased. A large proportion of the research uses a web-based game called Wikispeedia [61] to collect user data. In this game participants are required to find the shortest path between two random articles. The growing dataset collected by means of this online-game is used for several purposes. West et al. analyze differences from shortest paths [59], indicating a preference of participants to use hubs and extract missing links by analyzing the node centrality of pages and find evidence for the usefulness of these links by human subject ratings [60]. Takes and Kosters [57] try to understand why participants abort a specific navigation task and find evidence that users prefer landmark nodes, i.e. those with high in- and outdegrees in the network (see also [48]). Researchers, moreover, use the dataset to identify semantic relatedness of Wikipedia pages from human paths. Singer and colleagues [53] found evidence that, generally speaking, navigational paths are more useful to calculate semantic relations than given Wikipedia links are. Beyond the use of this particular dataset, methodological advancements have been made in recent years with respect to the comparison of human trails in web interaction in general [50,51] and have been successfully applied to Wikipedia: By matching user traces on Wikipedia with the users' goals – collected through 30,000 responses to a user survey – Singer et al. [52] apply these methods and find different user behaviour for different interests to be identifiable from server logs (e.g. explorers tend to have long sequences of pages at a considerably higher speed than others). Wikipedia server logs are also used to identify presumably useful links which do not yet exist in [41]. Lamprecht et al. [28] analyze eight different language versions of Wikipedia and find that navigability is heavily affected by restricted views on articles (i.e. lead section resp. the first paragraph vs. full article). This is in line with the findings of Dimitrov et al. [17], which indicate a high correlation between the position of a link and its successfulness (i.e. the more on top of the page and the more left on the screen the more successful). Moreover, they find that users prefer links with topical closeness to the current article and links pointing to the outer bounds of the network.

This overview of related work reveals while navigation in Wikipedia is a popular area of research, route learning and the effect of spatial abilities on navigation abilities – two aspects shown to be important in real world environments - have not yet been studied. This is of interest to our community because this kind of knowledge can help in the design of navigational aids for browsing behaviour based on personal factors. These can be part of a user profile, i.e. which is independent from the information repository currently browsed. It can, furthermore, have an impact on study designs, as large hypertexts are even more readily available than virtual environment setups.

3   Hypotheses

In their 2010 review article Wolbers and Hegarty [65, p. 141] provide a strong argument that real-world navigational abilities, which route learning is a part of, rely on spatial abilities and sense of direction. According to their model, spatial abilities can be measured by mental rotation ability, embedded figures and spatial memory span. Based on these insights about the omnipresence of navigation metaphors for user behaviour in hypertext and the fact that the influence of spatial abilities and sense of direction has not yet been analyzed, we derive the following two hypotheses for this exploratory study:

H1. The better an individual's spatial abilities and sense of direction the faster he or she refinds the memorized path.

H2. The poorer an individual's spatial abilities and sense of direction the more errors will be made during refinding.

4   Method

Data was collected by means of an online experiment. Participants were presented with routes (ordered sequences of Wikipedia pages reached by clicks on links) and then asked to refind these paths. We analyzed different facets of their ability to do this based on participant characteristics, i.e. dependent on their self-reported sense of direction and how they performed on spatial ability tests. Thus, this section has three parts. First, the routes in Wikipedia are described; second the way spatial abilities were assessed is presented, and, finally, the experimental setup is described. The experiments were conducted in German.

4.1   Determining Wikipedia Routes

We used the random article function of the German language Wikipedia to find four lemmas used as starting pages. For each starting lemma the destination page was found according to the following procedure. If the desired length of the path was not reached, a page was randomly selected from all content links the current Wikipedia page had. Table 1 presents the resulting random paths. Each of these paths comprises seven steps following the oft-cited 7 ± 2 rule for working memory capacity (see [34]). Path 1, however, comprises four steps only to familiarize participants with the task, i.e. this data was excluded from the analysis. By using random walks between start and destination lemma, we ensure that diverging interests in topics should not have an impact.

4.2   Measuring Spatial Abilities

Inspired by Wolbers and Hegarty [65, p. 141], we utilise measures of sense of direction, spatial memory and broad visual perception which include mental rotation and embedded figures tests:

Sense of direction. Participants were required to fill a self-report survey on their sense of direction. The scale presented by Münzer and Hölscher [37] comprises three different subscales: allocentric orientation strategy (7 questions), egocentric orientation (10), and cardinal direction orientation strategy (2). This survey is well-established, including norm data on a 4,000 participants sample published in 2016 [36,38].

Table 1. The paths participants had to learn by navigating Wikipedia.

	Path 1	Path 2	Path 3	Path 4
Start	Feiburger Beschwerdenliste	Kreis Samter	Subnetz	Kavadh I.
Step 1	Albert-Ludwigs-Universität Freiburg	Herzogtum Warschau	Supernetting	Belagerung
Step 2	Franz-Joseph-Bob	Erste Polnische Teilung	Netzklassen	Magister offociorum
Step 3	Volkswirtschaft	Weichsel	Netzmaske	Odoaker
Step 4	n/a	Nieszawa	Oktette	Noricum
Step 5	n/a	Estland	Digitaltechnik	Otto Helmut Urban
Step 6	n/a	Einheitssteuer	Datenbus	Hainburg
Destin.	n/a	Beitragsbe-messungsgrenze	Omnibus	Retz

Spatial memory. The spatial memory span of participants was assessed by a regular 4 × 4 field without any labeling variant of the corsi-block test [13], implemented in javascript. Participants have to repeat the order of colored highlighted fields starting with two fields. After a correct trail a new order with one more field was presented. After two mistakes the test ended. The measured value was number of field of the last correct trail. As Berch et al. [7, p. 330] pointed out, Corsi developed the block task as alternative to measure memory for verbal sequences, thereby noting "that the mental representations of verbal and spatial information in serial short-term memory are functionally equivalent".

Spatial abilities. Participants worked on a computer adapted version of three subtests of a general test of cognitive abilities (LPS-2, see [25]): No. 6: mental rotation, No. 7: visualization of 3D geometric bodies, No. 8: identify forms in line-pattern. These tests were constructed to represent *space* defined by Thurstone [58], which was the base for the *broad visual perception* of Carroll's Three-Stratum-Theory [10].

4.3 Experimental Setup

We developed a web application (see Fig. 2) as a Wikipedia-based data acquisition tool using Python 2.7 [1] and its framework called Django [2] to allow for a maximum of flexibility in the experimental design. The application captured the clicks on links and input of tests and questionnaires in a database. To restrict the number of potential participants, Internet Explorer, Chrome and Firefox were supported as browsers. The web application was not usable in mobile browsers in order to avoid confounding effects (e.g. differences in task time stemming from different rendering of Wikipedia pages on mobile devices).

A cookie ensured that an experiment was taken once and only once from within the same browser. All navigational meta elements (e.g. the navigation on the left-hand side and the search bar) were rendered non-clickable even though they were still part of the page. This means, category pages or description pages of pictures were not reachable to participants. Moreover, the change of color for clicked links from blue to purple was disabled. There was no way for the participants to leave Wikipedia from within the application.

Figure 1 shows the way experiments were conducted. Participants were first asked to provide their informed consent about the goals and the data analysis associated with this study. Next, the participants entered the learning phase of path 1, i.e. the start page was opened and participants were informed about the names of the start and destination page. On the instruction part of the page (see Fig. 2) participants were asked to remember the sequence of links they were guided. They were further instructed not to use CTRL+F or other shortcuts, but asked to find their way to the current decision point link (see Table 1) on their own. This had been repeated until they reached the destination page.

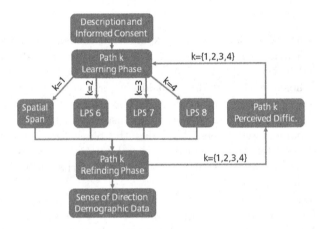

Fig. 1. A flowchart explaining the experimental setup. Every participant was subjected to $k = 4$ tasks, consisting of a route learning task, a test of spatial abilities, and a refinding phase. Having finished all tasks they were subject to a self-report sense of direction questionnaire and asked to provide demographic data.

Except for the first path, the paths were randomly assigned to each learning phase for every participant. Having finished a learning phase participants were asked to do one of the psychological tests (see above) to test their spatial abilities (see Fig. 1). Having finished the current test, participants entered the refinding phase. They were instructed to retrace the route they learned. During refinding the names of the start and the landing page were displayed on top of the page. In case of a mistake (i.e. when participants clicked on a wrong link) participants were instructed to return to the previous page via browser's back button. If participants did not reach the destination page within fifteen links, they were given the opportunity to stop the current task and continue with the remaining part of the experiment. On completion of each refinding phase, participants answered two questions, one about the perceived difficulty finding the links in the learning phase, the other about the difficulty of the refinding task. Having finished all tasks, participants were asked to provide demographic data as well as to fill in the sense of direction questionnaire (see [37]).

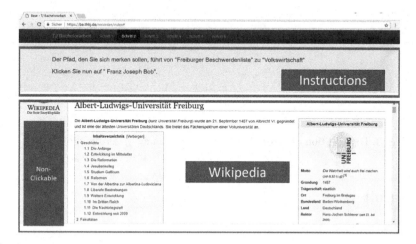

Fig. 2. A screenshot of the app used for data acquisition. The upper third of the application's website was used to provide instructions to the participants. The rest of the page contained the modified version of the Wikipedia.

4.4   Statistical Modeling

We use GNU R [42] and its packages dplyr [64], stringr [63], lavaan [45], psych [43], lme4 [5], lmerTest [26], xtable [14], ggplot2 [62] and texreg [31] to conduct our analysis. To explore if the Wikipedia-path-refind-paradigma is suitable for examination navigational abilities, we use duration (*dur*), i.e. the time needed to refind the right path, and the number of errors (*errors*) participants make as dependent variables. The independent variable we use to predict *dur* and *errors* are, first, the composite score of visual perception built with the three LPS-2 subtests (*LPS*); second, the composite overall score of the sense of direction questionnaire (*frs*), and third the spatial memory operationalized by the best level in the corsi task (*corsi*). To model the effects of spatial abilities, memory and sense of direction on working time we use a linear mixed model (LMM) in order to take individual working speed (*id*) and *task* specific attributes into account [19]. Additionally, we include the number of *errors* to control time consumption by mistakes. We also control for *age* and *gender* to take the ongoing discussion about different wayfinding strategies (see e.g. [22] resp. [30,56]) into account.

It would have been inappropriate to model *errors* with this approach due to the distribution of the error counts: 155 of 231 tasks (67%) were faultless. On average we find 1.6 errors ($SD = 3.5$, *skewness* $= 3.5$ and *kurtosis* $= 15.4$, see Fig. 3 and Table 2). To handle this floor effect, we modeled the probability of an error occurring as dependent variable by means of a logistic regression with random intercept within the Generalized Linear Mixed Model (GLMM) framework [15].

Fig. 3. Distribution of errors in all tasks (frequency of zero mistakes: 157)

5   Result

5.1   Descriptive Statistics

The data was collected from the August 25th to September 15th 2017. The application's disclaimer was viewed by approx. 300 different potential participants. 99 of the visitors completed the experiment. Of these, 13 participants were removed because they interrupted the experiment for more than 15 min. Furthermore, one record was not usable due to technical issues with storing the answers given to questionnaires. Therefore, 85 participants remain in the sample (46 female, 52 students, $\overline{x}_{age} = 27.34$ years, see Table 2). 78 out of 85 people participated from home, 6 from their office and one from a university building.

Due to the within groups design the 85 participants yield 255 trails. Of these, 18 trails were excluded from the analysis. 17 because the participants found a shorter path to the same target destination (1 for task 2, 11 trails for task 3, and 5 in task 4) and one trail because it took the participant longer than 40 min to finish. All statistical results reported below are based on the resulting $N_{trails} = 237$ usable trails. The figures presented in Table 2 reveal that task 3 is solved faster on average and with less variability compared to task 2 and 4 (see also Fig. 4). For all tasks the mean *duration* when solving it as first (position 1) is approximately 80 s longer than on position 2 and 3 ($M_{p1} = 280.37$ ($SD = 180.37$), $M_{p2} = 197.9$ ($SD = 156.85$), $M_{p3} = 199.89$ ($SD = 157.4$)). A 3×3 ANOVA shows main effects for *task* ($F(2, 228) = 8.22, p < .001$) and *position* ($F(2, 228) = 6.75, p < .01$), but not for their interaction ($F(4, 228) = 0.24, p = .92$). Neglecting the assumption for ANOVAs and apply it in the same way for *errors*, there are no effects for task or position (all F-values <1). The dependent variables are right-skewed, which is expected for time-based and

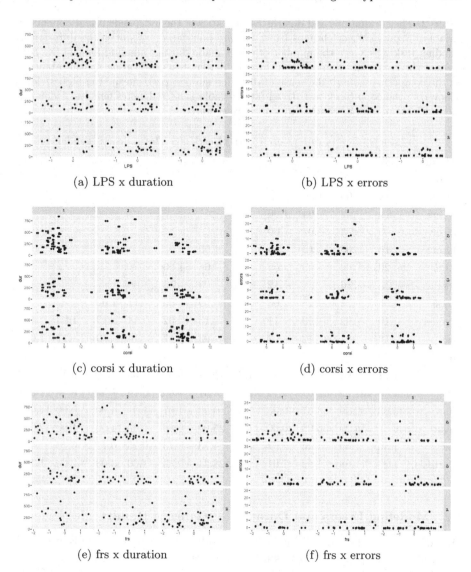

(a) LPS x duration

(b) LPS x errors

(c) corsi x duration

(d) corsi x errors

(e) frs x duration

(f) frs x errors

Fig. 4. Scatterplots of the independent variables against the time needed to find the path (*duration*) for each task (r2, r3, r4) at the particular position of the task (1, 2, 3).

error variables. Similarly, the *corsi* task results show a leptokurtic distribution because of high distribution around the mean of seven memorized steps and some outliers (see Fig. 4(c). The correlations between *duration* and number of *errors* for tasks 2 and 3 are rather high, whereas this is not the case for task 4. *frs* shows, furthermore, a similar pattern with lower coefficients. The remaining independent variables do not show any significant bivariate correlations neither with *duration* nor *error*.

Table 2. The correlations and descriptive statistics of the independent and dependent variables. Significant correlations ($\alpha = .05$) are bold-faced. *rX_dur* is the duration of refinding task X, *rX_err* the number of errors made during refinding for task X. *LPS* denotes the composite score of the three LPS-2 subtests indicating spatial abilities, *frs* the composite score of the sense of direction survey; *corsi* means the highest level achieved in the corsi-block-test. Level 0 of variable *gender* denotes females, 1 denotes males. Please note: The composite scores are centered.

	r2_dur	r3_dur	r4_dur	r2_err	r3_err	r4_err	LPS	frs	corsi	gender	age
r2_dur	1.00										
r3_dur	.11	1.00									
r4_dur	.13	.05	1.00								
r2_err	**.61**	.02	.04	1.00							
r3_err	.03	**.73**	−.01	.00	1.00						
r4_err	.14	.08	**.42**	**.30**	.09	1.00					
LPS	−.20	.00	−.09	.09	−.06	.06	1.00				
frs	**−.25**	**−.26**	.02	−.12	−.21	.03	**.23**	1.00			
corsi	−.05	−.21	−.15	.03	.01	−.09	.00	.11	1.00		
gender	−.10	−.02	−.20	.11	.04	−.15	.02	.14	.13	1.00	
age	.14	.21	.12	−.07	−.09	−.03	.17	.16	**−.30**	−.11	1.00
n	85	85	84	84	74	80	85	85	85	85	85
mean	241.07	164.03	260.28	2.11	1.36	1.31	0.00	0.00	7.12	0.46	27.34
sd	181.49	107.09	182.07	4.13	2.69	3.37	0.65	0.98	1.55	0.50	11.34
min	34.83	32.99	53.07	0.00	0.00	0.00	−1.67	−1.94	4.00	0.00	14.00
max	846.67	554.29	856.98	20.00	15.00	25.00	0.86	1.69	14.00	1.00	57.00
skew	1.30	1.39	1.46	2.64	2.85	4.73	−0.73	−0.25	0.77	0.16	1.59
kurtosis	1.23	1.68	1.63	7.01	9.78	28.41	−0.46	−1.00	3.08	−2.00	1.10

5.2   Modeling Errors and Duration – (G)LMM Results

Duration. Model 3 (see Table 3), i.e. including all variables, yields the best LMM fit with respect to Akaike's information criterion ($\Delta AIC_{Model1-Model3} = 92.39$) and the LR-test ($\Delta\chi^2_{Model1-Model3}(df = 7) = 106.39, p < .001$). Comparing the conditional R^2 (cR^2, i.e. the variance explained by both fixed and random factors [39]) reveals a significant increase when the number of *errors*, *gender* and *age* are used as control variables. The marginal R^2 (mR^2, variance explained by solely fixed factors) does not change for Model 3, but the coefficients of *LPS*, as well as *age* are now rendered significant. All coefficients, however, show the expected sign. The random effects *task* and *errors* are highly negatively correlated ($r = −.999$), a fact also evident from level 1 coefficients ($b_{r2} = −190.60 + 27.29 * errors$, $b_{r3} = −241.89 + 34.63 * errors$ and $b_{r4} = −140.26 + 20.08 * errors$).

Table 3. The fit of the LMM (model 1–3, left) to predict the time spent for a single task (*dur*) and the GLMM (model 4–6, right) results used to predict the probability of the occurrance of errors during a refinding task (*errordich*). Model 1 and 4 include only random factors (*id* and *task*); model 2 and 5 adds the fixed effects *LPS*, *frs* and *corsi*; model 3 includes *gender*, *age* and *errors* and model 6 just *gender* and *age*.

	Model 1	Model 2	Model 3		Model 4	Model 5	Model 6
(Intercept)	225.57***	308.53***	330.52***	(Intercept)	−0.82***	0.28	−0.08
	(23.44)	(56.53)	(55.97)		(0.00)	(0.88)	(1.17)
LPS		−22.77	−38.62**	LPS		−0.14	−0.16
		(17.65)	(13.87)			(0.29)	(0.29)
frs		−21.50	−13.53	frs		−0.27	−0.29
		(11.90)	(9.52)			(0.20)	(0.20)
corsi		−11.66	−3.95	corsi		−0.16	−0.14
		(7.24)	(5.92)			(0.12)	(0.13)
age			3.13***	age			0.01
			(0.85)				(0.02)
gender			−33.27	gender			0.00
(1=male, 0=female)			(17.88)	(1=male, 0=female)			(0.38)
AIC	3103.20	3100.39	3010.81	AIC	303.59	305.03	308.81
BIC	3117.07	3124.67	3048.96	BIC	314.00	325.84	336.56
Log Likelihood	-1547.60	-1543.20	-1494.41	Log Likelihood	-148.80	-146.51	-146.41
Num. obs.	237	237	237	Num. obs.	237	237	237
Num. groups: id	84	84	84	Num. groups: id	84	84	84
Num. groups: task	3	3	3	Num. groups: task	3	3	3
Var: id (Intercept)	3257.24	2010.36	787.75	Var: id (Intercept)	0.91	0.84	0.84
Var: task (Intercept)	1224.69	1251.98	38419.28	Var: task (Intercept)	0.01	0.01	0.01
Var: Residual	24061.00	24106.22	15716.09				
Var: task errors			787.37				
Cov: task (Intercept) errors			-5500.00				
marginal R^2		.04	.04	marginal R^2		.08	.08
conditional R^2		.16	.73	conditional R^2		.49	.50	.50

$^{***}p < .001, {}^{**}p < .01, {}^{*}p < .05$ $^{***}p < .001, {}^{**}p < .01, {}^{*}p < .05$

Errors. When modeling the probability of an *error* using GLMM, the fixed effects do not show any significant relevance. Taking just the random effects *task* and the personal factor into account (model 4, Table 3) results in the best fit looking at *AIC*. It shows, furthermore, a $\Delta\chi^2$ which is not statistically significantly worse than comparing the two other models χ^2 with more variables ($\Delta\chi^2_{Model1-Model2}(df = 3) = 4.65, p = .20$), but it explains just $cR^2 = .49$ variance. If fixed effects were, nevertheless, taken into account, they could explain $mR^2 = 8\%$ variance.

6   Discussion

A reasonable model fit for predicting *duration* can be achieved only by including the control variables age and gender ($cR^2 = .73$, model 3) – a finding in line with the controversy about the impact of gender and age mentioned above (see Sect. 4.4). In particular, considering the number of *errors* of each task shows an impact on *duration*. The variance of the *task* intercept increases heavily in model 3 compared to model 2 (see Table 3); similarly, with each error *duration* increases on average by 27, 34 or 20 s for task r2, r3 and r4, respectively. In model 3, however, *LPS* shows a statistically significant negative effect on *duration*, i.e. participants with lower abilities need more time. Spatial memory (*corsi*) has a lower impact for *duration* – presumably due to the floor effect. The weight of sense of direction (*frs*) shows a large standard error and is consequently not rendered statistically significant. The sign of the weight, however, is in line with prior expectations, i.e. better orientation skills yield shorter refinding time. *Men* seem to be a slightly faster than *women*, but high variability was again observed. Furthermore, *age* shows a statistically significant effect, with older participants taking on average 3 s longer for every year of age difference. These results are generally in line with the findings of studies in non-hypertext navigation contexts (see e.g. [22,40]), which consistently report weaker route learning abilities in older persons. In the logistic GLMM (models 4 to 6), however, the impact of *LPS*, *frs* and *corsi* on error probability is much weaker. All independent variables show weights signed as expected (i.e. the higher the score the lower the *error probability*), but the large standard errors render them statistically insignificant. Based on the informational criterion (*AIC*) model 4 is to be preferred. Even in a model with no personal factors at all, however, neither of the independent variables shows a significant effect. Taken together, these results indicate that personal factors beyond the measured abilities have a major impact. The subjects' ability to memorize words may be one of those aspects (see [3, p. 833ff.] for pointers to this idea). To test whether the low predictive power of all models in this study is in general caused by a differential effect on the different tasks, we calculate a model where the fixed effects for each task are taken into account. Compared with model 3 no statistically significant increase in likelihood ($\Delta\chi^2(df = 25) = 4.04, p > .99$) is found. The mean task duration is different and there is an influence if participants do the task for the first time (it took longer), but there is no interaction. There must be traits beside those measured interacting with tasks attributes, e.g. topical interest in the Wikipedia article.

From a methodological perspective there are two main conclusions from these results: First, longer paths need to be used in order to avoid the floor effect by inducing greater variance with respect to the number of errors. While the average length of seven in the *corsi* block test reinforces the finding by Miller [34], a path length of seven steps does not yield the theoretically and statistically desirable spread of error counts. Second, participants should be made aware of the importance of speed in refinding – either via the instructions given or through a visualization on the refinding pages. This will help to reduce biases which might, for example, be introduced by topical interest, i.e. participants who are interested in a topic might start reading the Wikipedia article during the refinding phase but ought to reach the current link as quickly as possible.

7   Conclusion and Future Work

Based on the importance of sense of direction and spatial abilities for real-world wayfinding performance we analyze the importance of these factors for route learning performance in hypertexts. We report on an online user study based on Wikipedia to research this question and fitted several models to predict refinding duration and whether errors are made by subjects using a LMM and a GLMM approach, respectively. The analysis yields a weak fit for all models discussed. These results suggest that personal factors other than spatial abilities and sense of direction and, in particular, task related aspects play an important role. We have also seen that these results leave room for methodological improvements. There are four lines of future work we would like to explore. First, we want to assess the influence landmarks have on route learning in hypertexts. Existing evidence suggests that landmarks are of high importance in gaining location knowledge (see [44, pp. 41–108] for an overview of cognitive aspects that make landmarks important). Second, we plan experiments to further investigate the role of other personal traits (e.g. Big five traits, in particular conscientiousness, [27]) in both, route learning and path finding. Third, we will conduct experiments based on different page structures presented to users, thereby analyzing if e.g. location of contents has an effect on the usefulness of spatial abilities. Finally, we plan to compare real-world wayfinding abilities of participants with their abilities in hypertexts in further within-subjects design studies.

References

1. Python Language Reference, version 2.7 (2010). http://www.python.org. Accessed 18 Feb 2018
2. Django (Version 1.11) (2017). https://djangoproject.com. Accessed 18 Feb 2018
3. Baddeley, A.: Working memory: looking back and forward. Nat. Rev. Neurosci. **4**, 829–839 (2003)
4. Barreau, D., Nardi, B.A.: Finding and reminding: file organization from the desktop. ACM SIGCHI Bull. **27**, 39–43 (1995)
5. Bates, D., Mächler, M., Bolker, B., Walker, S.: Fitting linear mixed-effects models using lme4. J. Stat. Softw. **67**(1), 1–48 (2015)
6. Benn, Y., Bergman, O., Glazer, L., Arent, P., Wilkinson, I.D., Varley, R., Whittaker, S.: Navigating through digital folders uses the same brain structures as real world navigation. Sci. Rep. **5**, 14719 (2015)
7. Berch, D.B., Krikorian, R., Huha, E.M.: The Corsi block-tapping task: methodological and theoretical considerations. Brain Cogn. **38**(3), 317–338 (1998)
8. Bergman, O., Gradovitch, N., Bar-Ilan, J., Beyth-Marom, R.: Folder versus tag preference in personal information management. J. Am. Soc. Inform. Sci. Techno. **64**(10), 1995–2012 (2013)
9. Burte, H., Montello, D.R.: How sense-of-direction and learning intentionality relate to spatial knowledge acquisition in the environment. Cogn. Res. **2**(1), 18 (2017)
10. Carroll, J.B.: The three-stratum theory of cognitive abilities. In: Flanagan, D.P., Genshaft, J.L., Harrison, P.L. (eds.) Contemporary Intellectual Assessment: Theories, Tests, and Issues, pp. 122–130. Guilford Press, New York (1997)

11. Chrastil, E.R., Warren, W.H.: Active and passive contributions to spatial learning. Psychon. Bull. Rev. **19**(1), 1–23 (2012)

12. Chrastil, E.R., Warren, W.H.: Active and passive spatial learning in human navigation: acquisition of graph knowledge. J. Exp. Psychol. Learn. Mem. Cogn. **41**(4), 1162–1178 (2015)

13. Corsi, P.M.: Human memory and the medial temporal region of the brain. Diss. Abstr. Int. **34**(2–B), 895 (1972)

14. Dahl, D.B.: xtable: Export Tables to LaTeX or HTML, r package version 1.8-2 (2016)

15. Demidenko, E.: Mixed Models: Theory and Applications with R. Wiley, Hoboken (2013)

16. Dillon, A., Richardson, J., McKnight, C.: Navigation in hypertext: a critical review of the concept. In: Diaper, D., Gilmore, D., Cockton, G., Shackel, B. (eds.) Human-Computer Interaction-INTERACT 1990, pp. 587–592. North Holland, Amsterdam (1990)

17. Dimitrov, D., Singer, P., Lemmerich, F., Strohmaier, M.: What makes a link successful on Wikipedia? In: Proceedings of the 26th International Conference on World Wide Web, WWW 2017, pp. 917–926 (2017)

18. Fabrikant, S.I.: Spatialized browsing in large data archives. Trans. GIS **4**(1), 65–78 (2000)

19. Gałecki, A., Burzykowski, T.: Linear Mixed-Effects Models Using R: A Step-by-Step Approach. Springer, New York (2013)

20. van der Ham, I.J.M., Claessen, M.H.: Navigation ability. In: Neuropsychology of Space. Spatial Functions of the Human Brain, Chap. 8, pp. 267–308. Academic Press, Amsterdam (2017)

21. van der Ham, I.J.M., Faber, A.M.E., Venselaar, M., van Kreveld, M.J., Löffler, M.: Ecological validity of virtual environments to assess human navigation ability. Front. Psychol. **6**, 637 (2015)

22. Hartmeyer, S., Grzeschik, R., Wolbers, T., Wiener, J.M.: The effects of attentional engagement on route learning performance in a virtual environment: an aging study. Front. Aging Neurosci. **9**, 235 (2017)

23. Hochmair, H.H., Luttich, K.: An analysis of the navigation metaphor - and why it works for the world wide web. Spat. Cogn. Comput. **6**(3), 235–278 (2006)

24. Hölscher, C., Meilinger, T., Vrachliotis, G., Brösamle, M., Knauff, M.: Finding the way inside: linking architectural design analysis and cognitive processes. In: Freksa, C., Knauff, M., Krieg-Brückner, B., Nebel, B., Barkowsky, T. (eds.) Spatial Cognition 2004. LNCS (LNAI), vol. 3343, pp. 1–23. Springer, Heidelberg (2005). https://doi.org/10.1007/978-3-540-32255-9_1

25. Kreuzpointner, L., Lukesch, H., Horn, W.: Leistungsprüfsystem 2. LPS-2. Manual. Hogrefe, Göttingen (2013). http://epub.uni-regensburg.de/27958

26. Kuznetsova, A., Brockhoff, P.B., Christensen, R.H.B.: lmerTest package: tests in linear mixed effects models. J. Stat. Softw. **82**(13), 1–26 (2017)

27. Kyritsis, M., Blathras, G., Gulliver, S., Varela, V.A.: Sense of direction and conscientiousness as predictors of performance in the Euclidean travelling salesman problem. Heliyon **3**(11), e00461 (2017). http://www.sciencedirect.com/science/article/pii/S2405844017306072

28. Lamprecht, D., Dimitrov, D., Helic, D., Strohmaier, M.: Evaluating and improving navigability of Wikipedia: a comparative study of eight language editions. In: Proceedings of the 12th International Symposium on Open Collaboration, OpenSym 2016, pp. 17:1–17:10. ACM, New York (2016)

29. Larrue, F., Sauzeon, H., Wallet, G., Foloppe, D., Cazalets, J.R., Gross, C., N'Kaoua, B.: Influence of body-centered information on the transfer of spatial learning from a virtual to a real environment. J. Cogn. Psychol. **26**(8), 906–918 (2014)

30. Lawton, C.A.: Strategies for indoor wayfinding: the role of orientation. J. Environ. Psychol. **16**(2), 137–145 (1996)

31. Leifeld, P.: texreg: conversion of statistical model output in R to LaTeX and HTML tables. J. Stat. Soft. **55**(8), 1–24 (2013)

32. Lingwood, J., Blades, M., Farran, E.K., Courbois, Y., Matthews, D.: Using virtual environments to investigate wayfinding in 8- to 12-year-olds and adults. J. Exp. Child Psychol. **166**, 178–189 (2018)

33. Lloyd, J., Persaud, N.V., Powell, T.E.: Equivalence of real-world and virtual-reality route learning: a pilot study. Cyberpsychol. Behav. **12**(4), 423–427 (2009)

34. Miller, G.A.: The magical number seven, plus or minus two: some limits on our capacity for processing information. Psychol. Rev. **101**(2), 343–352 (1994)

35. Montello, D.R.: Navigation. Cambridge Handbooks in Psychology, pp. 257–294. Cambridge University Press, Cambridge (2005)

36. Münzer, S., Fehringer, B.C., Kühl, T.: Validation of a 3-factor structure of spatial strategies and relations to possession and usage of navigational aids. J. Environ. Psychol. **47**, 66–78 (2016)

37. Münzer, S., Hölscher, C.: Entwicklung und Validierung eines Fragebogens zu räumlichen Strategien. Diagnostica **57**, 111–125 (2011)

38. Münzer, S., Hölscher, C.: Standardized norm data for three self-report scales on egocentric and allocentric environmental spatial strategies. Data Brief **8**, 803–811 (2016)

39. Nakagawa, S., Schielzeth, H.: A general and simple method for obtaining R2 from generalized linear mixed-effects models. Methods Ecol. Evol. **4**(2), 133–142 (2013)

40. O'Malley, M., Innes, A., Wiener, J.M.: How do we get there? Effects of cognitive aging on route memory. Mem. Cogn. **46**(2), 274–284 (2018)

41. Paranjape, A., West, R., Zia, L., Leskovec, J.: Improving website hyperlink structure using server logs. In: Proceedings of the Ninth ACM International Conference on Web Search and Data Mining, WSDM 2016, pp. 615–624. ACM, New York (2016)

42. R Core Team: R: A language and environment for statistical computing. R Foundation for Statistical Computing, Vienna, Austria (2017). https://www.R-project.org/

43. Revelle, W.: psych: Procedures for Psychological, Psychometric, and Personality Research. Northwestern University, Evanston, Illinois, r package version 1.7.8 (2017)

44. Richter, K.F., Winter, S.: Landmarks: Giscience for Intelligent Services. Springer, Cham (2014). https://doi.org/10.1007/978-3-319-05732-3

45. Rosseel, Y.: lavaan: an R package for structural equation modeling. J. Stat. Softw. **48**(2), 1–36 (2012). http://www.jstatsoft.org/v48/i02/

46. Ruddle, R.A., Lessels, S.: The benefits of using a walking interface to navigate virtual environments. ACM Trans. Comput.-Hum. Interact. **16**(1), 5:1–5:18 (2009)

47. Ruddle, R.A., Volkova, E., Bülthoff, H.H.: Walking improves your cognitive map in environments that are large-scale and large in extent. ACM Trans. Comput.-Hum. Interact. **18**(2), 10:1–10:20 (2011)

48. Scaria, A.T., Philip, R.M., West, R., Leskovec, J.: The last click: why users give up information network navigation. In: Proceedings of the 7th ACM International Conference on Web Search and Data Mining, WSDM 2014, pp. 213–222. ACM, New York (2014)

49. Siegel, A.W., White, S.H.: The development of spatial representations of large-scale environments. In: Reese, H. (ed.) Advances in Child Development and Behaviour, pp. 9–55. Academic Press, New York (1975)

50. Singer, P., Helic, D., Hotho, A., Strohmaier, M.: HypTrails: a Bayesian approach for comparing hypotheses about human trails on the web. In: Proceedings of the 24th International Conference on World Wide Web, WWW 2015, pp. 1003–1013. International World Wide Web Conferences Steering Committee, Republic and Canton of Geneva, Switzerland (2015)

51. Singer, P., Helic, D., Hotho, A., Strohmaier, M.: A Bayesian method for comparing hypotheses about human trails. ACM Trans. Web **11**(3), 14:1–14:29 (2017)

52. Singer, P., Lemmerich, F., West, R., Zia, L., Wulczyn, E., Strohmaier, M., Leskovec, J.: Why we read Wikipedia. In: Proceedings of the 26th International Conference on World Wide Web, WWW 2017, pp. 1591–1600 (2017)

53. Singer, P., Niebler, T., Strohmaier, M., Hotho, A.: Computing semantic relatedness from human navigational paths: a case study on Wikipedia. Int. J. Semant. Web Inf. Syst. **9**(4), 41–70 (2013)

54. So, W.C., Ching, T.H., Lim, P.E., Cheng, X., Ip, K.Y.: Producing gestures facilitates route learning. PLoS One **9**(11), e112543 (2014)

55. So, W.C., Shum, P.L., Wong, M.K.: Gesture is more effective than spatial language in encoding spatial information. Q. J. Exp. Psychol. **68**(12), 2384–2401 (2015)

56. Suzer, O.K., Olgunturk, N., Guvenc, D.: The effects of correlated colour temperature on wayfinding: a study in a virtual airport environment. Displays **51**, 9–19 (2018)

57. Takes, F.W., Kosters, W.A.: Mining user-generated path traversal patterns in an information network. In: Proceedings of the 2013 IEEE/WIC/ACM International Joint Conferences on Web Intelligence (WI) and Intelligent Agent Technologies (IAT), WI-IAT 2013, vol. 01, pp. 284–289. IEEE Computer Society, Washington, D.C. (2013)

58. Thurstone, L.L.: Primary Mental Abilities. University of Chicago Press, Chicago (1938)

59. West, R., Leskovec, J.: Human wayfinding in information networks. In: Proceedings of the 21st International Conference on World Wide Web, WWW 2012, pp. 619–628. ACM, New York (2012)

60. West, R., Paranjape, A., Leskovec, J.: Mining missing hyperlinks from human navigation traces: a case study of Wikipedia. In: Proceedings of the 24th International Conference on World Wide Web, WWW 2015, pp. 1242–1252. International World Wide Web Conferences Steering Committee, Republic and Canton of Geneva, Switzerland (2015)

61. West, R., Pineau, J., Precup, D.: Wikispeedia: an online game for inferring semantic distances between concepts. In: International Joint Conference on Artificial Intelligence (IJCAI 2009), Pasadena, California, pp. 1598–1603 (2009)

62. Wickham, H.: ggplot2: Elegant Graphics for Data Analysis. Springer, New York (2009). https://doi.org/10.1007/978-0-387-98141-3

63. Wickham, H.: stringr: simple, consistent wrappers for common string operations, r package version 1.2.0 (2017). https://CRAN.R-project.org/package=stringr
64. Wickham, H., Francois, R., Henry, L., Müller, K.: dplyr: a grammar of data manipulation, r package version 0.7.4 (2017). https://CRAN.R-project.org/package=dplyr
65. Wolbers, T., Hegarty, M.: What determines our navigational abilities? Trends Cogn. Sci. **14**(3), 138–146 (2010)

A Dissociation Between Two Classes of Spatial Abilities in Elementary School Children

Cathleen Heil[(✉)]

Institute of Mathematics and Its Didactics,
Leuphana University Lüneburg, Universitätsallee 1, 21335 Lüneburg, Germany
`cathleen.heil@leuphana.de`

Abstract. This study investigates whether the abilities to mentally manipulate an imagined object (object manipulation abilities) and the abilities to coordinate perspectives of mental movement of the imagined self (egocentric perspective transformation abilities) are distinct classes of spatial abilities in elementary school children. We developed a paper-and-pencil test with measures of mental rotations and folding and a wide range of perspective taking tasks. 240 fourth graders were tested. By comparing different models in a confirmatory factor analysis, we found that there is a partial dissociation between object manipulation spatial abilities and perspective transformation abilities. The results specify the degree of overlap, and sex differences concerning the measures but not the underlying constructs.

Keywords: Children · Dissociation · Gender · Spatial abilities

1 Introduction

The term *spatial abilities* refers to a conglomerate of cognitive capacities that allow individuals to mentally represent and transform spatial information [1]. Psychometric studies have revealed that the construct is adequately modeled in a multidimensional way [2]. Different models have been subject to intensive debate in research mainly involving adults, and only few studies have investigated basic components of spatial abilities in children. The main goal of this study was to address this gap. Understanding the basic components of spatial abilities might contribute to develop a comprehensive, empirically-based developmental model of spatial abilities. It may also advance research on the design of learning environments in STEM fields, for which spatial abilities have been as an important predictor of academic achievement [3,4].

S. Creem-Regehr et al. (Eds.): Spatial Cognition 2018, LNAI 11034, pp. 228–243, 2018.
https://doi.org/10.1007/978-3-319-96385-3_16

1.1 Object Manipulation Versus Perspective Transformation Abilities in Adults

Among the many models for spatial abilities proposed [5], contemporary research has highlighted two basic classes of spatial abilities: the abilities to mentally manipulate objects from a stationary point of view (*object manipulation abilities*) and the abilities to mentally transform the egocentric viewing perspective on spatially invariant objects (*egocentric perspective transformation abilities*) [6]. Spatial tasks demanding these transformations of visually perceivable information are logically equivalent, since they typically involve a spatial stimulus that can be seen from one vantage point and whose appearance from another one needs to be anticipated. Empirical studies have shown, however, that two separate classes of spatial abilities are needed to solve these tasks. Experimental studies have suggested that there are different cognitive processes involved [7,8], which is reflected in different patterns of errors [9] and different chronometrical profiles [10]. Moreover, the neurocognitive literature has suggested that there are different representational systems involved [11,12]. In particular, object manipulation abilities typically involve inferences based on an object-to-object representational system, that is, knowledge of object locations with respect to spatially invariant objects. In contrast, egocentric perspective transformation abilities typically involve a self-to-object-representational system, that is, knowledge of object locations with respect to the body of the observer [13].

The individual differences literature has suggested that the dissociation between object manipulation abilities and egocentric perspective transformation abilities can be found at the level of individual performances in measures that reflect those abilities [6,14]. These studies have reanalyzed classical measures of the psychometrical literature and suggested new strategy-homogenous measures of perspective taking. Depending of the measures used, those studies have reported that performances correlate by 0.7 [14] to 0.8 [6]. These findings have been related to those in the experimental and neuroscientific literature, and both studies have suggested that different cognitive processes tap different underlying classes of spatial abilities to an extent that whenever individuals excel in one class of abilities, they do not necessarily do so in the other one.

1.2 Transformation of Objects and Perspective in Children

Studies on children's spatial abilities date back to Piaget and Inhelder's work [15, 16], who conceptually separated the abilities to perform mental transformations of objects from the abilities to perform perspective transformations. Although Piaget and Inhelder did not experimentally compare both classes of abilities, they showed that object manipulation ability emerged by the age of 7 or 8 [16], whereas perspective transformation ability was still affected by egocentric judgements until the age of 9 and 10 [15]. This age discrepancy might point to a possible dissociation, but it is important to note that materials in both studies were different. Furthermore, purely developmental arguments on the emergence of those abilities do not necessarily require a dissociation of the two classes since the abilities to perform perspective transformations could be understood as an advanced developmental stage of the abilities to perform object transformations by means of enriching existing cognitive schemes.

Experimental studies with children aimed to contrast spatial tasks that demand mental rotations of a visually perceived object and tasks that demand mental rotations of the own perspective around an object under strictly identical experimental settings. In line with Piaget and Inhelder's findings, studies have shown that perspective tasks were harder for children than mental rotation tasks and that both tasks produced different pattern of errors [17]. Results of a subsequent study have suggested that each of the tasks required different cognitive processes involving different representational systems updated during the solution process [18].

Those classical findings have been taken up in recent studies that aimed to test whether object manipulation abilities and perspective transformation abilities can be described by divergent developmental trajectories and understood as dissociable classes of spatial abilities. For instance, motor imagery abilities (measured by left-right judgements of hands) have been shown to improve by the age of 7 or 8, when visual imagery abilities (measured by orientation judgement of letters) is almost fully developed. No evident relationship between both classes has been found in elementary school children aged from 7 to 12 [19]. These findings have been complemented by a study with 7- to 11-year old children, who were shown pairs of bodies and letters and who were asked to perform a series of left-right judgements in response to these visual stimuli [20]. Results confirmed that the performance in both tasks followed distinct developmental trajectories, with children improving later in perspective transformations tasks (from 8 to 9) than they do in object transformation tasks (from 7 onwards).

A recent study addressed the dissociation between the two classes of spatial abilities in children from an individual differences viewpoint [21]. The authors administered two paper-and-pencil tests and three tests with small objects to children between 8 and 12 and compared different multigroup CFA-models. Results suggested that a dissociation between both classes of spatial abilities may emerge by the age of 10.5 and specified the degree of overlap in the corresponding two-factor model ($r = 0.75$). Although the authors stated that both classes could not be separated for children between 9 and 10, the corresponding model showed also highly reasonable model fit indices and did not differ significantly from the preferred model of the authors. Furthermore, the descriptive statistics of some measures suggest that floor effects occurred for younger children, which might be due to a possible dissociation emerging before the age of 10.5.

1.3   Sex Differences in Children's Spatial Abilities

Sex differences concerning spatial abilities among adults in favor of men have been well documented [22,23], whereas for children they have not. Researchers emphasized that to demonstrate consistent sex differences in children, age-specific tests – ideally group-administered and in paper-and-pencil format – have to be conducted in a large sample [24]. Designing them was challenging and led to floor effects that might have obscured possible differences [23]. Despite this issue several studies focused on spatial tasks for children that involved 2D and 3D mental rotation, which allowed researchers to demonstrate robust advantages in favor of boys in infants [25], pre-schoolers [26] and older children [27,28]. Those findings were in line with a meta-analytical study, which demonstrated that significant sex differences in children are most likely to be found in measures of mental rotation [23]. For other spatial tasks that require different mental transformations, no consistent findings in favor of boys were reported but only exemplarily highlighted such as in the case of the Water-Level Task [28], the unwrapping of the surface of a cube [27], and a task to construct a 3D building from 2D plans [27]. Sex differences in perspective tasks have not been found in children [29] but reported in adults [30].

One study focused on the sex-specific correlational structure of a set of spatial tasks. Results suggested that performances in those tasks are more homogeneously intercorrelated for boys, indicating that spatial abilities might be a unified trait. In contrast, the heterogeneously correlated performances in girls indicated that spatial abilities might be treated as a multifaceted trait [28].

1.4   The Current Study

In this study, we examined whether the children's abilities to mentally manipulate an object from a stationary egocentric point of view is dissociable from the children's abilities to mentally taking another perspective on a stationary set of objects. This dissociation has been found in adults, and there is first evidence that the two different mental operations that are necessary to complete object manipulation and egocentric perspective transformation tasks might have different developmental patterns.

The first goal of this study was to develop a set of age-specific paper-and-pencil measures that reflect both classes of spatial abilities. Age-specific adoptions of existing object manipulation tests were developed, and a wide range of measures for perspective taking with different cognitive demands was proposed. We analyzed them statistically to examine whether those tasks can be used to measure individual performance of elementary school children in a differentiated way without showing floor or ceiling effects and represent reliable measures.

The second goal of our study was to empirically investigate whether, and to which extent both classes of spatial abilities are separable. We analyzed correlations of the performances in the paper-and-pencil tests using a confirmatory factor analysis (CFA) [31] by statistically comparing a hypothesized theoretical model to an alternative model. We assumed that whenever both classes of spatial abilities reflect the same underlying construct, a one-factor model should show the best fit to the empirical data. If both abilities are, however, dissociated, a two-factor model should outperform the alternative model, and the latent correlation between both factors would represent a statistical estimation of the degree of relationship between both constructs.

The third goal of this study was to use the proposed measures to investigate whether there are sex-differences both at the level of the single measures, and at the overall structural level of spatial abilities. We applied a group-wise approach in a comparison of individual performances and to the CFA. We assumed that sex-related differences at the level of the measures would become significant and tested measurement invariance at the level of the CFA-model.

2   Method

2.1   Participants

The sample consisted of N = 240 fourth graders (111 boys, 129 girls, mean age 10.29, $SD = .51$) from 13 different classes. They came from six different public schools and one Montessori school in a city in northern Germany. These schools are located in different parts of the town and attract a great variety of students with respect to their socio-economic background. All children in the sample were able to speak German well enough to understand the written instructions without supplementary help.

2.2   Materials

The paper-and-pencil test consisted of ten spatial tasks, four of them measuring performances in mental object transformation abilities (Table 1) and six measuring performances in egocentric perspective transformation abilities (Table 2).

Table 1. Description of measures reflecting object manipulation abilities

Measure	Description	Example item
LR	New measure requiring children to imagine going along a path on a map and to decide at each crossing whether they turned left or right by mentally rotating the map (4 pairs of items, dichotomously scored.)	
2DMR	Adoption of the Card Rotations Test [32] (4 items, polytomously scored)	
3DMR	Adoption of the Vandenberg Mental Rotation Test [33] (4 items, dichotomously scored).	
PFT	Adoption of the Paper Folding Task [32] (6 items, dichotomously scored).	

Table 2. Description of measures reflecting perspective transformation abilities

Measure	Description	Extract or example item
Boxes	Adoption of the classic Piaget Three-Mountain-Task [15]. Requires the children to sort the corresponding side views of an array of boxes that is presented in plan view. The children need to sort all four side views out of five possible solutions (3 items, polytomously scored)	
Claudia*	New measure requiring children to sort five pictures of field views to the corresponding locations in a plan view of a labyrinth (5 items, dichotomously scored)	
Emil*	New measure similar as the Claudia measure, but the locations are not predefined and the six pictures of the field views need to be sorted (single item, sorting is scored).	
Ben*	New measure similar to the Pictures Test [14] or Picture Show [34]. Requires children to sort five pictures of field views to a corresponding location in plan view (5 items, dichotomously scored).	
Cruise	Adoption of the Task Areal Orientation [34]. Requires the children to sort five pictures of field views that correspond to a trajectory given in the plan view (single item, sorting is scored).	
Meadow*	Adoption of the Guilford-Zimmermann Test [35]. Requires children to indicate horizontal (left/right) and depth (front/behind) changes of an imagined movement from Picture One to Picture Two (5 items, dichotomously scored).	

*Note: Tasks were designed with Sweet Home 3D, copyright (c) 2005-2017 E. Puybaret. Includes 3D models and textures distributed under a free license.

Tasks reflecting the first class of spatial abilities were mainly adoptions of existing tests for adults. In contrast, we developed measures reflecting the second class of spatial abilities from scratch, and designed them in a way such that different instructions to relate projected viewpoints to spatial locations were given.

We tested the quality of our tasks in a pilot study with N = 222 children to make sure that the test we developed had appropriate psychometrical characteristics.

2.3   Procedure

The paper-and-pencil test was presented in a small booklet. During the test instruction, the children were told that they were not allowed to turn the booklet. They further followed an oral presentation of the instruction of three reading-intensive tasks. Only during that phase, the children were allowed to ask questions. The children were given 45 min to work on their test booklets. During that time, the experimenter ensured that the children did not copy from each other.

3   Results

3.1   Descriptive Statistics and Reliability Analysis

Since we intended to use multivariate methods that assume normally distributed data, we first analyzed our data from a descriptive point of view. The descriptive statistics for the measures are shown in Table 3. All measures feature at least five distinct categories, which allowed us to treat them as continuous variables in the subsequent analysis. None of these measures departed considerably from normality [36] which allowed us to assume our data to be normal in further analysis.

Table 3. Descriptive statistics of all measures included in the paper-and-pencil test

Measure	Range	Mean	SD	Skew	Kurtosis	Min[%]	Max[%]
LR	[0,4]	2.23	1.54	-.14	-1.49	18.8	33.8
2DMR	[0,8]	5.00	2.10	-.62	-0.17	5.40	12.5
Claudia	[0,4]	2.22	1.48	-.14	-1.44	16.3	29.2
3DMR	[0,4]	2.03	1.24	-.06	-1.05	10.8	14.6
Boxes	[0,6]	3.44	1.97	-.44	-1.00	12.9	15.8
PFT	[0,6]	2.62	1.77	.42	-0.76	10.8	9.20
Emil	[0,6]	2.80	2.22	.32	-1.41	16.3	23.3
Ben	[0,5]	3.40	1.80	-.92	-0.54	16.3	38.8
Cruise	[0,4]	1.82	1.59	.12	-1.61	32.9	20.8
Meadow	[0,5]	2.62	1.96	.-14	-1.54	20.0	25.8

Half of the measures were particularly platykurtic (kurtosis < -1.4), which was due to bimodality effects in the distribution of observations. Indeed, for these tasks, a considerable number of children either did not score a single point, or received perfect score (last two columns of Table 3). This observation was particularly strong for the measures *Ben, LR, Cruise*. We furthermore observe that the measure *Ben* highly skewed $(-.92)$ and is subject to strong ceiling effects. All other measures do neither show ceiling, nor floor effects.

We computed Cronbach's α for all our measures that consisted of a set of different items (Table 4) but not for picture sorting measures. Most of the measures had an at least acceptable internal consistency, which was reflected by values for Cronbach's α that ranged from .75 to .84. In contrast, the measures *2DMR* and *3DMR* featured only questionable (.66) and poor (.54) reliabilities.

Table 4. Cronbach's α for the measures used in the study

LR	2DMR	Claudia	3DMR	Boxes	PFT	Emil	Ben	Cruise	Meadow
.81	.66	.80	.54	.77	.75	-	.84	-	.84

3.2 Analysis of Intraclass Correlation Effects

Since the data was collected class-wise, the intraclass coefficients (IC) for every measure were computed to detect possible biases in the following analysis due to an underlying multilevel structure. The results of the *Mplus* [37] analysis for computing the ICs (ρ_{IC}) are shown in Table 5.

Table 5. Intraclass coefficients for the measures used in the study

LR	2DMR	Claudia	3DMR	Boxes	PFT	Emil	Ben	Cruise	Meadow
.037	.026	.053	.011	.087	.044	.011	.011	.060	.020

Seven of the ten measures showed a $\rho_{IC} \leq 0.05$, indicating that variance in the measure is mainly due to individual differences but not to a considerable effect of belonging to a certain class [38]. The tasks *Claudia* ($\rho_{IC} = .053$), *Cruise* ($\rho_{IC} = .060$) and *Boxes* ($\rho_{IC} = .087$) show a clearer, yet not dramatically higher, effect of class-clustering (all $\rho_{IC} \leq 0.10$, see [38]).

3.3 Confirmatory Factor Analysis

To avoid sensitivity of the analysis to extreme outliers, we withdrew the upper and lower 5%-percentile from the sample, thus maintaining a sample of 215 children that did not receive particularly low (e.g. due to reading problems) or high scores (i.e., due to missing differentiation of the measures for high achievers). The correlations between the measures are shown in Table 6. To investigate patterns of correlations, in particular to examine whether object manipulation spatial abilities are separable from egocentric perspective transformation abilities, we conducted a confirmatory factor analysis (CFA) using R $lavaan$ [39]. Since our preliminary analysis revealed no considerable class-clustering effect, we neglected the influences of class-wise testing by performing a single-level analysis.

Table 6. Pearson correlations between the paper-and-pencil tasks (N = 215)

	1.	2.	3.	4.	5.	6.	7.	8.	9.	10.
1. LR	–	.28	.19	.28	.32	.32	.26	.17	.21	.23
2. 2DMR		–	.18	.31	.30	.33	.14	.15	.18	.11
3. Claudia			–	.17	.35	.35	.30	.17	.14	.22
4. 3DMR				–	.31	.38	.25	.14	.18	.10
5. Boxes					–	.42	.39	.24	.25	.37
6. PFT						–	.27	.33	.29	.32
7. Emil							–	.19	.16	.24
8. Ben								–	.12	.25
9. Cruise									–	.24
10. Meadow										–

As stipulated by our theoretical model, the tasks LR, $2DMR$, $3DMR$, and PFT load on a first class of spatial abilities, object-based manipulation abilities (OB), and the tasks $Claudia$, $Boxes$, $Emil$, Ben, $Cruise$ and $Meadow$ load on a second class of spatial abilities, egocentric perspective transformation abilities (EGO). However, since the measure Ben had been found to be highly skewed and subject to ceiling effects, we excluded it from the analysis. Furthermore, due to consistently low correlations with measures reflecting the factor EGO, there was a doubt whether the measure $Cruise$ is sufficiently well indicator of perspective transformation ability. To investigate this, we computed a preliminary model, in which the measure was allowed to load on both factors of spatial ability. We found that the measure neither loaded significantly on the first nor on the second factor. Therefore, we excluded $Cruise$ in subsequent analysis since it does not sufficiently reflect a single construct.

The fully standardized two-factor model solution is depicted in Fig. 1. Numbers above the single-headed arrow lines represent the standardized factor loadings. Since all measures load on one single factor, these loadings can be interpreted as standardized regression coefficients, but also as the empirical discrimination values of the measures. The shorter arrows that point to each measure represent error terms, that is, the percentage of variance in the measure not explained by the factors. The curved, two-headed arrow represents the latent correlation between both factors OB and EGO.

The values of the fit indices are reported in Table 7. All indices suggested that the model fits the empirical data very well. The model did produce a $\chi^2(19) = 15.98$-statistic that was not significant ($p = 0.66$), which indicates that the model did not derive considerably from the data. Moreover, the Root Mean Square Error of Approximation (RMSEA) is 0.00 with an 95%-confidence interval $CI =$ [.00, .05] and a non-significant test that the value is well beneath 0.05 ($p = 0.959$). Furthermore, the Bentler Comparative Index (CFI = 1.00), the Tucker-Lewis

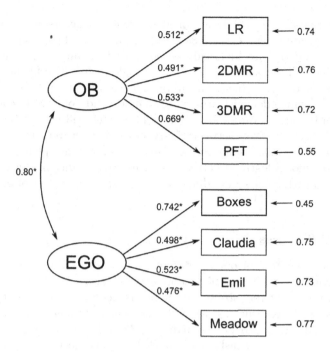

Fig. 1. Completely standardized solution of the confirmatory factor analysis revealing two distinct classes of spatial abilities (N = 215). *indicate significant path coefficients ($p < 0.001$).

Table 7. Comparison of the single-factor and two-factor models

Model	χ^2	df	χ^2/df	RMSEA(CI)	CFI	TLI	SRMR	AIC	BIC
1-factor-model	25.62	20	1.28	.03 (.00, .08)*	.97	.96	.045	6443	6496
2-factor-model	15.98	19	0.84	.00 (.00, .05)*	1.00	1.00	.034	6434	6491

*indicates if $p_{RMSEA \leq .05}$ is non-significant. The RMSEA is shown with its 90%-confidence interval (CI).

Index (TLI = 1.00), and the Standardized Root Mean Square Residual (SRMR = 0.034) were well beneath the commonly used criterion for good fit ($CFI \leq 0.95$, $TLI \leq 0.95$, $SRMR \leq 0.06$, see Hu and Bentler [40] for further information on fit indices).

The results indicated that the measure *PFT* is particularly suitable to discriminate between individual abilities to perform object manipulations (.669) and *Boxes* is a particularly suitable measure to discriminate between individual abilities to perform perspective transformations (.742). All other measures are moderately suitable ($\approx$.50) to capture individual differences. The reliabilities for both the OB-scale and the EGO-was almost acceptable (McDonald's [41] $\omega_{OB} = 0.64$, and $\omega_{EGO} = 0.65$) and the set of eight measures featured an acceptable reliabilities ($\omega_{total} = 0.76$).

The two-factor model solution indicated that both factors of spatial abilities are highly correlated factors ($r = 0.80$), thus sharing 64% of variance. To examine whether both factors are identical, we computed an alternative single-factor model in which all measures loaded on one single factor. The fit indices of this model are also shown in Table 7. The overall chi-square statistic for the model was non-significant which demonstrates that the model did not deviate considerably from the data, and the values for all other fit indices still met the criterion for good fit [40]. A comparison between the two models, however, revealed a better fit of the two-factor model solution. Both models, thus, can explain the data, but the two-factor model featured better fit indices. Significance in this observation was confirmed by the chi-square difference test comparing the fit of both models ($\chi^2(1) = 7.16, p = 0.007$).

3.4 Sex Differences

Table 8 shows the results on sex differences for all ten measures, including Cohen's d with the respective 95%-confidence interval [42], a measure of effect size for samples of different size (also denoted as Hedges's g). Boys outperformed girls in most of the measures. Boys performed better in measures that required 3D mental rotation (*3DMR*), but also in the (*PFT*). However, we did not observe this effect for the two other tasks that required mental object manipulation in two dimensions (*LR* and *2DMR*), and for the non-assignable measure *Cruise*. In contrast, consistent sex differences were found for all measures that required mental perspective transformations, with the largest differences in the labyrinth-based measures *Emil* and *Claudia*. For the reduced sample (N = 215), the same differences were found, but the significance testing became slightly non-significant for *PFT* ($p = 0.052$) and close to non-significance for *Meadow* ($p = 0.048$).

To examine whether sex has an influence on the extent of the dissociation between the two classes of spatial abilities, we computed a group-wise CFA. We ensured that the CFA-model closely matched the data for every group (not

Table 8. Sex differences for the measures included in the study (N = 240)

| Measure | Girls (N=129) | | Boys (N=111) | | t | df | Cohen's d |
	Mean	SD	Mean	SD			+ 95% CI
LR	2.05	1.47	2.43	1.60	1.91	238	.25 [-0.01, 0.50]
2DMR	4.90	2.14	5.12	2.16	0.78	238	.10 [-0.15, 0.36]
Claudia	1.88	2.62	1.44	1.43	4.01***	238	.51 [0.26, 0.77]
3DMR	1.78	1.23	2.32	1.18	3.50**	238	.44 [0.19, 0.704]
Boxes	3.10	1.94	3.84	1.93	2.94**	238	.38 [0.13, 0.64]
PFT	2.33	1.77	2.95	1.73	2.75**	238	.35 [0.10, 0.61]
Emil	2.11	1.96	3.60	2.24	5.51***	238	.71 [0.45, 0.97]
Ben	3.05	1.83	3.82	1.67	3.39**	238	.44 [0.18, 0.69]
Cruise	1.66	1.55	2.00	1.62	1.66	238	.22 [-0.04, 0.47]
Meadow	2.29	1.89	3.00	1.98	2.82**	238	.37 [0.11, 0.62]

Significance testing (two-tailed) was respectively based on independent samples t-tests with equal variance not assumed.
*$p < 0.05$, **$p < 0.01$, ***$p < 0.001$

reported here), and then we compared the estimated path coefficients and latent correlation (Table 9). To examine whether they differ significantly, we compared the confidence intervals for girls and boys for every path coefficient to test whether they overlap. We found only for the *Emil*-path coefficient significant differences.

Table 9. Comparison of completely standardized path coefficients for a sex-specific CFA model

Group	N	LR	2DMR	3DMR	PFT	Boxes	Claudia	Emil	Meadow	r
Girls	118	.60	.51	.58	.69	.79	.39	.28	.49	.79
Boys	97	.42	.51	.43	.68	.67	.55	.72	.44	.79

A final analysis of measurement invariance in our group-wise models showed partial weak invariance when fixing the loading of the measure *Emil* to be equal in both groups $(\Delta\chi^2(5) = 9.07, p = 0.11)$. Strong partial invariance was not attained $(\Delta\chi^2(6) = 15.35, p = 0.02)$. Therefore, both constructs, *OB* and *EGO*, are measured sex-robustly (except for *Emil*). Thus the factors themselves do not differ, but the intercepts (corresponding to group-specific mean values) are sex-sensitive.

4   Discussion and Conclusion

We proposed a set of paper-and-pencil measures that reflect two classes of spatial abilities, object manipulations abilities and perspective transformations abilities, for fourth-grade elementary school children. An analysis of these pointed towards a set of tasks with good psychometrical characteristics. The tasks *LR*, which requires children to mentally rotate a map to determine whether they turn left or right, and a child-specific adoption of the Paper Folding Task (*PFT*) were shown to be reliable measures that allowed us to differentiate among performances of object manipulation abilities. In line with previous findings [24], measures of 2D and 3D mental rotation suffer from poor reliabilities, a result that indicates the need for careful item re-analysis. Both labyrinth tasks (*Claudia* and *Emil*) and a paper-and pencil adoption of the Piaget Three-Mountains-Task (*Boxes*) were shown to be reliable measures that allowed us to differentiate among performances in transforming the perspective from aerial view to field views. Moreover, the task *Meadow*, an adoption of the Guilford-Zimmermann-Task, which requires perspective changes in depth and orientation, showed reasonable psychometrical characteristics as well.

Our results extend previous findings on adults that suggest that object manipulation abilities is dissociable from egocentric perspective transformation abilities. We showed that measures that require mental object manipulation to solve them do not reflect the same latent construct as measures that require individuals to mentally transform the egocentric viewpoint. In line with the differential spatial cognition literature for adults [6,14], the CFA demonstrated that a model assuming a dissociation assumed in this study has a statistically significant better fit than a model that is based on the assumption that spatial abilities are an undifferentiated construct. Although both classes are highly correlated ($r = 0.8$), object manipulation and perspective transformation abilities can therefore be separated in children as well. As a consequence, a child's ability to mentally manipulate an object stimulus from a stationary egocentric point of view does not necessarily reflect a child's ability to mentally take another perspective on a stationary set of object stimuli by the age of 9 to 12.

Our findings contribute to the literature by providing insights concerning sex differences with regard to elementary school children in spatial tasks. In line with the literature on sex differences in children [23], we found sex differences in a 3D Mental Rotation task. We also observed sex differences in a Paper Folding Task. However, sex differences in 2D mental rotation tasks have not been found. In line with the literature on sex differences in adults [30], we observed consistent sex differences among children in all the measures that demand perspective transformations. These differences were particularly high in the case of the two labyrinth tasks. Although there were sex-dependent invariances for these measures, a group-wise CFA demonstrated that the dissociation between object manipulation abilities and perspective transformation abilities is not sensitive to sex differences. Sex differences in the performance of specific measures were found, but our model of the latent construct of spatial abilities applied to boys and girls in an equal manner.

This study has three main limitations. First, although we presented individual differences in spatial abilities in children and provided empirical validation by means of examining correlations with other measures, we neither tacked individual differences in the use of specific strategies nor measured the underlying cognitive processes. We considered possible strategy choices of the children during the measure development but we did not provide an empirical verbal protocol analysis, which would have allowed us to test whether the measures used reflected the intended latent constructs. More research is needed to validate our measures and to develop comprehensive cognitive models for the two classes of spatial abilities that we separated.

Second, although all measures can be used to record individual differences among elementary school children, there is a limited range of differentiation in our measures, especially for low and high achievers. The paper-and-pencil test measures both classes of spatial abilities in a broad way. Consequently, each measure includes only a limited set of single items, which did not allow us to differentiate well enough among students on the margins of the performance spectrum. Furthermore, we did not control for individual differences in reading comprehension, attention span, or motivation. All of these factors may have influenced individual performances.

Third, our results might be limited since most of our participants were from the same town, and we tested them class-wise. It is important to replicate and refine our findings with a larger sample of elementary school children.

In conclusion, the most important finding of this study is that the dissociation between two classes of spatial abilities, object manipulation abilities and egocentric perspective transformation abilities, can already be found in elementary school children. Although boys outperform girls in some measures, the same degree of dissociation can be found for both sexes. Individual differences in spatial abilities measured by paper-and-pencil tests in children require more research, not only because they are being used to empirically test developmental theories of spatial cognition, but also because they play an important role in STEM education research.

References

1. Hegarty, M., Waller, D.: Individual differences in spatial abilities. In: Shah, P., Miyake, A. (eds.) The Cambridge handbook of Visuospatial Thinking, pp. 121–169. Cambridge University Press, New York (2005)
2. Carroll, J.B.: Human Cognitive Abilities: A Survey of Factor-Analytic Studies. Cambridge University Press, Cambridge (1993)
3. Andersen, L.: Visual-spatial ability: important in STEM, ignored in gifted education. Roeper Rev. **36**(2), 114–121 (2014)
4. Stieff, M., Uttal, D.: How much can spatial training improve STEM achievement? Educ. Psychol. Rev. **27**(4), 607–615 (2015)
5. Eliot, J.: Models of Psychological Space: Psychometric, Developmental, and Experimental Approaches. Springer, New York (1987)
6. Kozhevnikov, M., Hegarty, M.: A dissociation between object manipulation spatial ability and spatial orientation ability. Mem. Cogn. **29**(5), 745–756 (2001)
7. Wang, R.F., Simons, D.J.: Active and passive scene recognition across views. Cognition **70**(2), 191–210 (1999)
8. Zacks, J.M., Michelon, P.: Transformations of visuospatial images. Behav. Cogn. Neurosci. Rev. **4**(2), 96–118 (2005)
9. Presson, C.C.: Strategies in spatial reasoning. J. Exp. Psychol. Learn. Mem. Cogn. **8**(3), 243–251 (1982)
10. Zacks, J.M., Mires, J., Tversky, B., Hazeltine, E.: Mental spatial transformations of objects and perspective. Spat. Cogn. Comput. **2**(4), 315–332 (2000)
11. Creem, S.H., Wraga, M., Proffitt, D.R.: Imagining physically impossible self-rotations: geometry is more important than gravity. Cognition **81**(1), 41–64 (2001)
12. Zacks, J.M., Rypma, B., Gabrieli, J.D., Tversky, B., Glover, G.H.: Imagined transformations of bodies: an fMRI investigation. Neuropsychologia **37**(9), 1029–1040 (1999)
13. Easton, R.D., Sholl, M.J.: Object-array structure, frames of reference, and retrieval of spatial knowledge. J. Exp. Psychol. Learn. Mem. Cogn. **21**(2), 483–500 (1995)
14. Hegarty, M., Waller, D.: A dissociation between mental rotation and perspective-taking spatial abilities. Intelligence **32**(2), 175–191 (2004)
15. Piaget, J., Inhelder, B.: The child's conception of space: (Langdon, F.J. and Lunzer, J.L., Trans.). Norton (1948/1956)
16. Piaget, J., Inhelder, B.: Mental imagery in the child; a study of the development of imaginal representation: P.A. Chilton, Trans. Basic Books, New York (1966/1971)

17. Huttenlocher, J., Presson, C.C.: Mental rotation and the perspective problem. Cogn. Psychol. **4**(2), 277–299 (1973)

18. Huttenlocher, J., Presson, C.C.: The coding and transformation of spatial information. Cogn. Psychol. **11**(3), 375–394 (1979)

19. Caeyenberghs, K., Tsoupas, J., Wilson, P.H., Smits-Engelsman, B.C.M.: Motor imagery development in primary school children. Dev. Neuropsychol. **34**(1), 103–121 (2009)

20. Crescentini, C., Fabbro, F., Urgesi, C.: Mental spatial transformations of objects and bodies: different developmental trajectories in children from 7 to 11 years of age. Dev. Psychol. **50**(2), 370–383 (2014)

21. Vander Heyden, K.M., Huizinga, M., Kan, K.J., Jolles, J.: A developmental perspective on spatial reasoning: dissociating object transformation from viewer transformation ability. Cogn. Dev. **38**, 63–74 (2016)

22. Linn, M.C., Petersen, A.C.: Emergence and characterization of sex differences in spatial ability: a meta-analysis. Child Dev. **56**(6), 1479–1498 (1985)

23. Voyer, D., Voyer, S., Bryden, M.P.: Magnitude of sex differences in spatial abilities: a meta-analysis and consideration of critical variables. Psychol. Bull. **117**(2), 250–270 (1995)

24. Johnson, E.S., Meade, A.C.: Developmental patterns of spatial ability: an early sex difference. Child Dev. **58**, 725–740 (1987)

25. Quinn, P.C., Liben, L.S.: A sex difference in mental rotation in young infants. Psychol. Sci. **19**(11), 1067–1070 (2008)

26. Levine, S.C., Huttenlocher, J., Taylor, A., Langrock, A.: Early sex differences in spatial skill. Dev. Psychol. **35**(4), 940–949 (1999)

27. Kerns, K.A., Berenbaum, S.A.: Sex differences in spatial ability in children. Behav. Genet. **21**(4), 383–396 (1991)

28. Vederhus, L., Krekling, S.: Sex differences in visual spatial ability in 9-year-old children. Intelligence **23**(1), 33–43 (1996)

29. Frick, A., Möhring, W., Newcombe, N.S.: Picturing perspectives: development of perspective-taking abilities in 4- to 8-year-olds. Front. Psychol. **5**, 386 (2014)

30. Tarampi, M.R., Heydari, N., Hegarty, M.: A tale of two types of perspective taking: sex differences in spatial ability. Psychol. Sci. **27**(11), 1507–1516 (2016)

31. Kline, R.B.: Principles and Practice of Structural Equation Modeling. Guilford Press, New York (2015)

32. Ekstrom, R.B., French, J.W., Harman, H.H., Dermen, D.: Manual for Kit of Factor-Referenced Cognitive Tests. Educational Testing Service, Princeton (1976)

33. Vandenberg, S.G., Kuse, A.R.: Mental rotations, a group test of three-dimensional spatial visualization. Percept. Mot. Skills **47**(2), 599–604 (1978)

34. de Lange, J.: Geometry for all or: no geometry at all. Zentralblatt für Didaktik der Mathematik **3**, 90–97 (1984)

35. Guilford, J.P., Zimmerman, W.S.: The Guilford-Zimmerman aptitude survey. J. Appl. Psychol. **32**(1), 24–34 (1948)

36. West, S.G., Finch, J.F., Curran, P.J.: Structural equation models with nonnormal variables: problems and remedies. In: Hoyle, R.H. (ed.) Structural Equation Modeling: Concepts, Issues, and Applications, pp. 56–75. Sage, Thousand Oaks (1995)

37. Muthén, L.K., Muthén, B.O.: Mplus User's Guide: Statistical Analysis with Latent Variables: User's Guide: Computer Software Manual. Muthén & Muthén, Los Angeles (2004)

38. Geiser, C.: Data Analysis with Mplus. Guilford Press, New York (2012)

39. Rosseel, Y.: Lavaan: an R package for structural equation modeling. J. Stat. Softw. **48**(2), 1–36 (2012)
40. Hu, L.T., Bentler, P.M.: Cutoff criteria for fit indexes in covariance structure analysis: conventional criteria versus new alternatives. Struct. Equ. Model.: Multidisc. J. **6**(1), 1–55 (1999)
41. McDonald, R.P.: Test Theory: A Unified Treatment. Erlbaum, Mahwah (1999)
42. Olkin, I., Hedges, L.V., Hedges, L.V. (eds.): Statistical Methods for Meta-Analysis. Academic Press, New York (1985)

State Anxiety Influences Sex Differences in Spatial Learning

Ian T. Ruginski[(⊠)], Jeanine K. Stefanucci,
and Sarah H. Creem-Regehr

University of Utah, Salt Lake City, UT 08544, USA
Ian.Ruginski@gmail.com

Abstract. Past research shows consistent sex differences in survey-based spatial knowledge and wayfinding strategy. State anxiety may help to explain some of these differences. The current study tested if and how state anxiety influences sex differences in spatial learning during navigation. We used a virtual desktop spatial learning task and manipulated state anxiety between-subjects. Participants passively learned the locations of landmarks and then were tested using egocentric pointing and map landmark placement tasks. Results showed that males performed better than females overall, replicating past work. Further, state anxiety adversely affected pointing accuracy for females but not males. Males were more accurate in their cognitive maps and women's cognitive maps appeared to be more spatially compressed than men's across both anxiety conditions. Results are discussed in the context of how state anxiety might influence sex differences in the formation of survey representations dependent on spatial learning and assessment perspective.

Keywords: Spatial memory · Wayfinding · Sex differences · Anxiety

1 Introduction

Across numerous paradigms, individual differences are observed in spatial navigation tasks, often showing a male performance advantage in real and virtual environments [1–3]. While differences in abilities, strategies, and cue-use have been proposed to account for sex differences, our current study examined whether state anxiety affects sex differences in navigation. State anxiety can be defined as a subjective feeling of distress, often accompanied by physiological changes such as increased heart rate and/or skin conductance. Anxiety may be experienced during navigation in many circumstances, such as when one is late to a doctor's appointment, or lost in a new place. We expected state anxiety to affect sex differences in spatial learning given potential differences in neurobiological and behavioral stress responses in the context of spatial learning. For example, cortisol level at time of encoding positively predicts spatial memory in men, but predicts either no relationship or a negative relationship to memory in women [4]. Related research has found that spatial learning under stress impairs cognitive map formation in females, but not males [5, 6]. In contrast, similar research has found that stress did not affect male or female spatial learning performance

S. Creem-Regehr et al. (Eds.): Spatial Cognition 2018, LNAI 11034, pp. 244–257, 2018.
https://doi.org/10.1007/978-3-319-96385-3_17

as measured by an egocentric pointing task in a virtual environment [7]. Thus, although work exists testing an effect of state anxiety on sex differences in spatial learning, the direction and magnitude of the effect remains open to further investigation.

In the current study, we tested effects of state anxiety on a passive spatial learning task in a naturalistic, large-scale, outdoor virtual environment. We were particularly interested in the formation of survey knowledge—observer independent representations of the environment—because of its importance for efficient and flexible navigation and because it often shows sex differences [8]. Survey-based spatial knowledge supports flexible and global environmental representations of the relative spatial relationships, or configurations, between landmarks (as opposed to procedural, route-specific knowledge of landmark locations only). Men, more than women, tend to use distal (far-space) landmarks and a fixed allocentric coordinate system in learning of novel spaces that allows for efficient navigational shortcuts above and beyond previously traversed space, an indication of better survey spatial knowledge acquisition. Conversely, women often learn spaces in relation to proximal (near-space) landmarks and previously traversed routes [1, 9–11]. Self-reported spatial strategy and cue-use measures align with measures of wayfinding efficiency; orientation strategies and the use of distal-cues are more often reported by men, who navigate more effectively than women on average [12–17]. Based on attentional control theory [18], if anxiety typically affects global processing and results in attentional narrowing, then we would expect greatest effects of anxiety on survey spatial representations—spatial memory that relies on a global understanding of the environment—and on females, who may not have a tendency to use strategies or cues that support these types of representations.

Our approach contributes to existing work on the effect of acute anxiety on sex differences in spatial learning in three primary ways. First, many navigation studies have used geometrically rigid mazes/environments, which may favor preferred male strategies and cue selection. The larger scale, more naturalistic environment utilized in the current study increases the potential generalizability and external validity of findings. Second, the current study used measures of spatial learning from both egocentric (pointing) and allocentric (cognitive map) perspectives. Inclusion of both types of measures is important, given prior work indicates individual differences in spatial memory formation and retention dependent on frame of reference [19]. Previous work has shown that consistency between perspectives used in learning and testing matters, finding advantages when study and test match (e.g., egocentric learning of routes and egocentric test such as direct navigation to targets) and costs when they do not [20, 21]. Currently, there is no consensus as to whether anxiety affects the use of different perspectives in spatial memory retrieval.

Last, our study implemented a purely physiological (respiratory) manipulation of state anxiety. This manipulation was chosen to activate the sympathetic nervous system without introducing a confound of social stress or navigation-specific stress, and to test the hypothesis that male and female spatial memory would be differentially affected by high levels of stress. This high level of anxiety was targeted for manipulation due to work showing that anxiety at moderate levels of arousal sometimes increases performance [22], especially if reappraised as a positive emotion such as excitement or challenge [23, 24]. Overall, we aimed to test (1) whether anxiety would adversely affect women's spatial memory more than men's in a large-scale naturalistic virtual environment and

(2) whether the effects of anxiety would generalize to two different spatial memory retrieval tasks. We predicted an overall performance advantage for men on both measures, replicating past work. Previous indications of adverse effects of anxiety on female's spatial performance, and the notion that anxiety decreases global processing, led us to predict that women's acquisition of survey knowledge would be further impaired relative to men with the addition of a state anxiety manipulation. Given that both pointing and cognitive map measures relied on the formation of survey knowledge, we also expected that the anxiety effects on women would generalize across both measures. However, given previously established effects on the greater costs on memory when tested from a different perspective than learning, it is also possible that we would find differential effects on anxiety as a function of testing method.

2 Method

2.1 Participants

107 University of Utah students aged 18 to 47, ($M = 21$ years) participated for course credit. All participants provided informed consent before participation. Sample size was determined a priori using a GPower 3.1.7 power analysis [25] with a conservative effect size based on past literature (power = .80, $\eta_p^2 = 0.10$).

Six participants were excluded from data analysis as outliers due to Cook's distance (a measure of statistical influence) exceeding three times the mean distance of the sample [26] for either cognitive map distance or the pointing outcome measures. Three additional participants were excluded due to procedural errors. 98 participants were included in the final data analyses (26 F and 26 M in the anxiety condition; 22 F and 24 M in the control condition).

2.2 Virtual Environment

The large-scale virtual spatial learning task and environment were implemented using Unity 5.0.1. The experiment was presented on a high resolution, 24-in. Dell LCD monitor, updating at a frame rate of 60 Hz. The display was located 1.07 m from the chair where participants sat. The virtual environment spanned 1500 × 1500 m. There were six proximal landmarks present in the environment: a home, a truck, a well, a tent, a shed, and a column. Two separate spatial learning videos lasting 3 min 45 s each and containing 6 major (>45°) turns were shown through this virtual environment [27–29]. Three landmarks were directly encountered on dirt roads followed through the environment in each of the spatial learning videos, though other landmarks were visible in the distance. There were also distal cues, such as the sun, a waterfall, a beach, and surrounding mountainous terrain (see Fig. 1). Route learning order was counterbalanced.

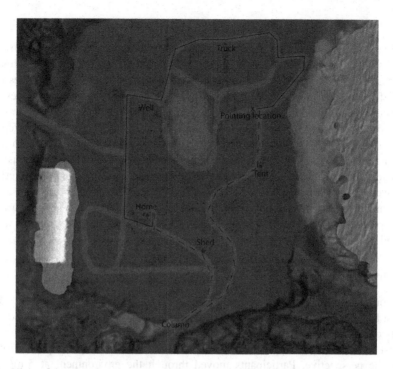

Fig. 1. View of the virtual environment from above. The two spatial learning paths are depicted using solid and dashed lines (participants did not see this aerial view during learning). The map landmark placement test was shown from the same perspective, but did not include labeled landmarks or indication of the paths taken (solid and dashed lines).

2.3 Anxiety Manipulation

Participants in the anxiety condition performed restricted breathing through a small coffee-stirrer straw for two minutes prior to encoding. This method has been utilized in clinical studies to elicit the physiological aspects of a panic attack [30] and more recently used to test effects of anxiety on perceptual judgments [31][1]. Individuals in the control condition breathed through a large straw for the same amount of time. The subjective units of distress scale (SUDS), which provides a subjective measure of distress on a scale from 1 (very calm and relaxed) to 100 (very agitated and anxious) was recorded as a manipulation check [33].

---

[1] This method was utilized instead of the Trier Social Stressor Task since men and women differentially respond to the Trier stressor [32]. Additionally, the stress response from the Trier might have lasted until the experimental testing phase, and we were interested in testing the effect of anxiety on spatial encoding, not testing.

2.4   Covariates

Participants completed a Corsi block test of spatial working memory for use as a covariate using Psychology Experiment Building Language (PEBL) software [34]. This was chosen as a covariate because our question of interest was about sex differences in the effect of anxiety on acquisition of survey knowledge, and alternative theories have posited that spatial working memory may explain these differences [35]. There were no gender differences ($t(95) = 1.7$, $p = 0.09$) or anxiety manipulation group differences ($t(95) = -0.1$, $p = 0.93$) in spatial working memory as measured by the Corsi. In addition, self-reported video game use (hours per week) was measured for use as a covariate to control for familiarity with virtual environments and computer interfaces. There were gender differences in video games played per week ($t(54) = -3.5, p < .001$), but no anxiety manipulation group differences ($t(91) = 0.3$, $p = 0.77$) in video games played per week. Men reported an average of 4.8 h played per week, while women reported an average of 0.7 h played per week.

2.5   Procedure

After completion of informed consent, a baseline SUDS measure was obtained. Then, the first breathing task was completed with either a large or small straw, depending on anxiety condition. After the manipulation, a follow-up SUDS measure was taken. Then, the first route video through the environment was shown to participants from an egocentric perspective. Participants moved through the environment at 5 m/s. Following spatial learning, participants were asked to accurately point to the unseen locations of each major environmental landmark from their stopping point on the path.

Fig. 2. Pointing test location in the virtual environment. Spatial learning paths through the environment were also viewed from this perspective without the appearance of the instructions and crosshair.

They moved a crosshair on the screen using an Xbox controller to indicate the direction of a particular landmark (see Fig. 2). They pointed twice to each landmark in random order for a total of six trials.

The spatial learning and testing procedure was then repeated once: the breathing task was performed a second time, a second video was played of a different path through the same environment, and a second series of pointing tests was completed. After this test, participants were asked to mark locations of major landmarks on a top-down map of the environment (see Fig. 1) as accurately as possible using the same controller. Finally, participants completed the Corsi task and were debriefed about the purpose of the experiment before leaving.

3   Results

3.1   Anxiety Manipulation Check

A 2 (sex) $\times$ 2 (anxiety condition) ANOVA was used to check the anxiety manipulation using the mean difference between SUDS ratings. Anxiety condition was significantly related to a change in SUDS from baseline, $F(1, 94) = 45.0$, $p < .001$, $\eta_p^2 = 0.32$. Individuals in the anxiety condition ($M = 25$, $SD = 20.20$) became significantly more anxious following the anxiety manipulation than individuals in the control condition ($M = 1$, $SD = 13.74$) (see Fig. 3).

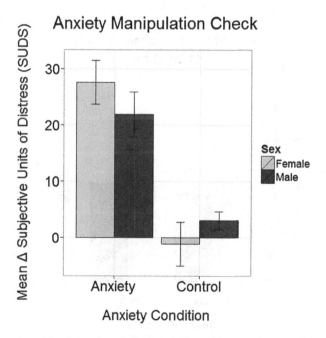

Fig. 3. Change in subjective units of distress ratings across anxiety conditions. Error bars indicate ± 1 SE. A positive value indicates that self-reported anxiety increased from baseline.

There were no differences in SUDS ratings between males and females (F(1, 94) = 0.1, $p = 0.77$, $\eta_p^2 = 0.001$) and no interaction between anxiety condition and sex (F(1, 94) = 1.9, $p = 0.16$, $\eta_p^2 = 0.02$).

Individuals were allowed to suspend the breathing task if uncomfortable, so a 2 × 2 ANOVA was used to determine if time (in seconds) spent breathing differed by sex. Overall, breathing was shorter in the anxiety condition ($M = 55.7$, $SD = 33.8$) than the control condition ($M = 115.1$, $SD = 18.35$), but male and female breathing time in the anxiety condition did not differ, F(1, 94) = 0.53, $p = 0.47$, $\eta_p^2 = 0.006$.

3.2 Survey Spatial Knowledge Tested from an Egocentric Perspective (Pointing Task)

For the pointing task, the absolute value of the difference between participants' answers and the correct angle was calculated for each trial and averaged across trials to yield the overall error score [8, 36, 37]. Guessing with no knowledge of the environment would yield an average score of 90°. The pointing errors of six participants were above the 90° threshold (maximum = 109.0°). These were left in the analysis since it was expected that anxiety would greatly affect pointing judgments and these values did not exceed the previously mentioned Cook's distance outlier threshold (three times pointing mean). There was large variability in performance overall, for both females ($M = 51.6°$, $SD = 27.6$, range = 95.9, n = 48) and males ($M = 32.3°$, $SD = 14.5$, range = 72.7, n = 50).

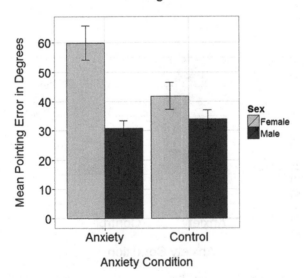

Fig. 4. Interaction between sex and anxiety condition predicting mean pointing error. Error bars indicate ±1 SE.

A two-way ANCOVA was conducted to test whether sex, anxiety condition, and the interaction between sex and anxiety condition significantly predicted pointing error while controlling for video game experience (hours played per week; $F = 0.004$, $p = 0.95$) and visuo-spatial working memory (Corsi block span; $F = 0.23$, $p = 0.63$). Males performed better than females on pointing, $F(1, 92) = 20.0, p < .001, \eta_p^2 = 0.18$. Participants in the anxiety condition ($M = 45.4°$, $SD = 27.2$) did not perform differently than controls ($M = 37.7°$, $SD = 18.91$) on the pointing task, $F(1, 92) = 2.8$, $p = 0.09$, $\eta_p^2 = 0.03$. However, there was a significant interaction between sex and anxiety condition, $F(1, 92) = 5.9$, $p = 0.016$, $\eta_p^2 = 0.06$ (see Fig. 4).

Post-hoc t-tests (Bonferroni-adjusted alpha at .025) revealed that females in the anxiety condition made greater pointing errors than females in the control condition (Mean difference = 18.2°, $SE = 6.2$, $t = 2.9$, p = 0.02, 95% CI [6.0, 30.4]), while males in the anxiety condition did not perform differently from males in the control condition (Mean difference = $-3.1°$, $SE = 6.1$, $t = 0.5, p = 0.96$, 95% CI [-14.9, 8.8]).

3.3   Survey Spatial Knowledge Tested from an Allocentric Perspective (Cognitive Map Formation)

A second measure of survey knowledge included assessing participants' cognitive maps after both paths were completed. Bidimensional regressions were conducted using the 'BiDimRegression' package for R software [38]. Bidimensional regression allows for comparison of two dimensional datasets and is a useful tool for assessing cognitive map accuracy [39]. Actual landmark locations (independent variable) predict remembered landmark locations (dependent variable). Bidimensional regression calculates a squared correlation coefficient (r^2) between remembered locations and actual locations, which describes the proportion of variance in the "real" map captured by individuals' cognitive maps.

Bidimensional regressions were conducted for each individual's cognitive map, and an ANCOVA mirroring the pointing analysis was conducted to determine if gender and anxiety predicted variance (r^2) captured by individuals' cognitive maps (akin to Weisberg et al. [37]). Similar to pointing, neither spatial working memory measured by Corsi block span ($F = 0.01$, $p = 0.92$) nor video game hours played per week ($F = 0.32$, $p = 0.57$) predicted mapping ability above and beyond gender and anxiety condition. Males ($M = 0.90$, $SD = 0.13$) performed better than females ($M = 0.77$, $SD = 0.25$) on cognitive map formation, $F(1, 92) = 10.86$, $p = .001$, $\eta_p^2 = 0.18$. Participants in the anxiety condition ($M = 0.84$, $SD = 0.21$) did not perform differently than controls ($M = 0.83$, $SD = 0.20$), $F(1, 92) = 0.07$, $p = 0.79$, $\eta_p^2 = 0.03$. Finally, there was no interaction between sex and anxiety condition, $F(1, 92) = 1.67, p = 0.20$, $\eta_p^2 = 0.06$. Overall, while the predicted gender difference was found, these results did not match the pattern of results from pointing accuracy analyses, as there was no interaction between anxiety condition and gender.

While the ANCOVA supported an overall advantage in accuracy for males compared to females, we were also interested in characterizing the patterns of these differences. To explore these differences, we ran bidimensional regressions on the data collapsed across individual participants for each sex x anxiety condition (4 groups). The resulting parameters are presented in Table 1 and further discussed in the next section.

Table 1. Bidimensional regression parameters. * indicates p < .05, ** indicates p < .001 for α1 and α2, and test whether these values are significantly different from zero. θ values greater than 0 indicate counterclockwise rotation relative to the real map; θ values less than 0 indicate clockwise rotation relative to the real map. Φ values greater than 1 indicate expansion of the cognitive map relative to the real map; values less than 1 indicate contraction.

Parameters	Female control	Male control	Female anxiety	Male anxiety
α_1, horizontal displacement	51.4	−20.8	108.9[*]	26.5
α_2, vertical displacement	267.3[**]	160.6[**]	325.3[**]	167.0[**]
θ, angle displacement	−7.6	−6.3	−7.2	−4.7
Φ, scaling	0.79	0.89	0.73	0.91
r^2	0.68	0.87	0.53	0.85

4 Discussion

The goal of the current study was to test whether state anxiety (induced during learning) would differentially affect male and female formation of survey spatial knowledge. To test this hypothesis, we utilized a passive, large-scale outdoor virtual environment spatial learning task with a straightforward, short-lasting physiological manipulation of stress that allowed for testing the influence of anxiety on spatial encoding, separate from social pressure and/or task demands. Our results support the hypothesis that anxiety influences sex differences in spatial learning, with the important caveat that perspective of assessment matters. Males performed better than females on two converging measures of spatial learning that draw on responses from either egocentric or allocentric perspectives [2, 8, 33]. Importantly, female performance was adversely affected (i.e., increased pointing error) with the induction of anxiety, whereas male performance was not. This result is consistent with previous work showing that women's spatial memory is impaired by state anxiety [4–6]. The inconsistent influence of anxiety across two survey spatial measures provides evidence for an effect of anxiety on spatial learning dependent on assessment method when learning the environment from an egocentric perspective.

Conflicting results between the pointing and cognitive map analyses raise interesting questions about how the formation of allocentric representations might differ depending on sex, state anxiety, and learning assessment methods. The finding that anxiety only adversely affected women's pointing is consistent with previous work finding differences as a function of match between learning and testing, as environments were learned from the same egocentric perspective as the pointing test. Given that women prefer egocentric, route-based strategies [12–15], anxiety may have only adversely affected the testing method that aligned with this preference. However, it may also be that anxiety differentially affected women's pointing because the pointing response measure immediately followed the learning phase whereas the map test came at the end of the study when state anxiety level could have decreased. As it stands, we cannot determine whether the inconsistent effect of anxiety on women between the map measure and pointing measure were due to timing or due to perspective because these two factors were confounded in the current study, opening the door for future work that further explores these factors. Future work might implement environment learning from a map-like perspective, and/or where map assessments precede pointing assessments. Both are critical factors to consider given anxiety's effects on attention to global features and the changing nature of anxiety over time [18]. Most importantly, manipulating these factors would help to assess whether anxiety affects pointing because of its alignment with learning perspective, or whether the persistence of the stress manipulation differentially affected the first task (pointing) more than the second (map formation).

On the group level, the bidimensional regression scaling parameter (Φ) suggests that women may compress cognitive maps compared to men. Women's memory of metric spatial relations between landmarks were not as accurate as men's, even though men also showed a slight compression overall. What might explain why women demonstrated fairly large compression? Kosslyn has proposed a distinction between coordinate and categorical spatial knowledge [40] and recent work has tested for individual differences in these types of spatial encoding [41]. Our current result may reflect men's greater reliance on metric information compared to women's greater reliance on categorical information during spatial learning, consistent with results from Holden et al. [42]. For example, in the current study, women placed landmarks more to the center of the map, around the visible locations of the dirt path. In addition, women in the anxiety condition were the only group who demonstrated a horizontal shift (α_1) of the cognitive map, compared to the physical layout of landmarks. Women in the anxiety condition tended to place landmarks generally closer to the water, biased to the side where most landmarks were located, which would also support an account of categorical encoding. It may be that categorical encoding is relied on as a more efficient cognitive strategy when working memory is consumed by task-irrelevant anxiety, but further testing is needed to address the role of cognitive mechanisms. In all, the bidimensional regression metrics supplementing r^2 provide additional information about the potential biases underlying individual differences in spatial learning and associated cognitive map formation.

4.1   Limitations

There are a few limitations related to the generalizability of the current study. First, the anxiety manipulation was not task specific. Breathing through a straw can be stressful, but does not necessarily have any functional relationship to spatial learning, navigation itself, or how anxiety might exert its influence outside of the laboratory, such as when someone feels lost while navigating. Future studies of the effects of anxiety on spatial learning could incorporate task-specific, threat-relevant stimuli, such as the presence of threat in the learned environment itself, or spatial-specific anxiety. For example, arousal alters estimates of vertical heights but not horizontal extents [43] and threatening stimuli, such as snakes, more easily draw attention than neutral stimuli [44].

An environment-specific threat may better elicit anxiety and test how anxiety affects spatial learning in a more ecologically valid way. Another possibility is that anxiety could affect spatial performance of men and women differently even when anxiety is not manipulated (via stereotype threat, for example) [45]. Future work that directly manipulates stereotype threat through planned instructions or scenarios could investigate this further in order to determine if type of anxiety matters.

Second, environments were learned passively rather than actively, but different mechanisms underlie passive and active navigation. For example, actively walking through an environment provides the proprioceptive and vestibular information necessary to form a metric survey representation of the traversed environment [46, c.f. 47]. Thus, the findings of the current study should only be generalized to passive spatial learning and not necessarily to the active spatial learning inherent to wayfinding. Future work would benefit from allowing individuals to actively learn the environment.

4.2   Future Directions and Open Questions

Despite these limitations, our findings provide initial evidence that state anxiety differentially affects male and female spatial learning and memory. Future research should test the underlying cognitive mechanisms of a sex-differentiated influence of anxiety on the formation and use of survey spatial representations. One potential mechanism may be that anxiety differentially affects attention in males and females, leading to individual differences in visual attention to environmental cues that could influence navigational strategies [15] or differences in the cognitive resources available for learning and memory [48, 49]. Future studies of the effect of anxiety on sex differences in spatial learning would benefit from eye tracking measures [50] to test whether anxiety differentially affects males and females' visual attention during spatial learning.

In addition, supplementary individual difference measures may help explain effects of anxiety on spatial learning. Recent work has shown that men high in trait anxiety and low in mental rotation ability navigate less effectively than other men [51]. Other trait variables, such as harm avoidance, can predict cautious exploration behavior, which leads to less accurate navigation [52]. More generally, individual differences exist in ability to integrate spatial knowledge from different routes traversed when navigating [34]. These trait-level individual factors could mediate sex differences in spatial learning performance.

In conclusion, the current study suggests that state anxiety should be considered when constructing and testing models of sex differences in survey spatial knowledge when learning under passive viewing conditions. In this case, a manipulation of state anxiety further exaggerated previously known sex differences in spatial learning, when knowledge was assessed from the perspective that the environment was learned. Work at the intersection between spatial cognition, emotion, and sex differences remains a large gap in the literature that merits further investigation, particularly since preliminary evidence across the fields of cognitive and neurobiological psychology suggest that emotional state may help to explain sex differences in spatial learning. This study serves as a first step for testing an influence of anxiety on spatial learning. Future research should investigate more subtle manipulations related to social factors and motivation using continuous measures of affective response and other individual differences across spatial tasks. A better understanding of the emotional underpinnings of sex differences in spatial performance could have far-reaching applications, from generating anxiety-based interventions for use with spatial tasks and tests during the lifespan (particularly during early development) to better understanding how different individuals navigate, learn, and remember spaces under stress.

References

1. Castelli, L., Latini-Corazzini, L., Geminiani, G.C.: Spatial navigation in large-scale virtual environments: gender differences in survey tasks. Comput. Hum. Behav. **24**(4), 1643–1667 (2008)
2. Coluccia, E., Iosue, G., Brandimonte, M.A.: The relationship between map drawing and spatial orientation abilities: a study of gender differences. J. Environ. Psychol. **27**(2), 135–144 (2007)
3. Shelton, A.L., Marchette, S.A., Furman, A.J.: A mechanistic approach to individual differences in spatial learning, memory, and navigation. Psychol. Learn. Motiv. **59**, 223–259 (2013)
4. Andreano, J.M., Cahill, L.: Sex influences on the neurobiology of learning and memory. Learn. Mem. **16**(4), 248–266 (2009)
5. Thomas, K.G., Laurance, H.E., Nadel, L., Jacobs, W.J.: Stress-induced impairment of spatial navigation in females. S. Afr. J. Psychol. **40**(1), 32–43 (2010)
6. Guenzel, F.M., Wolf, O.T., Schwabe, L.: Sex differences in stress effects on response and spatial memory formation. Neurobiol. Learn. Mem. **109**, 46–55 (2014)
7. Richardson, A.E., Tomasulo, M.M.V.: Influence of acute stress on spatial tasks in humans. Physiol. Behav. **103**(5), 459–466 (2011)
8. Wolbers, T., Hegarty, M.: What determines our navigational abilities? Trends Cogn. Sci. **14**(3), 138–146 (2010)
9. Ross, S.P., Skelton, R.W., Mueller, S.C.: Gender differences in spatial navigation in virtual space: implications when using virtual environments in instruction and assessment. Virtual Real. **10**(3), 175–184 (2006)
10. Sandstrom, N.J., Kaufman, J., Huettel, S.A.: Males and females use different distal cues in a virtual environment navigation task. Cogn. Brain. Res. **6**(4), 351–360 (1998)
11. Tlauka, M., Brolese, A., Pomeroy, D., Hobbs, W.: Gender differences in spatial knowledge acquired through simulated exploration of a virtual shopping centre. J. Environ. Psychol. **25**(1), 111–118 (2005)
12. Bosco, A., Longoni, A.M., Vecchi, T.: Gender effects in spatial orientation: cognitive profiles and mental strategies. Appl. Cogn. Psychol. **18**(5), 519–532 (2004)
13. Choi, J., McKillop, E., Ward, M., L'Hirondelle, N.: Sex-specific relationships between route-learning strategies and abilities in a large-scale environment. Environ. Behav. **38**(6), 791–801 (2006)
14. Dabbs Jr., J.M., Chang, E.L., Strong, R.A., Milun, R.: Spatial ability, navigation strategy, and geographic knowledge among men and women. Evol. Hum. Behav. **19**(2), 89–98 (1998)
15. Lawton, C.A.: Gender differences in way-finding strategies: relationship to spatial ability and spatial anxiety. Sex Roles **30**(11–12), 765–779 (1994)
16. Montello, D.R., Lovelace, K.L., Golledge, R.G., Self, C.M.: Sex-related differences and similarities in geographic and environmental spatial abilities. Ann. Assoc. Am. Geogr. **89**(3), 515–534 (1999)

17. Picucci, L., Caffò, A.O., Bosco, A.: Besides navigation accuracy: gender differences in strategy selection and level of spatial confidence. J. Environ. Psychol. **31**(4), 430–438 (2011)

18. Eysenck, M.W., Derakshan, N., Santos, R., Calvo, M.G.: Anxiety and cognitive performance: attentional control theory. Emotion **7**(2), 336 (2007)

19. Klatzky, R.L.: Allocentric and egocentric spatial representations: definitions, distinctions, and interconnections. In: Freksa, C., Habel, C., Wender, K.F. (eds.) Spatial Cognition. LNCS, vol. 1404, pp. 1–17. Springer, Heidelberg (1998). https://doi.org/10.1007/3-540-69342-4_1

20. Taylor, H.A., Naylor, S.J., Chechile, N.A.: Goal-specific influences on the representation of spatial perspective. Mem. Cogn. **27**(2), 309–319 (1999)

21. Brunyé, T.T., Taylor, H.A.: Extended experience benefits spatial mental model development with route but not survey descriptions. Acta Psychol. **127**(2), 340–354 (2008)

22. Sonstroem, R.J., Bernardo, P.: Intraindividual pregame state anxiety and basketball performance: a re-examination of the inverted-U curve. J. Sport Psychol. **4**(3), 235–245 (1982)

23. Brooks, A.W.: Get excited: reappraising pre-performance anxiety as excitement. J. Exp. Psychol. Gen. **143**(3), 1144 (2014)

24. Jamieson, J.P., Peters, B.J., Greenwood, E.J., Altose, A.J.: Reappraising stress arousal improves performance and reduces evaluation anxiety in classroom exam situations. Soc. Psychol. Pers. Sci. **7**(6), 579–587 (2016)

25. Faul, F., Erdfelder, E., Lang, A.G., Buchner, A.: G* Power 3: a flexible statistical power analysis program for the social, behavioral, and biomedical sciences. Behav. Res. Methods **39**(2), 175–191 (2007)

26. Cohen, J., Cohen, P., West, S.G., Aiken, L.S.: Applied Multiple Regression/Correlation Analysis for the Behavioral Sciences. Routledge, Abingdon (2013)

27. Meilinger, T., Knauff, M., Bülthoff, H.H.: Working memory in wayfinding—A dual task experiment in a virtual city. Cogn. Sci. **32**(4), 755–770 (2008)

28. Wen, W., Ishikawa, T., Sato, T.: Working memory in spatial knowledge acquisition: differences in encoding processes and sense of direction. Appl. Cogn. Psychol. **25**(4), 654–662 (2010)

29. Wen, W., Ishikawa, T., Sato, T.: Individual differences in the encoding processes of egocentric and allocentric survey knowledge. Cogn. Sci. **37**(1), 176–192 (2013)

30. Hofmann, S.G., Bufka, L.F., Barlow, D.H.: Panic provocation procedures in the treatment of panic disorder: early perspectives and case studies. Behav. Ther. **30**(2), 305–317 (1999)

31. Graydon, M.M., Linkenauger, S.A., Teachman, B.A., Proffitt, D.R.: Scared stiff: the influence of anxiety on the perception of action capabilities. Cogn. Emot. **26**(7), 1301–1315 (2012)

32. Kelly, M.M., Tyrka, A.R., Anderson, G.M., Price, L.H., Carpenter, L.L.: Sex differences in emotional and physiological responses to the Trier Social Stress Test. J. Behav. Ther. Exp. Psychiatry **39**(1), 87–98 (2008)

33. Morgan, C.A., Rasmusson, A.M., Wang, S., Hoyt, G., Hauger, R.L., Hazlett, G.: Neuropeptide-Y, cortisol, and subjective distress in humans exposed to acute stress: replication and extension of previous report. Biol. Psychiatry **52**(2), 136–142 (2002)

34. Mueller, S.T., Piper, B.J.: The psychology experiment building language (PEBL) and PEBL test battery. J. Neurosci. Methods **222**, 250–259 (2014)

35. Coluccia, E., Louse, G.: Gender differences in spatial orientation: a review. J. Environ. Psychol. **24**(3), 329–340 (2004)

36. Hegarty, M., Montello, D.R., Richardson, A.E., Ishikawa, T., Lovelace, K.: Spatial abilities at different scales: individual differences in aptitude-test performance and spatial-layout learning. Intelligence **34**(2), 151–176 (2006)

37. Weisberg, S.M., Schinazi, V.R., Newcombe, N.S., Shipley, T.F., Epstein, R.A.: Variations in cognitive maps: understanding individual differences in navigation. J. Exp. Psychol. Learn. Mem. Cogn. **40**(3), 669 (2014)

38. Carbon, C.C.: BiDimRegression: bidimensional regression modeling using R. J. Stat. Softw. Code Snippets **52**(1), 1–11 (2013)

39. Friedman, A., Kohler, B.: Bidimensional regression: assessing the configural similarity and accuracy of cognitive maps and other two-dimensional data sets. Psychol. Methods **8**(4), 468 (2003)

40. Kosslyn, S.M.: Seeing and imagining in the cerebral hemispheres: a computational approach. Psychol. Rev. **94**(2), 148 (1987)

41. Jager, G., Postma, A.: On the hemispheric specialization for categorical and coordinate spatial relations: a review of the current evidence. Neuropsychologia **41**(4), 504–515 (2003)

42. Holden, M.P., Duff-Canning, S.J., Hampson, E.: Sex differences in the weighting of metric and categorical information in spatial location memory. Psychol. Res. **79**(1), 1–18 (2015)

43. Stefanucci, J.K., Storbeck, J.: Don't look down: emotional arousal elevates height perception. J. Exp. Psychol. Gen. **138**(1), 131 (2009)

44. Öhman, A., Flykt, A., Esteves, F.: Emotion drives attention: detecting the snake in the grass. J. Exp. Psychol. Gen. **130**(3), 466 (2001)

45. Beilock, S.L., Rydell, R.J., McConnell, A.R.: Stereotype threat and working memory: mechanisms, alleviation, and spillover. J. Exp. Psychol. Gen. **136**(2), 256 (2007)

46. Chrastil, E.R., Warren, W.H.: Active and passive contributions to spatial learning. Psychon. Bull. Rev. **19**(1), 1–23 (2012)

47. Waller, D., Greenauer, N.: The role of body-based sensory information in the acquisition of enduring spatial representations. Psychol. Res. **71**(3), 322–332 (2007)

48. Stout, D.M., Shackman, A.J., Larson, C.L.: Failure to filter: anxious individuals show inefficient gating of threat from working memory. Front. Hum. Neurosci. **7**, 58 (2013)

49. Maloney, E.A., Sattizahn, J.R., Beilock, S.L.: Anxiety and cognition. Wiley Interdiscip. Rev.: Cogn. Sci. **5**(4), 403–411 (2014)

50. Mueller, S.C., Jackson, C.P., Skelton, R.W.: Sex differences in a virtual water maze: an eye tracking and pupillometry study. Behav. Brain Res. **193**(2), 209–215 (2008)

51. Thoresen, J.C., Francelet, R., Coltekin, A., Richter, K.F., Fabrikant, S.I., Sandi, C.: Not all anxious individuals get lost: trait anxiety and mental rotation ability interact to explain performance in map-based route learning in men. Neurobiol. Learn. Mem. **132**, 1–8 (2016)

52. Gagnon, K.T., Cashdan, E.A., Stefanucci, J.K., Creem-Regehr, S.H.: Sex differences in exploration behavior and the relationship to harm avoidance. Hum. Nat. **27**(1), 82–97 (2016)

Navigating in Space II

Electrocortical Evidence for Long-Term Incidental Spatial Learning Through Modified Navigation Instructions

Anna Wunderlich[1](✉) (iD) and Klaus Gramann[1,2,3] (iD)

[1] Biological Psychology and Neuroergonomics,
Berlin Institute of Technology, Berlin, Germany
{anna.wunderlich,klaus.gramann}@tu-berlin.de
[2] School of Software, University of Technology Sydney, Sydney, Australia
[3] Center for Advanced Neurological Engineering,
University of California, San Diego, CA, USA

Abstract. The use of Navigation Assistance Systems for spatial orienting has become increasingly popular. Such automated navigation support, however, comes with a reduced processing of the surrounding environment and often with a decline of spatial orienting ability. To prevent such deskilling and to support spatial learning, the present study investigated incidental spatial learning by comparing standard navigation instructions with two modified navigation instruction conditions. The first modified instruction condition highlighted landmarks and provided additional redundant information regarding the landmark (contrast condition), while the second highlighted landmarks and included information of personal interest to the participant (personal-reference condition). Participants' spatial knowledge of the previously unknown virtual city was tested three weeks later. Behavioral and electroencephalographic (EEG) data demonstrated enhanced spatial memory performance for participants in the modified navigation instruction conditions without further differentiating between modified instructions. Recognition performance of landmarks was better and the late positive complex of the event-related potential (ERP) revealed amplitude differences reflecting an increased amount of recollected information for modified navigation instructions. The results indicate a significant long-term spatial learning effect when landmarks are highlighted during navigation instructions.

Keywords: Spatial navigation · EEG · Navigation assistance system
Incidental learning

1 Introduction

Successful orienting in and navigating through the environment is one of the most important abilities of living creatures facing daily challenges in dynamic environments. Being an essential part of nearly all indoor and outdoor activities, spatial orientation is closely connected to general memory processes. However, technological developments in the last decades have changed the demands on individual navigation abilities and the

© Springer Nature Switzerland AG 2018
S. Creem-Regehr et al. (Eds.): Spatial Cognition 2018, LNAI 11034, pp. 261–278, 2018.
https://doi.org/10.1007/978-3-319-96385-3_18

way we memorize space. The use of motorized vehicles increased the speed of movement and, consequently, the spatial scale of the navigated environment. Using motorized vehicles also requires control processes that allow save driving and inter-action with other road users while keeping with traffic regulations. Navigation assis-tance systems were developed to help the driver in this multi-tasking situation and to provide the necessary directions enabling the driver to focus on the driving task while navigating to a goal location.

Due to these benefits, navigation assistance systems based on Global Positioning (GPS) are now widely used even when walking through familiar areas. With this growing trust in automation, new issues can be observed that are typically associated with automated systems. One important issue is over-trust [1, 2]: If a person is responsible for multiple tasks, and in addition, has to monitor an automated task that is based on seemingly reliable information, s/he tends to trust too much in the automation. In other words, in an orientation context the user outsources the navigation task completely to the assistance system [3] leading to decreased processing of environ-mental information including landmarks (salient orienting points) and their spatial relations. As a consequence, spatial knowledge acquisition degrades and spatial ori-enting skills decline with the use of navigation assistance systems [4].

Different methods have been tested to overcome the negative impact of navigation assistance. Such approaches aim at enhancing spatial learning by modifying the kind of spatial information and/or the modalities (tactile, visual and/or auditory) of navigation instructions provided to the user (see [5, 6] for an overview). Using the central role of landmarks in spatial orienting, Gramann and colleagues [5] demonstrated improved spatial learning with modified navigation instructions. In their study, participants were assigned to one of three conditions that differed regarding the information provided with the auditory navigation instruction. The acquired spatial knowledge was evaluated directly after the navigation phase demonstrating improved spatial knowledge for modified navigation instructions providing additional information as compared to the control group while the mental load for all instruction conditions was the same.

Spatial knowledge acquisition can be described at different levels. According to the model introduced by Siegel and White [7], a first level describes Landmark Knowledge representing knowledge about objects in space. A connection between those landmarks in space is described by Route Knowledge. A complex, map-like Survey Knowledge then includes spatial relations between landmarks enabling complex online and offline computations including short-cuts using previously unknown routes. While the original model proposes a sequential development from landmark to survey knowledge, several authors argue that the acquisition of spatial knowledge on different representational levels takes place in parallel [8–10]. In all accounts, however, encoding of landmarks and subsequent integration of the same into a spatial representation is essential to spatial knowledge acquisition. To experimentally address the encoding stage during spatial knowledge acquisition, the Levels of Processing (LoP) approach [10] offers a theoretical framework. Because navigation does not primarily demand semantic pro-cessing of the perceptible environment (e.g., different buildings at a street intersection), a cue augmenting an otherwise unnoticed building at a navigation-relevant intersection, attracts attention towards this building and renders a previously meaningless object salient and navigation-relevant. As a consequence, augmenting buildings by navigation instructions can initiate a deeper elaboration of the presented information that is associated with a spatial location. Extending the LoP model to spatial knowledge acquisition, the elaboration of specific landmark information should be associated with a longer maintenance of all information connected to the landmark and the surrounding. Moreover, the self-reference effect (for a review see [11]) should expand the elaboration of landmark information, further increasing the depth of processing and strengthening the memory trace [12]. Using navigation instructions referring to landmarks might thus lead to incidental spatial learning [13].

Based on the significant short-term improvement in spatial knowledge acquisition in the previous study [5], the current study used behavioral and neural measures to investigate whether modified navigation instructions can also lead to long-term improvement of spatial knowledge. To this end, we compared standard navigation instructions ("Please turn left at the junction.") with two modified navigation instruction conditions highlighting landmarks at navigation-relevant intersections and thus creating a contrast between the highlighted object and the remaining environment. Furthermore, the modified navigation instructions provided additional information related to the highlighted object. This was either a short description of the landmark (e.g., "Please turn left in front of the embassy. Here, the ambassador of a certain nation is working.") or information aligned to the participants' personal interests (e.g. in the case the participant was interested in New Zealand: "Please turn left in front of the embassy. This is the embassy of 'New Zealand'."). The first modification was named Contrast modified navigation instruction, because it created a contrast between the highlighted landmark and the surrounding without providing additional semantic meaningful information but having the same duration. The latter modification was dubbed Personal-reference modified navigation instruction as it highlighted a landmark to create contrast with its surrounding and, in addition, provided information that was of individual interest.

Beyond performance in navigation-related tasks, brain electrical activity recorded with EEG was used to investigate components of the event-related potential (ERP) in a landmark recognition task. The analysis focused on the late positive complex (LPC) of the ERP which is assumed to reflect information recollection (for a review see [14]). The amplitude of the posterior LPC increases with an increasing amount of information that is recollected [15, 16]. Based on the findings of Gramann and colleagues [5], we expected improved performance even after three weeks when using modified navigation instructions to navigate an unknown environment. In addition, increased LPC-amplitudes were expected for augmented landmarks with the most pronounced amplitudes for the personal-reference navigation instruction condition.

2   Materials and Methods

2.1   Participants

Forty-two participants with at least two years ownership of a driver license participated in the study. Participants were recruited through an existing database or direct contact. All volunteers received 10 Euro/h allowance for their participation. Gender distribution was kept constant for all conditions. For the analyses, 21 female and 21 male participants were included with an average age of 26.62 years ($SD = 4.36$ years, $Min = 19$ years, $Max = 37$ years). All had normal or corrected to normal vision and gave informed consent prior to the study. The study was approved by the local research ethics committee.

2.2 Measurements and Apparatus

The experiment took place in a driving simulator at TU Berlin consisting of a stripped VW Touran driver's seat environment and a projector screening the scene onto a white wall approximately two meters in front of the driver. The projection had a horizontal and vertical viewing angle of 90° and 54°, respectively. These angles depended on the individual body height (see Fig. 1A). The steering and pedal behavior was recorded through linking the seat box to the Game Controller, MOMO Racing Force Feedback Wheel (Logitech, Switzerland). This integration limited a realistic driving experience to a certain degree by reducing the maximum angle of the steering wheel to 110°. To compensate for this, the sensitivity of the control was increased. The Game Controller further provided two pedals to simulate an automatic transmission.

The virtual city model from Gramann et al. [5] was used, based on the open source simulator software OpenDS (www.opends.de). The size of the city was approximately 36 km^2 and the simulation restricted traffic to one single car at the beginning of the experiment to avoid an impact of traffic on the processing of environmental information. The route headed from one suburban quarter through an inner-city area to another suburban quarter, where the route ended. Along the way, different speed limits and stop signs or traffic lights were present and the route included seven direction changes at intersections with an unpredictable order of turning direction. Salient buildings that contrasted with the surrounding buildings, hereafter named landmarks, were placed in the virtual environment. Dependent on their location along the route, landmarks were categorized as either decision relevant (direction change) or decision irrelevant (straight route segment) for successful navigating (see Fig. 1C). The number of decision irrelevant landmarks between two direction changes varied from 0 to 2 ($M = 0.88$; $SD = 0.78$). The location of decision relevant landmarks at the intersections provided no indicator for turning directions. Navigation instructions were triggered whenever the vehicle passed a predefined point 100 m ahead of a direction change. Navigation instructions consisted of an auditory instruction (e.g., "In 100 m, turn right at the next intersection") and, in addition, a visually presented arrow that simulated a head-up display (a semitransparent hologram arrow projected onto the environment; see Fig. 1B). The augmented route guiding system with auditory instructions allowed participants to continuously direct their attention towards the environment [17, 18]. In case the participant left the predefined route, an automated resetting mechanism stopped the car and it was positioned back on the correct route facing the last intersection.

2.3   Study Design and Procedure

The experiment had a 3×2 factorial mixed measures design, with three different navigation instruction conditions (standard, contrast modified, and personal-reference modified) as between subject factor and a repeated measures factor experimental session (first and second navigation session) in which participants first navigated the route according to the navigation instructions and in the second session had to solve a series of spatial tasks as described below. The two sessions were separated by a three-week period ($M = 21.07$ days, $SD = 1.65$ days, $Min = 20$ days, $Max = 24$ days) to investigate the long-term impact of modified navigation instructions on spatial learning and memory. Participants were not aware that they would be tested on the same environment in the second session.

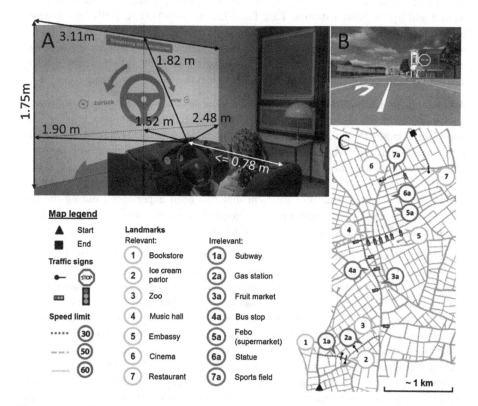

Fig. 1. (A) Setup of the experiment with driving simulator and projection area and the important distance measurements. (B) The visual navigation instruction is a semitransparent hologram arrow projected in the environment at decision points. (C) Map of the virtual city with the route and marker for the relevant and irrelevant landmarks and traffic details.

Pretest Questionnaire. Every participant, irrespective of the subsequent navigation instruction condition, had to answer a pretest questionnaire about her personal preferences regarding music, literature and other dimensions via e-mail. The answers were included in the auditory navigation instructions via text to speech software (Voice RSS, www.voicerss.org) for all participants, who were randomly assigned to the personal-reference condition.

Within the test sessions, participants answered several questionnaires between the tasks on a tablet (iPad 1, Apple Inc., Curtino, California using the software LimeSurvey, Hamburg, Germany). Overall, the first experimental session lasted approximately one hour and included the tasks described in the following.

Navigation Drive. Participants were instructed to abide traffic rules and were given five minutes to drive in a different environment to get accustomed to the wheel and pedal setup. Afterwards they were placed in the test environment and asked to follow the navigation instructions during driving. Participants' mental load during the navigation-guided drive was assessed using subjective (unweighted National Aeronautics and Space Administration Task Load Index, NASA-TLX, [19]) and objective measurements (driving parameters including velocity, distance to ideal line, pedal and steering wheel changes). Afterwards, the affective state of the participant was assessed by the Affect Grid [20] and three questions on a four-point Likert-scale regarding simulation sickness (nausea, headache, and dizziness).

Assessment of Individual Spatial Abilities. The first session included also several questionnaires focusing on driving and navigation habits, gaming experience, and spatial orientation (Santa Barbara Sense of Direction, SBSOD, [21]) as well as the Reference Frame Proclivity Test (RFPT) assessing the individual preference to use an egocentric or an allocentric reference frame during a path integration task [22, 23].

The second experimental session aimed at quantifying participants' spatial knowledge about the virtual environment that had been experienced during the first navigation session three weeks prior. Participants worked on five tasks measuring different levels of spatial knowledge in the following order.

Landmark Recognition Task. The landmark recognition task was designed to allow the analysis of event-related potentials and presented participants with snap-shots of 21 intersections from the test environment in the drivers' perspective in a random order. For every shown junction, participants had to decide whether the landmark was relevant, or irrelevant, or had not been present (novel landmark). For relevant landmarks, participants were instructed to steer into the direction that was instructed during the first navigation session. Furthermore, participants were instructed to push the gas pedal for irrelevant landmarks and to apply the brakes in case of novel landmarks. Overall, seven landmarks for each of the three landmark types (relevant, irrelevant, novel) were presented. The task included ten repetitions of all landmark stimuli to get a sufficient number of epochs for the analysis of event-related potentials. The landmark recognition task focused on landmark knowledge. However, because the responses required navigation decisions it also tested route knowledge (or Heading Orientation according to [24]) including stimulus-response associations. We expected improved landmark and route recognition for the modified navigation instruction conditions.

Scene Sorting Task. This task did also address landmark and route knowledge but was more focusing on the route representation as sequence of landmarks. Participants were asked to select the relevant and irrelevant landmarks out of all 21 landmarks (the same as in the landmark recognition task) and place them in the correct chronological order encountered during the first navigation session.

Sketch Mapping 1. Afterwards, participants were instructed to draw a map of the virtual environment including the route driven as well as any buildings, traffic lights, signs, or any other route-connected information the participant remembered on an empty DIN A3 page. This task combined all levels of spatial knowledge with a specific focus on survey knowledge.

Navigation Drive Without Assistance. Based on the assumption that the recall of information is best when learning and test situation are congruent [25], this task setting was identical to the learning situation. Participants were instructed to drive the identical route as in the first navigation session without navigation assistance. Participants got accustomed with the simulator setup before starting the task in a five-minute training session. Afterwards, the car was placed at the start of the route. In case of incorrect turns, the car was automatically set back to the last junction before the incorrect direction change. After reaching the destination, the NASA-TLX, Affect Grid, and simulation sickness questionnaire were filled out.

Sketch Mapping 2. Participants were asked to draw another sketch map of the virtual environment. The objective of this second map was to reveal differences in recovering survey knowledge after being confronted with the environment for a second time.

In a final questionnaire, participants provided feedback about the experiment and the modified navigation instructions.

2.4   Electroencephalography (EEG)

The EEG was recorded continuously for the complete second session using 64 channels (BrainAmps, Brain Products, Gilching, Germany) positioned in an elastic cap (EASYCAP, Herrsching, Germany) according to the extended 10% system [26]. All electrodes were referenced to FCz and the data was collected with a sampling rate of 500 Hz, band-passed from 0.016 Hz to 250 Hz. One electrode below the left eye (vEOG) was used to record vertical eye-movement. Time synchronization and disk recording of the data streams from the driving simulator and EEG was done using Lab Streaming Layer (LSL, [27]). Age of sample was corrected in the analyses by subtracting 50 ms for the delay induced by the EEG amplifier setup[1] and another 30 ms for the input lag of the projector[2].

---

[1] The test involves sending electrical impulses (n = 3600, 50 ms average recurrence) from a low-latency interface (the parallel port, controlled via MATLAB) of a PC directly to the ActiCap EEG electrodes. Impulse amplitude is limited to ∼150 mV via a voltage divider (ratio: 1:20). "At the same time" this PC sends "LSL markers" (string formatted irregularly sampled time series data) over the network, the "ground truth" in this setup. Another PC runs the BrainVisionRecorder (gathering data from the USB adapters), the BrainVision LSL application ("converting" these data samples into an LSL stream), and LSL's LabRecorder recording the "EEG data" (electrical impulses) and the markers sent from the first PC. The age of sample then is given by the time stamp difference of the markers and the corresponding impulse flanks in the BrainVision data.

[2] https://www.optoma.de/projectorproduct/gt1080e (last access: 23.02.2018).

For data processing, the interactive Matlab toolbox EEGLAB [28] was used. The raw data was high pass filtered at 0.5 Hz, low pass filtered at 75 Hz, and down sampled to 250 Hz. Subsequently, noisy channels and artifacts in the time domain were removed manually. Muscle activity and mechanical artifacts were rejected, while eye movements were kept in the data. The data was then re-referenced to average reference and submitted to independent component analysis (ICA, [29]). An equivalent dipole model for all independent components (IC) was computed using the Boundary Element Model (BEM) based on the MNI brain (Montreal Neurological Institute, MNI, Montreal, QC, Canada) as implemented by DIPFIT routines [30]. ICs reflecting eye movement and one frontal IC reflecting mainly 50 Hz noise were removed based on their scalp maps, component activity, and power spectrum. On average, 5 ICs per participant (*Min* = 2 ICs, *Max* = 11 ICs) were excluded before the data was back projected to the sensor space.

For the analysis of ERPs, the original sensor data was preprocessed using the identical processing steps as described above excluding the data cleaning in the time domain. The respective weights and spheres matrices from the ICA solution were copied to this data set. Afterwards, epochs were extracted from −500 ms to 1500 ms after stimulus onset of the landmark pictures in the landmark recognition test. The epochs were baseline corrected using the pre-stimulus period from −200 ms until stimulus onset. Only trials with correct response were accepted. Epochs of one landmark type (relevant, irrelevant, or novel) were aggregated to one dataset resulting in three datasets per subject. Subsequently, an automatic epoch rejection with a threshold of 100 μV for extremely large fluctuations and a rejection of improbable activity (probability threshold five standard deviations and a maximum rejection of five percent of the trials per iteration) was computed. The remaining 126 datasets (3 landmark types × 42 subjects) included on average 40 trials (*SD* = 16 trials, Min = 3 trials, Max = 67 trials) that were used to compute the averaged event-related potential. For the LPC an average voltage for a time window from 300 to 700 ms was computed. Parietal electrodes (P3, Pz, P4) were selected as the LPC was shown to be most pronounced over posterior regions [15, 16].

2.5 Statistical Analyses

Statistical analyses were performed using the statistic software SPSS (International Business Machines Corporation (IBM) Analytics, Armonk, USA). For the analysis of mental load, a 2 × 3 factorial mixed measures Analysis of Variance (ANOVA) was calculated with the factor navigation session (First and Second Navigation Session) as repeated measure and the factor navigation instruction condition (standard, contrast modified, personal-reference modified) as between subject measure. An additional 3 × 3 factorial mixed-measure ANOVA was computed focusing on the landmark recognition task using the between-subject factor navigation instruction condition and the within-subject factor landmark type (relevant, irrelevant, and novel). For the analyses of ERP amplitudes, the factor electrode was added to result in a 3 × 3 × 3 factorial mixed-measures ANOVA with the between subject factor navigation instruction condition, the repeated measures landmark type and electrode position, including the left, central, and right-hemispheric parietal electrodes (P3, Pz, and P4).

Post-hoc tests were adjusted for multiple comparisons with Fisher's Least Significant Difference (LSD) test. In case of violation of sphericicity, Greenhouse-Geisser corrected values and degrees of freedom are reported. As indicator for the effect size, the partial eta squared was calculated.

3   Results

3.1   Mental Load

The 2×3 factorial mixed-measure ANOVA revealed no effect of the factor navigation instruction condition ($F_{(2,40)} = 1.18$, $p = .318$, $\eta_p^2 = .056$) on subjectively experienced mental load (NASA-TLX subscale) of participants. A significant main effect was observed for the navigation session ($F_{(1,40)} = 14.4$, $p < .001$, $\eta_p^2 = .265$) indicating that the overall mental load during the navigation drive without navigation assistance was higher ($M = 61.6$, $SE = 3.01$) than during the navigation-guided drive ($M = 47.2$, $SE = 3.35$). There was no interaction effect of the two factors ($F_{(2,40)} = 2.38, p = .106$, $\eta_p^2 = .106$).

Driving performance parameters (mean distance to ideal line, mean velocity, number of pedal changes, and number of steering wheel changes) were investigated as objective indicators for mental load during driving. Route segments during wrong turns were excluded from calculations. The 2×3 factorial mixed-measure ANOVAs for the different dependent variables revealed similar statistical effects and thus only the results for the mean distance to the ideal line are reported here. There was no impact of navigation instruction conditions on the mean distance to the ideal line ($F_{(2,40)} = 0.91, p = .412$, $\eta_p^2 = .043$) and no interaction effect of navigation instruction condition and navigation session ($F_{(2,40)} = 0.38, p = .689, \eta_p^2 = .018$) was revealed. There was a significant main effect for navigation session ($F_{(1,40)} = 9.20$, $p = .004$, $\eta_p^2 = .187$) caused by a higher mean distance to ideal line during the second driving session without navigation assistance ($M = 1.39$ m, $SE = 0.02$ m) as compared to the first driving session ($M = 1.33$ m, $SE = 0.01$ m).

3.2   Performance

In the landmark recognition task, the rates of correct responses for each landmark type were taken as indicator for spatial knowledge acquisition during the assisted navigation session. The percentage of correct responses to relevant landmarks was defined as turning the steering wheel irrespective of the direction. The 3×3 mixed-measures ANOVA revealed a significant main effect of navigation instruction condition ($F_{(2,39)} = 4.01$, $p = .026$, $\eta_p^2 = .170$) and a significant main effect for landmark type ($F_{(2,78)} = 3.22$, $p = .045$, $\eta_p^2 = .076$). The interaction between navigation instruction condition and landmark type did not reach significance ($F_{(4,78)} = 2.24$, $p = .072$, $\eta_p^2 = .103$). Post hoc comparison revealed significantly lower recognition rates for participants in the standard instruction condition ($M = 51.7\%$, $SE = 2.3\%$) as compared to both modified navigation instruction conditions (contrast modified: $p = .034$, $M = 58.9\%$, $SE = 2.3\%$; personal-reference modified: $p = .012$, $M = 60.7\%$, $SE = 2.4\%$). Post hoc comparisons for the different landmark types revealed higher recognition rates for irrelevant landmarks ($p = .006$, $M = 64.1\%$, $SE = 3.2\%$) as compared to relevant landmarks ($M = 50.6\%$, $SE = 3.2\%$). This effect was driven by the pronounced differences between irrelevant and relevant landmarks in the standard navigation instruction condition (see Fig. 2). No other differences were significant.

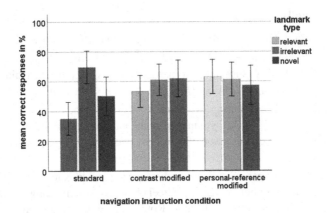

Fig. 2. Mean correct responses in % as a function of landmark type and navigation instruction condition. Error bars display ±2 standard error.

3.3 Event-Related Brain Activity

An overview of the event-related potentials with onset of landmark presentation is shown in Fig. 3 for nine representative channels of the 64 channel montage. While the differences between the navigation instruction conditions became noticeable over posterior recording sites, no such differences were present for different landmarks types.

The results of the mixed measures ANOVA revealed a significant main effect for the navigation instruction condition ($F_{(2,39)} = 4.18$, $p = .023$, $\eta_p^2 = .176$). The LPC for standard navigation instructions demonstrated significantly lower amplitudes ($M = 1.02\ \mu V$, $SE = 0.57\ \mu V$) than the LPC in both modified navigation instruction conditions (contrast condition: $p = .041$, $M = 2.69\ \mu V$, $SE = 0.55\ \mu V$, personal-reference condition: $p = .009$, $M = 3.27\ \mu V$, $SE = 0.59\ \mu V$). The main effect of electrode position ($F_{(2,78)} = 32.6$, $p < .001$, $\eta_p^2 = .455$) revealed higher LPC amplitudes over the right hemisphere ($M = 3.37\ \mu V$, $SE = 0.33\ \mu V$) as compared to the midline ($p < .001$, $M = 1.40\ \mu V$, $SE = 0.39\ \mu V$) and the left parietal leads ($p < .001$, $M = 2.21\ \mu V$, $SE = 0.39\ \mu V$). These main effects were qualified by a significant interaction effect between navigation instruction condition and electrode position ($F_{(4,78)} = 3.32$, $p = .015$, $\eta_p^2 = .145$; see Fig. 4). This interaction effect was mainly due to lowest LPC amplitudes but strongest differences between instruction conditions at Pz while the LPC-amplitudes were more pronounced and condition differences less

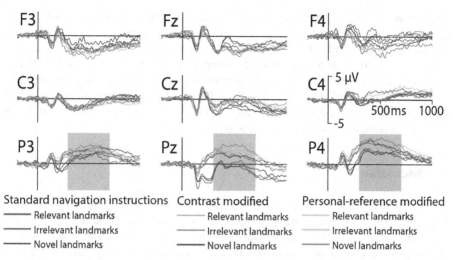

Fig. 3. Event-related potentials displayed at frontal (F), central (C) and parietal (P) electrodes over the left hemisphere (3), the midline (z), and the right hemisphere (4). Data is displayed from –200 ms until 1000 ms of stimulus onset. Navigation instruction conditions and landmark types are color coded with standard navigation instructions in red colors, contrast modified navigation instructions in violet colors, and personal reference navigation instructions in green colors. Landmark types are coded by color intensity. Voltage is displayed with positivity upwards. The grey bar at parietal leads indicates the time window used for statistical analysis of the LPC. (Color figure online)

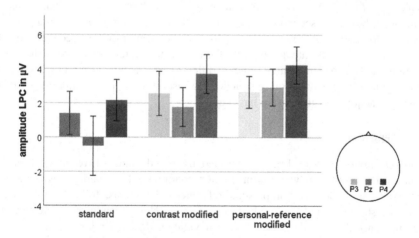

Fig. 4. Amplitude of the late positive complex in the time window 300 ms to 700 ms after stimulus onset for each navigation instruction condition and electrode position (P3, Pz, P4). Error bars display ±2 standard error.

pronounced at the left-parietal lead. At Pz, both modified navigation instruction conditions were associated with significantly increased LPC amplitudes compared to the control group (standard: $M = -0.50$ µV, $SE = 0.68$ µV; contrast modified: $p = .020$, $M = 1.78$ µV, $SE = 0.65$ µV; personal-reference modified: $p = .001$, $M = 2.94$ µV, $SE = 0.70$ µV). For the right-parietal electrode only the difference between personal-reference modification ($M = 4.23$ µV, $SE = 0.56$ µV) and standard instructions was significant ($p = .017$, $M = 2.16$ µV, $SE = 0.57$ µV. No effect including the factor landmark type reached significance ($p > .089$).

4   Discussion

This study investigated whether modified navigation instructions improve long-term spatial memory for an unknown environment. Participants navigated through a virtual city with the aid of standard or modified navigation instructions. The results demonstrated that, even after being exposed to a new environment only once and with a subsequent break of three weeks, landmark recognition performance was significantly improved for participants receiving modified navigation instructions. In addition, electrophysiological data revealed a significant difference between the navigation instruction conditions without differentiating between the landmark types.

4.1   Mental Load

To control that the modified navigation instructions did not increase the mental load of the user compared to a standard navigation assistance system, subjective (NASA-TLX) and objective (driving parameters) measurements were investigated. The analyses revealed no differences between the navigation instruction conditions but increased mental load during the second navigation drive that provided no navigation assistance. These results replicate the results of previous studies demonstrating decreased mental load during driving and navigating with the use of navigation assistance systems [31, 32]. Importantly, load measures did not differ for navigation instruction conditions rendering modified navigation instructions a useful option for improving spatial knowledge acquisition in assisted navigation.

4.2   Performance

Based on previous results [5], we expected improved landmark recognition performance in the modified navigation instruction conditions. Landmark recognition rates were expected to be best for personal-reference instructions, followed by contrast modified instructions and the standard instructions. Relevant landmarks were expected to be recognized better, because of their navigation decision relevant locations and because only those landmarks were accompanied by an auditory cue specifically mentioning the landmark.

The results of the recognition task showed the expected main effect of navigation instruction condition. A significant higher rate of correctly recognized landmarks was observed for participants in both modified instruction conditions as compared to the control group. These results support the assumption that highlighting an object along the route has a strong impact on spatial learning. Even though the improved landmark recognition effect was most pronounced for the personal-reference instructions, there was no statistical difference between both modified navigation instruction conditions. Thus, the present data cannot further clarify whether the improvement is caused by the mere reference to a landmark or by additional landmark-related information. It can be argued that redundant information already triggers further elaboration [33] and hence the investigated contrast modification might have already led to increased elaboration. These methodological ambiguities, however, do not diminish the result of significantly improved spatial memory for modified navigation instructions.

Against the hypothesis, the main effect of landmark type revealed higher recognition rates for irrelevant landmarks compared to relevant landmarks. This result is similar to previous findings [5] and questions the assumed predominance of relevant landmarks. Possible reasons for this might be found in the setup of the present study. First, driving the simulated car was a multitasking situation with steering as the main task and navigating plus abiding traffic rules as secondary tasks. Turning at decision points might thus require the focus of attention to be directed towards the main task leading to a suppression of processing environmental features. Especially, for the control group this attentional shift was possibly strengthened by the auditory navigation instructions pointing to the "next intersection" instead of an object in the environment. Second, the salience and superposition of the projected directional arrow as visual navigation instruction may have added to this general suppression of processing the surrounding area. Both factors were absent, when passing by irrelevant landmarks and thus, more attention might have been available to process aspects of the environment. This is supported by previous studies reporting reduced recollection of learned words when attention was divided during encoding by a secondary task [34]. Furthermore, passive passengers were reported to recall more landmarks compared to active drivers [35]. Another possible cause for improved recognition rates for irrelevant landmarks, especially in the control group, might have been a response bias. Overall responses revealed significantly more "irrelevant" responses (stepping on the gas pedal) than the chance level for the three response categories would have had predicted[3]. Additionally, incorrect responses were associated significantly more often with pushing the gas pedal than expected. These results supported the presence of a response bias presumably caused by the tendency of participants to respond that a landmark was alongside the route in case of uncertainty. The analyses of recognition performance based on

---

[3] The "irrelevant" responses (i.e., stepping on gas pedal) were significantly more often than one third of the trials ($M = 38.7\%$, $SE = 1.8\%$, $t_{(41)} = 3.13$, $p = .003$). The "relevant" responses (i.e., turning the steering wheel) were observed significantly less than in one third of the trials ($M = 27.1\%$, $SE = 2.1\%$, $t_{(41)} = -2.85$, $p = .007$). The rate of "unknown" decisions (i.e., stepping on the brake pedal) demonstrated the expected response distribution ($M = 34.3\%$, $SE = 2.5\%$, $p = .614$).

bias-corrected[4] responses revealed a main effect navigation instruction condition while the main effect of landmark type[5] could not be replicated.

In conclusion, the attention demanding requirements at navigation-relevant intersections and potential response biases may have negatively impacted the recognition performance for relevant landmarks. Consequently, the higher recognition performance observed in the modified navigation instruction conditions might reflect incidental learning of decision relevant landmarks by neutralizing a suppression effect present in standard navigation instructions.

4.3   Brain Activity

The amplitude of the LPC at parietal electrodes is considered an indicator for the recollection process of recognition memory [36]. Recollection is reflected in stronger amplitudes for a higher amount of retrieved information and consequently for "old" versus "new" stimuli. Against the hypothesis, the statistical analyses of the magnitude of the LPC revealed no impact of different landmark types. We expected higher LPC amplitudes for relevant landmarks reflecting improved recognition triggered by the contrasting information or additional personal information. The results implicate an absence of an "old" (relevant and irrelevant landmarks) versus "new" (novel landmarks) effect. This might be due to the long delay between learning and recognition leading to processes reflecting familiarity judgments rather than recollection of information. However, the generally pronounced amplitudes of the LPC and relatively good performance data contradict that explanation. In another study [37], an old/new effect was absent for stimuli presented with neutral backgrounds and could only be revealed for stimuli encoded within pleasant and unpleasant backgrounds. Thus, the neutral context of the virtual city might have had a similar impact in the present study.

The significant differences between navigation instruction conditions might be explained by a landmark independent recollection of the acquired spatial information. In this case, the onset of each landmark picture triggered the retrieval of context-related information to successfully solve the discrimination task. Thus, the modulation of the LPC amplitude would represent the general amount of retrieved information about the navigated environment instead of landmark-specific information retrieval. It is reasonable to assume that modified navigation instructions altered information processing in a more general rather than landmark-specific fashion as the landmarks were always embedded in the environmental context and not presented in isolation. This effect might have led to higher confidence in participants' decisions [38]. Thus, larger LPC amplitudes observed in the modified navigation instruction conditions might represent

---

[4] Bias correction was computed via multiplication of percentage correct with 33.3% divided by mean percentage reaction kind across all conditions respectively for each landmark type.

[5] Main effect landmark type: $F_{(1.7,66.9)} = 0.96$, $p = .376$, $\eta_p^2 = .0.24$; Main effect navigation instruction condition: $F_{(2,39)} = 2.24$, $p = .008$, $\eta_p^2 = .222$, with post hoc comparison showing a significant difference between standard ($M = 51.5\%$, $SE = 2.5\%$) and contrast condition ($p = .013$, $M = 60,6\%$, $SE = 2.4\%$) and personal-reference condition ($p = .004$, $M = 62,7\%$, $SE = 2.6\%$). The interaction effect of navigation instruction condition and landmark type is still not significant ($F_{(3.4,66.9)} = 2.24$, $p = .060$, $\eta_p^2 = .113$).

an increased amount of retrieved information covarying with higher confidence due to a generally increased environmental knowledge. A right hemispheric specialization was found in several studies investigating human spatial navigation [39, 40] as well as studies on attention that demonstrated a right-hemispheric asymmetry of activity in the parietal cortex (e.g. [16, 41, 42]). Furthermore, Tucker et al. [43], who examined spatial memory in terms of spatial-attention shift on the visual field and intentional memory of places of stimuli, described this activity of visual search as a negative attenuation of the LPC in the time frame from 400–500 ms of the ERP. This negativity was stronger at the contralateral hemisphere for an attentional shift towards one side of the visual field plus a superior spatial activity of the right hemisphere leading to lower LPC amplitudes through superposition [43].

In conclusion, pronounced differences in LPC amplitudes for different navigation instructions but not different landmark types might be explained by less effort required in visual search for relevant environmental features in the modified navigation conditions. This would support the assumption that the amount of recollected information and the confidence of the decision is higher and thus the spatial learning is enhanced in modified navigation instructions.

5 Outlook

This study provides a better understanding of spatial learning induced by modified navigation instructions and its underlying brain activity. The advantage of pointing out landmarks alongside the route was replicated providing a scientific basis for integrating modified navigation instructions in future navigation assistance systems to support spatial learning. The influence of emphasizing irrelevant landmarks and providing additional landmark related information should be investigated. Future studies will have to address the concept of the contrast modification including meaningful instead of redundant additional information. Finally, because GPS-based assistance systems are used repeatedly also in well-known environments, it is important to examine the effects of long-term spatial learning based on the repetitive use of modified navigation instructions.

Further studies will provide new insights into the basis of spatial memory and its cortical correlates connected to the use of navigation assistance systems. If such systems succeed to support the neural foundation of spatial cognition and more general memory processes, the implementation of the results in commercially available systems might help postponing dementia-based cognitive declines.

Acknowledgements. This work was supported by a stipend from the Stiftung der Deutschen Wirtschaft to AW. We would like to thank Matthias Rötting at TU Berlin for providing the car simulator facilities and Sabine Grieger for helping to conduct the experiment.

References

1. McKendrick, R., et al.: Into the wild: neuroergonomic differentiation of hand-held and augmented reality wearable displays during outdoor navigation with functional near infrared spectroscopy. Front. Hum. Neurosci. **10**(May), 1–15 (2016)
2. Parasuraman, R., Molloy, R., Singh, I.: The international journal of aviation psychology performance consequences of automation-induced complacency. Int. J. Aviat. Psychol. **3**(1), 1–23 (1993)
3. Forbes, N., Burnett, G.E.: Investigating the contexts in which in-vehicle navigation system users have received and followed inaccurate route guidance instructions. In: Dorn, L. (ed.) Driver Behavior and Training, vol. III, pp. 292–310. Ashgate Publishing Limited (2007)
4. Münzer, S., Zimmer, H.D., Schwalm, M., Baus, J.: Computer assisted navigation and the aquisition of route and survey knowledge. J. Environ. Psychol. **26**(4), 300–308 (2006)
5. Gramann, K., Hoepner, P., Karrer-Gauss, K.: Modified navigation instructions for spatial navigation assistance systems lead to incidental spatial learning. Front. Psychol. **8**(Feb), 193 (2017)
6. Giannopoulos, I., Kiefer, P., Raubal, M.: GazeNav: gaze based pedestrian navigation. Paper Presented at the MobileHCI, 17th International Conference on Human-Computer Interaction with Mobile Devices and Services, Copenhagen, Denmark (2015)
7. Siegel, A.W., White, S.H.: The development of spatial representations of large-scale environments. Adv. Child Dev. Behav. **10**(C), 9–55 (1975)
8. Gramann, K.: Embodiment of spatial reference frames and individual differences in reference frame proclivity. Spat. Cogn. Comput. **13**(1), 1–25 (2013)
9. Burgess, N.: Spatial memory: how egocentric and allocentric combine. Trends Cogn. Sci. **10** (12), 551–557 (2006)
10. Craik, F.I.M., Lockhart, R.S.: Levels of processing: a framework for memory research. J. Verbal Learn. Verbal Behav. **11**(6), 671–684 (1972)
11. Symons, C.S., Johnson, B.T.: The self-reference effect in memory: a meta-analysis. Psychol. Bull. **121**(3), 371–394 (1997)
12. Conway, M.A., Dewhurst, S.A.: Remembering, familiarity, and source monitoring. Q. J. Exp. Psychol. Sect. A **48**(1), 125–140 (1995)
13. Tresselt, M.E., Mayzner, M.S.: A study of incidental learning. J. Psychol. Interdiscip. Appl. **50**(January), 339–347 (1960)
14. Yonelinas, A.P.: The nature of recollection and familiarity: a review of 30 years of research. J. Mem. Lang. **46**(3), 441–517 (2002)
15. Vilberg, K.L., Moosavi, R.F., Rugg, M.D.: The relationship between electrophysiological correlates of recollection and amount of information retrieved. Brain Res. **1122**(1), 161–170 (2007)
16. Wilding, E.L.: In what way does the parietal ERP old/new effect index recollection? Int. J. Psychophysiol. **35**(1), 81–87 (2000)
17. Kun, A.L., Paek, T., Medenica, Ž., Memarović, N., Palinko, O.: Glancing at personal navigation devices can affect driving: experimental results and design implications. In: Proceedings of the 1st International Conference on Automotive User Interfaces and Interactive Vehicular Applications, AutomotiveUI 2009, p. 129 (2009)
18. Medenica, Z., Kun, A.L., Paek, T., Palinko, O.: Augmented reality vs. street views: a driving simulator study comparing two emerging navigation aids. Proceedings International Conference Human-Computer Interaction with Mobile Devices and Services (MobileHCI 2011), pp. 265–274 (2011)

19. Hart, S.G., Staveland, L.E.: Development of NASA-TLX (task load index): results of empirical and theoretical research. Adv. Psychol. **52**(C), 139–183 (1988)
20. Russell, J.A., Weiss, A., Mendelsohn, G.A.: Affect grid: a single-item scale of pleasure and arousal. J. Pers. Soc. Psychol. **57**(3), 493–502 (1989)
21. Hegarty, M., Richardson, A.E., Montello, D.R., Lovelace, K., Subbiah, I.: Development of a self-report measure of environmental spatial ability. Intelligence **30**, 425–448 (2003). Santa Barbara sense of direction scale questionnaire
22. Gramann, K., Müller, H.J., Eick, E.M., Schönebeck, B.: Evidence of separable spatial representations in a virtual navigation task. J. Exp. Psychol. Hum. Percept. Perform. **31**(6), 1199 (2005)
23. Goeke, C., Kornpetpanee, S., Köster, M., Fernández-Revelles, A.B., Gramann, K., König, P.: Cultural background shapes spatial reference frame proclivity. Sci. Rep. **5**, 1–13 (2015)
24. Arnold, A.E.G.F., et al.: Cognitive mapping in humans and its relationship to other orientation skills. Exp. Brain Res. **224**(3), 359–372 (2012)
25. Roediger, H., McDermott, K.: Implicit memory in normal human subjects. In: Boller, F., Grafman, J. (eds.) Handbook of Neuropsychology, vol. 8, pp. 63–131. Elsevier Science Publishers, Amsterdam (1993)
26. Oostenveld, R., Praamstra, P.: The five percent electrode system for high-resolution EEG and ERP measurements. Clin. Neurophysiol. **112**(4), 713–719 (2001)
27. Kothe, C.: Lab streaming layer (LSL) (2014). https://github.com/sccn/labstreaminglayer. Accessed 7 July 2018
28. Delorme, A., Makeig, S.: EEGLAB: an open source toolbox for analysis of single-trial EEG dynamics including independent component analysis. J. Neurosci. Methods **134**(1), 9–21 (2004)
29. Makeig, S., Bell, A.J., Jung, T.-P., Sejnowski, T.J.: Independent component analysis of electroencephalographic data. Adv. Neural Inf. Process. Syst. **8**, 145–151 (1996)
30. Oostenveld, R., Oostendorp, T.F.: Validating the boundary element method for forward and inverse EEG computations in the presence of a hole in the skull. Hum. Brain Mapp. **17**(3), 179–192 (2002)
31. Streeter, L.A., Vitello, D., Wonsiewicz, S.A.: How to tell people where to go: comparing navigational aids. Int. J. Man Mach. Stud. **22**(5), 549–562 (1985)
32. Liang, Y., Lee, J.D.: Combining cognitive and visual distraction: less than the sum of its parts. Accid. Anal. Prev. **42**(3), 881–890 (2010)
33. Kalyuga, S., Ayres, P., Chandler, P., Sweller, J.: The expertise reversal effect. Educ. Psychol. **38**(1), 23–31 (2003)
34. Yonelinas, A.P.: Consciousness, control, and confidence: the 3 Cs of recognition memory. J. Exp. Psychol. Gen. **130**(3), 361–379 (2001)
35. Sandamas, G., Foreman, N.: Drawing maps and remembering landmarks after driving in a virtual small town environment. J. Maps **3**(1), 35–45 (2007)
36. Friedman, D., Johnson, R.: Event-related potential (ERP) studies of memory encoding and retrieval: a selective review. Microsc. Res. Tech. **51**(April), 6–28 (2000)
37. Ventura-Bort, C., et al.: Binding neutral information to emotional contexts: brain dynamics of long-term recognition memory. Cogn. Affect. Behav. Neurosci. **16**(2), 234–247 (2016)
38. Paller, K.A., Kutas, M., Mayes, A.R.: Neural correlates of encoding in an incidental learning paradigm. Electroencephalogr. Clin. Neurophysiol. **67**(4), 360–371 (1987)
39. Maguire, E.A., Burgess, N., O'Keefe, J.: Human spatial navigation: cognitive maps, sexual dimorphism, and neural substrates. Curr. Opin. Neurobiol. **9**(2), 171–177 (1999)

40. Maguire, E.A., Burgess, N., Donnett, J.G., Frackowiak, R.S.J., Frith, C.D., Okeefe, J.: Knowing where and getting there: a human navigation network. Science **280**(5365), 921–924 (1998)

41. Rugg, M.D., Mark, R.E., Walla, P., Schloerscheidt, A.M., Birch, C.S., Allan, K.: Dissociation of the neural correlates of implicit and explicit memory. Nature **392**(6676), 595–598 (1998)

42. Johnson, R., Kreiter, K., Zhu, J., Russo, B.: A spatio-temporal comparison of semantic and episodic cued recall and recognition using event-related brain potentials. Cogn. Brain. Res. **7** (2), 119–136 (1998)

43. Tucker, D.M., Harty-Speiser, A., McDougal, L., Luu, P., deGrandpre, D.: Mood and spatial memory: emotion and right hemisphere contribution to spatial cognition. Biol. Psychol. **50** (2), 103–125 (1999)

Distinguishing Sketch Map Types: A Flexible Feature-Based Classification

Jakub Krukar[1]([⊠]), Stefan Münzer[2], Lucas Lörch[2],
Vanessa Joy Anacta[1], Stefan Fuest[1,2], and Angela Schwering[1]

[1] Institute for Geoinformatics, University of Münster,
Heisenbergstrasse 2, 48149 Münster, Germany
krukar@uni-muenster.de
[2] Psychology of Education, School of Social Sciences, University of Mannheim,
Mannheim, Germany

Abstract. Sketch maps are often used as a means of assessing participants' knowledge of spatial environments. However, the evaluation of sketch maps is challenging as they differ in many aspects and can be scored on many possible criteria. In particular, the classification of sketch maps into different types can be problematic, because participants rarely follow any of the identifiable formats consistently. This paper presents a set of criteria that can be used to score a sketch map on two dimensions simultaneously: its "route-likeness" and its "survey-likeness". The scoring is based on the presence or absence of six features for route-conveying information and six features of conveying survey information. In the present study, reliability estimates and factor structure of the approach were examined with 460 sketch maps with a high variability of spatial elements included. Results show that the two dimensions are largely independent. Sketch maps are found that score high on the route dimensions but low on the survey dimension and vice versa, as well as sketch maps that score high (or low) on both dimensions. It is concluded that the proposed two-dimensional scoring is useful for analysing sketch maps, however, results will also depend on the task and instruction when assessing participants' knowledge of spatial environments.

Keywords: Sketch maps · Factor analysis · Route knowledge
Survey knowledge

1 Introduction

Sketch maps are drawings of spatial environments, most often based on spatial memories of the drawer. Many readers might have drawn a sketch map before - for instance, when asked to describe a route in an area to their visiting friend. The task of drawing a sketch map is often used in spatial cognition studies as a measure of participant's spatial knowledge about the relevant area. While sketch maps are not exactly equivalent to the state of that knowledge, they can be interpreted to inform a number of commonly asked research questions.

© Springer Nature Switzerland AG 2018
S. Creem-Regehr et al. (Eds.): Spatial Cognition 2018, LNAI 11034, pp. 279–292, 2018.
https://doi.org/10.1007/978-3-319-96385-3_19

Among them, special attention has been given to interpreting sketch map types. Since there are many ways to draw a single spatial environment, it is interesting to observe repeatable patterns in the way the environment can be depicted. For example, while some sketch maps remain reminiscent of classic metric maps, others contain egocentric views of encountered locations, or choose to abstract locations and their connectivity by depicting a graph. Some sketches are rich in landmarks, while others use them scarcely; some provide more than necessary information, while other only depict the necessary minimum; some sketches schematize turns, distances, and area extents, while others try to scale the real-world spatial relations accurately. Depending on the theory and the investigated research question, sketch maps can be classified into infinitely many combinations of types. This makes it difficult to decide about the number and criteria of categories when analysing sketch maps in each new study.

Another common problem is the fact that a single drawing rarely follows any of the identifiable formats consistently. Thus, classifying sketch maps into types has been typically performed in a subjective manner, by multiple raters who must agree on the controversial cases. This approach is not only time-consuming, but also likely to yield very different results in a potential replication, if only a small change occurs in the subjective interpretation of a single minor aspect of the sketches. For this reason, the current approach proposes a set of features, which can be scored based on the presence or absence of the given feature in each drawing. The proposed sketch map analysis is performed by following a check list and by interpreting the resulting sum scores. The features are related to two dimensions, and accordingly, two sum scores will result for each sketch map. One dimension (score) represents the extent to which a sketch map conveys information that is typical for visually describing a route. The other dimension (score) represents the extent to which a sketch map conveys spatial survey information. These dimensions are thought to be largely independent of each other.

In the following sections, we first review existing approaches for interpreting and classifying sketch map types in previous research. Then, we provide two check lists that can be used to score sketch maps on two dimensions: its *route-likeness* and *survey-likeness* (reflective of the route-related and survey-related information present in the sketch). The check list for route-likeness has six features, and the check list for survey-likeness has six features. We examine the approach by performing a reliability analysis and a factor analysis. Furthermore, the paper provides suggestions for researchers wishing to apply the scoring method in their analysis of sketch maps.

2 Previous Work

2.1 Existing Classification Schemes

The study of sketch maps was inspired by the exploratory analysis of "imageability" of city elements (Lynch 1960). Appleyard (1970) presented an extensive analysis of sketch maps drawn by the residents of the Venezuelan Ciudad Guayana. He distinguished eight sketch types classified along two dimensions: level of accuracy (topological - positional) and predominant element type (sequential - spatial). In his approach, each map has been manually classified into one of the eight categories. This method has been long influential in the development of approaches to analyse sketch maps. For example, drawing sequences have been recently studied within this framework (Huynh et al. 2008).

Another classification was inspired by the developmental approach to spatial cognition. Moore (1976) suggested a three-level classification of the development of environmental representations. In order to demonstrate the differences between them, he described how sketch maps produced at each of these three levels would differ from each other. Sketch maps produced at Level I would only consist of egocentric viewpoints, reflecting a single, experience-based viewpoint on the subsets of the environment. At Level II, sketch maps would consist of clusters so that the quality of information within the clusters would be higher than the quality between the clusters. At Level III, sketch maps would consist of hierarchically organized clusters, related to each other on a consistent reference system.

This scheme inspired the analysis performed by Aginsky et al. (1997) where sixteen sketch maps were classified into one of three types: 0-D Place type, 1-D Place type, and 2-D Place type. These correspond to Moore's Levels I, II, and III. Nineteen percent of sketches analysed by the authors presented only egocentric views of – at most topologically related – locations (0-D Place type); half of all of the observed maps successfully connected visited places but often only with a straight line, while the individual locations were often enlarged and line distances were distorted (1-D Place type); 31% of maps had a consistent global structure, including accurate segment lengths, without disproportional enlargement of individual locations (2-D Place type). Further data analysis presented by the authors linked the 2-D Place type maps to a different learning strategy compared to the participants who produced 0-D or 1-D Place type sketches.

This work inspired the analysis later conducted in an indoor study described by Blajenkova et al. (2005). In this work, three types of sketch maps were named: 1-D, 2-D, and 3-D, based on the accuracy of spatial relations, as well as the type of topological features present in the sketches. A 1-D sketch map type was described as consisting of some turns present along the travelled route, by not including accurate relations between individual segments, and between the two floors on which the experiment took place. The 2-D drawings contained some relations between route segments, as well as approximately correct shape of the route, but did not differentiate between the two floors. The remaining drawings, named 3-D sketch maps, depicted the correct overall shape of the route and the two floors. Maps were classified as 3-D even if some of the turns they contained were incorrect. The authors use the classification into 1-D, 2-D, and 3-D sketch maps in order to derive the type of mental representation of the environment employed by the participants and use it for comparison with other wayfinding performance and memory measures.

A similar classification scheme was used by Zhong and Kozhevnikov (2016). In their experiment, participants were asked to sketch a route through a multi-level building. The authors classified 62 sketch maps into three categories: procedural route maps, allocentric-survey maps, and egocentric-survey maps. The first type consisted of maps including sequential information but no overall consistent layout of the environment. Those maps which included consistent global layout were classified as either allocentric-survey (if they employed a birds-eye view without clearly distinguishing between floors), or as egocentric-survey (if they included first-person views or clearly distinguished between the floors). The authors provide an empirical evidence for differences in cognitive strategies employed by the participants drawing these three different sketch map types, in the indoor context.

In the work presented above, the analysis of sketch map types has been proven useful in answering diverse research questions. It is possible, however, that sketch maps form a hybrid between more than one of the distinguished types. There seem to be at least two reasons for this. First, in the above analyses accuracy of information is analysed jointly with the form (type of elements) with which the information is being depicted. Second, these classification schemes force each map into a single category. This often suggests the superiority of the last category even when the quality of low-level route information in some of its maps is poorer, compared to the maps belonging to simpler categories.

2.2   Theoretical Constraints for the Two-Dimensional Scoring Approach

First, it appears essential to distinguish the *accuracy* of the information being depicted on a sketch map from the *type* of information that is being depicted. The accuracy of sketch maps is a separate research problem, for which some analytical methods have been provided both for quantitative (Friedman and Kohler 2003) and for qualitative aspects (Schwering et al. 2014; Wang and Schwering 2015). However, it can be questioned whether accuracy of sketch maps should at all be evaluated with respect to a metric correspondence with the real-world configuration, because the cognitive function of sketches is not to reflect the spatial reality, but to externalize the mental representation of an environment for the specific goal of the drawing. This includes the cognitive processing of spatial features and results in, among other characteristics, schematizing, omitting, and distorting of spatial information (Tversky 2002). Sketch maps in particular are subject to many systematic changes (Tversky 1992; Wang and Schwering 2015). For example, communicating the presence of a long, straight stretch of the route does not necessitate drawing it to scale and with the level of the surrounding detail equivalent to other parts of the sketch. Moreover, constructing a sketch enforces self-consistency in the model as well as the use of Euclidian metrics between its sub-parts, neither of which might be necessarily present in the mental representation of the environment (Montello 1991; Kirsh 2010). Therefore, it can be misleading to evaluate sketch maps based on their metric accuracy in relation to the real-world configuration. This issue is particularly problematic when the sketches are subjectively evaluated by raters, since there are multiple possible sources of errors and the source of error cannot be objectively distinguished based on the final drawing. An error can result, for instance, from an erroneous mental representation, from erroneous inferential processing during the construction of the sketch, or from limited drawing experience and poor drawing ability (which might be particularly problematic when the restricted size of the available paper sheet requires planning the drawing in advance). For these reasons, analysing sketch maps based on the *presence or absence* of particular features representing qualitative aspects of conveying spatial information might be a good alternative to analysing accuracy - especially when sketch map *types* are the focus of the analysis.

Second, there seem to be two dimensions that repeatedly form the basis for the differentiation of *sketch map types*. One of them is characterized by the egocentric disjoint experience of individual locations. The other is the survey-oriented way of depicting distant parts of the environment on a single reference system (although important differences exist within diverse survey depictions, as demonstrated by Zhong and Kozhevnikov (2016)). This is in line with the well-established classification of spatial knowledge types where landmark and route knowledge are distinguished from survey knowledge (Siegel and White 1975; Montello 1998). Within this framework, integrating information about separately experienced places is considered the most challenging aspect of learning an environment. Importantly, however, information relevant to route knowledge and to survey knowledge is gathered simultaneously (Montello 1998; Ishikawa and Montello 2006). Therefore, the aim of this work is to propose a scoring approach for sketch maps which considers these two dimensions simultaneously and accounts for cases in which both route and survey information co-exists within a single sketch map. This would be difficult to achieve when each sketch map is forced into only one pre-defined category type.

The current paper does not recommend to always substitute the analysis of sketch maps' accuracy by the analysis of their types. Instead, it argues that the typology of sketch maps and their accuracy are two separate variables, that should be assessed with methods that do not intermix them. The aim of this work is to propose a method for measuring the typology of sketch maps that is independent of their accuracy. In any experimental dataset, it is possible that many sketch maps that are classified as a "simpler" type are highly accurate, or that sketch maps that are classified as a "richer" type contain profound and multiple accuracy errors. The choice of an appropriate analytical method (i.e., focused on accuracy, on typology, or on the combination of the two) should be dictated by the investigated research question.

3 Defining *Route-Likeness* and *Survey-Likeness* of Sketch Maps

This paper focuses on evaluating sketches on two dimensions simultaneously: their *route-likeness* as well as their *survey-likeness*. These can be interpreted as the extent to which indications of route knowledge and survey knowledge information are present in the drawing, taking into account the possibility that a single map can contain elements indicative of only one or both of these dimensions. The scoring is based on the presence or absence of specific features on a sketch map, and was inspired by the studies of elements used in route instructions given by people to other people (Denis 1997; Schwering et al. 2013; Schwering et al. 2017; Anacta et al. 2016). The following checklists provide descriptions of the specific features (criterions) – six for route information, and six for survey information – and can be applied by answering the question "Does this element exist in the sketch map?". The scoring results from the sum of points given for the identified criteria, with one point given for each criterion identified in the sketch map (theoretical range 0 – 6 for both dimensions). The procedure implies that only one point is scored if the criterion is present on the map, regardless of the number of its instances. At this stage of analysis, it is not considered whether the depicted spatial features and spatial relations are accurate and whether they match the reality. Simply, a single point is given if the question concerned one specified criterion can be answered positively. With respect to the *route-likeness* dimension, the scoring procedure makes sense for sketch maps describing a path through the environment, which might depend on the participant's task and instruction. Multiple categories of landmarks, including their distinction into local and global landmarks, are defined based on the definitions presented in (Anacta et al. 2016). The way in which landmarks are depicted (Anacta et al. 2017) is not important for this assessment as long as the landmark can be uniquely identified by a potential sketch-map user unfamiliar with the area (e.g., a word label is enough if it describes a visible property of the landmark object).

3.1 Route-Likeness

Route-relevant information can be communicated by depictions of turns, landmarks, and side streets - information that helps a potential future user of the map to follow the visually indicated route and to make correct turning decisions. The route-likeness dimension is proposed to be reflected by the following six criteria.

(1) Continuous route: are there no "gaps", interruptions or "holes" in the depicted path (such that segments of the path are missing, making it impossible to determine how to move from one fragment of the path to the next)? Is the route continuous and not fragmented?

(2) Turns included: does the sketch depict clear turns indicative of approximate turning directions?

(3) Side streets at decision points: does the sketch include some indication (at least a single line or arrow) of possible choice alternatives at junctions? A roundabout is treated as a regular junction.

(4) Side streets outside decision points: does the sketch depict route alternatives along the straight stretches of the route, for instance indicating the number of junctions that need to be passed before turning?

(5) Local landmarks at decision points: does the sketch depict local landmarks at junctions?

(6) Local landmarks not at decision points, but along the route: does the sketch depict local landmarks along the route?

3.2 Survey-Likeness

Survey-relevant information can be communicated by depictions of various global landmarks, as well as hierarchical and configurational details and relations between elements not constituting a part of the main path. The survey-likeness dimension is proposed to be reflected by the following six criteria.

(1) Global landmark - point: does the sketch include a point-like landmark located off-route or visible from many parts of the route? Example: a city cathedral.

(2) Global landmark - line: does the sketch depict a line which does not constitute an integral path of the street network but provides structure to the sketch or a global spatial reference for other objects? This feature can include barriers to movement. Examples: a highway disjoint from the city streets, a river, a railroad.

(3) Global landmark - region: does the sketch include a region, either with clearly depicted, or vague boundaries, or with a label making it a uniquely identifiable area? Examples: a zoo, a city centre.

(4) Street network: are at least two streets connected outside the main path, so that taking an alternative route or a shortcut would be possible, at least at a short stretch of the route?

(5) Containment hierarchy: does the sketch depict containment of one object in another object, or in a region? Examples: a tower inside a zoo, a cathedral in a marked city centre.

(6) Spatial relation between distant objects: does the sketch depict an object which has a clear spatial relation to two other objects, which would be otherwise not directly connected to each other? Examples: A U-shaped street network with a building in the centre, where the building is clearly located between two otherwise opposite and disconnected streets.

Table 1 presents the summary of the scoring features. Figure 1 presents examples of sketch maps drawn by human participants varying on the two dimensions.

Table 1. Route-likeness and survey-likeness scoring features.

Dimension	Criterion
Route-likeness	r1 - Continuous route
	r2 - Turns included
	r3 - Side streets at decision points
	r4 - Side streets outside decision points
	r5 - Local landmarks at decision points
	r6 - Local landmarks outside decision points
Survey-likeness	s1 - Global landmark - point
	s2 - Global landmark - line
	s3 - Global landmark - region
	s4 - Street network
	s5 - Containment hierarchy
	s6 - Spatial relation between distant objects

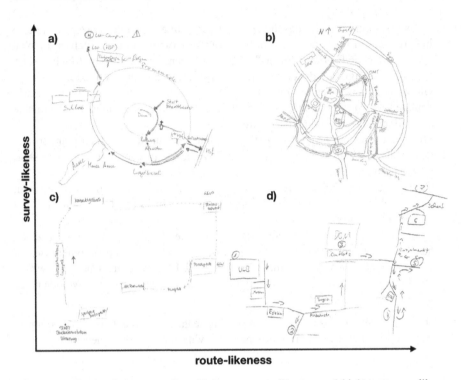

Fig. 1. Sample sketch maps scoring: (a) low on route-likeness and high on survey-likeness; (b) high on both dimensions; (c) low on both dimensions; (d) high on route-likeness and low on survey-likeness.

4   Examination of the Two-Dimensional Scoring Approach

The main goal of the analysis was to examine whether the assessment of spatial features in sketch maps on the proposed twelve criteria are reflected by two proposed dimensions (factors): *route-likeness* and *survey-likeness*. Therefore, we applied an exploratory factor analysis.

4.1   Data

The data included binary (yes/no) scores for all twelve criteria, manually coded for 460 sketch maps. The sketch maps were sourced from three studies not reported in this paper in detail. They depicted one American, two German, and two fictional cities either already known to or learned by the participants. The instructions of all three studies asked participants to draw a map for a friend visiting the city, including a path between specified locations. Being sourced from multiple experimental conditions and from participants with large individual differences, the sketches are diverse: they employ different styles to depict the elements of the urban layout. Table 2 presents raw count data of the criteria within the analysed 460 sketch maps.

Table 2. Number of maps (out of 460) containing each criterion.

Route-likeness						Survey-likeness					
r1	r2	r3	r4	r5	r6	s1	s2	s3	s4	s5	s6
352	366	171	215	253	235	129	210	213	172	255	253

4.2 Inter-rater Reliability

Three raters (one of the authors and two student assistants) independently assessed a subset of the sketch maps. Sixty-one sketch maps were randomly chosen from the 460 sketch maps. Each rater scored the same chosen 61 sketch maps based on a document detailing the scoring procedure that included descriptions and examples of criteria presented above (Table 1; the full document is available at: http://osf.io/3d97m). Inter-rater reliability was assessed using a two-way random, agreement-based, average-measures intra-class correlation (Hallgren 2012), calculated separately for *route-likeness* scores and *survey-likeness* scores using the irr R package (Gamer et al. 2012). Intra-class correlations (ICCs) were in the "good" range, ICC = 0.68 for the *route-likeness* dimension and ICC = 0.61 for the *survey-likeness* dimension.

4.3 Results

We employed exploratory factor analysis to analyse the sketch map classification. A scree plot inspection of Eigenvalues indicated that the data coming from twelve criteria might be described best using a three-factor solution. Further inspection revealed that two out of three suggested factors were sub-categories of the *survey-likeness* scale (i.e., criteria r1–r6, s1–s3, and s4–s6 loaded separate factors). On theory-motivated grounds, we performed factor analysis restricted to two factors, examining whether each criterion assumed to describe the *survey-likeness* factor indeed correlates the strongest with that factor, and not with the *route-likeness* factor. The analysis was

Table 3. Tetrachoric correlations between individual items.

	r1	r2	r3	r4	r5	r6	s1	s2	s3	s4	s5	s6
r1	1.00											
r2	0.93	1.00										
r3	0.52	0.58	1.00									
r4	0.68	0.75	0.69	1.00								
r5	0.39	0.51	0.43	0.50	1.00							
r6	0.50	0.64	0.51	0.61	0.69	1.00						
s1	0.03	−0.03	0.07	0.23	0.18	0.20	1.00					
s2	−0.05	−0.06	0.17	0.24	0.31	0.15	0.37	1.00				
s3	0.02	−0.04	0.24	0.39	0.32	0.03	0.56	0.53	1.00			
s4	0.36	0.30	0.47	0.55	0.14	−0.05	0.18	0.38	0.44	1.00		
s5	0.21	0.21	0.51	0.53	0.15	0.29	0.46	0.31	0.56	0.65	1.00	
s6	−0.20	−0.31	0.17	0.23	−0.02	−0.29	0.21	0.48	0.52	0.72	0.40	1.00

Table 4. Standardized factor loadings. The correlation between the two factors equals 0.14.

Criterion	Factor 1	Factor 2
r1	0.872	−0.097
r2	0.964	−0.170
r3	0.689	0.289
r4	0.786	0.368
r5	0.649	0.133
r6	0.819	−0.088
s1	0.022	0.564
s2	−0.024	0.685
s3	0.003	0.822
s4	0.214	0.737
s5	0.274	0.704
s6	−0.305	0.851

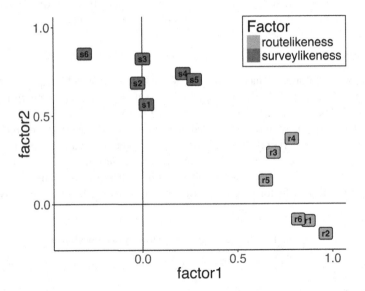

Fig. 2. The twelve analyzed criteria and their factor loadings.

performed in the psych R package (Revelle 2017), using the weighted least squares solution, the oblimin rotation, and the tetrachoric correlation method (suitable for binary data, such as the yes/no responses). This analytical method does not pre-impose any structure on the data and is thus suitable for examining whether the correlations found in the dataset are similar to those assumed on the theoretical grounds by the researchers. Raw correlations are presented in Table 3. Results of the factor analysis are presented in Table 4 and Fig. 2. Guttman's Lambda 6 was used to calculate reliability, as it is appropriate for binary data and for the joint assessment of multiple scales. Interpretation is similar to Cronbach's alpha with its values ranging from 0 to 1; the score of .70 is considered satisfactory for preliminary research, and scores above .90 are expected for decision-making tools (Nunnally 1978). Guttman's Lambda 6 was 0.82 for the route-likeness dimension and 0.73 for the survey-likeness dimension.

4.4 Discussion

The analysis confirms that twelve previously presented criteria can be seen as representative of two factors, in a structure as suggested in Table 1. It bears noting, that the purpose of this analysis was not to find the factorial structure reducing the data best to the fewest components, but rather to verify the assumption that twelve criteria can be used as indicators of two theoretically-motivated factors.

The correlation between both factors was small (0.14) and there was some moderate correlation between individual criteria belonging to two separate factors (Table 3, e.g., criteria r4 and s4). This is not surprising, given the fact that the characteristics of sketch maps tends to correlate with individual abilities, the knowledge of the environment, and the experimental task at hand. It is therefore likely that highly-skilled individuals draw information-richer maps in general ("richer" meaning sketches with more points on the presented classification), that higher familiarity contributes to richer maps on both dimensions, and that easier tasks result in richer maps on both dimensions. Overall, however, the correlation of 0.14 between the two factors is small. It is apparently meaningful to analyse the two dimensions – *route-likeness* and *survey-likeness* – separately, despite the fact that they are not completely orthogonal. The advantage of scoring sketch maps on two largely independent dimensions lies in the opportunity for making finer distinctions between sketch maps. It is possible, for instance, to consider maps that are high on one dimension, but low on the other, high on both, or low on both dimensions; and this can be done without creating new categories or manually re-classifying maps.

The two-dimensional scoring also contributes to the solution of the problem of hybrid sketches. In our dataset of 460 sketches, 327 scored at least one point on both dimension. Thus, most of the sketch maps are hybrids: they contain information relevant to both the information concerning a specified route and to the allocentric overview of the broader environment. The presented two-dimensional scoring approach does not involve forcing each hybrid map into a single category.

Nevertheless, more discrete categorizations can be derived, if needed. For instance, it is possible to calculate the mean *route-likeness* and mean *survey-likeness* scores and classify sketch maps into four relative categories, depending on their score below or above the two means (Fig. 1 contains some examples). Performing this operation on our 460 sketches resulted in 116 maps falling into the "low - low" category, 84 sketches in the "low route - high survey" category, 95 sketches in the "high route - low survey" category, and 165 in the "high - high" category. The spread of these numbers highlights the fact that the two-dimensional scoring approach can capture the diversity of sketch maps and does not result in a disproportionally large number of "poor" maps.

The implication for broader spatial cognition studies lies in the fact that the presented classification method appreciates the diversity in drawing strategies among individuals. For instance, it could be intuitively expected that higher amount of survey information is always associated with high amount of route detail. However, even poorly performing participants differ in their drawing strategies and it is possible that some participants aim to convey large amount of configurational information even when they do not have detailed knowledge of the route they are required to describe. This, as well as other nuanced relations, would be difficult to capture using a pre-defined set of sketch map categories, unless such a category is explicitly expected to occur among the sketches.

5 Limitations and Conclusion

The paper presented an approach that can be used for scoring sketch map types. Twelve criteria have been shown to load two separate factors, which correspond to the theoretically-supported concepts of *route-likeness* and *survey-likeness*. The scoring approach does not require forcing hybrid maps into a single category and makes it possible to distinguish higher and lower scores within each dimension.

The inter-rater agreement was not perfect in a situation when three raters scored the sketches based on a single document with descriptions and examples. An active communication between the raters might be necessary to ensure a shared understanding of all criteria. Since the sketches evaluated in our study came from three separate experiments, their diversity (and dissimilarity to the prototypical examples) might have been larger than it is typically the case for sketches derived from a single study.

It is important to note that the scores resulting from using the checklist are on the ordinal, and not on the continuous ratio scale. Limitations similar to likert-scale measures apply. Moreover, the distance of "1 point" should not always be interpreted in the equivalent way. If to consider three maps scoring 2, 3, and 3 points on the *survey-likeness* scale, the latter two maps are not necessarily "more survey-like" from the first map to the same extent, as their points might derive from different criteria. Likewise, two maps should not be considered disposing completely identical charac-teristics when they score the same number of points, as the points might be derived from distinct criteria. Researchers should consider relevant statistical tools for further analyses, depending on the case-specific application of the approach.

It also bears noting that the presented two-dimensional scoring approach does not consider the accuracy of information contained in sketch maps, but it offers the pos-sibility of including this aspect in the analysis. This could be done, for instance, by scoring the maps twice: once for the presence/absence of the criteria listed in Table 1, and the second time for the presence of correct vs erroneous instances of each criterion. A researcher investigating the accuracy of sketch maps would then be interested in the relation between these two values. Yet another alternative is to impose a threshold value of instances of each criterion that needs to be reached before a point is awarded on the checklist. This could either be a generic number (e.g. a point is awarded only if more than two *landmarks at decision points* are present on the sketch map), or it could be linked to a particular location of interest (e.g. a point is awarded only if a *landmark at decision point* other than the cathedral is present on the sketch map). The scoring can be also filtered by the informational value of the elements included in the sketch maps: for example, landmarks that are not visible from the route can be ignored in the scoring process. The presented scoring approach is flexible enough to support multiple application scenarios, without the need for deriving new category sets for each experimental dataset.

References

Aginsky, V., et al.: Two strategies for learning a route in a driving simulator. J. Environ. Psychol. **17**(4), 317–331 (1997)

Anacta, V.J.A., Humayun, M.I., Schwering, A., Krukar, J.: Investigating representations of places with unclear spatial extent in sketch maps. In: Bregt, A., Sarjakoski, T., van Lammeren, R., Rip, F. (eds.) GIScience 2017. LNGC, pp. 3–17. Springer, Cham (2017). https://doi.org/10.1007/978-3-319-56759-4_1

Anacta, V.J.A., et al.: Orientation information in wayfinding instructions: evidences from human verbal and visual instructions. GeoJournal **82**(3), 567–583 (2016)

Appleyard, D.: Styles and methods of structuring a city. Environ. Behav. **2**(1), 100–117 (1970)

Blajenkova, O., Motes, M.A., Kozhevnikov, M.: Individual differences in the representations of novel environments. J. Environ. Psychol. **25**(1), 97–109 (2005)

Denis, M.: The description of routes: a cognitive approach to the production of spatial discourse. Cah. Psychol. Cogn. **16**(4), 409–458 (1997)

Friedman, A., Kohler, B.: Bidimensional regression: assessing the configural similarity and accuracy of cognitive maps and other two-dimensional data sets. Psychol. Methods **8**(4), 468 (2003)

Gamer, M., Lemon, J., Singh, I.F.P.: irr: Various Coefficients of Interrater Reliability and Agreement (2012). https://cran.r-project.org/package=irr

Hallgren, K.A.: Computing inter-rater reliability for observational data: an overview and tutorial. Tutor. Quant. Methods Psychol. **8**(1), 23–34 (2012)

Huynh, N.T., et al.: Interpreting urban space through cognitive map sketching and sequence analysis. Can. Geogr./Le Geogr. Can. **52**(2), 222–240 (2008)

Ishikawa, T., Montello, D.R.: Spatial knowledge acquisition from direct experience in the environment: individual differences in the development of metric knowledge and the integration of separately learned places. Cogn. Psychol. **52**(2), 93–129 (2006)

Kirsh, D.: Thinking with external representations. AI Soc. **25**(4), 441–454 (2010)

Lynch, K.: The Image of the City. MIT Press, London (1960)

Montello, D.R.: A new framework for understanding the acquisition of spatial knowledge in large-scale environments. In: Egenhofer, M.J. (ed.) Spatial and Temporal Reasoning in Geographic Information Systems, pp. 143–154. Oxford University Press, New York (1998)

Montello, D.R.: The measurement of cognitive distance: methods and construct validity. J. Environ. Psychol. **11**(2), 101–122 (1991)

Moore, G.T.: Theory and research on the development of environmental knowing. In: Moore, G.T., Golledge, R.G. (eds.) Environmental Knowing: Theories, Research, and Methods. Stroudsburg, pp. 138–164. Dowden, Hutchinson & Ross, PA (1976)

Nunnally, J.C.: Psychometric Theory, 2nd edn. McGraw-Hill, New York (1978)

Revelle, W.: psych: Procedures for Psychological, Psychometric, and Personality Research (2017). https://cran.r-project.org/package=psych

Schwering, A., et al.: SketchMapia: qualitative representations for the alignment of sketch and metric maps. Spat. Cogn. Comput. **14**(3), 220–254 (2014)

Schwering, A., et al.: Wayfinding through orientation. Spat. Cogn. Comput. **17**(4), 273–303 (2017)

Schwering, A., Li, R., Anacta, V.J.A.: Orientation information in different forms of route instructions. In: Short Paper Proceedings of the 16th AGILE Conference on Geographic Information Science, Leuven, Belgium (2013)

Siegel, A.W., White, S.H.: The development of spatial representations of large-scale environments. Adv. Child Dev. Behav. **10**, 9–55 (1975)

Tversky, B.: Distortions in cognitive maps. Geoforum **23**(2), 131–138 (1992)

Tversky, B.: What do sketches say about thinking. In: Proceedings of AAAI Spring Symposium on Sketch Understanding, pp. 205–210 (2002)

Wang, J., Schwering, A.: Invariant spatial information in sketch maps—a study of survey sketch maps of urban areas. J. Spat. Inf. Sci. **11**(11), 31–52 (2015)

Zhong, J.Y., Kozhevnikov, M.: Relating allocentric and egocentric survey-based representations to the self-reported use of a navigation strategy of egocentric spatial updating. J. Environ. Psychol. **46**, 154–175 (2016)

The Invisible Maze Task (IMT): Interactive Exploration of Sparse Virtual Environments to Investigate Action-Driven Formation of Spatial Representations

Lukas Gehrke[1]([✉]) [iD], John R. Iversen[2], Scott Makeig[2], and Klaus Gramann[1,3,4]

[1] Biological Psychology and Neuroergnomics,
Technische Universität Berlin, Berlin, Germany
lukas.gehrke@tu-berlin.de
[2] Swartz Center for Computational Neuroscience,
University of California San Diego, San Diego, USA
[3] School of Software, University of Technology Sydney, Sydney, Australia
[4] Center for Advanced Neurological Engineering,
University of California San Diego, San Diego, USA

Abstract. The neuroscientific study of human navigation has been constrained by the prerequisite of traditional brain imaging studies that require participants to remain stationary. Such imaging approaches neglect a central component that characterizes navigation - the multisensory experience of self-movement. Navigation by active movement through space combines multisensory perception with internally generated self-motion cues. We investigated the spatial microgenesis during free ambulatory exploration of interactive sparse virtual environments using motion capture synchronized to high resolution electroencephalographic (EEG) data as well AS psychometric and self-report measures. In such environments, map-like allocentric representations must be constructed out of transient, egocentric first-person perspective 3-D spatial information. Considering individual differences of spatial learning ability, we studied if changes in exploration behavior coincide with spatial learning of an environment. To this end, we analyzed the quality of sketch maps (a description of spatial learning) that were produced after repeated learning trials for differently complex maze environments. We observed significant changes in active exploration behavior from the first to the last exploration of a maze: a decrease in time spent in the maze predicted an increase in subsequent sketch map quality. Furthermore, individual differences in spatial abilities as well as differences in the level of experienced immersion had an impact on the quality of spatial learning. Our results demonstrate converging evidence of observable behavioral changes associated with spatial learning in a framework that allows the study of cortical dynamics of navigation.

S. Creem-Regehr et al. (Eds.): Spatial Cognition 2018, LNAI 11034, pp. 293–310, 2018.
https://doi.org/10.1007/978-3-319-96385-3_20

Keywords: Invisible Maze Task · Spatial navigation
Active exploration · Virtual reality · Interactive environments

1   Introduction

Access to some form of mental spatial representation is a prerequisite for successful navigation from memory in known environments. Here, we introduce a new experimental paradigm, the Invisible Maze Task (IMT) for the study of navigation in which freely-moving participants must compute and use a spatial representation by relying on interactively triggered sparse visual or other sensory feedback defining the virtual walls of a maze. The maze as such is invisible, and stimuli defining the walls are only transiently revealed as the participant reaches out to "touch" the virtual walls.

Place yourself in the following scenario: waking up in a dark and unknown hotel room in the middle of the night, you need to visit the toilet. By reaching and touching the walls you manage to make your way without locating the light switch. On the way back, you contemplate whether to turn on the light or whether you had gained sufficient spatial knowledge to safely return to bed by confirming your internal spatial representation with a few select wall touches.

This example demonstrates our ability to use egocentric (body-centered, self-to-object relations) sensory information to compute a so-called allocentric spatial representation of the environment sufficiently detailed and accurate to guide future action. Egocentric tactile feedback from wall touches combined with vestibular and proprioceptive information as well as motor efference copies is used to compute a spatial representation of the room and corridor layout to allow navigation back to bed. The IMT captures the richness of such navigation, revealing in a tractable manner the multi-modal aspects involved in real-world navigation.

Real-world navigation has been difficult to study precisely because it involves a wide variety of information about location and orientation in space derived from self-motion cues that include motor efference copies, movement-related sensory information originating inside the body, and flow signals experienced in the auditory, visual and somatosensory modalities to successfully build complex spatial representations. The requirement of free movement has generally precluded the addition of brain measurement modalities. For example, in prior EEG neuroimaging experimental protocols to investigate the neural basis of spatial cognition, movement-related information is absent largely for fear of movement-induced artifacts. Limitations of other established imaging methods also do not allow participant movement because of physical constraints of the sensor [15,16,18,30]. As a consequence, neuroscientific studies investigating natural human behavior during free-roaming dynamic interactions with external environments are relatively rare. Knowledge about how and where the human brain processes sensory cues to form spatial representations, and about factors influencing individual's performance in spatial cognitive tasks, has been derived predominantly from stationary experiments [22,29].

Beyond greater realism, another argument in favor of an ambulatory paradigm is that animal studies have provided substantial new insights into the neural representations of location and direction in physically moving animals [31,48]. In providing evidence of selectively firing neuronal populations across several brain regions encoding spatial information about location, i.e. place-, grid- and boundary vector cells, and heading direction, these studies significantly contributed to the understanding of the neural representations of spatial cognition in settings with higher ecological validity, see [7,8] for a comprehensive overview. Meanwhile, studies with human participants addressing the connection of behavioral evidence and characterizing its neural correlates are missing key components of the *natural* subjective experience of space.

1.1 Formation of Spatial Representations Through Action-Oriented Percepts

A well-established theory of spatial learning in children assumes an ontogenetic sequence from egocentric to allocentric (external world-centered, object-to-object relations) representations of space implying a sequential development from coarse/simple to complex spatial representations [19,32,37]. In this framework, the first stage of spatial knowledge entails encoding sensory representations of landmarks. In the second stage, route knowledge develops through repetitive travel (and/or mental rehearsal of travel) along one or more routes between previously encountered landmarks. The final stage involves connection of different routes within a map-like model of the environment. This defines so-called survey knowledge, a spatial representation allowing planning of new routes, shortcuts, and detours. It is reasonable to assume an underlying continuum in the microgenesis of spatial knowledge as compared to a strictly categorical spatial learning [3,14]. For instance, presumably allocentric systems evaluating sensory spatial signals are active in parallel, e.g. place, grid and boundary cells in the rat brain [31,48] and process inputs continuously.

Taken together, survey knowledge, ultimately conceived in an allocentric reference frame, develops from egocentric representations of idiothetic spatial signals driving the buildup of metric representations, i.e. turn angles and distances [4,5], over repeated travels. Idiothetic signals generated at turns highlight and specify the association between the place in the environment and the action taken [4]. Prior findings indicate that bottom-up spatial microgenesis through active exploration of unknown environments is inherently ego-dependent [9].

1.2 A New Approach: The Invisible Maze Task

To allow investigation of behavior as well as human brain dynamics reflecting spatial learning in freely ambulating humans, we developed a virtual reality paradigm in which participants learn the spatial layout of mazes by active exploration. In this Invisible Maze Task (IMT), we task subjects to explore mazes by touching otherwise invisible walls to receive sensory feedback (visual, auditory or other) about the location of the wall. At the end of the exploration phase, participants have to produce a bird's eye view map representation that presumably requires mental transformations of egocentrically experienced spatial signals into allocentric representations. After exploring and building a survey representation of a previously unknown environment, the resultant spatial model can be tested through egocentric sampling of spatial information when the same environment is experienced again. This learning and confirming strategy of spatial representations highlights the interplay of egocentrically perceived information and the resultant spatial representation [9]. Hence, participants never experience an externalized, i.e. completely visible, representation of the entire maze structure but have to integrate many samples of spatial information involving significant spatiotemporal cognitive demands to complete the task.

In the following, we describe the paradigm based on *visually* sparse, interactive virtual exploration and describe behavioral parameters that can be extracted to investigate spatial learning. Specifically, we investigated whether self-report as well as psychometric measures in the spatial domain had predictive power explaining the production of allocentric spatial representations over time [21,40,45]. Understanding cognition as optimizing the outcome of behavior, we hypothesized changes in body dynamics occurring during formation and consolidation of spatial representations. Therefore, the number of wall touches and overall time spent exploring were tested as predictors of the buildup of spatial representations. Specifically, we hypothesized that the number of wall touches and time spent in mazes would be reduced as spatial representations become more accurate, possibly as a consequence of optimization of the energy costs of querying the spatial environment.

2   Methods

To test our hypotheses, we captured body motion while participants freely explored an interactive sparse "Invisible Maze" environment by walking and probing for virtual wall feedback with their hand. In the current study, wall touches were presented visually via a virtual reality (VR) headset. Participants explored four different mazes in three consecutive maze trials each. At the end of each maze trial, participants were asked to draw a sketch map of the maze from a bird's eye view as an index of spatial learning [26,38].

2.1   Subjects

Thirty-two healthy participants (aged 21–47 years, 14 men) took part in the experiment. All participants gave written informed consent to participation. Three participants were excluded from data analysis due to incomplete data caused by technical issues in two cases and difficulties in complying with the task requirements in one case.

2.2 Equipment

Data collection was performed at the Berlin Mobile Brain/Body Imaging Labs (BeMoBIL), a 10 m × 15 m research facility equipped with wireless high-density EEG synchronized to motion capture and virtual reality. Participants interactively explored virtual mazes walking around the lab space wearing a

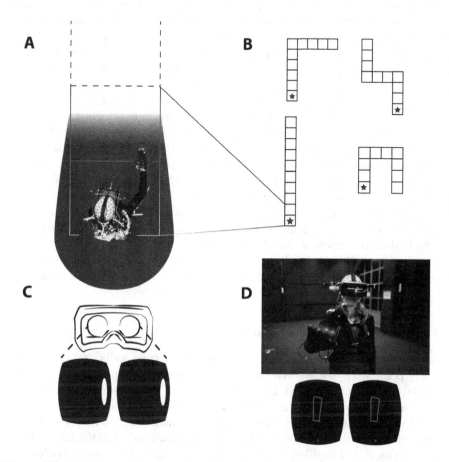

Fig. 1. (A) Participant displayed from a bird's eye view located at the starting point of an "I"-maze. The star marks the starting position but was not visible during the experiment. Participants were instructed to explore the maze and return to the start after full exploration of the maze. (B) Four mazes were used in the study including an "I", "L", "Z", and "U" shaped maze clockwise from lower left to lower right. Each maze was explored three times before the next maze was learned. (C) Exemplary visual feedback in first-person view in *binocular* "VR optics" of subject in A (above) touching the wall to the right. (D) Top: after returning to the starting location, participants drew a top-down view of the explored maze. The participant wears high-density wireless EEG, head-mounted virtual reality goggles and LEDs for motion capture attached to the hands, goggles, and torso. Bottom: screenshot of drawn sketch map. As a visual guidance during drawing, a small red dot was rendered at the position of the tracked hand. This figure is licensed CC-BY and available on Figshare [12]. (Color figure online)

head-mounted display (HMD). Visual stimulation was presented via an Oculus VR (Facebook Inc., Menlo Park, California, USA) Rift DK2 HMD (100° nominal field of view horizontally and vertically, 960 × 1080 pixels per eye, 75 Hz frame rate). Head position and orientation were updated by fusing data from the headset's internal inertial sensors and using a six-LED rigid body mounted to the headset and tracked via PhaseSpace (PhaseSpace Inc., San Leandro, California, USA) Impulse X2 system. To update the head position, motion capture data was sampled at 240 Hz and smoothed by averaging across one frame update of the HMD, approximately 13.3 ms. To correct orientation drifts originating from unstable inertial data, we continuously calculated an offset between the stable orientation of the motion capture rigid body and the unstable magnetometer data. A difference exceeding 3° in the Euler yaw direction triggered a correction in all three Euler dimensions by 1° per second until the difference approached 0°. Four further rigid bodies consisting of four LEDs each were attached to the lower arm, upper arm and both feet. To update the position of the right hand in VR, positional data from a PhaseSpace glove with 8 LEDs was smoothed by averaging across one frame update. Visual stimuli were generated on a MSI (MSI Co. Ltd, Zhonghe, Taiwan) Gaming Laptop (MSI GT72-6QD81FD, Intel i7-6700, Nvidia GTX 970M) using Worldviz (Santa Barbara, California, USA) Vizard Software worn in a backpack. Participants were further equipped with a microphone and headphones for audio communication and masking of auditory orientation cues. For EEG data collection, a 160 channel wireless BrainProducts MOVE System (Brain Products GmbH, Gilching, Germany) was administered with 128 channels applied on the head and 32 channels on the neck. Due to space limitations the results of the EEG analysis will be reported elsewhere.

2.3 Sparse Virtual Environments

Four different environments consisting of invisible virtual walls, 90° turns and a starting point were defined. All paths were composed of ten $1 \times 1\,m^2$ spatially arranged to different layouts (I, L, Z, U; see Fig. 1B). Participants were instructed to explore the space by walking and reaching in order to probe the walls to either side of the paths (see Fig. 1A). Upon collision of the hand with an invisible wall, a white disc was displayed 30 cm behind the collision point along the invisible wall (see Fig. 1C). The disc grew in size as participants further approached the disc and reached its maximum size (30 cm diameter) when the participant's hand was touching the disc, i.e. 30 cm deep into the wall collider. After two seconds the disk faded out. Another second later the disc reappeared colored red. The visual feedback was reset after participants retreated their hand back out of the wall. Participants were instructed to repeatedly touch the walls and not leave their hand *in the wall* to avoid the disc turning red. If participants collided with a wall head first, a red sphere was displayed as a warning instructing participants to step back until the warning dissappears. The sphere grew bigger the further participants moved into a wall.

2.4 Psychometric and Self-report Measures

After arrival to the lab, participants were given a number of questionnaires and self-report measures to complete, in order to characterize individual experience with virtual reality, individual differences in spatial abilities and preferred navigational styles:

Perspective Taking and Spatial Orientation Test, PTSOT: Participants viewed an array of objects on a sheet of paper and by taking the perspective of one of the objects judged the angle between two other objects in the array and sketch it in [27]. We recorded the absolute deviation from the correct angle to investigate the impact of perspective taking ability on the transformation of egocentric visual information into allocentric survey representations.

Santa Barbara Sense of Direction Scale (Freiburg Version), FSBSOD: This questionnaire is a measure of self-ascribed navigational ability consisting of 15 items [20]. We took the average of all correctly recoded items as the final measure. General navigational ability was of interest as a covariate in subsequent analysis.

Igroup's Immersion and Presence Questionnaire, IPQ: The IPQ measures the sense of presence experienced in a virtual environment (VE). We processed the results according to [36]. We were interested in whether immersion and presence had a positive influence on performance measures.

Gaming Experience: We asked participants to indicate how long they have been playing video games and further asked them to rate their gaming skills. A composite measure taking the sum of the two standardized scores was calculated as the final measure. As with the IPQ scale, we addressed whether general gaming experience positively affected measures of IMT performance.

Reference Frame Proclivity Test, RFP: This online available tool determines the proclivity of participants to preferentially use either an egocentric or an allocentric reference frame during a virtual path integration task [13,17]. For further correlation analysis, allocentric reference frame proclivity was coded as "1", egocentric as "0" and a tendency to switch reference frames as "2".

Simulator Sickness Questionnaire, SSQ: The SSQ measures simulator sickness on three factors: nausea, oculomotor and disorientation [24]. We administered SSQ twice, before and after the experiment and used the average value of each sub-scale as the resulting measure to test for significant effects of simulator sickness.

2.5 Procedure

The complete experiment, including EEG preparation took approximately 4 hours. Participants first completed the questionnaires and self-report measures. Subsequently, the EEG electrodes were prepped. Next, participants were instructed to explore a path until the end, i.e. reaching a dead end, and subsequently find their way back to the starting position. After exploration of at least three $1 \times 1\,\text{m}^2$ participants were free to return to the starting location. All participants explored the four mazes in the same order starting with the "I" maze and then increasing in number of turns in later mazes (I, L, Z, U).

Participants were informed that touching a wall with the right hand to either side of their body would temporarily illuminate a small part of the wall. Further, the participants were briefed that they will explore the same path three times in a row and that there will be four different paths to explore over the entire experiment. For all twelve trials, participants were oriented in the direction of the corridor by the experimenter after a short disorientation phase where participants were led walking in circles. A gamified feedback was displayed reporting back the performance in the current maze trial. The feedback measure was based on the progress made in the current path and provided information whether the end of a path was reached and how many wall collisions of the hands and the head were registered.

Drawing Task. After each exploration trial, participants were asked to draw a map of the environment from a top-down perspective whilst still being in VR. The experimenter entered the lab space at the end of each trial and handed the participant a computer mouse used to control the drawing functionality in VR. Participants were instructed to start drawing by clicking once with the left mouse button. A red sphere appeared in the VR goggles at the tracked position of the right hand holding the mouse. Holding down the left mouse button, participants were able to draw a red line by moving their hand in space (see Fig. 1D). Finally, participants were instructed to take a camera screenshot of their drawing by pressing down the mouse wheel once and holding their final drawing in view. Participants were allowed to erase their drawing and restart at any time by pressing the right mouse button.

2.6   Data Processing and Statistical Analysis

Motion Capture Measures. For quantification of changes in exploration behaviors we extracted the following measures for the time window between the start of each maze exploration and the return to the initial square: (1) the total number of wall touches, (2) the total duration of the exploration, and (3) the average velocity of participants in the maze. As participants were allowed to freely explore each maze, a change in duration could either be explained by a change in walking speed or a change in distance covered. Here, we decided to analyse the changes in walking speed.

Sketch Map Measure of Spatial Ability. Two independent raters judged each sketch map drawing of each maze trial per maze and subject. A total number of 29×12 sketch maps were rated. The raters were presented with the question: "Imagine that you can take the present sketch map with you into the virtual environment and use it as a navigational aid. How useful would the map be for you?" To give their rating between 0 (= no help at all) and 6 (= very helpful) they were given the correct shape of the maze to be rated side by side with the drawing to rate [2]. To test inter-rater reliability, we computed Cohen's Kappa with squared weights to emphasize larger rating differences using R (R Development Core Team), Version 3.4.3, and package *irr* [6,11].

Trial Rejection. Prior to the final statistical analysis, the data were cleaned. First, trials were rejected when more than ten wall collisions with the head were recorded. This resulted in the rejection of six out of a total of 348 trials. Second, four individual trials were rejected due to procedural problems during data collection. In one case, the battery of the LED driver of the motion capture system died, whereas in the remaining case a LED cable became loose and the trial had to be aborted. We deemed all trials incomplete where the path was not fully explored. With this criterion, 26 trials were rejected. Overall, 312 trials remained, amounting to 89.7 % of the total number of trials. Lastly, we checked the duration of each touch and confirmed that approximately 85% of all touches lasted less than one second.

Linear Mixed Effects Model. To investigate changes in exploration behavior, we performed linear mixed effects analyses of the relationship between (1) maze trials and (2) maze configurations and each dependent measure "number of wall touches", "duration" as well as "movement velocity" using R package *lme4* [33]. As fixed effects we entered "maze trial" with three repetitions for each maze and "maze" with four levels (different mazes) as well as their interaction. As random effects we considered intercepts for participants as well as by-maze trial random slopes for the effect of each dependent variable "number of wall touches", "duration" as well as "movement velocity". Subsequently, to examine changes in the sketch map drawings, we fit identical linear mixed effects models to the dependent measure sketch map usefulness. Ultimately, to make inferences about the relationship between the three measures of body dynamics on sketch map usefulness, we fit linear mixed effects models to the dependent variable "sketch map usefulness". As fixed effects we entered the body movement measures "number of wall touches", "duration" as well as "movement velocity". As random effects we considered intercepts for participants as well as by-maze trial random slopes for the effect of each sketch map usefulness. We assumed an underlying continuum in the sketch map ratings "usefulness" and hence conceived the variable as interval scaled. For all analyses, we obtained P-values by calculating likelihood-ratio tests of the full model with the effect in question against the model without it [44]. Post-hoc, we tested non-parametric pairwise differences using uncorrected Wilcoxon signed-rank tests [42]. We considered significant results with $\alpha < 0.05$. For report generation and data visualization purposes we used R packages *knitR*, *ggplot2*, *ggpubr*, *cowplot* and *corrplot* [23,39,41,43,47].

Correlation of Psychometric and Self-report Measures. We preprocessed all questionnaire and self-rating data to construct a full correlation matrix including dummy coding of binary variables. We added gender as an additional binary factor of interest with female participants coded "0". For better understanding, scores of perspective taking (PTSOT) were recoded, so that large numbers indicated better performance. Finally, we created a correlation matrix with the average ratings of the two sketch map raters together with the motion capture measures and the subjective data.

3   Results

First, we investigated if our experimental manipulation changed the exploration behavior of participants. Therefore, we tested if body movement measures were explained by repeated maze trials or changes in the maze configurations.

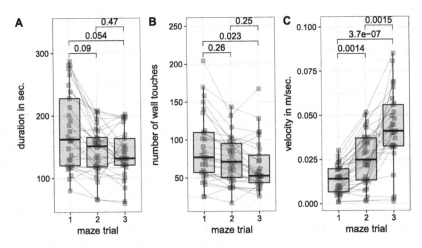

Fig. 2. Box-Whisker plots with individual observations of each participant averaged across maze configurations for each repeated maze trial 1 to 3. (A) Duration in seconds elapsed between the start and end of each exploration phase, (B) Number of wall touches during the exploration phase and (C) Movement Velocity in meters per second. P-values of pairwise comparisons are calculated by non-parametric Wilcoxon signed-rank tests.

Duration. The repeated measures factor maze trial affected the duration between start and end of each maze exploration ($\chi^2(2) = 15.521, p < 0.001$) lowering it by about $31.7 \, \text{s} \pm 8.1$ (standard errors) from the first to the second maze trial and $39.9 \, \text{s} \pm 9.4$ (standard errors) from the first to the third maze trial. Subsequent non-parametric pairwise comparisons revealed clear reductions in exploration times for the comparison of the first and second maze trial (p = 0.09), the first and third maze trial (p = 0.05), with a diminished reduction between the second and third maze trial (p = 0.47) (see Fig. 2A). Different maze configurations also affected the duration of maze exploration ($\chi^2(3) = 11.109, p < 0.05$). Initial exposure as well as increasingly complex maze configurations were associated with increasing exploration times (see Fig. 3A). The interaction of both factors revealed an effect of maze trials on exploration duration ($\chi^2(6) = 12.333, p = 0.05$).

Number of Wall Touches. The number of wall touches was significantly affected by repeated measurements across maze trials ($\chi^2(2) = 21.37, p < 0.001$) with a reduction in the number of wall touches by 15 touches $\pm$ 3.8 (standard errors) from the first to the second maze trial and 22 touches $\pm$ 4.1 (standard errors) from the first to the third maze trial. Neither the factor maze ($\chi^2(3) = 3.94, p = 0.27$) nor the interaction of both factors ($\chi^2(6) = 4.32, p = 0.63$) revealed an impact on the number of wall touches. Non-parametric pairwise comparisons between maze trial were not significant for the comparison of first and second maze trial or between second and third maze trial However, between the first and third maze trial ($p < 0.05$) the number of touches decreased significantly (see Fig. 2B).

Movement Velocity. Participants' movement speed was significantly increased across maze trials ($\chi^2(2) = 29.495, p < 0.001$) with an increase by 0.01 m/s $\pm$ 0.003 (standard errors) from the first to the second maze trial and 0.03 m/s $\pm$ 0.004 (standard errors) from the first to the third maze trial. Participants' movement speed was also affected by maze ($\chi^2(3) = 22.513, p < 0.001$) with a significant decrease after exploration of the "I" maze. We registered no interaction effect. Post-hoc multiple comparisons were significant for all comparisons between the three maze trials (1–2: $p < 0.01$, 2–3: $p < 0.01$, 1–3: $p < 0.001$) and between mazes "I" and "L" ($p < 0.05$), "I" and "Z" ($p < 0.05$) and "I" and "U" ($p < 0.01$), and did not show the same attenuation effect in later maze trials seen for maze duration. As an index of the consistency of this finding, all but one participant (28 of 29) moved faster in the third maze trial as compared to the first (see Fig. 2C).

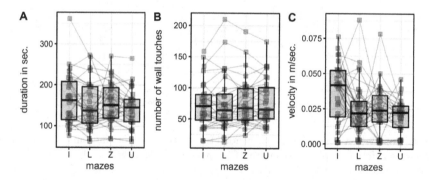

Fig. 3. Box-Whisker plots with individual observations of each participant averaged across maze trials exploring each maze configuration "I", "L", "U" and "Z". (A) Duration in seconds elapsed between the start and end of each exploration phase, (B) Number of wall touches during the exploration phase and (C) Movement Velocity in meters per second.

3.1   Sketch Map Ratings and Changes in Body Movement Behavior

Cohen's κ was calculated with squared weights of rating differences to determine if there was agreement between two raters judgments on the usefulness of a given sketch map to navigate a virtual environment. A total of 312 maps were rated. There was very high agreement between the two raters' judgements, $\kappa = 0.835, p < 0.001$. Next, to test for a general effect of the experiment exposure on the sketch map ratings a Wilcoxon signed rank test was run with the mean sketch map rating after the first trial run against the null hypothesis of a mean equal to zero. A deviation from 0 for the ratings of the first sketch maps would indicate that participants successfully built a mental representation of the invisible maze they explored for the first time. We observed a true location of the mean ($= 3.2$) different from 0 ($p < 0.001$) indicating successful spatial learning after the first trial. Investigating changes in the sketch map ratings over the repeated maze trial ($\chi^2(2) = 3.8123, p = 0.15$) and maze configurations ($\chi^2(3) = 3.2171, p = 0.36$) as well as their interaction ($\chi^2(6) = 4.3286, p = 0.63$) revealed no significant impact, however we did observe higher average sketch map ratings for 19 of 29 subjects after the third trial run as compared to the first (Fig. 4).

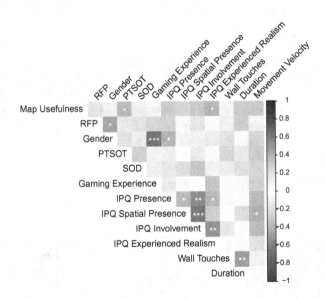

Fig. 4. Correlation matrix among psychometric- and self-report measures. Each cell is colored as a function of the strength of positive (red) or negative (blue) correlation. Significant correlations are indicated by $^*(p < 0.05)$, $^{**}(p < 0.01)$, or $^{***}(p < 0.001)$. (Color figure online)

To test the predictive power of body movement measures on the usefulness of the sketch maps, a null model was compared to three models each with one additional predictor. We subsequently added "duration", "number of wall touches", as well as "movement velocity" as predictors. The duration between start and end of each maze exploration affected the sketch map ratings ($\chi^2(1) = 17.160, p < 0.001$) as did the number of wall touches ($\chi^2(1) = 3.852, p < 0.05$)

with a decrease in duration and number of wall touches predicting an increase in sketch map ratings. We observed no impact of the head velocity on the sketch map ratings ($\chi^2(1) = 0.7221, p = 0.4$).

To examine the spatial exploration behavior and sketch map usefulness and their relation with subjective measures, a correlation matrix among all measured variables was calculated.

3.2   Correlation with Psychometric- and Self-report Measures

For the sketch map usefulness, we observed significant positive correlations with perspective taking skills ($r = 0.39, p < 0.05$) as well as experienced realism inside the VE ($r = 0.41, p < 0.05$). We observed a highly significant correlation between gender and gaming experience ($r = 0.65, p < 0.001$) with male participants scoring higher on gaming experience. Furthermore, male participants reported a higher general sense of presence ($r = 0.42, p < 0.05$) after the VE exposure with all presence sub-scales being correlated. Finally, we found a strong correlation between the duration of maze exploration and the number of wall touches ($r = 0.5, p < 0.01$) revealing more explorative touches the longer a maze was explored.

4   Discussion

We introduced a new paradigm, the Invisible Maze Task, to investigate realistic spatial learning as reflected through the computation and use of spatial representations derived from transient, discrete visual feedback in sparse (virtual) environments. We observed significant changes in body movement behavior across repeated explorations of the same environment. Participants moved faster, for a shorter period of time and with less touches of the surrounding walls supporting the assumption that each transient wall touch event may carry information used for formation and updating of some form of spatial representation. We hypothesize that the sparse environments were learnt in an efficient way that allows optimization of energy costs of repeated future explorations. Therefore, we argue, that the environment was incorporated in a useful way to guide future behavior.

To quantify the quality of sketch maps we chose the subjective rating measure "map usefulness" because it has been proven useful for within-subject investigation [2]. Although we observed a high variability between participants, 27 out of 29 participants clearly demonstrated spatial learning as reflected in the usefulness of their sketch maps after the initial exposure to the environment. Subsequent changes in the usefulness ratings were only minimal with a slight, albeit non-significant, increase with repeated exposures to the environment. In other words, we found that participants either drew a useful map after the first encounter with an environment and then maintained a level of usefulness in their sketch maps, or they never drew a meaningful map at all. In line with previous findings [1, 21], we noticed a substantial increase in sketch map quality over time in very few participants. The fact that some participants were able to draw a near perfect representation of the explored environment without ever witnessing full vista space may be interpreted against a linear, sequential development of spatial knowledge that should have been observable through incremental improvements of the drawn sketch maps usefulness [37].

To investigate a potential connection between spatial exploration behavior and sketch map quality we fitted linear mixed effects models of the spatial exploration parameters number of touches, times in a maze, and movement velocity to the sketch map ratings. The biggest impact on sketch map usefulness originated from the time spent exploring a maze with a decrease in duration predicting an increase in sketch map quality. In addition, a decrease in wall touches predicted higher sketch map quality. We conclude, that brief exploration phases are sufficient for most of the participants to form and maintain a spatial representation through discrete and localized samples of an otherwise invisible environment. Wall touches during repeated exposure to the same environment then serve as a probing mechanism for the correctness of the internal representations, just like finding your way back to bed in the middle of the night by confirming the location of walls and doors. This change in behavior reflects a more efficient means to navigate conserving energy when moving through a known environment. By administering several established measures of navigational abilities we investigated the impact of individual differences in spatial abilities and preferences on spatial learning in the invisible maze task. Contrary to previous findings we observed no impact of gaming experience on scores of the SOD, PTSOT and the spatial sketch mapping task [34]. However, most findings on the interplay between immersion, spatial presence, involvement and spatial abilities stem from experiments with 2-D displays. The recent surge of affordable head-mounted VR technologies will shed light on how accurate these new technologies map a three-dimensional reality. In the current study, we observed covariations between the feeling of presence experienced during exploration and the usefulness of the resulting sketch maps. One possible explanation for this correlation is that participants with a higher immersion score were able to better hold a realistic representation of the environment in memory and were subsequently better able to draw it.

Two widely used metrics of spatial abilities are the psychometric perspective taking and orientation test and the sense-of-direction scale [20,27]. PTSOT scores were significantly correlated with sketch map usefulness ratings. We instructed subjects to draw a top-down map moving their hand in the air imagining they were drawing on a chalkboard. Therefore, perspective taking processes, i.e. changing the viewpoint, were engaged during drawing of an accurate sketch map. A high correlation between perspective taking ability and sense-of-direction provides the ground for future group-based analysis approaches of good and bad spatial learners. Interestingly, we observed no substantial correlation of sense-of-direction with any other measure of interest. Finally, we investigated the impact of individual reference frame proclivities [13,17] on the performance in the invisible maze task. In an online test, participants were classified into three groups reflecting a preference for egocentric reference frames, a preference for allocentric reference, or the flexible switch between reference frames. We did not find any significant correlation of the preferred reference frame with spatial learning in the IMT. It is reasonable to assume that reference frame proclivities as measured in a passive visual flow paradigm without vestibular feedback do not play any role in a more natural active exploration setting such as the IMT. It is well established that vestibular information is used to update egocentric representations of position and orientation [25, 35]. The absence of any impact of reference frame proclivities as measures with the RFPT again indicates that traditional desktop-based measures of spatial abilities might not reflect behavior in natural three-dimensional environments accurately.

4.1   Limitations

In the current study, we used sketch maps as a dependent measure for the quality of internal spatial representations. We used a qualitative assessment instead of quantifiable data, e.g. segment lengths and angular accuracy between segments. This approach is prone to subjective tendencies but was countered in the present study by measuring the agreement between two raters. Still, other sketch map measures might provide a deeper insight into the variables that affect the accuracy of mental spatial representations derived from exploration of the environment. Sketch maps are always subject to individual's capabilities to draw and their belief in their skill as well as the interpretation of the rater [10]. Furthermore, participants were required to carry a substantial amount of equipment to render our virtual environment. Therefore, participants were restricted, to a certain degree, in their ability to move as they would naturally move without the equipment. We may use more explicit tests of spatial knowledge in future environments, such as asking how many turns it would take to get from one point to another or asking for a bearing to a distant point such as the entrance.

4.2   Summary and Future Directions

We introduce the Invisible Maze Task to study spatial learning behavior during ambulatory exploration of sparse environments that provide only transient feedback, therefore breaking down spatial explorative inputs into discrete moments in time. Our paradigm provides the basis for investigations of "atoms of spatial thought" that ultimately allow computation of spatial representations of an environment that has never been seen as a whole. This approach, which we have behaviorally validated here, will enable investigation of the tight link of physical behavior and cognitive processes during spatial learning. Furthermore, the multimodal nature of the IMT may serve (a) as a testing framework to disentangle modality-specific and modality-independent processes of spatial navigation and (b) to investigate differential spatiotemporal parameters of cross-modal syntheses supporting the build up of spatial representations [28, 46].

In the future, we plan to use event-related EEG neuroimaging to test existing models of spatial cognition and to gain a deeper understanding of the relationship of cognition, active spatial exploration behavior, and brain dynamics [3]. The results from this initial study offer a new perspective on the interplay between body dynamics and common assessments of spatial orientation skills during the formation of spatial representations.

Acknowledgments. This research was supported by a grant from the German Federal Ministry of Education and Research (01GQ1511) to KG and a grant from the US National Science Foundation (1516107) to SM.

References

1. Arnold, A.E.G.F., Burles, F., Krivoruchko, T., Liu, I., Rey, C.D., Levy, R.M., Iaria, G.: Cognitive mapping in humans and its relationship to other orientation skills. Exp. Brain Res. **224**(3), 359–372 (2013)
2. Billinghurst, M., Weghorst, S.: The use of sketch maps to measure cognitive maps of virtual environments. In: Proceedings of the Virtual Reality Annual International Symposium (VRAIS 1995), p. 40. IEEE Computer Society, Washington, DC (1995)
3. Byrne, P., Becker, S., Burgess, N.: Remembering the past and imagining the future: a neural model of spatial memory and imagery. Psychol. Rev. **114**(2), 340–375 (2007)
4. Chrastil, E.R., Warren, W.H.: Active and passive spatial learning in human navigation: acquisition of survey knowledge. J. Exp. Psychol. Learn. Mem. Cogn. **39**(5), 1520–1537 (2013)
5. Chrastil, E.R., Warren, W.H.: Active and passive spatial learning in human navigation: acquisition of graph knowledge. J. Exp. Psychol. Learn. Mem. Cogn. **41**(4), 1162–1178 (2015)
6. Cohen, J.: A coefficient of agreement for nominal scales. Educ. Psychol. Measur. **20**(1), 37–46 (1960)
7. Cullen, K.E., Taube, J.S.: Our sense of direction: progress, controversies and challenges. Nat. Neurosci. **20**(11), 1465–1473 (2017)
8. Epstein, R.A., Patai, E.Z., Julian, J.B., Spiers, H.J.: The cognitive map in humans: spatial navigation and beyond. Nat. Neurosci. **20**(11), 1504–1513 (2017)
9. Filimon, F.: Are all spatial reference frames egocentric? Reinterpreting evidence for allocentric, object-centered, or world-centered reference frames. Front. Hum. Neurosci. **9**, 648 (2015). https://doi.org/10.3389/fnhum.2015.00648
10. Friedman, A., Kohler, B.: Bidimensional regression: assessing the configural similarity and accuracy of cognitive maps and other two-dimensional data sets. Psychol. Methods **8**(4), 468–491 (2003)
11. Gamer, M., Lemon, J., Gamer, M.M., Robinson, A., Kendall's, W.: Package 'irr': Various coefficients of interrater reliability and agreement (2012)
12. Gehrke, L.: Invisible Maze Task (IMT): Procedure. Figshare (2018). https://doi.org/10.6084/m9.figshare.5946970.v1
13. Goeke, C., Kornpetpanee, S., Köster, M., Fernández-Revelles, A.B., Gramann, K., König, P.: Cultural background shapes spatial reference frame proclivity. Sci. Rep. **5**, 11426 (2015)
14. Gramann, K.: Embodiment of spatial reference frames and individual differences in reference frame proclivity. Spat. Cogn. Comput. **13**(1), 1–25 (2013)
15. Gramann, K., Gwin, J.T., Ferris, D.P., Oie, K., Jung, T.P., Lin, C.T., Liao, L.D., Makeig, S.: Cognition in action: imaging brain/body dynamics in mobile humans. Rev. Neurosci. **22**(6), 593–608 (2011)

16. Gramann, K., Jung, T.P., Ferris, D.P., Lin, C.T., Makeig, S.: Toward a new cognitive neuroscience: modeling natural brain dynamics. Front. Hum. Neurosci. **8**(6), 444 (2014)

17. Gramann, K., Müller, H.J., Eick, E.M., Schönebeck, B.: Evidence of separable spatial representations in a virtual navigation task. J. Exp. Psychol. Hum. Percept. Perform. **31**(6), 1199–1223 (2005)

18. Gwin, J.T., Gramann, K., Makeig, S., Ferris, D.P.: Removal of movement artifact from high-density EEG recorded during walking and running. J. Neurophysiol. **103**(6), 3526–3534 (2010)

19. Hazen, N.L., Lockman, J.J., Pick, H.L.: The development of children's representations of large-scale environments. Child Dev. **49**(3), 623–636 (1978)

20. Hegarty, M., Richardson, A.E., Montello, D.R., Lovelace, K.L., Subbiah, I.: Development of a self-report measure of environmental spatial ability. Intelligence **30**(5), 425–447 (2002)

21. Ishikawa, T., Montello, D.R.: Spatial knowledge acquisition from direct experience in the environment: individual differences in the development of metric knowledge and the integration of separately learned places. Cogn. Psychol. **52**(2), 93–129 (2006)

22. Janzen, G., van Turennout, M.: Selective neural representation of objects relevant for navigation. Nat. Neurosci. **7**(6), 673–677 (2004)

23. Kassambara, A.: ggpubr: 'ggplot2' based publication ready plots (2017)

24. Kennedy, R.S., Lane, N.E., Berbaum, K.S., Lilienthal, M.G.: Simulator sickness questionnaire: an enhanced method for quantifying simulator sickness. Int. J. Aviat. Psychol. **3**(3), 203–220 (1993)

25. Klatzky, R.L., Loomis, J.M., Beall, A.C., Chance, S.S., Golledge, R.G.: Spatial updating of self-position and orientation during real, imagined, and virtual locomotion. Psychol. Sci. **9**(4), 293–298 (1998)

26. Klippel, A., Hirtle, S., Davies, C.: You-are-here maps: creating spatial awareness through map-like representations. Spat. Cogn. Comput. **10**(2–3), 83–93 (2010)

27. Kozhevnikov, M., Hegarty, M.: A dissociation between object manipulation spatial ability and spatial orientation ability. Mem. Cogn. **29**(5), 745–756 (2001)

28. Loomis, J.M., Klatzky, R.L., Giudice, N.A.: Representing 3D space in working memory: spatial images from vision, hearing, touch, and language. In: Lacey, S., Lawson, R. (eds.) Multisensory Imagery, pp. 131–155. Springer, New York (2013). https://doi.org/10.1007/978-1-4614-5879-1_8

29. Maguire, E.A., Burgess, N., Donnett, J.G., Frackowiak, R.S., Frith, C.D., O'Keefe, J.: Knowing where and getting there: a human navigation network. Science **280**(5365), 921–924 (1998)

30. Makeig, S., Gramann, K., Jung, T.P., Sejnowski, T.J., Poizner, H.: Linking brain, mind and behavior. Int. J. Psychophysiol. **73**(2), 95–100 (2009)

31. Moser, E.I., Kropff, E., Moser, M.B.: Place cells, grid cells, and the brain's spatial representation system. Annu. Rev. Neurosci. **31**(1), 69–89 (2008)

32. Piaget, J., Inhelder, B.: The Child's Conception of Space. Routledge & K. Paul, London (1956)

33. Pinheiro, J., Bates, D., DebRoy, S., Sarkar, D.: nlme: linear and nonlinear mixed effects models (2007)

34. Richardson, A.E., Collaer, M.L.: Virtual navigation performance: the relationship to field of view and prior video gaming experience. Percept. Mot. Skills **112**(2), 477–498 (2011)

35. Riecke, B.E., Cunningham, D.W., Bülthoff, H.H.: Spatial updating in virtual reality: the sufficiency of visual information. Psychol. Res. **71**(3), 298–313 (2007)

36. Schubert, T.W.: The sense of presence in virtual environments: a three-component scale measuring spatial presence, involvement, and realness. Zeitschrift für Medienpsychologie **2**, 69–71 (2003)
37. Siegel, A.W., White, S.H.: The development of spatial representations of large-scale environments. Adv. Child Dev. Behav. **10**(C), 9–55 (1975)
38. Tversky, B., Lee, P.U.: Pictorial and verbal tools for conveying routes. In: Freksa, C., Mark, D.M. (eds.) COSIT 1999. LNCS, vol. 1661, pp. 51–64. Springer, Heidelberg (1999). https://doi.org/10.1007/3-540-48384-5_4
39. Wei, T., Simko, V.: Package 'corrplot: visualization of a correlation matrix' (v.0.77) (2016)
40. Weisberg, S.M., Schinazi, V.R., Newcombe, N.S., Shipley, T.F., Epstein, R.A.: Variations in cognitive maps: understanding individual differences in navigation. J. Exp. Psychol. Learn. Mem. Cogn. **40**(3), 669–682 (2014)
41. Wickham, H.: ggplot2: elegant graphics for data analysis, vol. 35 (2009)
42. Wilcoxon, F.: Individual comparisons by ranking methods. Biom. Bull. **1**(6), 80 (1945)
43. Wilke, C.O.: Cowplot: streamlined plot theme and plot annotations for ggplot2 (2015)
44. Winter, B.: Linear models and linear mixed effects models in R with linguistic applications. arXiv preprint arXiv:1308.5499 (Tutorial 2), pp. 1–42 (2013)
45. Wolbers, T., Hegarty, M.: What determines our navigational abilities? Trends Cogn. Sci. **14**(3), 138–146 (2010)
46. Wolbers, T., Klatzky, R.L., Loomis, J.M., Wutte, M.G., Giudice, N.A.: Modality-independent coding of spatial layout in the human brain. Curr. Biol. **21**(11), 984–989 (2011)
47. Xie, Y.: knitr: a general-purpose tool for dynamic report generation in R. Documentation **8**(1), 1–12 (2012)
48. Yoder, R.M., Taube, J.S.: The vestibular contribution to the head direction signal and navigation. Front. Integr. Neurosci. **8**(April), 32 (2014)

Memory for Salient Landmarks: Empirical Findings and a Cognitive Model

Rebecca Albrecht[1(✉)] and Rul von Stuelpnagel[2]

[1] Center for Economic Psychology, University of Basel,
Missionsstrasse 62a, 4055 Basel, Switzerland
`rebecca.albrecht@unibas.ch`
[2] Center for Cognitive Science, University of Freiburg,
Hebelstraße 10, 79104 Freiburg, Germany

Abstract. We test the effect of a landmark's visual and structural salience on memory retrieval of turning directions at choice points in a VR environment. We find a higher probability for a correct turning decision at intersections where the location of the visually salient landmark converges with the turning direction as compared to intersections where the location of the visually salient landmark diverges from the turning direction. Although altered versions of the intersections were mostly recognized as being novel, we found systematic error patterns depending on the placement in the original intersection. A cognitive model in the ACT-R architecture grounds these findings in an established framework of human memory. Our findings have implications, for example, for the selection of suitable landmarks for navigation assistance systems.

Keywords: Landmark memory · Visual salience · Structural salience
ACT-R

1 Introduction

Landmarks are a core element of human navigation and orientation, included in some of the most prominent frameworks of spatial information processing [29]. However, the definitions of what exactly constitutes a landmark remain fuzzy and under-specified [17]. Thus, it is still a challenge to determine which landmark represents the optimal landmark among the basically infinite number of alternatives in real-world navigation [23]. Let us, for example, consider the statement "I turned right after the post office". Most researchers agree that a landmark (i.e., the post office) is more likely to be referenced when positioned at a decision point [6,13], and that most people prefer a landmark located in their turning direction [27]: The mentioned post office is likely to be preferred over, for example, the gas station located on the opposite side of the street (and thus against the turning direction. In reality, however, the most striking landmark element might not be located where most people would prefer it, thus creating a potential conflict between different affordances. Even less is known about how a

© Springer Nature Switzerland AG 2018
S. Creem-Regehr et al. (Eds.): Spatial Cognition 2018, LNAI 11034, pp. 311–325, 2018.
https://doi.org/10.1007/978-3-319-96385-3_21

landmark's position in relation to the required turn affects memory performance. In other words, it is so far unknown whether memorizing "I turned right after the post office" allows for better retrieval of the correct turning direction at a later point in time as compared to "Before the gas station on the left side, I turned right". We address this gap by running a VR-based study and present a cognitive model within the ACT-R framework to ground the empirical findings in a formalized framework.

1.1 Research on Landmark Salience at Decision Points.

A prominent approach distinguished between a landmark's semantic, visual, and structural salience [30]. A landmark's semantic salience consists of its historical and cultural significance. It remains conceptually ambiguous as well as difficult to address empirically due to the inherently high individual variance [19]. Visual salience refers to a landmark's distinctiveness regarding its size, color, and shape as compared to the surrounding environment, and appears to be the most important relevant factor in the processing of a scene [9]. Finally, structural salience it thought to be affected by a landmark's position relative to a specific route [27,32]. It is assumed that the overall salience of a landmark results from weighting and combining these three sub-saliences. Previous research has used theoretical considerations to identify the optimal landmarks for wayfinding assistance in a scenery [21]. However, the relative importance of visual, structural, and semantic salience as well as their interactions are still not fully understood.

So far, research on this issue has been mostly concerned with the investigation of landmark selection for route descriptions. In [6,15], the authors analyzed real world route descriptions for the mentioned landmarks' positions relative to the route. In [13], the authors distinguished between choice point landmarks at intersections, potential choice point landmarks at passed intersections, on-route landmarks along paths with no choice, and off-route landmarks (distant but visible from the route). Findings from both research groups converge on the importance of landmarks at choice points for good route descriptions. In [18], the authors found that landmark references in descriptions of a route through a virtual environment were tightly linked to the landmarks' advance visibility as well as their structural salience (operationalized by the algorithm from [12]).

The experimentally most controlled investigation of structural salience has been achieved by [24,27]. In the so-called SQUARELAND paradigm, participants are presented a step-by-step path through a regular grid-like virtual environment [7,8]. At each intersection, participants have to indicate which of the corners (uniquely identifiable but controlled for visual and semantic salience) they would prefer as a landmark for future navigation. From an egocentric perspective, participants show a strong preference for landmarks located at the corners in the turning direction. In the same experimental paradigm, the authors also compared landmark selection for instances where the visually and the structurally salient landmark were located at either converging or diverging corners [25]: In a converging instance, one visually salient landmark (i.e., colored differently, with all other landmarks colored uniformly, cf. Fig. 2) is positioned in the turning direction (i.e., the structurally salient positions). In the diverging case, the visually salient landmark is located opposite to the turning direction. Despite the fact that from a rational point of view, the only sensible choice in the diverging case was the visually salient landmark, there was an about 45% probability that participants still selected one of the two uniformly colored, structurally salient landmarks. The authors conclude that landmark selection is affected by both structural and visual salience, and neither aspect obliterates the other. These findings have recently been extended to gaze behavior in a real-world setting [32]: Landmarks with a higher level of visual salience attracted generally more fixation time. Additionally, participants looked more at landmarks at structurally salient locations close to the route (e.g., at decision points as compared to potential decision points; and more into turning direction as compared to against turning direction).

The picture becomes less clear if landmark salience is linked to memory retrieval. Landmarks at turns were better recognized than landmarks passed straight-by on a virtual route [31], but visual salience was not considered in this study. In [16], the authors converged on a differentiation between visual and structural salience by investigating recognition performance and spatial descriptions of landmarks in a virtual museum tour. The authors report that higher visual salience benefited recognition performance, but not the probability to be included in spatial descriptions or sketch maps. Vice versa, landmarks located at choice points were more frequently included in spatial descriptions and recognized more quickly (also see [10]). Using the SQUARELAND paradigm, participants in [11] learned short routes of eight consecutive regular intersections, which always consisted of a turn towards the left or the right (i.e., the structurally salient landmark positions), and one visually salient landmark. Decision accuracy during route recall was independent of the landmarks' visual and structural salience. As the authors note themselves, it is likely that route recall might have relied on a serial memorization of direction changes [5] rather than on the encoding of landmarks with varying visual salience.

1.2   Aims of This Research

A landmark's visual and structural salience both appear to support its encoding and retrieval, but potential interactions between the salience forms have seen little attention so far. We hypothesize that intersections with a visually salient landmark located at a structurally salient position (i.e., displaying convergent evidence for a turning direction) are more likely to be responded to correctly than intersections where a visually salient landmark is not located at a structurally salient position (i.e., displaying divergent evidence for a turning direction). We apply an experimental paradigm that does not allow participants to shortcut the processing of landmark information. Furthermore, we investigate whether altered versions of the studied intersections are recognized more easily, depending on an intersection being an instance of convergent or divergent landmark salience, respectively. Finally, we formalize the encoding and memory retrieval processes for landmark information and their relation to turning directions in a cognitive model implemented in the ACT-R architecture.

Fig. 1. Illustration of an intersection as presented to the participants. The visually salient landmark position (red color) converges with the structurally salient landmark positions (i.e., the left turning direction indicated by the colored line on the floor). (Color figure online)

2 Experiment

2.1 Methods

Participants. We tested 34 students of the University of Freiburg (23 of them women; $M_{age} = 20.15$ years, $SD = 1.68$, range: 18–25 years). They received course credit for their participation in the experiment.

Stimuli and Procedure. During the experiment participants saw a series of intersections from an egocentric perspective (illustrated in Fig. 1). Intersections were implemented within the SQUARELAND paradigm [7] and all pictures were generated with the SQUARELAND 2.0 virtual environment [8]. In SQUARELAND, intersections are symmetrical and consist of four buildings placed in the four corners, also see [24, 27]. At each intersection, we highlighted one building (colors: red, blue, green, violet, black) in order to increase its visual salience, with the other three buildings all sharing the same grey color, see [11, 25]. The turning direction (left or right), if given, was indicated by a yellow line.

The experiment consisted of 24 blocks, with each block consisting of two phases. In the route learning phase, participants studied subsequent pictures of five unique intersections with a given turning direction. They proceeded from one intersection to the next by pressing the correct arrow key (i.e., left or right, according to the yellow line). In the *decision phase*, they were presented with one intersection without an indicated turning direction (i.e., target blocks). The first and last intersection were never presented in the decision phase in order to avoid primacy and recency effects. In order to prevent participants from using a directional strategy (see [11]), we also included intersection where the position of the visually salient landmark was changed (i.e., foil blocks, see below). Thus, it was not sufficient to mentally link the visually salient landmark's color to the turning direction, but the position of the visually salient landmark had to be encoded as well. Participants were instructed to recall and indicate the previously encountered turning direction by using the arrow keys "left" or "right", or to press the "down"-arrow if they believed the intersection to be novel. At the four untested intersections of each block (distractors), positions of the visually salient landmarks and turning directions were randomized and balanced within participant and condition.

In 16 of the 24 blocks, the decision phase used an intersection that was also presented during the route learning phase (target blocks). The 16 target blocks included the four possible placements of the visually salient landmark (the four corner buildings) and the two turning directions (left and right), two times each. This resulted in 8 blocks with convergent placement of the visually salient landmark (i.e., on the same side as the indicated turning direction), and 8 blocks with divergent placement (on the opposite side of the turning direction). The correct response in a target block was the arrow key corresponding to the turning direction learned for that intersection (uniquely identifiable by the color and position of the visually salient landmark) during the route learning phase (see Fig. 2 for an illustration).

In the other 8 blocks, the decision phase consisted of an intersection that was not presented during the route learning phase (foil blocks). Foil blocks were constructed as follows: For each of the 8 possible combinations of visually salient landmark placements and turning directions, one foil was created that inverted the learned intersection with respect to the placement type (convergent vs. divergent). For example, for a convergent intersection presented during route learning (e.g., with the visually salient landmark located at the upper left corner and left turning direction), the respective foil intersection presented during the decision phase would present the visually salient landmark (with the same color) positioned at one of the corners opposing the left turning direction (e.g., the upper right building or the lower right building), thus now constituting a divergent intersection. The concrete placement of the foil (upper or lower building) was randomized and balanced within participants. The correct response in a foil block was rejecting it as novel by pressing the down-arrow key (see Fig. 2). In total, each participant completed 4 foil blocks with a switch from a convergent to a divergent placement and 4 foil blocks with the opposite switch.

Prior to the main experiment, participants completed a training phase with one target block and one foil block, each consisting of four intersections. Colors of both the visually salient and the visually not salient buildings differed from the main experiment.

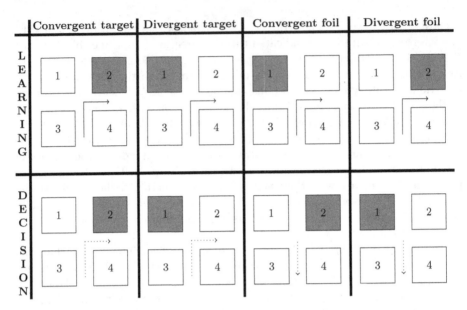

Fig. 2. Illustrations of all task combinations. The visually salient corner is colored grey. The arrow indicates an exemplary turning direction. (Right and left turning directions were counterbalanced.) In the target condition, participants had to make a decision for an intersection they encountered during the route learning phase. In the foil condition, they had to make a decision for an intersection they had not encountered during the route learning phase. In the convergent condition, the visually salient landmark lies in the (structurally salient) turning direction. In the divergent condition, the visually salient landmark lies on the opposite side of the turning direction.

2.2   Results and Discussion

Descriptive Statistics. First, we looked at the probability for a correct response across all participants. Figure 3 shows the proportion of correct responses for targets and foils as well as for convergent and divergent intersections, respectively. In the target condition, response accuracy (i.e., a correct decision for the left or the right direction) is higher for convergent intersections as compared to divergent intersection. In the foil condition, this pattern is inverted with a higher accuracy (i.e., a correct rejection) in the divergent condition (i.e., a convergent intersection presented during route learning and the position of the visually salient landmark changed to the opposite side in the decision phase) as compared to the opposite case. In other words, participants showed an enhanced recall accuracy when the visually salient landmark was aligned with the turning direction. They were also less likely to identify such an intersection as novel when it was presented in an altered foil version.

Second, we took a closer look at the distribution of incorrect responses: Participants could, for example, not only mistake the turning direction (i.e., making a turning error), but also mistake a target for a foil (i.e., making an identification

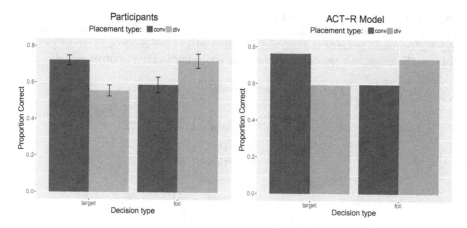

Fig. 3. Left subfigure shows participant data; right subfigure results from the evaluation of the cognitive model. Bar height represents the mean value; error bars the standard error; placement type: convergent (visually salient landmark in turning direction) vs. divergent (visually salient landmark opposite of turning direction); decision type: target vs. foil. A convergent foil block refers to a the case where, for example, a divergent intersection was presented during the study phase, and changed to a convergent intersection in the decision phase (or vice versa).

error). All descriptive data, separately for all conditions, are provided in Table 1. For convergent target blocks, participants showed a similar number of turning and identification errors. For divergent target blocks, however, the errors seem to shift towards turning errors: in case of an incorrect response, participants were more likely to turn into the direction of the visually salient landmark rather than rejecting the intersection as novel.

We found a different bias in the foil blocks. For convergent foils (where a studied divergent intersection was changed into a convergent one), participants produced about twice as many errors towards the direction of the current position of the visually salient landmark. For divergent foils (where a studied convergent intersection was changed into a divergent one), this pattern was reversed: participants tended to choose the direction away from the currently visually salient landmark. We will scrutinize these descriptive impressions more closely in the next paragraph.

Inferential Statistics. We used R [20] with the package "lme4" [4] and followed the procedure described in [33] to conduct a mixed effects model analyses. We used a generalized mixed effects model ("glmer") with a binomial error distribution and a logistic link to estimate the effects of our conditions on response accuracy. In all the following analyses we included subject and item (combination of visually salient landmark and turning direction) intercepts as random factors, because there are repeated measures of each in our data.

Table 1. Descriptive numbers and percentages of all possible responses, separately for all intersection conditions. [1] indicates a correct response in the respective condition and [2] a response towards the learned direction in the foil condition. Model percent displays the respective response's probability according to the cognitive model.

Decision type	Placement type	Response	Participants		Model
			Number	Percent	Percent
Target	Convergent	Convergent	196[1]	.72	.76
		Divergent	35	.13	.01
		Rejection	41	.15	.23
	Divergent	Convergent	72	.26	.07
		Divergent	151[1]	.56	.60
		Rejection	49	.18	.33
Foil	Convergent	Convergent	38[2]	.28	.40
		Divergent	18	.13	.01
		Rejection	80[1]	.59	.59
	Divergent	Convergent	12	.09	.14
		Divergent	26[2]	.19	.12
		Rejection	98[1]	.72	.74

First, we analyzed the overall response accuracy. We included the relative placement of the visually salient landmark (placement type: convergent vs. divergent, decision type: target vs. foil, and an interaction term as predictors of correctness into the mixed effects model (full model), and compared it with every less complex model that can be constructed using a likelihood ratio test. The full model ($AIC^1 = 1{,}045$) differs significantly from all other models: A baseline model only considering random effects ($AIC = 1{,}053$; $\chi^2(3) = 14.03, p = .003$), a model with random effects and placement type: convergent vs. divergent ($AIC = 1{,}055$; $\chi^2(2) = 13.98, p = .0009$), a model with random effects and decision type: target vs. foil ($AIC = 1{,}055$; $\chi^2(2) = 13.97, p = .0009$), and a model with random effects and both conditions but not interaction term ($AIC = 1{,}057$; $\chi^2(1) = 13.92, p = .0002$). All of the less complex models did not differ significantly from the baseline model including only random intercepts. Estimates obtained from the full mixed model analysis are displayed in Table 2.

We also analyzed the qualitative biases found in the distribution of incorrect responses shown in Table 1. We only considered trials with incorrect responses and split our analysis between the target and foil condition (because we are not interested in the interaction between conditions in this case). The baseline model again considered random intercepts for the participant and item level. First, we checked for a bias towards convergent responses between convergent and divergent target blocks. In contrast to the descriptive impression, this model

---

[1] Alkaike Information Criterion [1].

(AIC = 276) does not differ significantly from the baseline model (AIC = 278; $\chi^2(2) = 3.4, p = .07$). Considering foil blocks, the model that predicts a difference between incorrect responses in the convergent and divergent direction between the convergent and divergent condition (AIC = 126) differs significantly from the baseline model (AIC = 134; $\chi^2(2) = 12.2, p = .002$). The direction of the estimated effect ($b = 1.52$, from factor levels divergent with coding $-.5$ to convergent with coding $+.5$) supports the assumption that there is a bias towards responding incorrectly by answering the learned turning direction.

Table 2. Results from the full mixed effects model. Conditions with factor levels and used coding (presented in brackets). Estimates (Est.) are calculated by the mixed model (log odds ratio), confidence Intervals 95% bootstrapped in brackets. Proportions of correct responses (Correct) predicted by mixed effects model for the different conditions (relative to second level; second level of Decision Type for the interaction) obtained from the estimates with the inverse logit function.

Condition	Est.	Correct
Intercept	.65 [.42, .90]	.66
Placement type: divergent $(-.5)$ vs. convergent $(+.5)$	$-.07$ [$-.25, .42$]	.67
Decision type: foil $(-.5)$ vs. target $(+.5)$	$-.07$ [$-.46, .30$]	.64
Interaction: Cond 1 $\times$ Cond 2	1.37 [.70, 2.03]	.73

Discussion. As expected, a landmark featuring convergent visual and structural salience makes it easier to remember the correct turning direction. Interestingly, the results in the foil condition are inverse; if a visually salient landmark is falsely placed at a convergent position a correct rejection is less likely compared to a false divergent placement. The mixed model analysis of the responses, especially the distribution of incorrect responses in the foil conditions, suggests that this is not a general bias towards a convergent response (i.e. always turning towards the position of the visually salient landmark). In the foil condition, participants tended to turn into the direction they learned during the route learning phase, even if this is now a divergent response given the now falsely placed visually salient landmark.

3   Cognitive Model

3.1   ACT-R

In order to explicate and explore the behavioral patterns found in the experiment, we implement our ideas in a cognitive model. The ACT-R framework is an established framework frequently used to model human memory. ACT-R is a modular cognitive architecture with an underlying production system operating on symbolic representations of declarative memory items – so-called chunks [2, 3]. The system defines specific modules corresponding to cognitive functions, e.g. a module for constructing internal representations (imaginal module), and a module to store and retrieve memory items (declarative module). A special status is assigned to the procedural module which comprises production rules that are used to define the behavior of a model.

The access to items of the declarative memory is influenced by several sub-symbolic components. The probability to recall an item from declarative memory depends on its memory activation. Memory activation decays over time if a chunk is not used and is boosted otherwise (base-level learning). Additionally, the context at the time of memory retrieval (spreading activation) and the similarity between the context and the items in memory (partial matching) affect a chunk's activation value. There is also a subsymbolic component for the procedural system (utility learning) we do not consider in this work.

To our knowledge, there are only a handful of attempts to model spatial cognition in ACT-R. Previous approaches using ACT-R with the aim of modeling spatial representations were mostly concerned with survey knowledge [14,22], but not with landmark knowledge (for a comprehensive overview, see [34]).

3.2 Model Concepts

Intersections are represented as chunks which include the three qualitatively relevant pieces of information, namely the color of the visually salient landmark, its location (simplified to left or right side only), and the turning direction (left or right). We restricted the context to this information because all other context information is invariant with respect to the different task conditions.

The process model is as follows: During the route learning phase, each intersection is internalized as an intersection chunk and stored in the declarative memory. During the decision phase, an intersection with a visually salient landmark at a certain position is presented to the participants. This information is used to request an intersection chunk from the declarative memory. If an intersection can be recalled, the stored turning direction is translated into pressing the left or right arrow key as a response. If no intersection can be recalled, the response is pressing the down arrow key to indicate that the intersection is unknown.

In our model, we use all three ACT-R memory mechanisms that influence chunk activation. Two of the memory mechanisms explicitly explain the empirical patterns found in the experiment, partial matching and spreading activation. Firstly, we assume that spatial locations can get confused. This is made worse by the task at hand; because both the turning direction and the position of the visually salient landmark represent knowledge of the feature type "location", they may get mixed up. We model this by using the partial matching functionality. Conceptually, partial matching allows the occurrence of commission errors (i.e., that a chunk with similar features as requested still has a chance to be recalled from memory). In our case, we assume that the similarity between different locations is higher than the similarity between colors. As a result, colors and locations can be confused in principle, but it is more likely to confuse locations.

The second important memory mechanism used to model the empirical pattern is spreading activation. Conceptually, spreading activation models the influence of context on memory retrieval; the more features are shared between a chunk in declarative memory and the current context, the more likely this chunk is recalled from memory. In our task, the context during the retrieval request in the decision phase is given by the color and position of a visually salient landmark. Table 3 shows the number of location features the target (or the foil chunk, respectively) has in common with the context in each task condition. For convergent targets, for example, the location given by the context (the position of the visually salient landmark) is the same as the visually salient landmark position and turning direction in the associated target chunk in memory. Thus, the target chunk is boosted twice. In divergent targets, on the other hand, the target is only boosted with one common feature (i.e., the visually salient landmark position). As a result, accuracy is higher in convergent targets. For foils, the situation is similar but with an inverse outcome. A convergent foil is boosted by one common feature because the new and false location of the landmark is the same as the turning direction associated with the landmark's color in memory. The probability to recall the chunk is, thus, higher than in the divergent case, where the new placement has no features in common with the associated intersection in memory. In case of a foil, however, this corresponds to a false reply. Note that it is still more likely to recall a convergent target than a convergent foil. The reason is the aforementioned partial matching functionality. The retrieval action requests an intersection specifying a landmark with a certain color and position. For foils, however, the position does not match and the respective chunk is therefore penalized.

3.3   Model Evaluation and and Discussion

We evaluated the absolute fit of our model by running a simulation. The simulation results were compared to the participants' responses on an aggregate level. All declarative memory mechanisms were enabled (base-level learning, partial matching, spreading activation). We kept all free, numeric parameters at their defaults except the parameters that need to be estimated to fit specific data (the retrieval threshold [value 1.35], the similarity between locations left and right [value .21], and the overall noise [value .35]). These parameters were estimated with an R procedure (function "nlminb") minimizing the least square deviation between participants' and the model's mean response accuracy over all four task conditions. To obtain model responses, ACT-R activation mechanisms and our process model were implemented in R. The obtained parameter values were inserted into the ACT-R model, which was then executed for a 1000 times for each task condition with the Lisp ACT-R interpreter. All results shown in this paper are based on this simulation.

The accuracy in the four task conditions as predicted by the ACT-R model is shown on the right side of Fig. 3; the predicted response for each condition is shown in the in the rightmost column in Table 1. We conclude that the sketched mechanisms were able to predict human recall accuracy found in the experiment.

However, the distribution of incorrect responses was not predicted well. One possible explanation is that we did not include the ability to guess a response into the model. Including a guessing procedure would require adding production rules which are applied with a certain probability (via setting the utility associated with a rule by hand). This, however, would make the model much more flexible in predicting empirical pattern and might overshadow the actual explanation we want explore in this work. For this reason, we did not include this additional layer of complexity into our model. Another potential reason is that we do not allow the model to recall an intersection chunk from a previous block for a similar reason. Adding this layer of noise would clutter the model predictions.

Table 3. Impact of spreading activation (number of common features) in the different task conditions. Turning direction and position of visually salient landmark (LM; study phase) correspond to the information presented during the study phase and are stored in the declarative memory. Position of the visually salient LM (decision phase) indicates the side of a visual landmark during the decision phase and provides the context for the retrieval request. Number of common features conceptualizes how often the direction in the context corresponds to the directions in the declarative memory.

	Declarative memory:		Context:	
	Turning direction	Position of visually salient LM (study phase)	Position of visually salient LM (decision phase)	Number of common features
Convergent target	Left	Left	*Left*	2
Divergent target	Left	Right	*Right*	1
Convergent foil	Left	Right	*Left*	1
Divergent foil	Left	Left	*Right*	0

4   General Discussion

The question of a landmark's optimal position for good route instructions has been extensively studied [13,15,21,27]. However, the literature has been mostly mute about the influence of landmarks as a factor mediating route recall from memory (but see [11,16,31]). In this work, we manipulated the placement of a visually salient landmark located either in (convergent placement) or opposite (divergent placement) to a learned turning direction for both familiar and novel intersections. We found that a convergent placement increased response accuracy as compared to a divergent placement for familiar intersections. Interestingly, we found the opposite pattern for novel intersections: a convergent placement leads to a higher number of false identification errors and thus to a lower response accuracy in correct rejections as compared to a divergent placement.

We present a cognitive model build within the ACT-R framework to show that the empirical patterns found in the experiment can be explained within established models of human memory. In this model, we assume that two factors moderate the ability to recall an intersection from memory: (1) the context given at the time of recall (i.e. the placement of a visually salient landmark) and (2) potential errors of commission for location information (i.e. confusing the position of the visually salient landmark with the turning direction). These two assumptions predict the empirical pattern found in the experiment. More specifically, the overlap in the number of features between the context at the time of recall and an intersection chunk stored in memory influences the ability to recall the intersection. As convergent intersection share more features (turning direction and landmark placement are aligned) they are easier to recall. This leads to a higher accuracy for known intersections but also a lower accuracy in correct rejections.

In an applied context, these findings suggest that people are more likely to memorize a turn correctly if a visually salient landmark is positioned in the turning direction. This finding is intuitive and in line with research using landmark selection tasks [25,26]. However, if an intersection is encountered from a different direction (thus resulting in an altered position of the visually salient landmark's position), people might still identify the intersection from the previous perspective and move towards according turning direction. This means that if they remember that they turned right a the post office (which was located on the right side), they are still more likely to turn right when they encounter the intersection from a perspective putting the post office on the left side. We hypothesize that at least in the very controlled setup of our study, the directional information of the turning direction was deeply encoded with the visually salient landmark - but not the position of the visually salient landmark itself. Although there are still limitations to our work, specifically in the ability to generalize the results to more complex (virtual or real) environments as well for a more heterogeneous population, we believe that our findings and cognitive model build important ground work for further investigations of human memory processing of landmark knowledge.

Our findings have implications for the selection of suitable landmarks for navigation assistance systems (e.g., [23]), and could be extended to approaches aimed at supporting the processing and memorization of spatial information when navigation assistance systems are used [28]. While using a visually salient landmark to guide navigation is very helpful if it is located in the turning direction, it might even be harmful if it is located opposite to the turning direction.

Acknowledgements. We thank Benedikt Solf for collecting the data and his idea of including foil blocks and Karoline Greger for implementing the SQUARELAND ACT-R environment.

References

1. Akaike, H.: A new look at the statistical model identification. IEEE Trans. Autom. Control **19**(6), 716–723 (1974)
2. Anderson, J.R., Lebiere, C.J.: The Atomic Components of Thought. Psychology Press, Hove (1998)
3. Anderson, J.R., Bothell, D., Byrne, M.D., Douglass, S., Lebiere, C., Qin, Y.: An integrated theory of the mind. Psychol. Rev. **111**(4), 1036 (2004)
4. Bates, D., Mächler, M., Bolker, B., Walker, S.: Fitting linear mixed-effects models using lme4. J. Stat. Softw. **67**(1), 1–48 (2015)
5. Buchner, A., Jansen-Osmann, P.: Is route learning more than serial learning? Spat. Cogn. Comput. **8**(4), 289–305 (2008)
6. Denis, M., Pazzaglia, F., Cornoldi, C., Bertolo, L.: Spatial discourse and navigation: an analysis of route directions in the city of venice. Appl. Cogn. Psychol. **13**(2), 145–174 (1999)
7. Hamburger, K., Knauff, M.: SQUARELAND: a virtual environment for investigating cognitive processes in human wayfinding. PsychNology J. **9**, 137–163 (2011)
8. Hinterecker, T., Roser, F., Strickrodt, M., Hamburger, K.: SQUARELAND 2.0: a flexible and realistic virtual environment for investigating cognitive processes in human wayfinding. In: Proceedings of the Annual Meeting of the Cognitive Science Society, vol. 36 (2014)
9. Itti, L., Koch, C.: Computational modelling of visual attention. Nat. Rev. Neurosci. **2**(3), 194 (2001)
10. Janzen, G.: Memory for object location and route direction in virtual large-scale space. Q. J. Exp. Psychol. **59**(3), 493–508 (2006)
11. Karimpur, H., Röser, F., Hamburger, K.: Finding the return path: landmark position effects and the influence of perspective. Front. Psychol. **7**, 1956 (2016)
12. Klippel, A., Winter, S.: Structural salience of landmarks for route directions. In: Cohn, A.G., Mark, D.M. (eds.) COSIT 2005. LNCS, vol. 3693, pp. 347–362. Springer, Heidelberg (2005). https://doi.org/10.1007/11556114_22
13. Lovelace, K.L., Hegarty, M., Montello, D.R.: Elements of good route directions in familiar and unfamiliar environments. In: Freksa, C., Mark, D.M. (eds.) COSIT 1999. LNCS, vol. 1661, pp. 65–82. Springer, Heidelberg (1999). https://doi.org/10.1007/3-540-48384-5_5
14. Lyon, D.R., Gunzelmann, G., Gluck, K.A.: A computational model of spatial visualization capacity. Cogn. Psychol. **57**(2), 122–152 (2008)
15. Michon, P.-E., Denis, M.: When and why are visual landmarks used in giving directions? In: Montello, D.R. (ed.) COSIT 2001. LNCS, vol. 2205, pp. 292–305. Springer, Heidelberg (2001). https://doi.org/10.1007/3-540-45424-1_20
16. Miller, J., Carlson, L.: Selecting landmarks in novel environments. Psychon. Bull. Rev. **18**(1), 184–191 (2011)
17. Montello, D.R.: Landmarks are exaggerated. KI-Künstliche Intelligenz **31**(2), 193–197 (2017)
18. Peters, D., Wu, Y., Winter, S.: Testing landmark identification theories in virtual environments. In: Hölscher, C., Shipley, T.F., Olivetti Belardinelli, M., Bateman, J.A., Newcombe, N.S. (eds.) Spatial Cognition 2010. LNCS (LNAI), vol. 6222, pp. 54–69. Springer, Heidelberg (2010). https://doi.org/10.1007/978-3-642-14749-4_8
19. Quesnot, T., Roche, S.: Measure of landmark semantic salience through geosocial data streams. ISPRS Int. J. Geo-Inf. **4**(1), 1–31 (2014)

20. R Core Team: R: a language and environment for statistical computing. R Foundation for Statistical Computing, Vienna, Austria (2016). https://www.R-project.org/

21. Raubal, M., Winter, S.: Enriching wayfinding instructions with local landmarks. In: Egenhofer, M.J., Mark, D.M. (eds.) GIScience 2002. LNCS, vol. 2478, pp. 243–259. Springer, Heidelberg (2002). https://doi.org/10.1007/3-540-45799-2_17

22. Reitter, D., Lebiere, C.: A cognitive model of spatial path-planning. Comput. Math. Organ. Theory **16**(3), 220–245 (2010)

23. Richter, K.F., Winter, S.: Landmarks, vol. 10. Springer, Heidelberg (2014). https://doi.org/10.1007/978-3-319-05732-3., pp. 978–983

24. Röser, F., Hamburger, K., Knauff, M.: The giessen virtual environment laboratory: human wayfinding and landmark salience. Cogn. Process. **12**(2), 209–214 (2011)

25. Röser, F., Krumnack, A., Hamburger, K.: The influence of perceptual and structural salience. In: Proceedings of the Annual Meeting of the Cognitive Science Society, vol. 35 (2013)

26. Röser, F., Krumnack, A., Hamburger, K., Knauff, M.: A four factor model of landmark salience, a new approach. In: Krüger, A., Butz, A., Oliver, P. (eds.) Proceedings of the 11th International Conference on Cognitive Modeling (ICCM), pp. 82–87. Springer, Heidelberg (2012)

27. Röser, F., Hamburger, K., Krumnack, A., Knauff, M.: The structural salience of landmarks: results from an on-line study and a virtual environment experiment. J. Spat. Sci. **57**(1), 37–50 (2012)

28. Schwering, A., Krukar, J., Li, R., Anacta, V.J., Fuest, S.: Wayfinding through orientation. Spat. Cogn. Comput. **17**(4), 273–303 (2017)

29. Siegel, A.W., White, S.H.: The development of spatial representations of large-scale environments. In: Advances in Child Development and Behavior, vol. 10, pp. 9–55. Elsevier (1975)

30. Sorrows, M.E., Hirtle, S.C.: The nature of landmarks for real and electronic spaces. In: Freksa, C., Mark, D.M. (eds.) COSIT 1999. LNCS, vol. 1661, pp. 37–50. Springer, Heidelberg (1999). https://doi.org/10.1007/3-540-48384-5_3

31. von Stülpnagel, R., Steffens, M.C.: Active route learning in virtual environments: disentangling movement control from intention, instruction specificity, and navigation control. Psychol. Res. **77**(5), 555–574 (2013)

32. Wenczel, F., Hepperle, L., von Stülpnagel, R.: Gaze behavior during incidental and intentional navigation in an outdoor environment. Spat. Cogn. Comput. **17**(1–2), 121–142 (2017)

33. Winter, B.: Linear models and linear mixed effects models in R with linguistic applications. arXiv preprint arXiv:1308.5499 (2013)

34. Zhao, C.: Understanding human spatial navigation behaviors: a novel cognitive modeling approach. The Pennsylvania State University (2016)

A System of Automatic Generation of Landmark-Based Pedestrian Navigation Instructions and Its Effectiveness for Wayfinding

Jue Wang and Toru Ishikawa[✉]

Graduate School of Interdisciplinary Information Studies,
University of Tokyo, Tokyo, Japan
ishikawa@csis.u-tokyo.ac.jp

Abstract. Websites of hotels, restaurants, and other businesses often provide navigation instructions from a nearby railway station. One form of such navigation instructions could combine street-view photographs and verbal directions, which may be intuitive and easy to understand. This study developed a method of generating landmark-based navigation instructions automatically using a digital map database available, and examined their effectiveness in navigating the user in comparison to a commercial GPS-based navigation application. Results showed that participants tended to travel longer distances and deviate from directed routes more frequently when using a GPS-based navigation application; the tendency was greater for people with a poor sense of direction. These people, however, did not have difficulty with wayfinding when using the landmark-based instructions. The present method of providing landmark-based navigation instructions was thus found to help the user, especially people with a poor sense of direction, find their way in a new environment.

Keywords: Pedestrian navigation · Navigational directions · Landmarks
Wayfinding · Sense of direction

1 Introduction

1.1 Navigation Tools

Nowadays many kinds of navigation tools and methods are available for human wayfinding, such as paper maps, Global Positioning System (GPS)–based navigation applications, audio guidance, and augmented reality (AR) navigation. Paper maps have been a major navigation tool, but with the advances in information technology, various GPS-based mobile navigation applications are now widely used [16]. Those mobile applications can locate the user's position dynamically and provide turn-by-turn navigation instructions to the user.

Although some argue that digital maps and navigation applications take the place of conventional paper maps, previous studies showed that mobile users, compared to map users, traveled longer distances and stopped more frequently during navigation [9] and

S. Creem-Regehr et al. (Eds.): Spatial Cognition 2018, LNAI 11034, pp. 326–340, 2018.
https://doi.org/10.1007/978-3-319-96385-3_22

acquired fragmented knowledge about traveled routes [25]. Latest navigation applications, however, offer various advanced options, for example, showing photographs of street views or updating the traveler's heading automatically on the screen, which may contribute to improving the usability and efficacy of mobile navigation applications.

Successful navigation assistance requires that information about a route and wayfinding clues, particularly landmarks, is provided in a timely manner. Websites of hotels, restaurants, and other businesses often provide navigation instructions from a nearby railway station (Fig. 1). Such navigation instructions combine photographs of street views and verbal directions, assuming that they are intuitive and easy to understand for the traveler. A previous study [11] showed that spatial orientation could be done faster by viewing pictures than viewing maps. In particular, pictures annotated by an arrow indicating the direction of travel helped people with a poor sense of direction in spatial orientation. Thus, this research focuses on landmark-based navigation instructions in the form of street view photographs combined with text instructions and direction arrows as shown in Fig. 1. Specifically, it develops a system of automatically generating landmark-based navigation instructions using digital map databases, and examines the effectiveness of such instructions for the user's wayfinding in an unfamiliar environment.

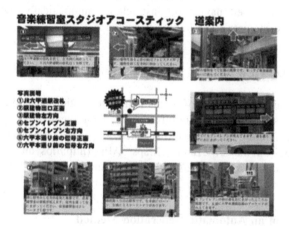

Fig. 1. An example of landmark-based navigation instructions provided on a website. Seven street view photographs and a map around the shop are shown in the instructions. Arrows denote the directions of travel. Verbal navigational instructions are shown in the text boxes on the photographs. (Image from: http://www.studio-acoustic.com/info/2015/1020_779.html)

1.2 Landmarks

Landmarks can be defined in various different ways, but in the context of navigation, they may be defined as geographic objects that stand out in the environment and structure people's mental representations of it [20]. Importantly, landmarks have been shown to play important roles in wayfinding and navigation. For example, navigation instructions based on landmarks yielded better wayfinding performance and quicker route recalls than did instructions based on street names [23, 24]. Landmark-based pedestrian navigation assistance was particularly helpful for older adults [6], and instructions based on landmarks were preferred to those based on metric distance information [18].

Researchers noted the relative nature of the properties that make objects "landmarks," and proposed a formal model of landmark salience on the basis of visual, semantic, and structural attraction [12, 15, 17, 21]. Also, based on the evaluations of these three types of salience, a landmark-based pedestrian navigation data model was proposed [4]. Furthermore, relationship with sense of direction and other variables is reported, such that when walking unfamiliar routes, people tended to identify buildings with larger facades or of more saturated color as landmarks more frequently [10].

There is a good potential to take landmark information into navigation instructions on mobile applications more specifically, as is popularly done on many websites (Fig. 1). At the same time, however, there are some issues to consider for effective landmark-based navigation instructions. First, developing landmark-based navigation instructions is time consuming, because one needs to take photographs with an appropriate viewing angle and add verbal and graphic directions that are easy to understand. Second, the effectiveness of such landmark-based navigation instructions awaits empirical examination in comparison to, for example, commonly used commercial navigation applications. Therefore, this research aims to propose a method of generating landmark-based navigation instructions automatically, and to examine whether they assist the user's wayfinding behavior.

2   System Overview

This section explains the method of an automatic generation of landmark-based navigation instructions for pedestrians in urban areas. To implement the system, any map application programming interface (API), such as the Google Maps API (https://developers.google.com/maps/), Baidu Maps API (http://lbsyun.baidu.com/), and OpenStreetMap Editing API (https://wiki.openstreetmap.org/wiki/API_v0.6/), may be used.

2.1   Procedure of an Automatic Generation Method

Shortest Path Generation. First, the shortest walking path (nodes and edges of the path) from the starting point to the goal needs to be determined as the basic information for generating pedestrian navigation instructions. It is done in this system by using a map API.

Determining Decision Points. Second, the system determines decision points, or landmarks located at decision points, along the path [2, 16]. Previous studies discussed four types of decision points: (a) choice points (intersections where actions such as turning left or turning right are needed); (b) potential choice points (intersections where no turns are made); (c) on-route points (located along the traveler's path); and (d) off-route points (located off the traveler's path and used to provide global orientation information [13, 16]). The decision points identified by the system therefore included the starting point, the goal, intersections where the traveler needs to perform an action, and intermediate points along a path longer than 200 m that assure the traveler that he or she is walking on the right path [26]. Since the address system used in the study area is street based, intersections where street names change were also identified as important decision points (Fig. 2).

Fig. 2. Decision points along a route. Solid lines denote a route from the start to the goal and circular markers denote decision points. (Map data from Baidu Maps.)

Selecting Street View Photographs. Third, the system selects, from a panoramic database, photographs of landmarks at decision points using a street view API. To select a "good" photograph that shows the whole view of a decision point, four parameters, location, heading, pitch, and field of view, are considered. The parameter *location* consists of the latitude and longitude of a position where the photograph is taken. For decision points other than the starting point and the goal, location was set to a position 20 m before each decision point (Fig. 3). For the starting point, location was set to the exact position of the starting point, and for the goal, it was set to a position 5 m before the goal so that the destination was clearly shown in the photograph. The parameter *heading* is the horizontal angle of a camera's heading. It was set to the forward direction at the location where the photograph was taken (Fig. 3). The parameter *pitch* is the upward or downward angle of a camera relative to a street view vehicle. It was set to 0°, a common vertical angle of sight for pedestrians. The parameter *field of view* is the horizontal field of view of the photograph. In this system, it was set to 170° to ensure that the user can obtain panoramic information not only in the front, but also sideways around a decision point. Figure 4 shows an example of a street view photograph selected by the system in this procedure.

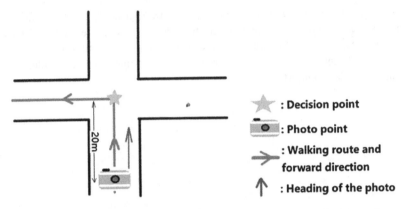

Fig. 3. The location and heading of a photograph selected for a decision point.

Fig. 4. An example of a street view photograph selected by the system. (Street view image data from Baidu Maps.)

Extraction of "Helpful" Landmarks. Fourth, the system extracts up to three objects which can serve as helpful landmarks for the traveler to identify each decision point. Since the research focuses on pedestrian navigation in urban areas and the map databases only include the locations and names of buildings along street networks, the system considers buildings as candidates for landmarks, excluding for example street furniture, plants, or other objects. Also, it takes only local landmarks into consideration, landmarks at decision points and course-maintenance landmarks intermediate along a route. The principle of extracting "good" landmarks was based on the evaluation of the degree of attraction in terms of structural, visual, and semantic salience [1, 10, 17, 21].

With respect to structural attraction, the system extracted landmarks that are close to a decision point and functionally relevant for the action at the decision point [1, 19]. Figure 5 illustrates candidate buildings that are considered relevant or not relevant to the action at the decision point in this research.

With respect to visual attraction, the system considered the visibility of a building in the street view photograph, such that buildings that were located far away from the decision point (>30 m) or off the heading direction (out of the field of view of 170°) were eliminated (Fig. 6). Previous research found the color and facade area of a building to be important variables of visual attraction [10], but because of the difficulty of determining those values from a photograph automatically, they were not considered by the system in this study.

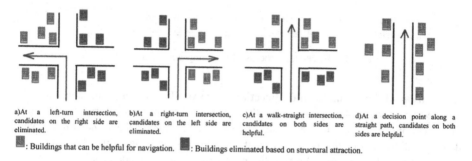

a)At a left-turn intersection, candidates on the right side are eliminated.

b)At a right-turn intersection, candidates on the left side are eliminated.

c)At a walk-straight intersection, candidates on both sides are helpful.

d)At a decision point along a straight path, candidates on both sides are helpful.

■ : Buildings that can be helpful for navigation. ■ : Buildings eliminated based on structural attraction.

Fig. 5. Evaluation of the salience of candidate landmarks in terms of structural attraction.

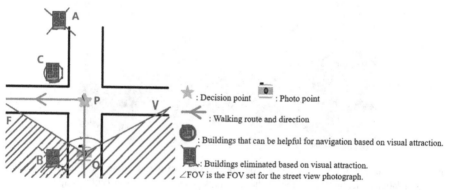

★ : Decision point   📷 : Photo point

← : Walking route and direction

● : Buildings that can be helpful for navigation based on visual attraction.

■ : Buildings eliminated based on visual attraction.

∠FOV is the FOV set for the street view photograph.

Fig. 6. Evaluation of the salience of candidate landmarks in terms of visual attraction. Candidate A is located far away from the decision point, P (AP > 30 m). Candidate B is out of the field of view at the photograph location, O. Candidate C is near the decision point P and within the field of view.

To evaluate semantic attraction, the system refers to the scoring scheme proposed in previous studies [3, 4]. In their scoring scheme, colleges, parks, theaters, restaurants, banks, hotels, hospitals, libraries, and stations had relatively high scores. The system thus selected buildings in these categories as landmarks with high semantic attraction.

In sum, for each decision point, the system searches for information about all buildings nearby from a map API database, and extracts up to three landmarks on the basis of salience determined by the three-step elimination process described above (Fig. 7).

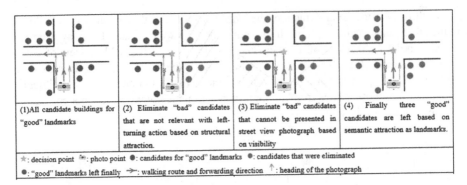

(1)All candidate buildings for "good" landmarks	(2) Eliminate "bad" candidates that are not relevant with left-turning action based on structural attraction.	(3) Eliminate "bad" candidates that cannot be presented in street view photograph based on visibility	(4) Finally three "good" candidates are left based on semantic attraction as landmarks.

☆ : decision point ▣ : photo point ● : candidates for "good" landmarks ◐ : candidates that were eliminated
● : "good" landmarks left finally ➤ : walking route and forwarding direction ↑ : heading of the photograph

Fig. 7. Three-step process of selecting good landmarks.

Annotation of Landmarks and Direction Arrows. The system then annotates the selected street view photographs with the names of landmarks and arrows indicating the directions of travel (Fig. 8). The positions of the name labels and arrows were determined by taking the positions of the landmarks and the center line, location, heading, field of view, and width of the photographs into consideration.

Fig. 8. An example of a street view photograph with an arrow indicating the direction of travel and a text label indicating the name of the landmark. (Image data from Baidu Maps.)

Generation of a Route Overview Map. Finally, the system generates a route overview map that shows the route and the locations of decision points (see Fig. 2).

2.2   Advantages of This System

The present method of automatic generation of landmark-based navigation instructions has some advantages. For its implementation, this study used the Baidu Maps API, but other map APIs that have map data and street view information available may also be used. The method provides an efficient way of generating navigation instructions composed of landmark-embedded street view photographs, a route overview map, and text instructions, which may be flexibly modified according to possible updates of a map database. Compared to other landmark-based navigation applications such as the "Whereis" service [3], this system not only extracts landmarks at decision points along a route, but also displays the direction of travel and landmark information embedded on street view photographs.

3   Differences Between Two Different Navigation Tools

Table 1 illustrates several differences between the landmark-based navigation instructions developed herein and commercial GPS-based navigation applications.

Commercial GPS-based navigation applications possess massive map databases and allow the user to view maps at different scales, while the landmark-based navigation instructions have a static representation of a route, which cannot be rescaled. Commercial GPS-based navigation applications, with GPS positioning and gyroscopes, can display and update the user's position and heading in real time. In the landmark-based navigation instructions, the user needs to understand one's position and heading based on the street view photographs and the route overview map. However, as an advantage of the landmark-based navigation instructions, the street view photographs provide information about decision points in a visual and intuitive manner to the user. On the street view photographs, landmark information and travel directions are annotated, which can enhance the user's confidence and trust during navigation as predominant navigation clues [5, 14]. In addition, the landmark-based navigation instructions provide street view photographs at intermediate points of a route segment longer than 200 m, which assures the user that he or she is on the right path. Finally, commercial GPS-based mobile navigation applications rely on electronic devices, internet connection, and GPS signals.

Table 1. Differences between commercial GPS-based mobile navigation applications and the landmark-based navigation instructions generated by the system in this research.

Commercial GPS-based mobile applications	Landmark-based instructions generated by the current system
- Richer map data	- Limited map data
- With GPS positioning/a gyroscope/a compass	- No positioning or orientation aid
- Show and update the current position and heading	- Users need to understand one's position and heading
- No panoramic information	- Panoramic photographs with arrows embedded
- No annotation of landmark information	- With annotation of landmark information
- No information about intermediate points along a long straight path	- Providing visual information of intermediate points of a path longer than 200 m
- Need mobile electronic devices with internet connection and GPS signals	- Can be printed out (paper-based)/offline on electronic equipment

4 Experiment

4.1 Purpose

We conducted a behavioral experiment to examine whether the landmark-based navigation instructions, generated by the system illustrated in Sect. 2, were effective in assisting the user's wayfinding, compared to a commercial GPS-based mobile navigation application. As long as the salience of landmarks can be assessed in terms of their structural, visual, and semantic attraction [1, 10, 17, 21] and landmarks can be effectively used in navigation instructions [6, 18, 23, 24], the instructions generated by the current system would lead to a better wayfinding performance. Also, given that people with a poor sense of direction have difficulty identifying effective landmarks [10], the provision of good landmarks by the system would help those people in navigation.

4.2 Participants

Twenty adults (7 men and 13 women) participated in the experiment. Their ages ranged from 22 to 29 years. All of them had the experience of using a mobile navigation application in their daily lives. None of the participants was familiar with the study area or routes prior to the experiment.

4.3 Materials

Study Routes. The study area was located in the Huangpu district, Shanghai, China. In this area, mixed with residential and commercial land uses, two routes with a similar structural complexity (980 m in length) were chosen (Fig. 9). The system identified decision points and salient landmarks on each route, and generated nine and ten street view photographs for Route 1 and Route 2, respectively.

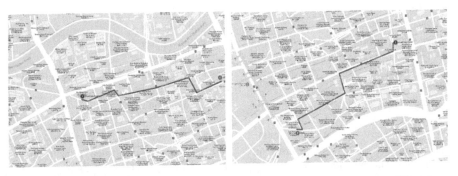

Fig. 9. Map of the study routes: Route 1 (left) and Route 2 (right). Both routes are 980 m long. Circular icons represent the starting point and the goal of the route. (Map data ©2018 Google.)

Experimental Tools. For the wayfinding task with a commercial mobile navigation application, participants used a Baidu Maps navigation application on a smartphone (Fig. 10). It displayed the user's position, heading, a route from the starting point to the goal, and text instructions on the screen, which were updated dynamically as the user walked. The user could drag and zoom in and out on the map.

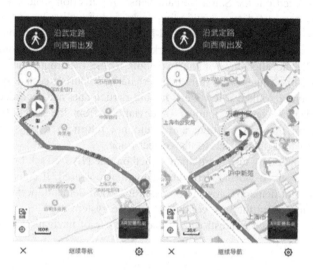

Fig. 10. Screenshots of the Baidu Maps navigation application used in the experiment. The arrow indicates the user's current position and heading. The solid line indicates the route. Verbal navigational instructions are shown on the top of the screen. The user could view the entire route (left) and also the detail of route segments (right) by zooming in and out.

For the wayfinding task with the landmark-based navigation instructions, participants used a booklet which contained navigation instructions generated automatically by the system as described in Sect. 2, showing street view photographs and a route overview map (Fig. 11).

Fig. 11. Booklet of the landmark-based navigation instructions used in the experiment. (Map data from Baidu Maps.)

4.4   Experimental Procedure

The experiment was conducted in the daytime and it took 45–60 min for each participant. The specific experimental procedure was as follows:

1. The experimenter explained the procedure of the experiment and introduced the two navigation tools to participants.
2. Participants filled out the Santa Barbara Sense-of-Direction scale [8].
3. Participants conducted two wayfinding tasks individually. In one of the tasks, participants used the commercial GPS-based navigation application, and in the other task, participants used the landmark-based navigation instructions, mentioned in Sect. 4.3. The allocation of the two tools to the two routes and the order of traveling the two routes were fully counterbalanced. During each wayfinding task, the experimenter walked a few steps behind participants and recorded their travel time and distance and the number of deviations from the route. If participants deviated from the correct route and could not return to it by themselves, the experimenter took them back to the correct route.
4. After each wayfinding task, participants filled out the NASA Task Load Index [7] to assess the perceived workload of the navigation tool used. It consists of six subscales of mental demand, physical demand, temporal demand, performance, effort, and frustration about the task conducted and the system used.
5. Participants answered a questionnaire about the use of navigation applications.

5   Experimental Results

The measured variables of travel time, the distance traveled, the number of deviations, and self-assessed workload were examined in an analysis of covariance, with the tools (the landmark-based instructions generated by the system and the commercial navigation application) as a within-subject variable and sense of direction as a covariate (descriptive statistics and correlations are shown in Tables 2 and 3). For the present sample of participants, no significant male-female differences were observed for any variable, t's(18) < 1.63, p's > .120.

5.1   Travel Time and Workload

For travel time, there was not a significant main effect of tool, $F(1, 18) = 1.29$, $p = 0.271$, or sense of direction, $F(1, 18) = 0.15, p = 0.700$; nor was there a significant interaction between the two, $F(1, 18) = 1.58, p = 0.475$.

For workload, there was not a significant main effect of tool, $F(1, 18) = 0.53$, $p = 0.475$, or sense of direction, $F(1, 18) = 0.10, p = 0.759$; nor was there a significant interaction between the two, $F(1, 18) = 1.34, p = 0.263$.

5.2 Distance Travelled

For the distance traveled, there was a significant main effect of tool, $F(1, 18) = 5.87$, $p = 0.026$, and sense of direction, $F(1, 18) = 5.40$ and $p = 0.032$. The interaction was also significant, $F(1, 18) = 5.19$ and $p = 0.035$.

Participants traveled a longer distance when using the commercial navigation application than when using the landmark-based navigation instructions (Table 2). Participants with a poorer sense of direction tended to travel a longer distance when using the commercial navigation application, but such a negative effect of sense of direction was not observed when they used the landmark-based navigation instructions (Table 3 and Fig. 12). Thus, the navigation instructions generated by the system particularly helped people with a poor sense of direction.

Table 2. Means (and standard deviations) for each measured variable for the two tools.

Measured variable	Tool	
	Commercial mobile application	Landmark-based instructions
Travel time (s)	786.75 (83.3)	788.8 (83.73)
Distance traveled (m)	1,011.5 (50.8)	1,001.5 (26.81)
Number of deviations	0.15 (0.37)	0.05 (0.22)
Workload	20.0 (17.3)	25.7 (15.9)

Table 3. Correlations between measured variables and sense of direction.

	APP time	LM time	APP distance	LM distance	APP deviation	LM deviation	APP workload	LM workload
SOD	−.15	−.03	−.54*	.01	−.61**	.25	−.20	.08

Note. $*p < .05$; $**p < .01$. APP = commercial mobile application; LM = landmark-based instructions generated by the system; SOD = sense of direction.

5.3 Number of Deviations

For the number of deviations, there was a significant main effect of tool, $F(1, 18) = 12.64$, $p = 0.002$, and a significant interaction between tool and sense of direction, $F(1, 18) = 11.19$ and $p = 0.004$.

Participants deviated from the route more frequently when using the commercial navigation application than when using the landmark-based navigation instructions (Table 2). Participants with a poorer sense of direction tended to deviate more frequently when using the commercial navigation application, but not when using the landmark-based navigation instructions (Table 3 and Fig. 12). With this measure, again, the navigation instructions generated by the system particularly helped people with a poor sense of direction.

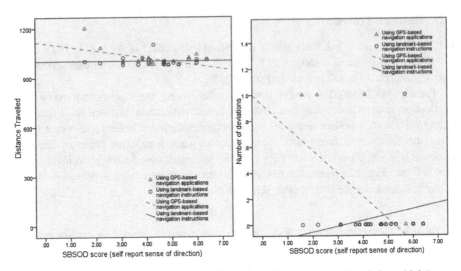

Fig. 12. Scatter plots of the distance travelled (left) and the number of deviations (right) as a function of sense of direction.

Among the measured variables, there was a significant correlation between travel time and the distance traveled ($r = .50$, $p = .025$) and between the distance traveled and the number of deviations ($r = .75$, $p < .001$) with the commercial navigation application. No significant correlations were observed between measured variables for the landmark-based navigation instructions.

6   Conclusions and Future Work

This research developed a system of generating landmark-based navigation instructions automatically using a digital map API. The system determines decision points, selects street view photographs, extracts good landmarks at the decision points, annotates the selected photographs with landmark information and direction arrows, and generates a route overview map. The selection of landmarks is based on the evaluation of landmark salience in terms of structural, visual, and semantic attraction.

Results from the behavioral experiment showed that the landmark-based navigation instructions generated by the system decreased the user's travel distance and deviations. The effect was particularly noticeable for people with a poor sense of direction: when using the landmark-based navigation instructions, they did equivalently to people with a good sense of direction. The present results thus empirically showed the effectiveness of the current system and the instructions automatically generated by it for wayfinding, as compared to a widely used commercial navigation application. The two tools compared in this study differ in several respects, as shown in Table 1, and the differences were not systematically varied in the present experiment. Identifying possible reasons for the positive effects of the landmark-based navigation instructions in a more controlled experiment should be an issue for future research.

The current system may be applied to various situations, for example, when business owners intend to provide potential customers with access information intuitively or when navigation assistance is needed in situations without internet access or for older adults and children, and particularly people with a poor sense of direction.

Other future research questions include:

1. To recognize visually attractive objects and buildings in a street view photograph automatically through the technique of computer vision or the development of richer geospatial data infrastructures.
2. To examine different orders of considering the three types of salience. In the present case, structural, visual, and semantic attraction was considered in this order.
3. To examine the practical significance of observed differences and the effectiveness of the current system for more complex environments and in a real-time setting.
4. To come up with different principles of extracting landmarks depending on the spatial aptitudes of users or the time of day, to improve user-friendliness of navigation tools. Previous research showed differences in the number of landmarks identified and the routes selected depending on sense of direction [10, 22]. Such a consideration would lead to a higher degree of context awareness for location services and geospatial technologies.

References

1. Burnett, G., Smith, D., May, A.: Supporting the navigation task: characteristics of 'good' landmarks. In: Hanson, M.A. (ed.) Contemporary Ergonomics 2001, pp. 441–446. Taylor and Francis, London (2001)
2. Daniel, M.-P., Denis, M.: Spatial descriptions as navigational aids: a cognitive analysis of route directions. Kognitionswissenschaft 7(1), 45–52 (1998)
3. Duckham, M., Winter, S., Robinson, M.: Including landmarks in routing instructions. J. Locat. Based Serv. 4(1), 28–52 (2010)
4. Fang, Z., Li, Q., Zhang, X., Shaw, S.-L.: A GIS data model for landmark-based pedestrian navigation. Int. J. Geogr. Inf. Sci. 26(5), 817–838 (2012)
5. Furukawa, H.: Empirical evaluation of the pedestrian navigation method for easy wayfinding. In: Proceedings of the 2015 International Conference and Workshop on Computing and Communication, article no. 113. IEEE, New York (2015)
6. Goodman, J., Brewster, S.A., Gray, P.: How can we best use landmarks to support older people in navigation? J. Behav. Inf. Technol. 24(1), 3–20 (2005)
7. Hart, S.G., Staveland, L.E.: Development of NASA-TLX (Task Load Index): results of empirical and theoretical research. Adv. Psychol. 52, 139–183 (1988)
8. Hegarty, M., Richardson, A.E., Montello, D.R., Lovelace, K., Subbiah, I.: Development of a self-report measure of environmental spatial ability. Intelligence 30(5), 425–447 (2002)
9. Ishikawa, T., Fujiwara, H., Imai, O., Okabe, A.: Wayfinding with a GPS-based mobile navigation system: a comparison with maps and direct experience. J. Environ. Psychol. 28(1), 74–82 (2008)
10. Ishikawa, T., Nakamura, U.: Landmark selection in the environment: relationships with object characteristics and sense of direction. Spat. Cogn. Comput. 12(1), 1–22 (2012)

11. Ishikawa, T., Yamazaki, T.: Showing where to go by maps or pictures: an empirical case study at subway exits. In: Hornsby, K.S., Claramunt, C., Denis, M., Ligozat, G. (eds.) COSIT 2009. LNCS, vol. 5756, pp. 330–341. Springer, Heidelberg (2009). https://doi.org/10.1007/978-3-642-03832-7_20

12. Klippel, A., Winter, S.: Structural salience of landmarks for route directions. In: Cohn, A.G., Mark, D.M. (eds.) COSIT 2005. LNCS, vol. 3693, pp. 347–362. Springer, Heidelberg (2005). https://doi.org/10.1007/11556114_22

13. Lovelace, K., Hegarty, M., Montello, D.: Elements of good route directions in familiar and unfamiliar environments. In: Freksa, C., Mark, David M. (eds.) COSIT 1999. LNCS, vol. 1661, pp. 65–82. Springer, Heidelberg (1999). https://doi.org/10.1007/3-540-48384-5_5

14. May, A.J., Ross, T., Bayer, S.H., Tarkiainen, M.J.: Pedestrian navigation aids: information requirements and design implications. Pers. Ubiquit. Comput. 7(6), 331–338 (2003)

15. Nothegger, C., Winter, S., Raubal, M.: Selection of salient features for route directions. Spat. Cogn. Comput. 4(2), 113–136 (2004)

16. Quesnot, T., Roche, S.: Measure of landmark semantic salience through geosocial data streams. ISPRS Int. J. Geo-Inf. 4(1), 1–31 (2014)

17. Raubal, M., Winter, S.: Enriching wayfinding instructions with local landmarks. In: Egenhofer, M.J., Mark, D.M. (eds.) GIScience 2002. LNCS, vol. 2478, pp. 243–259. Springer, Heidelberg (2002). https://doi.org/10.1007/3-540-45799-2_17

18. Rehrl, K., Häusler, E., Leitinger, S.: Comparing the effectiveness of GPS-enhanced voice guidance for pedestrians with metric- and landmark-based instruction sets. In: Fabrikant, S. I., Reichenbacher, T., van Kreveld, M., Schlieder, C. (eds.) GIScience 2010. LNCS, vol. 6292, pp. 189–203. Springer, Heidelberg (2010). https://doi.org/10.1007/978-3-642-15300-6_14

19. Richter, K.-F.: A uniform handling of different landmark types in route directions. In: Winter, S., Duckham, M., Kulik, L., Kuipers, B. (eds.) COSIT 2007. LNCS, vol. 4736, pp. 373–389. Springer, Heidelberg (2007). https://doi.org/10.1007/978-3-540-74788-8_23

20. Richter, K.-F., Winter, S.: Landmarks. Springer, Cham (2014). https://doi.org/10.1007/978-3-319-05732-3

21. Sorrows, M.E., Hirtle, S.C.: The nature of landmarks for real and electronic spaces. In: Freksa, C., Mark, D.M. (eds.) COSIT 1999. LNCS, vol. 1661, pp. 37–50. Springer, Heidelberg (1999). https://doi.org/10.1007/3-540-48384-5_3

22. Takemiya, M., Ishikawa, T.: I can tell by the way you use your walk: real-time classification of wayfinding performance. In: Egenhofer, M., Giudice, N., Moratz, R., Worboys, M. (eds.) COSIT 2011. LNCS, vol. 6899, pp. 90–109. Springer, Heidelberg (2011). https://doi.org/10.1007/978-3-642-23196-4_6

23. Tom, A., Denis, M.: Referring to landmark or street information in route directions: what difference does it make? In: Kuhn, W., Worboys, Michael F., Timpf, S. (eds.) COSIT 2003. LNCS, vol. 2825, pp. 362–374. Springer, Heidelberg (2003). https://doi.org/10.1007/978-3-540-39923-0_24

24. Tom, A., Denis, M.: Language and spatial cognition: comparing the roles of landmarks and street names in route instructions. Appl. Cogn. Psychol. 18(9), 1213–1230 (2004)

25. Willis, K.S., Hölscher, C., Wilbertz, G., Li, C.: A comparison of spatial knowledge acquisition with maps and mobile maps. Comput. Environ. Urban Syst. 33(2), 100–110 (2009)

26. Wither, J., Au, C.E., Rischpater, R., Grzeszczuk, R.: Moving beyond the map: automated landmark based pedestrian guidance using street level panoramas. In: Proceedings of the 15th International Conference on Human-Computer Interaction with Mobile Devices and Services, pp. 203–212. ACM, New York (2013)

Author Index

Printed in the United States
By Bookmasters